THE COMPLETE MANUAL OF

CORPORATE
AND
INDUSTRIAL
SECURITY

RUSSELL L. BINTLIFF

PRENTICE HALL

Prentice-Hall International (UK) Limited, *London*
Prentice-Hall of Australia Pty. Limited, *Sydney*
Prentice-Hall Canada, Inc., *Toronto*
Prentice-Hall Hispanoamericana, S.A., *Mexico*
Prentice-Hall of India Private Limited, *New Delhi*
Prentice-Hall of Japan, Inc., *Tokyo*
Simon & Schuster Asia Pte. Ltd., *Singapore*
Editora Prentice-Hall do Brasil, Ltda., *Rio de Janeiro*

10 9 8 7 6 5 4 3

Library of Congress Cataloging-in-Publication Data

Bintliff, Russell L.
  The complete manual of corporate and industrial security / by
Russell L. Bintliff.

    p. cm.
  Includes index.
  ISBN 0-13-159641-1
  1. Industry—Security measures—Management.   2. Office buildings—

United States—Security measures.   3. Industrial buildings—United
States—Security measures.   I. Title.
HV8290.B56 1992
658.4'7—dc20   92-19744
                                                          CIP

ISBN 0-13-159641-1

90000>

9 780131 596412

PRENTICE HALL
Professional Publishing
Englewood Cliffs, NJ 07632

Simon & Schuster, A Paramount Communications Company

PRINTED IN THE UNITED STATES OF AMERICA

To my family:
My wife Janie
Our sons Roger and Mark

Introduction

When a giant corporation files bankruptcy, it shocks the nation. The blame and excuses center on a bad economy, lack of company leadership, an incompetent marketing department, the comptroller, or anyone else handy. No one talks about the security director, quietly sacked, cleaning out his desk and wondering about the future. The mainstream business publications feature long stories about the corporate mistakes, microanalyzing why a prosperous company went belly up, and during times when it seemed to have unprecedented growth. No one notices, or maybe doesn't recognize, the real reason this corporate model of success moved from number one position to a shell of its past, is now struggling to survive and salvage something from the business rubble.

The truth, however, of the corporation's demise is known to a few insiders. It stems from management error, but primarily fueled from systematic "thievery," from the systematic internal and external diversified looting of company products, property, and information. As the company growth and success reached new highs the security director could have anything he wanted. He succumbed to persistent persuasion by manufacturers' reps about the infallible "bells and whistles" of high-tech security equipment. Everyone in the company leadership believed in the new security arrangements, because in the long term, they were convinced the transition to high tech would save the company money. The thieves, eagerly waiting in the wings, watched as this vast storehouse of wealth steadily grew into a ripe plum ready for picking.

The systematic stealing began and grew with the company, eroding its seemingly impregnable foundations. Collectively, they stole information, products, supplies, and equipment. The thieves also converted vehicles and equipment for their personal sideline businesses and used them to haul the company's products to buyers of stolen property. Small, tightly knit conspiracies developed, each having its own niche. Others acted alone, stealing whatever opportunity made available. While armies of thieves went about their murky business, neither the security director, nor anyone in the company leadership, had a clue about the activities; after all, the high-tech security equipment called nothing about the problem to their attention.

The first sign of trouble came from the corporate comptroller and others who discovered the bills began to exceed the receipts. In a futile effort, they tried to solve the problem by cracking down on expense accounts, examining marketing practices, and implementing other cost-cutting measures. When those processes had little effect, they implemented a strong effort of creating better purchasing deals. Then, they started department reorganizing to gain more efficiency in production, shipping, and receiving coupled with a purge of managers supplying convenient blame. As the company leadership pondered and probed the increasing problem, no one could imagine or admit their problem involved theft. From a business philosophy sense, loss must stem from an accounting error. Through all this, the corporate executives deliberated, while the thieves, like multiplying groups of ants, continued to systematically plunder the company assets.

Finally, when the creditor and stockholder pressure on company leadership became intense, they called in brigades of auditors to descend on the company, taking it apart piece by piece. After weeks of unrelenting dissection, the truth began to emerge. The auditors concluded the reason causing the problem stemmed from the mysterious disappearance of company property that far exceeded profit. Their gloomy report declared the company suffered not only the loss of products, but supplies and equipment that doubled costs because they needed replacements. When the dread finally spread to the boardroom, they hired a security expert to probe further into the workings of the company and supply them with a face-saving and financial solution. His report to the board concluded the security program effectively controlled people but overlooked control of the property and assets the employees, visitors, vendors, and trespassers accessed and then stole from the company areas. The security expert also found another major flaw. The security department training included a two-hour orientation about the company and its history and a couple more hours on how to operate the bells and whistles in nearly totally automated security systems.

That crippled company survived, you would recognize its name immediately. It did go into bankruptcy, but it will be years before its wounds heal. The security director became unemployed, clearly destroying his budding career.

When you hear about a corporation or industry in shocking financial trouble, look behind all the excuses, blame, news releases, and magazine and newspaper stories, and more often than not you'll find a seriously flawed security program created the dilemma. However, often the security director tries hard, but the business philosophy of corporate leadership doesn't allow him or her to develop an effective security program. There's often a lack of understanding about what can happen when security remains weak, and how important the security needs an active place and role in the business operations.

THREE IMPORTANT STEPS YOU NEED TO TAKE IMMEDIATELY

The story just related did happen, and I'm the expert mentioned in the story. Don't you be responsible for bringing down a huge corporation because you've listened to whistle and bells sales reps. No matter how sophisticated any system might be, there's an adage we always need to remember: "Whatever man creates, another man can defeat." However, the secret key to genuine security remains layering, improving, and changing. A crook can't defeat what he doesn't know is there. Now, let's get to those three important steps:

- If you're reading this book, you've already taken the important first step—*buying this book!*

- However, there's a critical second step. *Use this book regularly.* Don't leave your situation and career to chance. Instead, include winning and success in your primary goals. This book will help you achieve those goals.

- Your third step comes in two parts. *When you have problems, refer to this book. When your problem involves resistance from the business executives, buy them a copy!*

WHAT THIS BOOK WILL DO FOR YOU

I'm supplying you with a book that makes sure you can have success as a security professional. I decided to write this book because I'm often called, when as in the case just cited, it's far too late for anything beyond defining the reasons and trying to establish a new security program to salvage what's left after the plunder of a company. I have packed this book with valuable techniques, procedures, and illustrations so you have the complete guidelines in one resource. I'm offering you unequaled advantage and benefit plus the opportunity to excel.

FIVE MAJOR BENEFITS YOU'LL GAIN FROM THIS BOOK

- The secret of effective security involves the creation of a "total" program. That process begins with administrative management and includes the dreaded task of making and following budgets. But in my book, you'll learn how to create and develop winning budgets. Added benefits include how to manage your department resources efficiently and to your best advantage. You'll get important techniques enabling you to demonstrate strong leadership and procedures of creating forms and method of keeping excellent records. Collectively, each of these important elements creates a strong administrative foundation necessary when your goal includes success.

- How you can ensure your security system has a solid foundation offering total protection without the bells and whistles of high-tech equipment. There's nothing wrong with high-tech security; however, you need to use this equipment as a supplement to your security systems, not view it as the only system. I show you how to create and manage your basic foundation of security, including control of people, barriers, and lighting; structural hardening; and management of locks and keys.

- How to integrate high-technology equipment into your basic security "foundation" effectively creating "layers" that stop the crooks cold. You'll also learn the reality and marketing of high-tech equipment showing that high-tech equipment designed for a specific task compares to buying an automobile. Why buy a luxury car loaded with unnecessary features when a less costly compact car with just the basics accomplishes the need you have? I show you how to determine your high-tech needs, how to choose the system that's right for your needs, how to weigh the cost-benefit factors, and how to use the equipment effectively.

- Your security role may cover a broad spectrum of situations, even within the same company. Although the same basic foundations always apply, you might need added specific needs. I show you how to achieve success in these several areas including sea or river ports, protecting the executives in your company, cargo in transit, buildings, financial institutions, and others. Whatever your needs, you'll find the details and techniques about how to do it effectively in my book.

- There's no substitute for quality training in any profession and that holds true in the security fields. In this book you'll learn how to establish a variety of quality training programs at each level necessary. You'll also benefit by learning how to create and manage your department's career development program effectively for its security officers.

SOME OF THE OTHER BENEFITS YOU'LL GAIN FROM THIS BOOK

Besides the benefits and advantages I've just given you, here are seven more valuable dividends that will be yours:

1. A physical security plan guide takes you step by step through the process of accurately assessing what you now have in place and what you need to do to create better security.

2. A physical security checklist gives you the advantage of checking your security systems regularly either independently or collectively.

3. A section on bomb threats shows you how to deal effectively with bomb threats made to your company.

4. A quick reference crime checklist ensures that your officers will approach a situation properly and not overlook important information or evidence.

5. A detailed illustrated criminal description guide and checklist puts you and officers at a big advantage when describing a person or helping a victim or witnesses to supply a credible description.

6. A directory, state by state, of colleges and universities across the country and in Canada lists those institutions that offer courses, some of which award degrees in the security profession.

7. A complete manual about corporate and industrial security is at your fingertips with techniques and procedures that work anywhere, anytime, and for any situation.

Table of Contents

Chapter Six Managing Protective Barriers 128

Chapter Seven Protective Lighting Management 159

Chapter Eleven Electronic Countermeasures 310

PART FOUR HOW TO IMPLEMENT SPECIALIZED PROTECTION 349

Chapter Twelve Security for Corporate Headquarters and Financial Institutions 351

Chapter Thirteen Security Management for Port, Harbor, and River Terminals 362

Chapter Fourteen Intransit Shipments and Cargo Security Management 377

Chapter Eighteen Training Security Supervisors 464

Chaper Nineteen Important Basic Security Training 484

Chapter Twenty In-service Training for Security
Departments 499

Table of Illustrations

P A R T 1

Results-Oriented Security Management

Taking charge of your corporate and industrial security responsibilities and getting results begins with techniques that supply you with the keystones of security management. They include a series of coordinated, goal-directed actions increasing use of your four key resources: human, financial, administrative, and operational. You gain advantage by using your resources to achieve specific security management goals through attentive planning, organizing, staffing, leading, controlling, coordinating, and directing or implementing. The decisions you make and the actions you take hinge on these important resource elements separately and collectively.

MANAGING YOUR IMPORTANT RESOURCES

Each resource has separate importance but remains necessarily interrelated. One resource alone cannot enable your security department and systems to function properly. In the chapters following, and throughout the book, you will discover techniques of managing these resources separately and together. Your key resources include the following:

Human Resources

A critical element in your security department is people, or human resources. Your management skills must include accurately identifying current and future staffing needs. Also, you need to know the techniques of choosing the right people to satisfy those needs effectively. Key techniques to learn include recruiting, selection, training, leading, and retaining.

Financial Resources

Your success of protecting company assets also depends heavily on your department's budget. Your budget interrelates with the quality and retention of human resources, plus supplying the operational and administrative resources.

Administrative Resources

Your third resource includes the security department's assets that enable performance daily. These include offices and supplies, furniture and office equipment, computers, machines, physical inventories of equipment and spare parts, uniforms, firearms, and the basic equipment for your security officers.

Operational Resources

Your corporate and industrial security management depends on basic and technology-based equipment, barriers, and other elements arranged in layered systems to protect company assets. The effectiveness of your security effort relies on how you select and use this important resource.

Part One gives you the step-by-step techniques and processes you will need on a continuing basis to plan, organize, staff, lead, coordinate, control, and direct your resources.

Illustration P1–1 supplies you with an example of how your security management decisions relate to resources, actions, and results, essential to achieve effective security management performance.

Illustration P1–1

Management Decisions and Actions in Terms of Resources, Actions, and Results

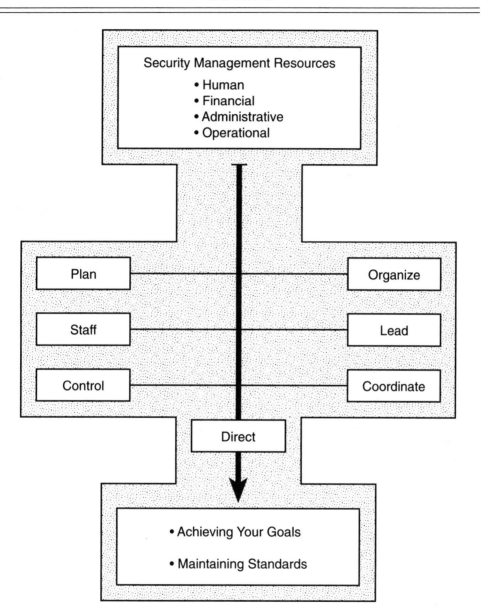

1 Profit from Your Budget

About once a year the corporate budget committee strikes terror in the hearts of security managers by sending around a request for next year's security budget. It strikes terror because making a budget can involve a confusing, time-consuming process. However, it is easier than it seems, and your budget supplies you with a way of achieving goals and helping the company with better protective security. It is the dollar and resource representation of your planned security activities over a period of time, normally the next corporate fiscal year. This chapter shows you the benefits, advantages, and techniques of developing a performance-oriented budget that provides the important financial resource you need.

WHERE YOU FIT IN THE COMPANY BUDGET

In developing your security department budget, you need a clear understanding about where your protective services fit into the company budget, your only financial resource. When you know where you fit in, your approach and requests take on a new meaning. For example, instead of portraying your department as a "deadweight," you can show that it is a part of the business effort and in a different way helps the company earn more profits and have a healthier bottom line. You are helping the profit margin by reducing or preventing losses of company assets. That keeps company assets within the company for use or sale as they were intended. Also, assets stolen, such as computers, office supplies and equipment, and other types of support items, have to be replaced. Your security prevention of that type loss also enhances the bottom line by reducing money spent replacing stolen or pilfered items. The third advantage of your security supplies the company with protection of its information. Competitor intelligence has grown to a huge industry with companies having internal researchers or hiring experts to develop information about competitors. Parts of that enterprise can be legal or illegal depending on the approach; however, legality applies only when value, tangible evidence, and other circumstances are provable. Competitor intelligence is so murky that prosecution should rarely be the concern. Instead, it is protecting the information sources within the company that enables your department to increase company profits.

Although you recognize how your security department efforts aid company profitability, never assume others do. You need to tell management, and aside from your planning, your budget and its structure helps get the message up the line. When that happens, you will receive the necessary financial resources to perform the protective services activity with dynamic dimensions.

QUICK REFERENCE REVIEW

THREE KEY POINTS HELPING YOU GET THE BUDGET YOU NEED

Your Security Department helps the Company Profit by

- Reducing or eliminating theft of company assets from internal or external threats. That includes systematic or opportunity-oriented pilferage by employees, vendors, visitors, or contractors.

- Increasing company profits by reducing or eliminating a need to replace stolen merchandise, office equipment, and other materials, such as tools, building materials, and other items. Also included in this category is the conversion of company property to personal gain on a temporary basis, for example, using company vehicles for personal use, such as operating a delivery service in the evenings with a company van.

- Preventing competitors from obtaining classified information including research and develop data, clients lists, advertising plans and budgets, personnel records, and others that help a competitor increase its profits and decrease your company's profit—or jeopardize the entire company existence by creating huge losses.

SEVEN IMPORTANT BEGINNING STEPS IN YOUR BUDGET PROCESS

Developing a goal-directed budget process is a dreary task that needs to be accomplished—because the company requires you to do it. However, with the five important beginning steps, you can learn that your budget becomes your opportunity.

● The First Step—Recognizing Five Key Factors Influencing Your Budget

From your company's viewpoint of security, five key factors play a primary role in the total resources your department receives. All resources hinge on one main resource—money.

1. *There is demand for protecting company assets.* Corporations are made up of people, and people have a tendency to discard or diminish things believed no longer in need. When your security efforts or other conditions have reduced or eliminated losses from theft, stopped intrusions, and created a safe environment, people managing the company might begin thinking there's no longer a need for strong security. Of course, logic tells us that reduction nearly guarantees that the problems will return and that more money will be spent to compensate for the losses.

2. *Your company leadership must see your value.* Achieving this goal requires strong self-promotion, often a difficult task. Most of us don't like to brag; instead, we go about our professional duties believing others recognize the effort. Don't believe that for a minute, or you will be lost in the budget shuffle. You need to show what your security department accomplishes daily and how outside trends show you are the only thing between the company assets and criminal enterprise. Use the information discussed earlier as your guide in this area.

3. *Clearly identify and document the threat.* Just telling the company leadership it's a dangerous world and the bad guys are constantly looking for ways to rob the company will not help you to achieve your goal. You have to use precise examples and document and prove your case with information from a wide variety of sources. Examples of credible sources include professional publications, coupled with information from local, regional, and national law enforcement agencies.

4. *The company must have the money.* Often, corporations that appear huge, powerful, and rich have their own financial problems. However, corporate leadership isn't likely to tell you the reason your budget is chopped severely stems from the company being in financial straits. You need to communicate and read between the lines. Fighting for money when there isn't much to go around can push leadership into a corner. That can have a significant effect on your future company relationship. But, when you know business isn't so good now but probably will be back, use common sense, compromise, and be diplomatic. The tactic may get you to the top of the list when better times return.

5. *Make sure your performance justifies the request.* From a business point of view, throwing good money after bad does not constitute competent management. When your department's performance is less than top drawer, you're going to have a hard time proving that more money will solve the loss problems. Often, your performance stems from a lack of resources,

specifically money, but you can't approach it that way. When money is a factor in your department's performance, recognize the problems you'll have with the new budget and take action. Since you can't do everything with limited resources, consolidate and concentrate your security on the most important areas. That leaves the thinned security on other areas where problems already exist, but at least you can stop about 50%. You can prove your performance has a direct relationship to resources, letting the facts and figures make your point.

● The Second Step—Understanding Two Important Business Viewpoints

The attitude of your company's management to security is important because in any given year, profits can be increased by reducing expenses. On the annual corporate report to stockholders, the belt tightening and climbing profits look good. However, it's an illusion that eventually catches up unless the company can increase sales and increase profits genuinely. You probably have to deal with two "schools" of executives and middle managers with an eye to the executive washroom.

1. *The "expense" school of thought.* Management that belongs to the "expense" school believes that their company's security effort should be kept to a minimum. They begrudge every penny the company spends on security. When they must cut expenses, security is one of the first things to go. It is an easily reducible expense. Decreasing security will not have an immediate effect on the company's operations since the problems that action creates won't begin showing up on the books for several months and there's always the security manager to blame.

2. *The "investment" school of thought.* Corporate management that belongs to the "investment" school believes that security is an investment. They also believe any investment made by the company should have a predictable rate of return. In their minds, security is similar to an investment in bonds or in shares of stock. They feel that devoting an adequate amount of money to security operations will yield a certain percentage of return through loss reduction that is comparable to cutting expenses resulting in increasing profits. The investment school is your best ally in the budget process. However, when you know who they are, help them prove their point with credible, accurate performance data. Help them prove your security department is a good investment.

● The Third Step—Change Your Personal Attitude About Budgets

The term "budget," like the terms "restriction" or "rationing," evokes negative emotions. Most of us view our budget as force imposing a restriction or restraint. We don't look upon budgets with much enthusiasm. The discipline and control of your budget, however, are necessary, and you can turn it around to be a major positive factor that helps you achieve your goals. Be enthusiastic and take advantage of finding creative ways to get the financial resources you want. There are many examples throughout this chapter.

● The Fourth Step—Be Creative and Realistic

Corporate security is vitally important; however, you need to let the budget committee and others in the executive management circles know how important. You do that through seizing the opportunity of creating a realistic, well-documented, and skillfully prepared budget document as opposed to filling out a form with numbers. With your strategic and annual plans you know exactly what you need and where you want the department to go and that's the first large hurdle. It's a large hurdle for most, because they don't use the advantage of planning. Many companies ask department heads to fill out a form or two and send them in for someone else to second guess, normally an accountant who has no idea what the security department does. He or she sees an officer at the gate and entrance to the office building and for them, that's "security." When they send you a form, fill it out and comply but attach your "budget packet" of documents, worksheets, plans, and spreadsheets. They might be surprised to see what you really do and might help you get the resources you need.

● The Fifth Step—Always Show a Profit

Companies operate with a profitable bottom line in mind. You can use that knowledge to your benefit. When formulating your budget request, ensure you always emphasize the money you receive through the budget *saves* the company money. It's no secret that the corporate bean counters probably view the security department as they do the utility bills. They need the service but neither turns a profit. Show them why they need to view security differently.

● The Sixth Step—Don't Slash Your Budget to the Bone

There is an old myth about budgets and turning back money ending the year. Doing that not only reduces your security performance, but sets a precedent that caused the downfall of many security professionals. When you request a specific amount of financial resources, you should need and use every penny. There are people who always request more than they need so ending the year they can turn back the unused part. It doesn't take long for the company leadership to catch on, although for a time you might be a hero. Later, however, they'll start cutting, and it might be a time when you would really need it. Ask for what you honestly need and use it all—to benefit the company. When you don't need the operating money, don't ask for it. Remember, your budget must request only the amounts you perceive have valid purpose as an expert in the profession assessing the security needs.

• **The Seventh Step—Separate Your Budget into Assets and Win**

When you submit your budget estimate or request to the budget committee, break down and document your security department assets. Don't just ask for money; also show them where last year's company money went, and that from in years past. Your equipment, and all the security department property, often including lighting, fences, vehicles, and other items, form an impressive list of assets. In the corporate environment, controlling assets projects an image of management and responsibility. That makes it easier to get recognition and the financial resources you need.

CREATING YOUR RESULTS-ORIENTED BUDGET

Your company may supply you with a budget forecast and request worksheets. However, the following guidelines assume that you are faced with figuring it out for yourself.

What Belongs in Your Budget Request?

With the refined and accurate annual security plan as your guide, you can begin to forecast the cost. You also need last year's budget and an asset list and other records applicable to your situation. Now you are ready to begin drafting your budget request.

TEN IMPORTANT ELEMENTS TO SUPPORT YOUR BUDGET

Begin your budget request document with concise, but well-crafted summaries of the security department responsibilities. This section of your budget request involves historical data. Never assume the budget committee and other approval authority knows exactly what you do or the extent of the security task. The following "items" list minimum examples that you need to include; however, your company might call for more information or ask for more in-depth information in certain categories or may not ask for anything beyond what you want for the upcoming year. However, always support your request with a recent history of what you're doing to make it easier to justify asking for financial resources.

Element 1: Dates of the Budget Period for This Document.   Show the date the budget begins and ends.

Element 2: Describe Your Security Department Mission.   Include general information, such as "The Security Department, XYZ Corporation protects company assets at (list each facility location). That protective security function includes (number of buildings, open storage areas, number of acres, industrial complexes, etc.). These elements need to be listed with an item heading and shown separately in subelements.

Element 3: List Performance During the Past Year. This section allows you to let the budget committee know how much routine and administrative work is done daily. Often, the security role is envisioned by business-oriented persons as "guards" checking identification at building entrances, gates, and walking along fences. You need to show there is more to the security role. Examples of this processing and administrative actions list follow:

SECURITY DEPARTMENT ACTIVITY ADMINISTRATIVE SUMMARY

Security badges issued	2,816	Security badges repaired	612
Lost badge reports	612	Employee fingerprints	1,925
Visitor passes	4,300	Vendor parking permits	1,410
Employee parking decals	3,410	Employee ID cards	2,330
Security badges destroyed	745	ID cards destroyed	832
Laminations	4,592	Decal terminations	1,423

Accumulative cost of services: $ _____

Element 4: List Actions and Activities. You also need to show the committee how busy the security department and officers are during the past year in other matters. Explain in your opening summary to this section that figures show the "response and investigation" activity by security officers.

RESPONSE AND INVESTIGATIVE ACTIVITIES BY SECURITY OFFICERS

Apprehension of intruders	291	Forced entry alarms	783
Fire alarms	192	Telephone complaints	239
Minor vehicle accidents	210	Law enforcement aid	18

Accumulative cost of services: $ _____

Element 5: Security Personnel Requirements. In this section show the actual placement and requirements of security officers. Also, explain any abbreviations or terms, such as noting "a shift as shown here indicates 8 hours." It's a good idea to include a concise statement below each requirement identifying the need for the activity, or depending on the situation, your decision or recommendation of omitting it from next year's operations. Also, include a summary recapping the information.

SECURITY DEPARTMENT ACTIVITIES AND OFFICER REQUIREMENTS

Placement	Days per Week	Hours	Officers
Security Control Center	7	24	2 per shift

(The security control center monitors CCTV systems, alarm boards and radio dispatches of mobile units to investigate possible security breaches. Officers assigned to this duty also maintain radio and telephone contact with security officers throughout the complex and have responsibility for requesting fire and police assistance when needed.)

Placement	Days per Week	Hours	Officers
Entrance Gate 1 (summary of need and responsibilities)	7	24	2 per shift
Entrance Gate 2 (summary of need and responsibilities)	5	16	1 per shift
Exit Gate 1 (summary of need and responsibilities)	5	16	1 per shift
Exit Gate 2	5	16	1 per shift

(Exit Gate 2, established during 1989 to handle flow of additional employees hired to fulfill government contracts, will no longer be needed after November 29, 19XX when the contract is completed and work in that section of the company no longer requires the numbers of employees as in the past. The current planning includes closing this gate and transferring the officers used to work the gate to other duties within the complex.)

Placement	Days per Week	Hours	Officers
Warehouse 1 (summary of need and responsibilities)	7	24	1 per shift
Warehouse 1 (loading dock) (Summary of need and responsibilities)	5	16	1 per shift
Open Storage Area 2 (summary of need and responsibilities)	7	24	1 per shift
Mobile Patrol 1 (summary of need and responsibilities)	7	16	1 per shift
Supervisor Patrol (summary of need and responsibilities)	7	24	1 per shift

1 Security Manager

1 Assistant Security Manager/Trainer

94 Security Officers

5 Security Supervisors

4 Sentry Dog Handlers and Dogs

3 Equipment Maintenance Technicians

2 Administrative Clerks

Cumulative cost of salaries, benefits, and other personnel expenses: $ _____

Element 6: Personnel Use Summary. Having shown the activities and work force numbers, describe briefly what the job of each category is in relationship to your security mission. Do not assume that it's obvious to the budget committee what each person does specifically.

> *Security Supervisor (show personnel category number, if applicable, rank, or grade beyond job title)* The security supervisor has responsibility for ensuring that the plans, rules and regulations, policies and procedures, and special instructions of the company and security department are known and followed by all officers and other security employees under his or her supervision during the period of duty. He or she conducts roll call, presents briefing, inspects officers and ensures they are posted, maintains schedules, and records and supervises all incidents. (This description can continue to include other duties, depending on your situation.)

Element 7: Security Department Assets Inventory. *List* all the equipment and tangible (physical) assets and its approximate value based on depreciation that you have within your department when the company shows them to be your responsibility. Depending on the situation you have, the assets you can claim vary, but they all need to be listed in this section to show the budget committee what exists along with their age and condition. This information supports later requests for financial resources needed to increase, upgrade, repair, or replace equipment.

Element 8: Maintenance and Support. Depending on the configuration of your company, a maintenance department may support your security department on request or you might be authorized to contract that type of service. Whatever processes you use, summarize the cost of maintenance in your budget request.

Repairs to perimeter fence (by independent contractor)	$0,000.00
Support generator servicing and repairs	$0,000.00
Computer repairs	$0,000.00

Element 9: Training and Equipment Cost. In this section show the budget committee the cost of training and equipment from the past year's operations. You may want to attach supporting documents detailing the training subjects, hours, and other expense documentation.

Basic security training for 12 new employees	$0,000.00
In-service training for security officers	$0,000.00
Training equipment and aids	$0,000.00
Firearms qualification training	$0,000.00

Element 10: Administrative Expenses. Here, you need to itemize all the expenses that fall into administrative resource categories. They include operating the security department along with those items already covered, such as supplies,

furniture, and equipment. In some companies, you might need to include lease of space expenses, utility costs, and other expenses such as insurance, bonding, and telephone charges. When your company does not require that, you need to list only your direct administrative costs.

Accumulative administrative costs: $ _____

Using Spreadsheets to Support Your Budget Request

You may choose to support each of the foregoing items using a spreadsheet or series of spreadsheets. That method enables a variety of options and can be drawn from other information and records within your computer systems. Spreadsheets can also be compiled with a typewriter or by hand. Illustration 1–1 on the following page suggests one possibility for the spreadsheet in developing your budget request.

Illustration 1–1

SUMMARY OF DAILY SECURITY ACTIVITIES—XYZ CORPORATION

ACTIVITY LOCATION	OPERATION TIMES	PERSONNEL REQUIREMENT	DURATION OF OPNS	TOTAL OFFICERS	COST PER DAY
Gate 1	24-hour post	2 officers per shift	7-day operation	6 officers	$0.00
Gate 2	16-hour post	1 officer per shift	5-day operation	3 officers	$0.00
Gate 3	16-hour post	1 officer per shift	5-day operation	3 officers	$0.00
Warehouse 1	16-hour post	2 officers per shift	5-day operation	6 officers	$0.00
Warehouse 2	16-hour post	1 officer per shift	5-day operation	3 officers	$0.00
Warehouse 3	24-hour post	2 officers per shift	7-day operation	6 officers	$0.00
Perimeter 1	16-hour post	1 officer per shift	7-day operation	3 officers	$0.00
Perimeter 2	16-hour post	1 officer per shift	7-day operation	3 officers	$0.00
Perimeter 3	16-hour post	1 officer per shift	7-day operation	3 officers	$0.00
Perimeter 4	16-hour post	1 officer per shift	7-day operation	3 officers	$0.00
Tower 1	24-hour post	1 officer per shift	7-day operation	3 officers	$0.00
Tower 2	24-hour post	1 officer per shift	7-day operation	3 officers	$0.00
HQs Entrance	24-hour post	1 officer per shift	7-day operation	3 officers	$0.00
Visitor Reg	8-hour post	1 officer per shift	5-day operation	3 officers	$0.00
Pass & ID	8-hour post	1 officer per shift	5-day operation	3 officers	$0.00
Parking Control	16-hour post	2 officers per shift	5-day operation	6 officers	$0.00
Control Center	24-hour post	2 officers per shift	7-day operation	6 officers	$0.00
Training	8-hour post	2 officers per shift	5-day operation	6 officers	$0.00
Supervisors	24-hour post	3 officers per shift	7-day operation	6 officers	$0.00
Asst Chief	8-hour post	1 officer per shift	5-day operation	1 officer	$0.00
Chief	8-hour post	1 officer per shift	5-day operation	1 officer	$0.00

Recapitulation:

322 staffing hours per day
 33 officers per 8-hour shift requiring 80 officers per day at a cost of $0,000.00 per day

Relief Force					$0.00
Overtime	24-hour post	5 officers per shift	7-day operation	15 officers	$0.00

This summary of daily security activities serves only as an example of how you can plot each activity and attach to your budget request. You may also develop a spreadsheet for applications of each resource including human, financial, operational, and administrative. The spreadsheet supplies a means of listing and showing a variety of corresponding information such as how, when, and why the item is needed and how it is used, plus the daily, monthly, and yearly costs.

You may also enter information from your worksheets and other records into an ongoing spreadsheet daily or weekly, which saves valuable time when the budget preparation requirement comes down from your company budget committee.

HOW TO CREATE YOUR FINANCIAL RESOURCES

Having established your importance to the budget committee and approving authority in the company, now it's time to ask for next year's resources. Support that request with a copy of your annual plan and reference each request for the same or added (or less) money to the items already discussed. Also, provide a brief explanation of why you reached the decision. For example, discuss your prebudget research and normal liaison with local police that revealed that the crime rate in the area has increased. Also, cite local and national economic trend information as reasons to base your request for increased security officers and equipment.

Often, you are competing with other departments in the company for financial resources. Each believes it has a need, and maybe their arguments are credible. However, your chance of achieving your goals depends on your budget, and just maintaining a high performance level of security costs more each year. Your chances increase when you offer clear, concise historical information and then make clear, concise requests fully and accurately supported with all possible information, including that coming from independent sources. There is only so much money available to be split among many departments. How well you fare depends on your efforts to convince the budget committee security is a priority service in the company, and in its way through prevention of losses, is helping the company make a profit. Examples of how you might structure a request for added resources follow:

Example A: Request for Salary Increases (Human and Financial Resources)

1. Compare security officer salaries and benefits with other comparable position levels in the company.
2. Compare security officer salaries and benefits with those of other companies and national statistics.
3. Stress advantages of an increase such as quality recruiting, retention, and motivation compared to long-term saving resulting from the improved salaries.
4. Consider alternatives such as overtime authorization instead of salary increases. This serves as a temporary measure because within the pay grades companywide an increase for security officers might require a complex restructuring for all employees.

Example B: Additional Security Personnel (Human Resources)

1. Show the number now in your security force compared to current and projected responsibilities.
2. Show specifically where added officers will be used and why.

3. Document benefit and disadvantage to the company if the added numbers are not approved, such as reducing hours on gates, or other areas that might lead to theft or inconvenience for employees coming and going.
4. Include projected turnover rates based on tangible reasons. These might include retirements, other companies aggressively hiring security officers for an expansion, and offering better salaries and benefits.
5. Consider other companies aggressively hiring for an expansion although not in security positions, which may provide enticing opportunities for your security officers to leave.

Example C: Increased Administrative Facilities and Equipment (Administrative Resources)

1. Show a need for added office space and equipment often based on your administrative work loads as cited in Elements 3 and 4, compared with projected increases.
2. Show greater efficiency and long-term cost reduction through use of better equipment such as computers, programs, and computer forms.
3. Show a need for more space to ease increased work loads and promote better and more efficient service to employees and visitors.

Example D: Increased or Replacement of Security Equipment (Operational Resources)

1. Compare need to situation if not approved.
2. Show probable saving resulting from upgraded equipment.
3. Compare cost now with later increased costs resulting in saving.
4. Point out problem areas the resources target and determine savings from theft reduction.

Close Your Budget Process with a Summary Sheet

Earlier I noted that you are dealing with "bottom-line"–oriented businesspeople as well as people who are busy. You also must keep in mind the principle of good salesmanship since you are competing with dozens of other departments and activities for a fair share of the money available to meet expenses of security operations in the coming corporate year. That principle tells us to show the needs, demonstrate the want, support it all quickly, and then close the sale. Your summary sheet closes the sale. It needs to show all the general resource categories you support in the request with last year's cost and the projected cost of next year.

A monthly summary example shown in the following section also can serve as your year-end summary with minor modification. You can consolidate totals from each monthly summary and attach it to your budget. It also serves as an excellent analysis tool month to month when you take your yearly budget and divide it into monthly increments. You can maintain an accurate tracking of how much you have available to spend according to the approved budget and how much you are spending.

HOW TO SELL THE BUDGET COMMITTEE

Depending on the size of your company and its operational procedures, your budget request may involve two steps. The second step probably includes an invitation for you to sit with the committee and go over your budget request to clarify questions or negotiate compromise. When you go to that meeting, you'll need to support your position and demonstrate to the committee you have made reasonable, beneficial requests supported with facts and figures. However, you need to begin now keeping the right type of budget supporting records or "working papers." Illustration 1–2 supplies guidelines for creating your monthly budget working papers, although you need to keep in mind that you need to tailor them to your specific situation. You can also use the same format to create a cumulative year-end worksheet by adding the month-end totals. Often, companies use an accounting code preceding any expenditure, and you should include that when applicable.

Illustration 1–2

Security Department Budget Working Paper Example

Month of: _____

ACCT. CODE	ITEM	EXPENDITURE	BUDGET ALLOWANCE
	SALARY DATA		
0000	Salaries, regular	$ _____	$ _____
0000	Salaries, overtime	$ _____	$ _____
0000	Benefits	$ _____	$ _____
0000	Employee expense items	$ _____	$ _____
	Total _____	$ _____	$ _____
	EQUIPMENT AND VEHICLE MAINTENANCE EXPENSES		
0000	Utility vehicles	$ _____	$ _____
0000	Patrol vehicles	$ _____	$ _____
0000	Motor fuel	$ _____	$ _____
0000	Communications (portable)	$ _____	$ _____
0000	Communications (vehicle)	$ _____	$ _____
0000	Communications (other)	$ _____	$ _____
0000	Typewriters	$ _____	$ _____
0000	Computers	$ _____	$ _____
0000	Office and other lighting	$ _____	$ _____
0000	Generators	$ _____	$ _____
0000	Firearms	$ _____	$ _____
0000	Office furniture/items	$ _____	$ _____
0000	Other	$ _____	$ _____
	Total _____	$ _____	$ _____
	OPERATIONAL EQUIPMENT MAINTENANCE		
0000	Security lighting	$ _____	$ _____
0000	Fencing	$ _____	$ _____
0000	Intrusion alarms	$ _____	$ _____
0000	CCTV equipment	$ _____	$ _____
0000	Screening/other	$ _____	$ _____
0000	Alarm boards	$ _____	$ _____
0000	Locks	$ _____	$ _____
0000	Sensor equipment	$ _____	$ _____

(continued)

Illustration 1–2 (continued)

ACCT. CODE	ITEM	EXPENDITURE	BUDGET ALLOWANCE
0000	ID systems	$ _____	$ _____
	Total _____	$ _____	$ _____

ACQUISITION OF NEW OPERATIONAL EQUIPMENT

ACCT. CODE	ITEM	EXPENDITURE	BUDGET ALLOWANCE
0000	Locks and keys	$ _____	$ _____
0000	Alarm systems	$ _____	$ _____
0000	Security lighting	$ _____	$ _____
0000	Barrier construction	$ _____	$ _____
0000	Sensors	$ _____	$ _____
0000	ID readers	$ _____	$ _____
0000	CCTV equipment	$ _____	$ _____
	Total _____	$ _____	$ _____

ACQUISITION OF NEW ADMINISTRATIVE EQUIPMENT

ACCT. CODE	ITEM	EXPENDITURE	BUDGET ALLOWANCE
0000	Office furniture	$ _____	$ _____
0000	Typewriters	$ _____	$ _____
0000	Computers	$ _____	$ _____
0000	Computer software	$ _____	$ _____
0000	Firearms (handgun)	$ _____	$ _____
0000	Firearms (shotguns)	$ _____	$ _____
0000	Uniforms	$ _____	$ _____
0000	Flashlights	$ _____	$ _____
0000	Office supplies	$ _____	$ _____
0000	Forms	$ _____	$ _____
0000	Company forms (ID, etc.)	$ _____	$ _____
0000	Custodial service	$ _____	$ _____
0000	Lease (rent)	$ _____	$ _____
0000	Telephone	$ _____	$ _____
0000	Electric utilities	$ _____	$ _____
	Total _____	$ _____	$ _____

RECRUITMENT, SELECTION, AND TRAINING

ACCT. CODE	ITEM	EXPENDITURE	BUDGET ALLOWANCE
0000	Recruiting expenses (ads, etc.)	$ _____	$ _____
0000	Selection process	$ _____	$ _____
0000	Basic training	$ _____	$ _____

(continued)

Illustration 1–2 (continued)

ACCT. CODE	ITEM	EXPENDITURE	BUDGET ALLOWANCE
0000	In-service training	$ _____	$ _____
0000	Firearms ammunition	$ _____	$ _____
0000	Targets and ranges	$ _____	$ _____
0000	Training aids	$ _____	$ _____
	Total _____	$ _____	$ _____

— Continue this worksheet tailored to your situation —

Illustration 1–3

QUICK REFERENCE GUIDE
FOR
CREATING YOUR ANNUAL SECURITY DEPARTMENT BUDGET

What You Need to Start

Your Annual Plan (for next year) _____

Your Current Department Budget _____

Your Monthly Expenditure Worksheets _____

Notes, Company Memos, Information
Helpful in Creating Your Budget _____

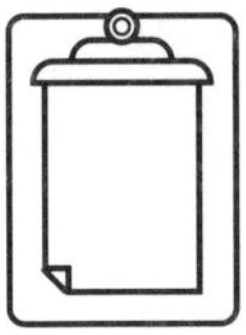

QUICK REFERENCE GUIDE
FOR
CREATING YOUR ANNUAL SECURITY DEPARTMENT BUDGET

How to Put It Together—Minimum Information

Date of Budget Period _____ ☐

Concise Description of the Security Mission _____ ☐

A Summary of Past Year's Performance _____ ☐

A Summary of Security Actions and Activities _____ ☐

Security Personnel Requirements _____ ☐

Security Personnel Utilization _____ ☐

Security Department Assets _____ ☐

Maintenance Requirements _____ ☐

Training and Equipment Costs _____ ☐

Administrative Expenses _____ ☐

2 Human Resource Management

An integral part of your security management staffing process includes the important resource of human resources staffing. Developing a quality staff requires careful planning, beginning with recruiting people to fill security department positions. Although finding, hiring, training, evaluating and developing have important roles in your staffing process, you need to create a solid foundation for it, and that comes from attentive planning. Your staff planning process involves three important analyses:

1. Analysis of the levels of skill in your department (often called a "skills" inventory)
2. Analysis of current and expected vacancies resulting from retirements, discharges, transfers, promotions, sick leaves, leaves of absence, or other reasons
3. Analysis of current and expected expansions or curtailments in your department stemming from company cutbacks, expansions, or replacing one security measure for another (e.g., use of sentry dog teams that decreases a need for larger numbers of regular officers or high-tech equipment that replaces human presence in a specific area).

After determining what you have, what you'll probably need, and when you need it, you're ready to start deciding how you're going to find, hire, train, and retain replacements or increased numbers of security officers, technicians, and administrative staff.

DRAFTING ACCURATE JOB DESCRIPTIONS AND SPECIFICATIONS

You cannot recruit the type of person or develop skills you need when you aren't sure yourself. However, you can find out through a defining process for each position with a concise, accurate description of the job and the specifications (or requirements). Your company has legal counsel and human resource experts who will help you and always ensure they review and approve your job descriptions and specifications. Your first concern when creating a job description and specifications is to ensure no part of them violates any of the many laws governing employment. It is not feasible for you to make any assumptions, for example, on what you may have done last year or six months ago, because hiring and employment laws, regulations, policies, and court decisions change frequently. This section helps you "draft" these documents. Neither the process nor the examples should be construed to be "legally correct" for the reasons already noted. Always keep in mind when drafting your job descriptions and specifications always to strive for accuracy and list genuine skill requirements fairly and without any type of prejudice. Although the many laws and regulations often raise objections from those having to hire and employ people, the reason for the strict rules stems from a variety of problems that developed over decades. Instead of viewing these rules as obstacles, look at them with positive views, understand their purpose, and integrate that reasoning into your staffing process.

The Accuracy of Your Job Description

Describing exactly what the job you want to fill includes isn't easy. You need to think about that carefully. For example, when a security position in your department calls for an officer to be armed, the first thing you must consider is the necessity for arming security officers in that position. That has nothing to do with the concept of arming security officers; rather, that kind of thinking helps you to prove the need when drafting your job description. Remember, much of what you say in the job description has far greater impact than just recruiting and hiring. It shapes training policies and procedures, as well as how you manage the department and officer careers. When you can genuinely prove a necessity, you need to state clearly in the job description and specifications that the position calls for "an Armed Security Officer." Exactness throughout your job description creates an inherent fairness to interested applicants and a solid foundation for your management techniques to develop. It also helps attract skills that otherwise might be missed, such as a person who might not apply for an security position thinking it to be only a "watchman" job.

Develop Precise Job Specifications

Your job specifications tell the applicant, trainers, and others concerned exactly what skills are needed in that specific position. For example, when the security officer position must be armed, the applicant doesn't necessarily need experience with firearms; however, the candidate must be willing (and able) to attend firearms training and through that process meet minimum qualification standards. The training difficulty level must also correspond to proven need to prevent creation of a "discreet" form of discrimination. A complete discussion of security officer training aspects appears throughout Part Five.

The development of job specifications deserves more attention than it usually gets. Knowing specifically what to look for in applicants helps you decide how and where to recruit, the selection process to use, and how to assess competing candidates. Job specifications increase your objectivity in making selection decisions and reduce the likelihood that irrelevant criteria and personal bias will influence your judgment.

Illustration 2–1 shows a "draft" job description and specification example. This is an "example only" and should not be construed to satisfy all the laws, regulations, policies, and court decisions. Use it only as a "guide" for "drafting" your requirements. Ensure that each job description draft be approved by your company legal and human resources experts. Since the position of security officers might be regulated by state law, ensure your description and specifications meet those special requirements.

Illustration 2-1

EXAMPLE OF JOB DESCRIPTION WITH JOB SPECIFICATIONS

Position and Grade:	Armed Security Officer Grade 1
Company and Location:	XYZ Manufacturing Company, Inc., Any City, Any State
Opening Date:	These items have relevance when using the description and specifications as a "job announcement" or providing it to applicants who are free to take it with them. Be sure to specify an opening and closing date so no misunderstanding emerges that the job is always open.
Closing Date:	

Position Duties

1. This is a 40-hour-per-week position with periodic overtime requirements.

2. The position offers a company benefit package, including health, life and other types of insurance, vacation and retirement plans, and other programs. Many are optional and offer various levels of participation.

3. Daily duties include:
   a. Reporting for duty in uniform and attending a preshift briefing by a Supervisor.
   b. Working alone for long periods of time, including days, nights, weekends, and holidays.
   c. Regularly walking a patrol area during a dutyshift lasting about one hour each patrol, four times per shift minimum. This includes all types of weather, day or night. (All equipment is furnished.)
   d. Carrying an issued .357 magnum revolver on duty. (Handgun is issued at beginning of shift and turned in at end of shift.)

   (Continue your job description duties according to your situation.)

Job Specifications

1. Must attend and successfully complete an 80-hour basic preassignment security course provided by the company.

2. Must attend and successfully complete a certified first aid and CPR course.

3. Must attend a 16-hour firearms training course and successfully qualify with the issued duty handgun and other firearms as needed. Must requalify twice each year to maintain qualification for this position.

4. Must attend scheduled in-service training throughout employment period.

5. Must have an average knowledge of the English language and be able to read and understand instructions and other documents, interview persons, fill out forms, and write reports.

(continued)

Illustration 2–1 (continued)

6. Must have ability to communicate effectively with a wide variety of persons encountered on duty.

7. Must wear furnished uniform during duty period and present a neat, professional image.

8. Must be physically fit and have correctable sight of minimum 20/40.

(Continue your specifications to include all aspects relevant to the position.)

Qualification Brief

This section allows you to offer alternatives when applicable, as when your job description calls for a specific type of experience, for example, "Must have 5 years general security experience." This might be the situation when looking for a supervisor or some other position that needs special skill. You should list the specific experience qualifications in two ways:

• General Requirements

Except for the substitutions explained below, candidates must have

1. Three years of progressively responsible general experience. Such experience must show skill in (a) list skill, (b) list skill, (c) list skill.

2. Two years supervisory experience including demonstrated skills in (a), (b), (c).

3. Others as applicable.

• Substitutions for General Requirements

1. Five or more years as a certified police officer

2. Two years college and two years experience as a security officer

3. Two years experience as a military police person

4. Others as applicable

Note to Applicant: Combinations of education, training, and experience may also serve as a means to satisfy total qualification requirements. Past training and certifications may apply to requirements.

How to Apply

Add this section when you use description and specifications to announce a position, supplied to interested persons considering application, during recruiting, or posting on bulletin boards.

(continued)

Illustration 2–1 (continued)

1. State any special needs, ensuring each is a genuine job necessity and following the employment laws, for example, a birth certificate, military DD214 (needed for many defense contract positions), proof of education when that is one of the specifications, or other documents specified.

2. Letters of recommendation if available or other documents that further qualify the applicant for the position; for example, a retired police officer or a person having significant training in security or law enforcement fields should attach copies to his or her application.

3. Instructions about where to apply, or call, or write for applications. In this section you need to explain the options of application, where to get the applications, and any special instructions about submitting it.

4. Include any other instructions relevant to application.

Company Policy Statement

You should normally show this on job descriptions and specifications and applications. Your company can decide the necessity; however, inclusion reminds interested persons, applicants, and your own employees of good faith intentions about staffing the security department.

"All qualified applicants will receive consideration for employment without regard to race, creed, color, national origin, or any other nonmerit factor."

MANAGING THE RECRUITING EFFORT

Once you have the staff planning, job descriptions, and hiring authorization budget in place, it's time to find potential security officers. The key word of recruiting remains "qualified" or "quality" when seeking persons for security positions. They must be willing to attend training; work odd hours, weekends, and holidays; wear a uniform; and perform responsible duty in all kinds of weather. These types of special considerations, coupled with salaries that rarely pay enough for that commitment, make your job of attracting a flood of quality applicants who have a career in mind difficult. The solution is to get out and beat the bushes, and convince people that the security profession is improving and that with the right people, it will improve faster. Also, with improvement, professionalism, and strong leadership, the salaries and benefits for security officers will increase.

Eight Places to Find and Recruit Security Officers

When you project a positive attitude and enthusiasm, the recruiting effort becomes easier. Often, one of the problems involving security positions stems from an apologetic attitude about what you have to offer or have a willingness to take whoever you can get and hope for the best. In the eight areas discussed here, you can find quality people who have the need and motivation to learn and develop into solid security officers.

1. The Internal Market

Often, your own company can provide some or all your human resource needs. Possibilities include

- *Laid-off employees.* For example, large industrial firms periodically lay off employees when the firm has completed a manufacturing phase or government contract or is undergoing a slowdown in business. When you can successfully recruit these employees, you gain advantage. They already have familiarity with the area, the company, and other employees. A major part of the hiring process has already been satisfied. Often, with good coordination you can recruit persons needed before the layoff, and your company personnel department can transfer them to the security department when the layoff takes place.

- *Employees seeking advancement or career change.* A company employee, for example, a secretary or warehouse clerk might find transferring to the security department an advancement, not only income, but for building a career. Your coordination with the personnel department can help. It's easier and less costly for the company to recruit a secretary or warehouse clerk than a security officer who must receive basic and continuing training and uniforms and fulfill other requirements not applicable to many other company employees.

2. Direct Applications (Write-ins or Walk-ins)

Often a person seeking a job will make the rounds to corporations filling out applications and hoping for a job opening even when the company isn't hiring. Coordination with your personnel department might identify applicants you can recruit to fill a security officer position. Even if the person asked about a position with the sales department, his or her qualifications might be just right for your security department.

3. Private Employment Agencies

Often, job seekers go to a private employment agency and ask them to find a job. Often these persons include those already employed in some other company or position, but looking for a change or career for a variety of reasons. This is a valuable resource for you because the agency manages much of the screening and qualification you would have to do. These agencies normally have clients who look for long-term, career-oriented positions and might be candidates for security department recruiting.

4. Public Employment Service

Government-operated employment service offices (about 2,600) throughout the country are a good security recruiting source. These offices collect a variety of qualification information from job seekers, much the same as the private agencies, and enable an effective screening process matching qualifications with your requirements. Many now use a computerized process of matching "transferable skills" with those you cite in your job description and specifications. Most also have a network among their offices to search for the right person nearby or in a distant location who voiced a willingness to relocate.

5. Classified Advertising

Depending on the geographical area, this type of recruiting can supply candidates. However, the problem with classified advertising is that it draws more curiosity than genuinely interested persons, and a study of replies to classified advertising shows a majority often turn out as underqualified persons (people not willing or able to perform as needed). It's far too expensive to put your entire job description and specifications in a classified ad, so readers of normal advertising rarely have a meaningful understanding about the job is or its requirements. To find out they have to come in, write, or call. Many companies now use blind ads because the administrative work load of just answering questions about the advertised job becomes awesome.

6. College Placement Offices

Depending on your needs and circumstances, you might consider local colleges. This works often when the vacancy is some time off such as a known retirement. While most college graduates feel they can do better than becoming a security officer, depending on the person, and the position and benefits you have to offer, he or she might be willing start at the bottom and move up. There are about 3,280 college placement officers across the country who could supply you with a good resource for recruiting.

7. Drawing on Retiring Public Servants

Police departments, sheriff's offices, and other law enforcement and regulatory agencies in the area might supply you with names of officers preparing to retire and looking for a less arduous job within the same general profession. Most will also allow you to post your announcement of vacancies and job descriptions on their bulletin boards. Much of the security industry has retired law enforcement officers, especially security positions that require an officer be armed, or dealing with large numbers of people and problems. That recruiting possibility also applies to a variety of state agencies.

8. Associations and Trade Magazines

Depending on the type of security officer you're seeking, you might identify candidates from ads placed in professional magazines for security and law enforcement officers. For example, a person might want to live in your city and seeing your advertisement supplies a potential opportunity for him or her to move from a current security job in another city to yours. Other possibilities include those noted for local law enforcement retiring officers who are looking for a security position in your area after retirement.

THE SELECTION PROCESS

When your recruiting efforts work, you might have a stack of applications, maybe 50 for 5 security officer jobs, and that creates a new dilemma. Choosing the best candidates is a difficult task, since you have 50 hopeful people at the beginning and 45 disappointed people at the end. There are also other considerations that relate to the legal factors much like your job description and specifications. Before scheduling interviews, or selecting which applicants you want to interview, always obtain guidance from your company human resource expert and legal counsel. Excluding an applicant needs a reason beyond the common dismissal of "not qualified." Also, innocent, well-meaning questions during an interview might get you and your company in trouble when a candidate believes you have prejudices or discrimination in mind. For example, the following checklist helps you to avoid a few established areas during an interview. Keep in mind that some of the prohibitive questions can be asked depending on special circumstances, especially those involving security positions that involve government contacts and classified materials and information. In such cases, a government security clearance might be needed, and that involves additional rules and latitudes. Always try to record your interviews, but ensure you inform the applicant that you're doing so and explain that your interview is a part of and an extension of the written application with the recording becoming a part of that record. If the applicant objects, you must respect that and be satisfied with notes. Illustration 2–2 supplies guidelines in a may or may not questions checklist.

Illustration 2–2

CHECKLIST FOR ANTIDISCRIMINATORY INTERVIEWS

(Intended as Guidelines Only)

1. **Race or color**
   - ☐ Inquiries NOT permitted regarding:
     - Complexion or color of skin
     - Coloring

2. **Religion**
   - ☐ Inquiries NOT permitted regarding:
     - Religious denomination
     - Religious affiliations
     - Church
     - Parish
     - Pastor
     - Religious holidays observed
   - ☐ It is also NOT permissible for the interviewer to say, "This is a (Catholic, Protestant, or Jewish) organization."

3. **National Origin**
   - ☐ Inquiries NOT permitted about any of the following topics:
     - Lineage
     - Ancestry
     - National origin
     - Descent
     - Parentage
     - Nationality
     - Nationality of family (e.g., parents or spouse)
     - Mother tongue

4. **Sex**
   - ☐ *A preemployment inquiry regarding sex on an application form is* UNLAWFUL.

5. **Marital status**
   - ☐ The interviewer MAY NOT ask questions such as
     - Are you married?
     - Where does your spouse work?
     - How old are your children, if any?

6. **Age**
   - ☐ The interviewer MAY ask questions such as
     - Are you over 18 years of age? If not, state your age.
   - ☐ The interviewer MAY NOT ask questions such as
     - How old are you?
     - What is your date of birth?

7. **Disability**
   - ☐ The interviewer MAY ask questions such as
     - Do you have any impairments, physical or mental that would interfere with your ability to perform the job for which you have applied?
     - If there are any positions or types of positions for which you should not be considered or job duties you cannot perform because of a physical handicap, please explain.

(continued)

Illustration 2–2 (continued)

☐   The interviewer MAY NOT ask questions such as
- Do you have a disability?
- Have you ever been treated for any of the following diseases? (reading or reciting a list of diseases)
- Has any member of your family ever had any of the following diseases? (reading or reciting a list of diseases)

8. **Name**

☐   The interviewer MAY ask questions such as
- Have you ever worked for this company under a different name?
- Any more information about change of name, uses of an assumed name, or nickname necessary to enable a check of your work record? If yes, explain.

☐   The interviewer MAY NOT ask questions about
- The original name of an applicant whose name changed by court order or otherwise.

☐   The maiden name of a married female.

☐   Whether the applicant has ever worked under another name, and if so, where and when.

9. **Address or duration of residence**

☐   The interviewer MAY ask questions such as
- What is your address?
- How long have you resided in the state or city?

10. **Birthplace**

☐   The interviewer MAY NOT ask questions such as
- Where were you born?
- Where were your parents, spouse, or other close relatives born?

11. **Photographs**

☐   There MAY NOT be a requirement that the applicant affix a photograph to the employment form before hiring.

12. **Citizenship**

☐   The interviewer MAY ask questions such as
- Are you a U.S. citizen?
- If not, do you intend to become a U.S. citizen?
- Have you ever been interned or arrested as an enemy alien?

☐   The interviewer MAY NOT ask questions such as
- Of what country are you a citizen?
- Are you a naturalized or native-born citizen?
- On what date did you receive citizenship?
- Were your parents or is your spouse naturalized or native-born citizens of the United States?
- On what date(s) did your parents or your spouse receive citizenship?

Note: The Immigration Reform and Control Act of 1986 calls for a newly hired employee to furnish, within three business days of starting work, original documents that prove his or her right to work in the United States.

(continued)

Illustration 2–2 (continued)

13. **Languages**
    - ☐ The interviewer MAY ask questions like:
      - What foreign language(s) do you read fluently?
      - Write fluently?
      - Speak fluently?
    - ☐ The interviewer MAY NOT inquire about how the applicant acquired the abilities to read, write, or speak a foreign language.

14. **Education**
    - ☐ The interviewer MAY ask questions about the academic, vocational, or professional education of the applicant.
    - ☐ The interviewer MAY NOT require that an applicant have a minimum of a high school or college education unless such education can be proven to be a bona fide occupational requirement.
      (*Griggs* v. *Duke Power*, 401 U.S. 424, 1971)
    - ☐ The interviewer MAY ask about the public and private schools the applicant has attended.

15. **Experience**
    - ☐ The interviewer MAY ask about the applicant's work experience and visits to other countries.

16. **Character**
    - ☐ The interviewer MAY ask questions such as
      - Have you ever been convicted of any crime? If so, please specify when, where, and disposition of offense.
    - ☐ The interviewer MAY NOT ask questions such as
      - Have you ever been arrested?

Note: An employer's use of an individual's arrest record to deny employment would, without proven necessity, be a violation of the human rights laws.

17. **Relatives**
    - ☐ The interviewer MAY ask questions such as
      - The names of any of the applicant's relatives who are already employed by the company.
    - ☐ The interviewer MAY NOT ask questions about
      - Names, addresses, ages, number, or other information about applicant's children or other relatives not employed by the company.

18. **Notice in case of emergency**
    - ☐ The interviewer MAY ask the name and address of the person to be notified in case of an accident or emergency.

19. **Military experience**
    - ☐ The interviewer MAY ask questions such as
      - Have you ever been a member of the U.S. armed services or a state militia? If so, did your military experience have any relationship to the position for which you have applied?
    - ☐ The interviewer MAY NOT ask about an applicant's general military experience.

(continued)

Illustration 2–2 (continued)

20. **Organizations**
    - ☐ The interviewer MAY ask questions such as
      - Are you a member of any clubs or organizations? Exclude organizations whose name or character indicates the race, creed, color, or national origin of its members.
    - ☐ The interviewer MAY NOT ask questions such as
      - List all the clubs, societies, and lodges where you have or have had membership.

21. **References**
    - ☐ The interviewer MAY ask who suggested that the applicant apply for a position with the company.

POSTINTERVIEW ACTION

After conducting your interviews, and you've chosen probable candidates for the job based on a complete assessment, you need to verify the information on their applications plus develop standard information about their character and reputation. Just as with job descriptions, applications, and interviews, seek guidance from your company's legal counsel and human resources expert before proceeding. However, providing they allow you to move forward, the traditional steps that follow are commonly used in the selection of applicants in part or totally depending on the situation and needs.

1. Testing

There are always controversies about testing, with the primary argument that a test can be a discreet form of discrimination. There is also the question of validity and accuracy referring to certain people who are experts in a skill yet flunk written tests on the same subject. Studies show that some people can fare better in a written test than others and the outcome can often be misleading. There are few valid reasons to give tests for a security officer position unless you need to determine a candidate's ability to read and follow instructions and to complete forms and write reports if that requirement is important to performance of the job. There is always a problem of illiteracy, and those who fall victim to that problem devise excellent defensive measures to prevent discovery. For example, a recent U.S. Department of Education survey of young adults found that only 11% could read a bus schedule successfully. That type of testing (administrative) can disclose that type of problem that may disqualify the candidate from your position. Other forms of testing are used and your company human resources experts offer the best guidance on what's available and those that might help you in the qualification and selection process.

2. Physical Examinations

Many companies routinely ask applicants to have a physical examination at company expense before further consideration for a position. One reason is a job related need, as when employees are exposed to strenuous labor or are in a sensitive and dangerous work environment. While a physical exam is always a good idea, calling for the examination and using it to disqualify a person from a job needs attentive planning and be legally justified. Primarily you must show and prove the job needs to be a specific physical parameter before the search for employees begins.

3. Reference Checks

Your job application must include a clear statement understood and signed and dated by the applicant before you can legally become involved in a background investigation. The applicant needs to know that you will or may conduct that kind of investigation based on his or her application, interviews, and other pertinent information collected from a variety of sources. The depth of your investigation depends on the need. For example, when a company receives a government contract that involves classified information, a security officer working in or around the area may need a strict background check based on government standards. When the position doesn't provide access to anything important and the officer always works in a crowded environment, the need for an intense background investigation diminishes. Regardless of the circumstances, ensure the applicant agrees to a background investigation and signs that agreement. Also, ensure the applicant can read and understand it before allowing him or her to sign it. The statement should have an agreement similar to the one following shown as Illustration 2–3.

Illustration 2–3

APPLICANT'S STATEMENT ON JOB APPLICATION

- I certify that answers given herein are true and complete to the best of my knowledge.
- I authorize investigation of all statements in this application for employment as may be necessary in arriving at an employment decision.
- I consent to the release of information about my ability and fitness for the position I have applied for by employers, schools, law enforcement agencies, and other individuals and organizations to investigators, personnel staffing specialists, and other authorized employees of this company.
- If hired, I understand that false or misleading information given in my application or interview(s) may lead to discharge.

[signature of applicant]	Date

4. Five Basic Steps of Qualifying an Applicant

Security personnel have nearly unlimited access to all areas of the company without suspicion or challenge by other employees. Their integrity and loyalty needs verification before having that access through employment. Before embarking on any background investigation, ensure that you coordinate with your company's legal counsel and human resources expert to determine the legality of what you plan to do for each specific employee. The steps you should follow when justified and legal according to the position include

1. Systematically verifying all information supplied by the applicant on the application or during a recorded interview.
2. Conducting a search for criminal convictions. This is public information and does not disclose number of arrests, only cases resolved by court actions.
3. Conducting a driver's license records search (when the applicant is required to operate a company vehicle).
4. Conducting a credit history profile when the applicant will have access to money or other items of high value such as diamonds, gold or other precious metals, or negotiable securities, or other similar items. (Note: Bad credit doesn't necessarily mean the applicant is a bad risk. For example, a person who has good credit could be keeping it that way by stealing or be a person who honors his or her obligations. The report in itself cannot identify which; that comes through your analysis process.) For credit information to be accurate in the selection process, you need to analyze derogatory credit

information with other circumstances within the time parameter of that shown on credit reports. The applicant might have been laid off, suffered illness, had a family crisis, or been subject to any number of happenings that created the bad credit. Often, too much credence is placed on credit reports in the selection process. When everything else is positive, and the credit report is the only problem, at least give the applicant an opportunity to explain. Often that is satisfactory. Also, remember that credit bureaus do make mistakes.

5. Undertaking background investigation steps as might be necessary depending on the situation. For example, when the company has government contracts for classified work and the security officer might have access to it, additional investigation supported by the FBI often occurs.

PLACEMENT AND APPRAISAL MANAGEMENT

When you've assessed all the information and are satisfied that the selected applicants supply the quality and potential you need to fill the security officer vacancies, an offer of employment leading to acceptance brings you to the next staffing phase, training, placement, and appraisals. (The training aspects are discussed in Part Five.) Considering that each applicant has attended and successfully completed the required training, you need to decide how to integrate the new officers into the security department's operational mission. When you have the officers working under supervisors, the management task continues. Aside from in-service training (also discussed in Part Five), you need to ensure each new officer hired receives a performance appraisal within six months of beginning work. All other officers and employees in the security department should receive a performance appraisal at least once each year. Conducting performance appraisals creates significant benefit to your management efforts, the department, and company.

Your Performance Appraisal Creates 5 Key Benefits

1. The appraisal helps the officer to maintain an understanding of their job and how it relates to the present company operations.
2. It provides officers with an awareness of your goals for the security department and makes them feel a part of the development process.
3. Your appraisal process helps the officer and you to develop each officer's full potential and encourages career-oriented thinking.
4. It provides an effective means of recognizing exceptional performance.
5. It serves as a basis for improving the performance of each officer and resulting collectively in improving the performance of the department.

Your Performance Appraisal Provides Management Advantage

Your performance appraisal system is task oriented and uses clear measurement standards to determine the officer's level of performance. It assures security officers that you are aware of their performance and interested in their professional growth and development. It also provides a mechanism for you to plan constructively for any needed improvement in your officer and department performance collectively. Most important, it yields opportunities for interaction and communication regularly between officers and supervisors who normally conduct the appraisal and reviewed by you. To create this appraisal system you need to develop uniform performance standards that remove the "personality" element from supervisor's prerogative. The following guide supplies the technique of developing your performance standards for appraisals.

Six Key Points to Developing Performance Standards

Your *performance standard* is a stated *measure* of expected performance an officer needs to achieve or the goal an officer must accomplish. When developing your performance standards, keep the following key points in mind.

1. *Standards must be stated resolutely and precisely.* They must enable the officer to know what their responsibilities include and ways to achieve the standard. It also must enable the supervisor to measure the officer's actual performance against the standard. During that process, both supervisor and officer can determine whether the performance standard was achieved.

2. *Standards must be practical to measure.* They need to provide the necessary information about performance in terms of cost, accuracy, and availability of data in the most efficient manner possible.

3. *Standards must be meaningful.* They need to assess what is important and connected to the job and to the achievement of goals.

4. *Standards must be realistic and based on sound rationale.* Expectations of performance must be realistic and achievable. The standard level or difficulty is determined through historical information (e.g., the level achieved in a previous year), comparison (e.g., the level achieved by other officers in a like setting), or a more job-specific procedure. To the extent possible, arbitrariness in setting standards should be avoided. Sometimes, however, when no historical precedents or logical sources for comparison are available, the supervisor will have to choose the level that seems most reasonable.

5. *Officers who are doing similar jobs should have similar performance standards.* Certainly some variations might be reasonable because of differences in work requirements. But take care to ensure that officers who are performing identical jobs are treated uniformly and that differences in standards reflect only real differences in jobs.

6. *Standards may be expressed in positive or negative terms:*
  a. *Positive standards.* State exactly what's expected. They may also establish a requirement for an increase in a particular aspect of the job.
  b. *Negative standards.* Explain what's not wanted or establish a requirement for a reduction in a particular aspect of the job.

Seven Common Dimensions of Measurement

Because of the differences in jobs, they cannot all be measured in the same dimensions. Most security officer positions need to be measured about results. However, some might be in positions production oriented, for example, processing passes, managing gates, and other activities where numbers of people, vehicles or paperwork must be handled efficiently. The following dimension guidelines enable you to match the measurement to the position appraised.

  1. *Quality.* This describes how well or how thoroughly the work is performed; it refers to accuracy, appearance, usefulness, or effectiveness. It may be expressed in terms of an error rate, such as a number or percentage of errors allowable per unit of work, or as general results necessary if numerical rates are not feasible. For measurements involving quality, consider usefulness, responsibleness, error rate, and feedback from those being served.

  2. *Quantity.* This specifies how much work must be completed within a specific time. For measurements involving quantity, use numbers or percentages only when using tracking systems, for example, managing traffic and parking, inspecting cargo, processing trucks or visitors, or moving employees in and out of company areas.

  3. *Timeliness.* This specifies how quickly work must be performed. It answers questions such as when, how soon, or within what period. Where definite quantity standards cannot be set, it may be possible to set time limits. Also, when work tends to fluctuate or there are seasonal trends in work loads, a time per unit requirement may be a more practical means of measurement. For measurements involving timeliness, consider the best performance indicator and what's easiest to track, for example, processing applications for employee and visitor passes.

  4. *Cost effectiveness.* This measurement works when performance can be assessed in terms of money saved, earned, collected, or expended.

  5. *Results desired.* This is used when the standard can best be expressed in terms of the results obtained.

  6. *Manner of performance.* This dimension is often helpful in establishing standards of performance for positions in which personal contacts are an important factor, or when the officer's personal attitude, mannerism, and behavior affect performance.

7. *Method of accomplishment.* This measurement is used when there's a standard procedure or method for completion of a task and when the use of other than prescribed procedures is unacceptable.

Illustration 2–4 shows how these guidelines might be integrated into a performance standards appraisal worksheet for the officer and supervisor.

Illustration 2–4

SAMPLE PERFORMANCE STANDARDS
CLASS TITLE: SECURITY OFFICER

Numerical Rating Schedule:
(1) Outstanding (2) Satisfactory (3) Acceptable and Improving (4) Needs Improvement (5) Unacceptable

DUTIES AND RESPONSIBILITIES	PERFORMANCE STANDARDS	RATING
1. Reports for duty at scheduled time.	1. Wears clean, pressed, and neat uniform.	[ ]
	2. Keeps working equipment clean and serviceable.	[ ]
	3. Exhibits presentable grooming according to company and department policy.	[ ]
	4. Reports punctually and prepared for work.	[ ]
2. Observes receiving operations at warehouse 1 outside docks	1. Checks and initials all manifests.	[ ]
	2. Ensures checkers actively count all cargo as it is unloaded.	
	3. Ensures manifest accuracy.	[ ]
	4. Inspects cargo and verifies condition.	[ ]
	5. Inspects each truck to ensure all cargo on manifest is unloaded.	[ ]
3. Reports all discrepancies to supervisor and in reports.	1. Contacts supervisor immediately.	[ ]
	2. Completes forms accurately.	[ ]
	3. Writes clear, concise reports.	[ ]
4. Maintains appropriate attitude and demeanor.	1. Exhibits cordial and firm work demeanor.	[ ]
	2. Exhibits positive work attitude.	[ ]

Other examples of duties and responsibilities can include work, punctuality, planning and organizing work, or others according to your security department positions and situations.

Eight Key Preparation Steps to a Performance Appraisal Process

To prepare and conduct the performance appraisal process successfully, it's important for you or a supervisor you designate to collect certain materials. The appraisal is not criticism in a strict sense; however, it is always focused on being constructive for career development and must be conducted efficiently, fairly and with a helping, counseling attitude. A successful security officer brings superior performance that benefits the department and company. Assemble the following:

1. *Description of the department's goals and objectives.* The basis for the appraisal of an officer's performance is a description of your department's responsibility and how the officer's job relates to the goals of the department. That information condenses from your strategic, annual, and operational plans.

2. *Current job description.* You need to provide the officer with a current position description that outlines his or her duties and responsibilities. It is crucial that the supervisor and officer mutually understand the job as described in your position description.

3. *Specific guidelines from management.* This includes your situational plan coupled with any special instructions or applicable company policies.

4. *Appraisal forms.* Appraisals need to be a matter of record and the information recorded on a standard department form. An example is shown as Illustration 2–4.

5. *Review job duties, activities and objectives, performance standards, special assignments, and other relevant aspects.*

6. *Determine developmental needs and solutions to be discussed with the officer.*

7. *Identify activities and objectives for concentration during the next appraisal period.*

8. *Ensure the officer knows the appraisal interview time and place in advance.*

Three Major Elements of Conducting the Appraisal Interview

How you conduct an appraisal interview determines its value as intended. The following guidelines help you develop the three major elements and factors within each to achieve the maximum results.

1. **Beginning Your Interview**
   a. Anticipate the officer's attitude.
   b. Set the stage: a natural, friendly, but businesslike atmosphere.
   c. Explain the purpose for the interview even when done often before.

    d. Make it clear that the interview is to be a two-way conversation, a mutual problem-solving and goal-setting exchange.

    e. Select time when you and officer aren't under great pressure or time constraints.

    f. Select location with strict privacy.

    g. Have all the information needed.

2. Body of Your Interview

    a. Listen for facts and feelings.

    b. Talk about job performance: evaluate results of performance against objectives set during last performance planning meeting.

    c. Talk about strong points first, alternating and blending discussion of improvement needs with discussion of strong points.

    d. Cite specific observations for each point you want to discuss, not accomplishments, show interest, encourage the officer to conduct a self-appraisal.

    e. Ask direct and open-ended questions.

    f. Before discussing possible developmental plans, ensure that the officer responds to the evaluation.

    g. Reach agreement on developmental plans with the officer: plans should explain what's expected of the officer, supervisor, and department.

    h. Establish performance standards for next period or set a time to do so.

3. Ending the Appraisal Interview

    a. Summarize major points discussed and stress future actions.

    b. Give the officer an opportunity to make suggestions and voice opinions from his or her perspective.

    c. Close the interview on a positive note.

A CLOSING SUMMARY ABOUT STAFFING YOUR DEPARTMENT

Chapter Two has presented an overview of the staffing process for security managers, with much of the actions keyed to your company policies. However, your company relies on you to contribute to their decision process, and security mangers need regularly to try to increase the importance of their mission and gain positive recognition of corporate executives. Much of your success depends on your officers and others in the department. That begins with aggressive recruiting of quality officer candidates, careful selection processes, training, and the appraisal process to ensure the officer maintains a sound, progressive professional development. Often, "bosses" criticize employees among themselves. They complain that an employee's work and performance are substandard but they fail to take positive action, first, to let the officer know and, second, to offer specific solutions instead of generalities. The appraisal process ensures fairness. The success of your appraisal system depends on the combined efforts of officers, supervisors, and managers. The system accomplishes the following objectives:

- Clarifies the roles, responsibilities, and working relationships of employees.
- Helps supervisors know their staff and how to best develop and use their knowledge, skills, and abilities.
- Defines ways to improve performance.
- Provides and opportunity for officers, supervisors, and managers to work together to define expectations for successful job performance, set goals, and review results.
- Provides feedback to employees about assigned tasks, motivating them to perform at optimal levels.
- Stimulates and fosters personal and career growth and development.

Once these systems and processes have clear focus and implementation, the benefits of aggressive, positive leadership begin to emerge. Leadership, like staffing, is a systematic process that's not an easy task. However, when approached, developed, and practiced correctly, the benefits and advantages of sound leadership management create strong professionalism and performance. Chapter Three helps you to learn, understand, and apply the basic foundation blocks of security management leadership, another vital element of your effective management responsibilities.

Illustration 2–5

QUICK REFERENCE GUIDE
A SECURITY DEPARTMENT STAFFING MODEL

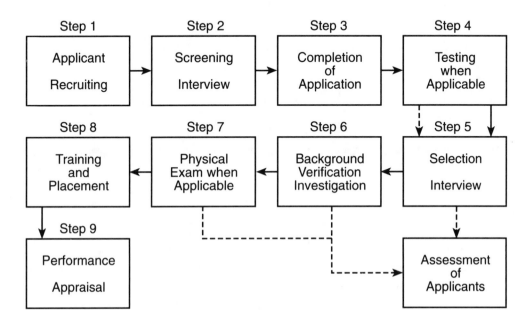

3 Pace-Setting Management and Leadership

An effective security manager has unique responsibilities when compared with other management positions in a corporation. Responsibility of asset protection management begins with planning and organizing and then moves to directing and controlling resources to achieve goals, and that requires dynamic leadership. Management and leadership permanently intertwine, and one without the other creates the environment for failure. Often, men or women promoted or hired to security management roles experience a dilemma because they don't perceive the relationship of leadership. This chapter outlines the principles of pace-setting management and leadership as two inseparable elements you must create, develop, and practice. The old myth of "born leaders" is untrue because leadership, like management, is a developed skill for those who decide they want to accept the responsibilities of management with its credit and criticism. To become and remain effective, you need to set a specific course that brings results for you. Although the elements of management and leadership remain consistent, each person must use the principles to develop his or her own style. Don't fall into the common trap of trying to mimic someone else you perceive to be successful. Although that person might be effective and successful, the management and leadership style he or she applies probably won't work for you. The first rule of management and leadership success stems from following the tested principles, but always be yourself.

Earlier in the book, we talked about techniques for effectively using your four *security resources*—human, financial, operational, and administrative—to achieve security management goals, namely,

- Planning
- Organizing

- Staffing
- Leading
- Controlling
- Coordinating
- Directing or implementing

The first three—planning, organizing, and staffing—involve management; the last four call for the principles of leadership coupled with management. Moving into this phase, you have *leadership and management resources*, including

- *Time*—demanding performance efficiency, conserving money and material
- *Money*—controlled by your department budget
- *Material*—requiring preventive maintenance, accountability, maximum use
- *People*—the engine of your department and essential asset.

In the same way the human element of security resources is essential, so it is with the management resources. Without people to manage, there is no management. Without people to lead, there is no leadership. View the human resource as a foundation for applying the others. Each has its importance and calls for your attention collectively if you shall succeed as a security manager and leader. With each of the management resources come a daily decision-making responsibility. It is a critical aspect of your position. It requires attentive thought and analysis. The following techniques can help you develop, apply, and perfect this important leadership and management skill.

THE EIGHT KEY STEPS IN A DECISION-MAKING PROCESS

The eight steps that you need to use when making a decision (or solving a problem) build on a logical analysis:

● Recognizing and Analyzing the Problem

Your first prerequisite of problem solving includes correctly defining the problem. There's a myth about believing that problem recognition is easy. Often, managers are easily influenced by a solution-oriented view that forces them to ignore the first and necessary condition in the decision-making process. *You must solve the "right" problem.*

To do this, you need to define the factors causing the problem. *When you define the symptoms as the problem, all your subsequent activity will only create more problems.* For example, if two security officers are constantly arguing about the assignments and work schedule, accusing the other of trying to gain advantage, the symptoms might suggest an awkward difference in personality. However, the causal factor could be more profound; it could be a supervisor's failure to delineate job duties between the two officers. If the problem were defined as a personality clash, the solution would be to ignore, tolerate, or try to pacify the situation. If you define other factors as the cause, a different approach would be necessary. The problem definition means recognizing the causal factors and not confusing the symptoms with the problem itself.

After definition, you must analyze the problem. Analysis, in this instance, means identifying the important facts connected to the problem as you define it. These facts can be tangible, or intangible. The tangible facts could involve the assignment of work, the work schedule, or an order given by your supervisor. Intangible elements could include morale, motivation, and personal feelings and impressions.

● Determining Workable Solutions (Alternatives)

Now that you can identify the specific problem you need to solve and can isolate the facts pertinent to the problem, your next step must be to search for and create workable, alternative solutions. The term "workable" eliminates possible alternative solutions proving too costly, time consuming, or elaborate.

Your best approach to determine workable solutions includes listing all possible solutions and then eliminating those not workable. The remaining alternative solutions provide you with a basis for later decision-making steps. Exploring all the possible solutions help you to prevent eliminating the "most desirable" one. A decision is as good as the best alternative solution evaluated.

● Identifying Key Uncertainties

Your key uncertainties are the unknown variables that result from simple chance. Despite the solution you choose, the key uncertainties play an important role. They can be pluses or minuses in the process. For example, consider the key uncertainties that could exist by the quarreling security officers. If you or your supervisor reschedule and place these two officers on different shifts, what would other employees think or demand? How would the others perceive the action? Would they, for example, think you showed "favoritism," or would they accept the action. Another chance variable could be the reaction of both or either one of the officers involved. What would happen to their morale and motivation if they know you might transfer them to separate shifts and lead to personal embarrassment involving other employees? Which way would these variables fall, relative to each of your workable solutions?

● Gathering Information

Now, you know where you're going. You need to begin the function of how to get there. You should postpone research or gathering facts until thinking through all aspects of the problem. This includes identifying, stating, and analyzing the problem; listing all the workable solutions; and identifying the key uncertainties of the problem.

In your course of gathering data, it is quite possible that new insights will develop and lead you to return to earlier steps for a redefinition of the problem. For example, it may happen that by talking with the two quarreling security officers, you learn that the problem is not laxity on the supervisor's part, and has nothing to do with the security department, but the fact that they live as neighbors and have experienced personal disputes at home they bring to work. This information might require you and your supervisor to establish new workable alternatives and identify new key uncertainties. You might consider counseling, shift changes, or disciplinary action if the situation continues.

● Estimating the Value of Each Alternative

After reviewing the data gathered in the previous step, you (including your supervisor) must now begin to analyze each alternative. You must judge what would happen with each choice, its effect on the problem, and the department's protective role. Consider possible chance factors when evaluating each alternative. Consider the possibility of risk, uncertainty, and ignorance. Since there's no single best criterion for decision making where a perfect knowledge of all the facts are present, use a set of criteria that fits the perceived problem. Risk is a state of imperfect knowledge where you can judge the different possible outcomes of each alternative and determine the probabilities of success for each. Uncertainty is a state where you can judge the different possible outcomes of each alternative but lack any feeling for their probability of success. Ignorance is a state in which you cannot judge the different possible outcomes of each alternative, or their probabilities.

Timing is another facet for your evaluation of each alternative. The effect of a probable result, its advantages versus its disadvantages, happens according to the time of implementation of your alternative solution. The most appropriate alternative may be the one you feel is most proper at a given time. The checklist in Illustration 3–1 contains key questions you should ask yourself before making a decision in a problem situation.

Illustration 3–1

DECISION-MAKING SUPPORT CHECKLIST

☐ What seems to be the problem? Is it serious?

☐ Why is the situation causing the problem? Does it disrupt operations?

☐ What are the causal factors? Who is responsible?

☐ What can you do in all possibilities?

☐ Are these possibilities workable?

☐ What is success probability for each of my solutions?

☐ What are the appropriate alternatives?

☐ Have I logically eliminated the other choices?

☐ When and how can the solution be implemented?

☐ What is the best way to implement the solution?

☐ Have I planned, organized, and provided control of actions leading to solutions?

● Choosing a Solution (Decision)

You must make a choice among the alternatives or compromise by choosing a combination of alternatives. You can aid your decision with information supplied through your supervisor's experience, past judgment, advice from others, or even hunch (but with high probability of success), but you must remain responsible for the result. You must also be responsible for implementing and following up your decision.

● Acting on Your Decision

There is a long road between making a decision (determining a plan of action) and the action itself. You plan, organize, and control the action so that the entire effort exerted in the preceding steps isn't wasted. You need to work with and through your supervisors and others, and your action calls for communication, motivation and leadership skills.

● Following up Your Action

After acting to implement your decision, you must follow up and appraise your solution. This last step can take many forms, depending on the problem, type of decision, environment, working conditions, desires of superiors and subordinate supervisors, the employees involved, and technical problems. The main function of your follow-up involves knowing the problem no longer exists.

Illustration 3–2 serves as a tool to clarify and focus approaches to problem solving and decision making.

Illustration 3—2

WORKSHEET: DECISION MAKING

PROBLEM DEFINITION:

Workable Alternatives

Key Uncertainties

Research Data

Evaluation of Each Alternative

DECISION:

Action

Follow-up

LEADERSHIP AND PERSONAL STYLE

Two common threads run through the most frequently used definitions of leadership. First, leadership is a relationship between people in which there is a legitimate difference between the power and influence of leaders and followers. Second, there are no leaders without followers. Another generally accepted aspect of leadership is that a person may be able to lead effectively in one situation and fail in another. This is true because the kind of behavior that effectively influences a certain person or group under a given set of circumstances may be inappropriate when conditions or objectives are different.

Three Styles of Leadership

For many years, the human relations approach in corporations tended to concentrate on increasing pay raises and fringe benefits. Although both continue to have importance, emphasis has shifted from wages and benefits as a way of securing adequate performance. Experience shows that employees will perform better under certain motivating conditions affecting their group participation, sense of belonging, and many similar nonmonetary factors. Now, accepted management and leadership philosophy emphasizes the practice of "goal-oriented" management and leadership. The three broad styles of leadership normally recognized are: (1) Autocratic ("boss"), (2) democratic (participative), and (3) laissez-faire (free rein).

Autocratic Leadership ("Boss")

If you are an autocratic leader, you make your decisions alone. You centralize power and decision making within yourself. Your subordinates do exactly as they are told and have no input to any aspect of operational control. You also assume full authority and responsibility. When an autocratic leader becomes oppressive, the subordinates may become insecure and begin looking for another job.

However, the autocratic leader can become a benevolent autocrat. He or she can deal with subordinates effectively. Some employees find a sense of security and satisfaction under this style of leadership. In turn, this type of leadership provides strong motivation and psychological rewards to the leader. Within the definition of a benevolent autocrat, there are also three types:

- The leader who simply gives orders
- The leader who uses praise and demands loyalty
- The leader who makes subordinates feel they are participating in decisions although they are doing what the boss wants

Autocratic leadership often risks building resentment among the employees, especially if carried to extremes or if tried among strong subordinates who also wanted to exercise authority.

Democratic Leadership (Participative)

If you are a democratic leader, you share some of your decision-making responsibility with your subordinate supervisors and allow general employee input. You consult with your supervisors on questions especially those to which they can make a genuine contribution. There are obviously some decisions for which you cannot do this. However, you try to develop the supervisors' sense of responsibility for their accomplishments, and those achievements of their shifts. You might use both praise and criticism. Although you share the decision making with supervisors, the ultimate responsibility of the department's performance still rests with you.

There are several ways you can share the decision-making process with your supervisors: (1) by creating situations they can learn naturally, (2) by enabling them to check out their own performance, (3) by allowing them to set challenging goals, (4) by supplying opportunities for them to improve work methods, (5) by supplying opportunities to pursue job growth, and (6) by recognizing achievements and helping them to learn from their errors.

Laissez-faire Leadership (Free Rein)

If you use the laissez-faire style of leadership, you essentially avoid power by delegating it to your supervisors. You depend on them to establish their own goals and solve their own problems. The department tends to be leaderless unless you include dealing with outside persons to bring the department personnel necessary information, materials, and resources. You give little or no direction and allow your supervisors freedom to manage operations. Most often, this style works best for professionals engaged in research work to prevent inhibiting their independent thinking. It is difficult leadership, demanding much understanding and perseverance by you.

Analyzing Leadership Styles

In actual practice, you cannot use any of these three styles exclusively. The ideal scenario uses all leadership styles to the best advantage. You may use the autocratic style when necessary. You may use the free-rein style to serve a particular purpose. You may use the democratic (participative) style to develop the talents of security officers. The skill of leadership lies largely in knowing when to use each style and how far to go with each. Your problem as a security manager is to vary styles to fit the changing conditions under which your subordinates are working.

See the accompanying Quick Reference Review and Guide for the leadership styles.

Illustration 3–3

QUICK REFERENCE REVIEW AND GUIDE
FOR
THREE STYLES OF LEADERSHIP

Democratic
(participant)

Autocratic
"Boss"

Laissez-Faire
(free-rent)

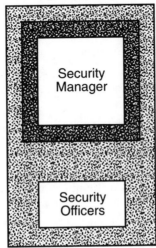

FIVE IMPORTANT LEADERSHIP TECHNIQUES

Challenge and opportunity characterize the role of a corporate or industrial security manager. He or she is challenged by the scope and diversity of asset protection and seeks continuing opportunity to assume responsibility and develop resourcefulness. Often, a security manager finds an urgent need to use all his or her personal resources in perhaps the most demanding of all tasks—leadership of people. First, you need to understand decision-making, and the overviews of leadership, and then learn the skill of being a leader. The following five leadership techniques frame the principles needed to meet the challenge of being an effective security leader.

Technique One: Secure Cooperation

A successful leader must secure the cooperation of those whom he or she has the responsibility to lead. This task becomes easier when security officers have proper orientation and understand where you're leading them and why. They must also understand their relationships to one another and how they as a team will achieve their personal goals and those of the department and company.

Develop your performance criteria so subordinates can understand their success in progressing toward those goals. You must follow up each subordinate's performance. This follow-up technique tends to encourage confidence. When you establish the goals of the department and communicate them to the officers and other employees, you establish criteria for measurement of performance and you communicate these to the officers.

Within the operations of your security department, friction among members happens no matter how diligent you or your supervisors are. Some members of the department will undoubtedly have complaints or grievances. Their willingness to continue cooperation depends on how fairly you and supervisors handle their grievances. You need clear lines of communication so grievances come to your attention quickly and you can act effectively to eliminate or resolve the problems.

During your security operations, plans and goals may change. It is important that you communicate these changes and the reasons for them. Confusion has a devastating effect on employees and begins harmful rumors and that might lead to a lack of cooperation because officers fear they are on the losing side or are receiving unfair treatment.

Technique Two: Use Authority Effectively

You have authority inherent to your position of security manager. However, your authority becomes useless unless you apply it effectively. To maintain the effectiveness of your authority, you must be fair in your dealings with department officers, and they must consider you as a fair, open-minded, reasonable manager. You cannot hope to maintain effectiveness if you discipline a subordinate for sloppy performance when you have no standards to make it clear what you expect him or her to do. However, when you do have clear performance standards, and communicate them regularly, then members of your department will support your critical evaluations and demands for competent performance.

Technique Three: Direct and Communicate

You must exhibit a unity of command. When you need help occasionally, your subordinates must know precisely how much authority you delegate to them. You must also be clear about whether anyone outside the security department has authority to direct their activities. The most effective leader represents a single command.

Personal contact with subordinates is important. It is impossible to determine the opinions of your subordinates without talking with them. Also, it is impossible for them to understand you if their sole contact with you is by memorandum or directive passed from you through supervisors.

Second only to the unity of command is the clarity of command. Communication is a "two-way" activity. The officers need to understand all your instructions clearly. Also, your instructions must be feasible to execute and acceptable to the persons receiving them.

And you must be a good listener. Often, managers listen poorly. For example, a subordinate has a problem and wants your help or advice. Your preoccupation with other problems prevents your full attention. Although you invite the subordinate to speak, and you nod periodically and smile sympathetically, your mind is elsewhere and you might not be listening. Subordinates or anyone else can sense whether you are listening genuinely, and when they perceive you are not they lose confidence in you as a leader. Everyone has problems, and when your subordinates seek your help or advice; set aside other matters temporarily and listen carefully. Always show genuine interest, and do all you can to help them with their problem. Your actions here, when genuine, will pay large dividends later throughout the department.

Technique Four: Maintain Discipline

Effective discipline and maintenance of it stem from the clarity of your standards and rules. You must ensure that each has been clearly communicated and understood. When employees break rules, your disciplinary measures must be consistent and reasonable. You should generally look at discipline as a means of effecting corrective action, not as a means of punishment. However, there are occasions when employees will specifically break recognized rules; when that happens, your response must be firm, consistent, and clear.

Technique Five: Develop Department Morale

You can maintain high department morale only if all officers and employees understand the department's goals and if there is a clear measure for their job performance. Each officer must thoroughly understand that achieving department and company goals call for departmental teamwork. You must think of your officers in the department as individuals and regard each person's personal goals, and then help him or her to see how achieving those goals is consistent with the department's goals and responsibilities.

HOW TO DEVELOP SUCCESSFUL LEADERSHIP PATTERNS

You must have or develop certain personal behavioral patterns that help you to implement your leadership techniques. These behavioral patterns affect your relationships with subordinates, but also importantly with higher corporate management, other company departments, and unions (when applicable). The following tips can help you develop successful leadership patterns.

Tip One: With Subordinates

You can convey your leadership by clearly defining performance objectives for the members of the security department. You should make certain they understand their performance obligations. You should see that they are aware of their relationship to other departments and functions within the company. By presenting these matters clearly, you establish that each person in the security department is part of the security team, and the company team, and that they share a responsibility in these matters. Always maintain a genuine attitude to subordinates and ensure that they understand your willingness to help them.

Tip Two: With Higher Management

Often, you show department subordinates your true attitude toward them through actions defending their interests with higher company management. You need to act as a buffer between them and higher management. If an officer makes an honest error, you must take responsibility for it and not try to offer him or her as a scapegoat to protect your interests. If there are complaints lodged by upper management, you must absorb these personally instead of allowing them to come to your subordinates.

There is one other point often neglected. When higher management sets a policy with which you do not wholeheartedly agree, it is your responsibility to convey this policy to your subordinates as though it came from you alone. You should never blame company management for establishing unpopular policies. Instead, spend your time helping subordinates understand what is behind an unpopular policy and their duty to fulfill them.

Tip Three: With Other Company Departments

You must always recognize your relationship with other company departments. You can achieve more by working with other departments to meet corporate goals and ensure your subordinates understand the importance of cooperation throughout the company. Strong interdepartment working relationships also bring your department a vast amount of resources that otherwise would not be readily available.

Tip Four: With Unions (When Applicable)

You must recognize that unions have an important place in an industrial society. Although you may not like some of their methods or motives, you must recognize that they perform a service by supplying management with a united group with which to deal. You should acquaint yourself with the union contract and its provisions. You should recognize that this is an operating agreement between your company and employees. It is a contract to be honored like any other contract.

Here, you have the opportunity to establish your credibility. When you administer the union contract justly and cooperate with union leaders fully within the spirit and letter of the contract, then you can expect they will trust you and your judgment. That trust may become important at some later date.

The following checklist and Quick Reference Review will help you to consider the useful attitudes that an effective manager-leader should maintain. Use the checklist to determine areas you might need to develop.

Illustration 3–4

CHECKLIST AND QUICK REFERENCE REVIEW
FOR
DEVELOPING LEADERSHIP PATTERNS

☐ Have I clearly defined the goals for my security department subordinates?

☐ Am I receptive to the opinions of my subordinates?

☐ Do I expect the best performance from my department personnel?

☐ Am I fair and unbiased in discipline?

☐ Do I involve my subordinates in setting performance goals?

☐ Do I bear responsibility for my subordinates' mistakes?

☐ Do I represent management to subordinates?

☐ Am I fair with managers of other company departments?

☐ Do I cooperate and work with managers of other company departments?

☐ Do I consider myself a part of the company management team?

☐ Am I attentive to follow the provisions of a company-union contract when it's applicable to the security department or related protective activity?

☐ Do I manage department assets properly?

☐ Do I encourage suggestions of improved efficiency and performance?

☐ Do I set fair standards?

☐ Do I ensure my standards apply to the department as a whole?

BENEFIT FROM STUDYING HUMAN BEHAVIOR

The study of human behavior, often neglected, plays an important role in your effective management and leadership. Trying to cope with the way people act and do what they do remains one of the frustrating elements of management. Learning why people act and react in certain ways, identifying various types of behavior, and learning how to influence the behavior of subordinates have important advantages for achieving your company and security department goals. You also need to know how to motivate your officers and get the self-disciplined responses you need from them. This section helps you to understand a range of common human behavior you might experience among your security officers and employees, including how to analyze, predict, and influence their behavior.

THE IMPORTANCE OF VALUES AND ATTITUDES

Everyone lives according to what he or she feels is worthwhile, or according to his or her personal value system. A person's value system motivates his or her thinking and actions. Each person develops his or her own value system through experience with society. Because of the impact of differing cultures, classes, ethnic backgrounds, intelligence, family characteristics, and the like, there are many variations in what people believe and the way they behave. Managers often make the critical mistake of failing to note these differences. Value and attitude differences cause people to see things differently and to act or react differently. Values and attitudes are two of the factors you must consider and understand in the human behavior of your subordinates.

What Are Values?

A value includes an attitude for or against an event. It is a personal view that a specific event or situation helps or harms some person, group, or company. A value has a recognizable outward display of behavior and is observable and measurable. Often, values lead to or are called "attitudes" and enable people to determine what they believe to be worthwhile or right. Values, like needs, can have either a direct or indirect effect on views and beliefs. Also, values include "learned goals" that begin to develop from the moment of birth.

What Do Values Do?

Values are at the center of people, for example, their character. A phrase heard often today is that society must work out a new set of values. Others are saying in response, "There's nothing wrong with the values of the past—such as honesty and loyalty—we simply need to bring them back." Because values are the basis for our beliefs and attitudes, we may become emotional regarding certain issues. These values begin early in life and develop throughout adulthood. They become building blocks for each person's value system and play an important role in personal behavior on the job.

To identify and understand a person's values, it is necessary for you to understand that person. It's an important element of management and leadership to be aware of social values of your various officers.

How Can You Identify Personal Values?

Because the subject of values is often vague, you need a method for value identification. For better understanding divide values into the following five categories:

• Personal Values

Each person has traits that represent his or her moral character. They may have an order of importance such as: honesty, responsibility, loyalty, moral courage, and friendliness. Common values can be as diverse as success and prestige and an interest in others and an appreciation of beauty. The values a person integrates into their character become apparent by their attitudes, beliefs, and actions.

• Social Values

These values include social responsibility, honesty in interpersonal relationships, social consciousness, equality, justice, liberty, freedom, and pride in country. Social values "are learned" and often alter or change dramatically throughout a person's life. They involve one's relationship to society and other people. For example, many parents teach their children right from wrong, and what goals to pursue in their lives. Social values generally divide into four distinct classes:

1. *Folkways*—values people accept out of habit
2. *Mores*—morality that governs values
3. *Institutional ways*—practices established under law
4. *Taboos*—the determined do's and don'ts of a particular society

• Economic Values

You can identify these values through employee views involving equal employ-ment, salaries, benefits, a stable economy, private property, pride of ownership, and taxes. For example, one economic value is affluence: a rise in our living standards will help us realize a goal based on our economic values.

● Religious Values

These values are characterized by reverence for life, human dignity, and freedom to worship. Religious values often become clear by expressed belief by some employees while others tend to keep this value private. Often, religious values involve a strong desire for observance of various religious holidays, a Sabbath, or other beliefs within the religious context.

● Political Values

These include a loyalty to country, concern for national welfare, democracy, public service, voting, elections, and civic responsibility. A person's political views reflect his or her political values.

When you understand the development and role of values and attitudes, you move into a more favorable position to deal with the behavioral problems of your officers and other employees. When you acknowledge that your subordinates will not always act and react as you do to a given situation, or that they will not understand things or feel about them as you do, your approach to problems and situations emerge as one of management and leadership success.

Review Tips for Creating Better Subordinate Attitudes

Solving attitude problems within your security department might be perplexing. However, there are a few basic and often successful tips to apply. They include the following:

Providing Accurate Information

Often an employee's attitude stems from misconceptions, and supplying the correct facts personally could lead to a marked improvement of their attitude.

Showing Genuine Concern

Often a simple act of kindness or an indication that you care about your subordinate employees can change a poor attitude to a better one. Listening to an employee who is bitter or hostile permits him or her to "blow off steam" and feel better having done so.

Changing an Employee's Status

Often giving an employee a new job, position, or responsibilities will enable him or her to identify with new roles and frames of reference. This gives the employee a new slant on the situation. You might change a bad attitude to a good one simply by changing the situation.

Have Personal Discussions with Your Subordinates

Often leader-subordinate discussions help to correct negative attitudes because communicating encourages the person to express his or her feelings and problems. This can be one of the best methods used to improve attitudes. When you talk to employees about their interests and desires, you will uncover some of their attitudes and the underlying causes for them. Then, you can evaluate ways of correcting poor attitudes within the department.

How to Solve the Human Needs Problem

For years, scholars studied human behavior and offered hundreds of explanations about human nature and how the various needs affect people's actions. Although behaviorists do not always present the same concepts, they do agree that certain factors, elements, or needs play a major role in the way people behave in certain ways and cause them to do certain things. The most basic of these factors are the "human needs."

Human needs have meaningful importance in your leadership role. They are those elements necessary for a person's existence, but also include his or her mental and emotional stability, important considerations for security officers. Those human needs required for existence are called "physical needs," including, for example, food, water, shelter, clothing. Human needs are the same for all people, but their importance differs from person to person. The essential human needs you must understand include those "learned needs" that create and regulate mental and emotional stability.

The Four Basic Learned Needs

• *Safety*   The safety needs are the most basic of the learned needs and include the desire for personal safety. For example, you need to ensure that each officer assignment affords every precaution possible to assure him or her that his or her job has no needless risks. This might include assigning one officer to a dangerous area when two would be prudent and lessen the chance of injury. Another example might be an industrial complex where dangerous and hazardous chemicals or toxic waste are present and next to security officer positions. Although the situation might not be dangerous, the officer's perception of danger needs to be addressed. Supply accurate information and assurance of you attention to their safety needs to dispel the concern, and their need for personal safety.

• *Social Acceptance (Belonging)*   The employee's personal need for belonging or having social acceptance includes a common human desire to be an accepted company member in the workplace. A security officer needs good personal relationships with other members of the security department. The problem created by a perception of "not belonging" portrays the feeling of many more employees than managers often recognize. The people who believe that they don't fit in or that others don't accept them within the group can think of little else and their performance becomes substandard. You must remain alert for that need, especially in new officers. When observed or suspected, take immediate corrective action. For example, having personal discussions with your officers and others in the department generally contributes to finding ways of identifying such problems and showing what action might work to bring the person around to feeling a part of the team. Often, the perception has no real basis except in the person's mind. This feeling regularly strikes a person who comes from another work environment and has fears of making mistakes when he or she wants to perform perfectly. His or her desire for perfection often strikes others in the department as a sign of "superiority" or "arrogance," and that leads to the problem.

● *Esteem* People need self-esteem and the esteem of others. Self-esteem (or self-respect) includes personal feelings and perceptions of competence, autonomy, independence, dominance, achievement, acquisition, and retention. These needs may be an outgrowth of the more basic physiological and safety needs. The need for esteem or respect from others includes the need for recognition and acclamation, attention, appreciation, prestige, and status. These needs obviously overlap with the needs for belonging.

Esteem follows in the progression and, next to physical needs, is the one most easily satisfied by your leadership. You can directly recognize subordinates in the department for their performance and show your appreciation by intangible rewards such as a simple, "Well done." You can also create and offer tangible rewards, including paid time off, award programs, and promotions.

● *Self-fulfillment* The highest need remains that of self-fulfillment or the achievement of full potentials. Because learned personal needs are progressive, satisfying this final need stems from at least partial satisfaction of those that precede it. Although the percentage of people who reach self-fulfillment is small, intermediate goals achieved create a level of satisfaction that encourages them to continue trying. For example, you might have an officer who wants to be a supervisor or the security manager. Although you know he or she doesn't now have the intangible attributes to achieve that goal, or maybe the education, training, and experience, you can help by encouraging, and recognizing achievements. You can also support continued training and education that might one day enable the person to reach his or her goals.

YOUR SOLUTIONS FOR THE MOTIVATION ENIGMA

While individual differences in ability undoubtedly establish limits of human performance, motivation is also clearly a powerful factor. Motivation (or motive) determines whether a person will put his or her abilities to use and want to perform well. The task of motivating your security officers and other employees rests squarely on your shoulders. Motivation relates to how people perform their jobs and is associated with the needs described earlier. The degree to which a person desires to satisfy these needs usually determines how productive and creative he or she will be on the job. If the job environment is dissatisfying, the officer becomes concerned with his or her own well-being to the point of excluding all activities that do not lead to this satisfaction. Most begin thinking about or actively seeking another job.

It is noteworthy, however, that elimination of dissatisfiers does not in itself motivate people. That action alone does not create motivation, but simply supplies a neutral environment where motivation can develop. The satisfaction of needs on the positive side of the scale motivates subordinates, while failure to satisfy these needs results in dissatisfaction. For example, a security officer who consistently does well but no one recognizes that extra effort and consistency may become dissatisfied.

Motivation is a complete process determined by the interaction of all the needs. It relies on those needs created by the situation and on a combination of personal and group needs. Because the requirements of the situation, personal needs, and group or department commitment are always present, you may correctly conclude that everyone has some type of motivation to do something. For example, everyone needs food resulting in a motivation to eat. Rational people, when their lives are threatened, try to reduce the threat, and most people want social or group acceptance and are motivated to achieve that end. The key motivators, often called the "Herzberg motivation factors" because he and colleagues developed the theory during a study of behavior and motivations, include

- Achievement
- Recognition for achievement
- Work satisfaction itself
- Responsibility
- Advancement

HOW YOU CAN MOTIVATE PERFORMANCE

Everyone has motives, so your question should *not* be, "How can my officers be motivated?" Instead, ask yourself, "How can I channel the motives of my officers performing well and achieve department and company goals and objectives?" To answer your question, consider these factors that influence a security officer's motivation to perform well:

- *The feeling that he or she can succeed and climb the career ladder.* The motives fulfill other needs, but also have an economic basis. Our society often judges success or ability in financial terms opposed to separating craft excellence from wealth. However, the motive here stems from a strong desire to enhance a personal quality of living, and when that exists, motivation to perform well remains high.

- *The feeling that he or she will receive recognition for their performance*, with either tangible or intangible rewards, preferably both. When officers put extra effort into their performance or make an effort to increase their education or skills, they expect and need solid recognition. Your recognition must be consistent with the accomplishment and be attentive not to create a feeling within the department that an officer excelling is your "favorite." However, with thought, discretion, and other techniques, you can recognize excellence and effort in ways that help to motivate others to perform better.

- *The value of that recognition.* Often, managers don't mean what they say; instead they try to enhance their own interests by "appearing" to be "interested" in their employees. However, employees can recognize the facade and place no value on it.

- *The estimate of the discipline probability when not trying.* When you have clear standards of performance rules and officers deliberately fall short of them, and you do nothing, the employees will come to see the rules and standards as "eyewash" as opposed to being there for strict compliance. (Never make rules or set standards that you do not or cannot enforce.)

Motivation to Try

Experience shows that people will have little motivation to try something they think they cannot do. You must know your officer's capabilities and establish challenging attainable goals within their capabilities. You can build the officers' confidence in themselves by offering support, encouragement, and assistance. Also, showing them that when they give their best effort and fail or make honest errors, you never impose disciplinary action. This is important because on difficult tasks, people encouraged to keep trying may ultimately succeed; without encouragement, they may simply quit. For example, when you have a security assignment that involves operating sophisticated devices, inspecting documents, or training other officers, the average person used to performing easy, routine tasks might believe he or she cannot possibly do these things. Your responsibilities as a leader involve recognizing the strengths and limitations and encouraging those officers you have certainty can succeed if they try.

Expectation of Recognition for Good Performance

When people are convinced that their chances of success are good enough to warrant the effort to try, their belief that success will help them complete personal goals or needs becomes important. However, when people are not convinced that good performance is the best way to satisfy these needs, their motivation will be low, and they will have little or no interest in doing their best. Creating assurance that good performance will be rewarded based on three things:

1. You must have a consistent record of checking and evaluating performance.
2. You must have a consistent record of using the rewards.
3. You must recognize when performance has exceptional merit.

The Best Technique You Can Use for Motivation

The best technique to use for aligning personal and department goals and providing personal satisfaction motivation is to give the officer increased authority and responsibility. Often, these elements already exist but are not recognized by the officer. One way stems from changing a title, for example, instead of just posting an officer at a gate, make the officer working the gate a "manager" of the specific operation during their shift. Perception of responsibility and authority plays a major role in motivation. Another example can include placing a senior security officer as the "assistant shift supervisor" or "warehouse 5 security manager." You can motivate supervisors by changing their department title to "Shift 3 security manager." The idea is to remove their perception of the job from the mundane to one of importance. The benefits of this technique are far reaching. Added to increasing motivation, this technique gives your officers the opportunity to grow professionally through a process of challenging their abilities.

A Valuable Tip on Motivation Versus Ability

When you observe a security officer performing poorly, you must determine whether performance is poor because of a lack of motivation or because of a lack of ability. In departments or companies that have no effective training programs, the latter might prove to be the case. When you assess the problem of motivation, consider that ability might be the real problem and solve that through meaningful training.

Often, the problem of motivation and ability stems from other problems that create stifling stress in the workplace. They can be problems from within the work environment, at home or other location. The stress might emerge from a combination of all those sources.

HOW STRESS AFFECTS THE BEHAVIOR PROBLEM

A common security management problem involves dealing with the stress experienced by their officers. Because stress can reduce the level of discipline and efficiency important in asset protection, you must identify stress-producing situations and behavior resulting from stress to avoid or correct the situation or behavior.

In the physical sciences, the term "stress" describes a force directed at an object. The term has the same meaning when used by a social scientist, because stress stems from forces of frustration and pressure directed at human beings. Because the forces of frustration and pressure are so interrelated, it is difficult to separate the two.

Everyone seeks the fulfillment of his or her needs or goals, but such fulfillment is not always easy to achieve. Failures or delays in fulfilling needs and goals cause frustration—a behavior pattern that results when one is hampered by external or internal obstacles. Most frustrations are small, temporary, easily resolved, and unimportant. However, recurring small frustrations lead to big frustrations that produce a wide range of problems from inefficiency, and poor performance and can lead to mental illness.

How to Identify the Causes of Frustration

The causes of frustration can be categorized in two major types: delaying or blocking causes and conflicting causes. You are accustomed to scheduling daily activities on a time basis, and, when a delay causes change to your schedule, a degree of frustration results. For example, officers arrive late for duty or call in sick and on a day when the company gives you added security requirements because of an incoming shipment. This might cause the entire security schedule and officer assignment roster to be shuffled, maybe calling for overtime or working through a holiday, and that causes frustrations in the officers.

You also need to consider frustration by conflict that happens when trying to achieve two or more goals and finding that satisfying one causes the denial of the other. Conflict also happens when you must choose between two unpleasant goals. An example of this type conflict is a choice between working on Christmas day or working on Christmas night when the original schedule allowed you to be off duty. Conflict can also include a pleasant and unpleasant situation, for example, a security officer receiving a promotion that necessitates working under a disliked supervisor.

Recognizing the Symptoms of Frustration

You can be certain that frustrating events stimulate some type of behavior. The resulting behavior varies with the person and the situation, and it can cover a wide range of reactions. Behaviors induced by frustration can involve either good or bad reactions. Good reactions are those that happen because of increased drive and can help a person to overcome the obstacle that prevents him or her from reaching the original goal. Good reactions to frustration are not uncommon. Studies show that certain types of people perform at their best when subject to some minor form of frustration. However, frustration can produce various bad reactions such as aggression, rationalization for poor performance, regression, fixation, resignation, and negativism that cause concern for you. The following symptoms identify what you need to watch for within your department:

The Aggression Reaction

One common reaction to frustration is aggression, though, other responses to frustration may precede it. Aggression is particularly difficult for a security manager to handle when a security officer works in contact with other company employees, such as a gate, a building entrance, or a warehouse. It is also a problem because frustration and aggressive behavior tends to spread throughout the department. Symptoms of aggressive frustration include hostility, vicious gossip, snide remarks, and worse.

The Hostility Reaction

Another serious reaction of frustration to identify and correct is hostility, or "scapegoating." If a person cannot attack the cause of the frustration directly, he or she often takes out the frustration on another person or object having nothing to do with the original cause of frustration.

The Rationalization Reaction

This is a common reaction that leads to poor security performance. It often occurs when an officer becomes frustrated and blames someone else for his or her inability to achieve some goal and talks himself or herself out of the desirability of that goal. For example, an officer might expect a promotion to shift supervisor but you hire another person from the outside to fill the position. The frustrated officer rationalizes that he or she really doesn't want the added responsibility anyway and decides to just wave people through the gate instead of checking them carefully. The secondary rationalization stems from deciding that he or she has done exceptionally and received nothing in return so now a mediocre performance or less will get him or her by.

The Regressive Reaction

This behavioral reaction happens when a person becomes unable to deal constructively with reality and retreats to the behavior of an earlier age that seems more satisfying; this person is showing symptoms of regression. These symptoms include pouting, temper tantrums, and other immature actions.

The Fixation Reaction

This is a severe and serious reaction to frustration stress factors and is characterized by compulsive, stereotyped, repetitive behavior. An officer may exhibit the same behavior repeatedly with no attempt to adjust to the situation. An example of fixation is the security officer who persists in trying to unlock a padlock with the wrong key although it's apparent the key will not work in the lock.

The Resignation Reaction (Apathy)

This symptom shows a reaction to frustration stress characterized with an officer experiencing loss of hope, escape from reality, withdrawal, and retreat from the source of frustration. The person becomes apathetic and resigned to failure.

The Negativism Reaction

The most common reaction to frustration stress is negativism. In this reaction, the person adopts a negative resistive attitude toward the situation. For example, a security supervisor becomes frustrated with a situation and you direct that, whether he or she agrees or disagrees, the employee must follow the company policy exactly. The supervisor displays a defensive, negative attitude to all company policies, department policies, and you when talking with others.

How to Solve the Frustration Stress Problem

Once you determine that an officer or employee is frustrated, identify the source of the frustration and try to solve the problem. In doing so, you must be cause oriented and not symptom oriented. Do not make a snap judgment. If frustration is the problem, remember that frustration is cumulative. What may appear to be the primary cause of the frustration may only be "the straw that broke the camel's back," the last in a long series of causes of frustrations. By discussing an officer's problem with him or her, you can often help them determine the cause of the problem and find a viable solution.

There are many problems that can arise relating to the job, the department or the company that you may be able to solve. The cause of an officer's frustration stress may be his or her inability to get along with members of his shift. Here, you can eliminate the cause by finding out why he or she is not getting along and helping the person understand what adjustments he or she can make to resolve the problem Sometimes it may benefit the department and the officer by transferring him or her to another shift or position. Other causes of frustration such as personal problems may call for you to prompt the officer to seek professional help from counselors. Still other problems dictate that the officer remains the only person to develop a solution. In these cases, you may help eliminate the cause by suggesting ways to overcome the problem or by suggesting alternate goals.

Solving a problem is not your final step. After identifying and eliminating the cause of the frustration, you must prevent a recurrence and future frustration. It is easier to put oil into your automobile engine than it is to replace a burned-out engine, and it is easier for you to prevent frustration within your security department than it is to correct it. There are several steps you can take to prevent frustration within your department:

- *Conduct an honest self-evaluation to determine if you are causing frustration.* Your personality, your method of managing, and your manner of communicating with the members of your department are some things that may frustrate your officers. For example, your sarcastic replies to their questions may build up a resistance to your leadership.
- *See that your officers have meaningful assignments.* Don't assign an aggressive, dynamic young officer to an obscure position that doesn't allow him or her to have challenging responsibility.
- *Keep your channels of communication open so officers have a credible outlet for their problems.*
- *Establish logical and reasonable rules, regulations, and operating procedures.*
- *Ensure satisfaction of human needs and that officers stay motivated and well-trained.*
- *The efforts of the leader to prevent frustrations are not always completely successful.*

Some frustration is inevitable. Fortunately, most people can tolerate frustration to some degree.

COPING WITH THE PRESSURE STRESS PROBLEM

Stress created by pressures involves internal feelings of tension, anxiety, or fear experienced by a person in situations that he or she sees as demanding or threatening.

Internal Pressure Stress Symptoms

Internal sources of pressure center on our own aspirations and egos. When a person has high ideals about work requirements and achieving required standards, the pressure may be severe and continuous. For example, the career-oriented security officer or supervisor who wants to get a college degree, become a security manager, or establish his or her own company may experience pressure for years. Generally, the well-motivated person who wants to do a good job is more likely to experience pressure than is the unmotivated person. Many persons drive themselves relentlessly and try to attain unrealistic standards of work and social acceptance. They may feel that they should work harder, get along with everyone, and be better persons than they are. This may be good because it can motivate many people to do well, but they will have to cope with the resulting pressure.

External Pressure Stress Symptoms

There are many sources of external pressure. There is pressure to succeed in a competitive society, pressure to produce well over an extended period, pressure to adjust to constantly changing conditions, and pressure to satisfy wishes of family, peers, and superiors. These are only a few of the more prevalent sources of pressure that we face daily.

A person may maintain an outwardly calm behavior through a long series of minor pressures and suddenly explode over some seemingly minor incident. Those around the officer normally express complete surprise by the reaction, not realizing that it represents the culmination of a long series of minor pressures. Normally, pressure will remain suppressed by a person until he or she reaches his or her personal "overload point," the point when he or she is no longer able to function effectively under the pressure felt.

Five Key Common Causes of Pressure Stress

● Competitive Pressure

In our highly competitive society, people grow up learning to compete for every-thing—grades in school, athletic honors, popularity, jobs, leadership positions, money, and social status. Some people are more competitive than others, and some are better equipped to handle the pressures created by competition. Not everyone can be a winner continually. Striving to do the impossible invites frustration and self-devaluation. While competitive pressure drives many to greater productivity and higher standards of excellence, such pressure may be harmful if it leads to constant "overloading" of a person's ability to adjust or to cope with the pressure. This type of pressure is more severe among motivated persons who perceive success to be dependent on competitive performance.

● Sustained Concentration of Effort

This is another source of pressure stress that all persons experience at one time or another. This pressure often occurs in a job where many demands are felt for a prolonged period. Generally, the higher the position or the higher the standards of performance required, the greater the pressure.

● Suddenness and Complexities of a Problem

Often, this type of stress affects new officers unfamiliar with the setting or duties yet who have a desire to do well. This is also true of many people promoted to supervisory or other management-level positions.

• Situational Threats

Situations that include a possibility of physical harm or a perception of such a threat can bring pressure stress. Generally, a situation believed to be threatening creates more strain than does a situation presenting a difficult, but manageable, problem.

• Anticipation of Pressure

This expectation factor itself can cause pressure stress as the pressure inducing event becomes imminent. You may have felt pressure build up inside you as the time approached for you to address a group of people, particularly people with whom you are closely associated or those who can influence your career. This type of stress might affect officers who have to attend an appraisal or some type of qualification training.

The Problems and Solutions Involving Pressure Stress

The severity or level of pressure relates to how much strain (tension, anxiety, or fear) is produced within a person. Intensity of strain felt depends on several factors. First is the importance attached to the situation. The second factor is that the longer a pressure situation continues, the more severe the strain. Increasing demand made simultaneous also has a direct bearing on intensity of pressure felt. Each person has a different level of pressure that he or she can stand. That level depends on the person's maturity and personal characteristics, the situation, and the presence or absence of support from others. For example, under mild pressure, a person normally adjusts easily with little or no loss of efficiency. Under moderate pressure, adjustment may be difficult and some efficiency lost. Under severe pressure, ability to adjust is overtaxed and inefficiency results.

Stressful situations may not cause any strain in some people. When the person is confident that he or she can handle the situation, then the person probably feels very little pressure. However, when confidence is lacking, he or she will feel great pressure. Levels of competence, perception, the presence or absence of threat, and self-confidence all contribute to a person's ability to withstand pressure stress.

The best things you can do as manager and leader are reduce the pressure. If you cannot eliminate the source of pressure, ensure your presence and support in stressful situations. If the leader stays calm and confident, the officers will gain strength to withstand the pressure. You cannot expect your officers to show less effect of pressure than you do, and you must conceal the effects of pressure you feel. Don't deny that you are under pressure, but be present with cool confidence.

You must always be alert for situations in your department or the company environment that produce frustration and pressure. You must strive to reduce the bad effects through training, counseling, arranging for professional assist-ance, providing external support, and setting a good example. Your security officers perform well only when their pressure and frustration stay at an ac-ceptable level.

QUICK REFERENCE GUIDE
FOR
MANAGEMENT-LEADERSHIP REVIEW

- Maximize use of your management resources.

- Develop your decision-making skills.

- Develop your leadership skills.

- Develop your leadership patterns.

- Study human behavior problems and solutions.

- Become a pace-setting manager-leader.

✓ **Management:** The process of utilizing organizational resources to achieve specific goals and objectives by planning, organizing, leading, and controlling.

✓ **Leadership:** The process of influencing others to achieve specific objectives in specific situations without using unduly coercive methods or techniques.

✓ **Leadership style:** The consistent pattern of behaviors that characterizes a leader.

4 Operational Records and Reports

The operations level is the management core of your security, the entire reason for the department's existence. It is at the operations level where all your resources and administrative effort come together to enable effective asset protection. Throughout this book, you'll find the many "tools" of security management and operations; however, this chapter discloses the "catalyst" of all these things—operational records and reports.

Throughout the country, and in many foreign countries, proprietary and contract security forces outnumber law enforcement 5 to 1. The rate of increase for security compared to law enforcement is higher. Law enforcement agencies, understaffed and overworked with ordinary and extraordinary crime, have little time (or interest) when a major corporation reports that someone stole its assets. The security profession clearly must accept greater responsibility for recording, investigating, and record keeping.

There also remains another important aspect for recording, investigating, and record keeping by your security department. Most criminal activity and other incidents in the corporate and industrial environments happen totally or partly on private property. Corporate and industrial management has certain rights and obligations to decide what actions to take, and you must work within their policy. Also, private action is often more expedient, less costly, and less embarrassing to a company. The threat of lawsuits or protecting an offender from a criminal record may be, within a business logic, in the company's best interest. Your company then, preferably with your advice and counsel, decides what the policy will be for reporting misdemeanors and felonies to law enforcement agencies. That decision stems from whether the company wants to prosecute offenders and whether prosecution serves any purpose in the long term. Such crimes as murders, rape, or assaults involving employees pose different problems. The magnitude of the crime dictates the policy, removing the company prerogatives of involving criminal justice agencies. In those events, you must immediately report the crime to the proper law enforcement agency. However, most criminal activity confronting corporate or industrial security forces involves some form of theft or destruction of company property and other crimes that offer a choice. A good rule of thumb to follow suggests that you report all crimes against employees and other persons to law enforcement agencies immediately, and let company policy determine those that involve their assets.

Whatever your company management policies dictate, you need to maintain good records and the guidelines for key operational records follow in this chapter. Many reports, investigations, and records and their formats depend on the type of facility, company, or industry you protect. However, those discussed and shown here supply the "foundation," applying common principles and procedures that serve as a basis of development for your department.

RECORDING DAILY SECURITY ACTIVITIES

You should link all phases of security records to form an integrated system. The mere introduction of various forms will accomplish little and often create a nightmarish administrative load. The system you design must remain administratively simple, flowing from one set of controls, yet meet the operating needs of your security department and support your company with documents needed. The level of complexity also depends greatly on the size of your operations.

EVALUATING YOUR NEED FOR SECURITY RECORDS

You have a responsibility to maintain appropriate data to give corporate management a basis for determining the value and effectiveness of your security services and to help pinpoint specific needs. The importance of keeping accurate crime statistics and other records by law enforcement agencies has long been recognized. Records remained one of the basic principles of the Peelian Reforms written in 1829 by Sir Robert Peel, the person who organized the London Metropolitan Police Department. Peel wrote "Police records are necessary to correct distribution of police strength." That principle remains as pertinent today as when it was written. It also applies to modern security operations that increasingly assume greater and more professional responsibilities.

Records can help you in determining patrol areas, work schedules, use of preventive measures, and other factors that lead to efficient application of security officers and physical resources. For example, if accurate records point out a trend or significant increase in thefts at a given location, you can initiate special actions. As another example, maybe several assaults happen in a particular company parking lot justifying assignment of an added security patrol in the area during the time employees are reporting to or leaving work. Imaginative planning, based on an accurate record system, can be an effective crime prevention and enforcement tool.

The main purposes for maintaining internal data on criminal activities, such as pilferage, are to develop, improve, and assess effectiveness of your crime reduction programs. Never create this system for or intend it as a record system on company employees; rather, view it as a data base for proper security management planning. The scope of your records system within that category could depend on many factors, such as size of the facility, criticalness and vulnerability of protected company resources, and location of facility. The general purpose of the crime reduction data effort must enable you to meet a management objective instead of being an end in itself. Law enforcement agencies have long used a "criminal information" and "criminal intelligence" effort to develop crime trends and to help identify persons probably involved in criminal activities. Your efforts should stay focused on specific problems reported by other department managers regarding asset losses and your case reports discussed and shown later.

Added importance on security records stems from the liability problems that face persons and companies. Often, a lawsuit involving a security officer also names the company as a defendant. Presumably, when a grievance against a security officer is filed, it assumes that he or she represented the company. Also, since a security officer probably has no meaningful financial resources to offer as a settlement even when a court finds him or her liable for some improper action, the company proves to be a better source. Many lawsuits today stem from greed as opposed to genuine injury (the legal term for any type of wrong directed at and received by a person). Without good records, your security officer and the company can suffer from an alleged situation. When there is no true cause for liability, and your records cannot document or prove the actual facts, a court probably will decide for the plaintiff.

Also, when law enforcement becomes involved in a case involving your company, and a decision to prosecute an offender is made, the success or failure of the action often depends on the accuracy and thoroughness of your security reports, investigations, and records. Within the corporate or industrial environment, a security officer normally discovers a crime or is called to the scene by another employee or detection system. The information and follow-up investigation have important effect on the result of the event, either handled internally or involving the criminal justice system.

CREATING A SECURITY RECORDS SYSTEM

The forms and procedures discussed in this chapter are appropriate in any security environment, each being essential to creating an efficient and effective reporting and records system. Any system must have a logical starting point, and security actions, like law enforcement, begin at the scene of an event or crime. What the security officer does at the time can have a profound impact on all that happens or doesn't happen. However, you need control over officer response activity and that centers on a case or event numbering system.

CREATING A CONTROL SYSTEM

Reports have little benefit without a catalyst. You need a central numbering system that all reports reference and enable you to develop statistical information for your planning, budgeting, and resource management. You can accomplish that with one sequential numbering system to prevent confusion and excessive administration. The control system needs a central location and must be administered by limited numbers of supervisory or administrative persons. It begins with the creation of a numbering sequence that best serves your needs. You may use the following guidelines as they appear or as a concept to develop your own system.

• Begin with Identifiers

The first three digits of your control numbering system should identify the event, offense, or crime. For example, categorize the possible and probable events arising from your protective security situation, such as

- Company property theft—assign the identifying number 01.
- Personal property theft—assign the identifying number 02.
- Motor vehicle collision—assign the identifying number 03.
- Assault or personal injury—assign the identifying number 04.

Continue the process until you've identified all the categories.

• Follow with the Calendar Year

An integral part of your control number must tell at a glance the year written. That designation follows the identifier number with a hyphen separating them. For example: For the year 1992, use only 92. Your number to now involving company property theft appears 01-92.

• Continue with an Accounting Number

Your control number ends with a sequential number beginning immediately after midnight on the first day of January and continues through December 31 at midnight. For example, you begin the accounting number with 0001 that notes the first case report for that year. This number not only serves as a retrieval and reference number, but one that helps you determine at any given moment how many responses your officer has made during that year. Your control or case number would now appear as 01-92-0001. That tells you instantly, without reading the report that the case or event is about company property theft, during the year 1992, and it's the first case of the year.

● **Adding Information to Your Control Numbers**

Depending on your administrative management needs, you may want to add numbers or letters to the control number. For example, you might also want to use the control number to identify company theft in value increments, such as $500, $1,000, and so on, and use letter suffixes such as "A" for a $500 loss. When the suffix is integrated into the previous example it appears as follows: 01-92-0001-A. You might identify a $1,000 loss with "B," and so on. Other possibilities, primarily for fast collection and tally of statistical information might include a suffix letter showing if a vehicle collision involved only company vehicles, one or two vehicles; whether only employee-owned vehicles were involved; and whether personal injury resulted. The limits of information and benefit from your control number depend entirely on you. However, an important tip includes having a comprehensive master list and ensuring whoever in your department assigns control numbers use the list attentively to avoid confusion and guarantee accuracy. With a control numbering system in place, you're ready to put it to use with case reports.

CREATING AN EFFECTIVE CASE REPORT

A variety of titles can apply to this report, and a sheaf of different forms can be developed to cover different types of events. However, the first rule of effective, efficient, and cost-benefit security reports and records points us logically to simplicity. The case reports apply to any situation, from an alarm activation, damage from a storm, theft of an employee's purse, or to an entire warehouse being cleaned out. It is primarily a standardized form of reporting any event a security officer responds to investigate or becomes involved in while on duty.

Your case reports also must have a design that enables the officer first at the scene to obtain sufficient information. Stumbling around haphazardly trying to remember what to write in a pocket notebook adds to the confusion. Your officers need to approach a situation systematically, and the case report design can guide them through the procedures. Illustration 4–1 shows a case report form. Keep in mind that the example is not fixed, and you should use it as a guide to develop your own case reports meeting specific information needs. However, the format shown includes the essential elements. An added tip: Don't try to be economical by trying to squeeze your case reports on one sheet of paper. One of the greatest flaws in "forms" continues to be many confused blanks so tiny no human can complete the information properly or add anything that might have importance. Give your officers plenty of space to supply all the information and still be legible while keeping the form simple.

Normally, in a security report much of the personal or other type of identifying information necessary or found in law enforcement reports is obtainable from company personnel files later when or if needed. Some examples include dates of birth, social security numbers, and other information that might be necessary should you refer the case to a law enforcement or other criminal justice agency. When a person (intruder) is apprehended trespassing, stealing property, or committing another offense, they're normally released to law enforcement officials promptly. Although your case report applies in such cases, further identifying information is obtained by the law enforcement agency taking the person into custody, and when needed, you can obtain that information from them. The concept of security reports is keeping a light administrative burden on security officers, avoiding confusion and unnecessary information easily obtainable from other records when needed. Illustration 4–1 is a working example you can use as an effective guide to develop your case report forms.

Illustration 4–1

EXAMPLE OF A SECURITY CASE REPORT

**Security Department
HYZ Industries, Any City**

CASE REPORT

Case Control Number: _____ *00-00-0000*

Date and Time of Report: _____ *Friday, June 23, 0000 – 4:30 p.m.*

Officer Making Report: _____ *Corporal John Doe – Badge 431*

Event Identification: _____ *Theft of Company Property*

_____ *Assault on Company Employee*

Location of Event: _____ *Warehouse 42*

_____ *South Beach Street, Any City*

Time of Event: _____ *4:00 p.m.* _____ Date of Event: _____ *Friday, June 23, 0000*

Reported by: _____ *Samuel Roberts*

Address: _____ *Maintenance Department, XYZ Industries* _____ (work)

_____ *32 Elm Street, Apartment 12, Any City* _____ (home)

Telephone: _____ *000-0000* _____ (work)

_____ *000-0000* _____ (home)

Victim of Event: _____ *John Smith*

Address: _____ *Warehouse 42 – Shipping* _____ (work)

_____ *824 Hillsdale Blvd., Any City* _____ (home)

Telephone: _____ *000-000* _____ (work)

_____ *000-000* _____ (home)

Personal injury involved? ☐ Yes ☐ No ☐ Not applicable

(continued)

Illustration 4–1 (continued)

Action taken when personal injury involved (i.e. first aid, hospital):

Paramedics called from company dispensary

Paramedics transported Smith to County Hospital for examination

Law enforcement agency involved: ☐ Yes ☐ No ☐ Not applicable

If so, identify agency and responding officers' names:

Johnson County Sheriff's Department, Deputy Clint Rockwell

Any City Police Department, Patrol Officer Marvin O'Hara

Describe action taken by law enforcement agency representatives:

Filled out their department forms and will interview Smith later.

Vehicle involved?   ☐ Yes   ☐ No

Damage to vehicle?   ☐ Yes   ☐ No

Collision report completed: ☐ Yes   ☐ No

Other comments: _____

Person(s) apprehended? ☐ Yes   ☐ No   ☐ Not applicable

If so, identify each: (Name, Address, Social Security No., Date of Birth)

Joe Robinson, 57 East Elm St., Any City 000-00-0000, May 10, 00

Pete Mulligan, 84 West Pine St., Any City 000-00-0000, Oct. 4, 00

Suspects released to law enforcement? ☐ Yes   ☐ No

If not, why? _____

(continued)

Illustration 4–1 (continued)

If yes, identify agency and officer taking custody:

Deputy Sheriff George Samuels – Johnson County Sheriff's Dept.

Deputy Sheriff John Overby – Johnson County Sheriff's Dept.

Check the appropriate box for enclosures to this report:

☐ Statement of victim   ☐ Statement of witness(s)

☐ Photographs   ☐ Sketches

☐ Physical evidence   ☐ Property receipts

☐ Security officer statement   ☐ Other items, show below

Item: _____

Item: _____

Item: _____

Comments and memorandum:

The suspects were apprehended by Security Officer Jim Richards.

near the south perimeter fence (section 21) when they tried to

climb over it from the inside to the outside. Contact with the

central control by Richards revealed the Warehouse 42 event

and further investigation disclosed the suspects assaulted Smith.

Further investigation by the Johnson County Sheriff's Dept.

ADVANTAGES OF A SECURITY BLOTTER

The security blotter has been a law enforcement tool from the beginning. It is a daily chronological record of security activity developed from reports and other information sources. The blotter does not serve as a substitute for your case reports. Entries are normally in brief narrative form and contain only the essentials of the report, concisely stating the who, what, when, where, and how, and identity of persons related to the event and directing reference to the case report for details.

Your security blotter also serves as a journal for personnel changes or any operational item wanted as a permanent record. The security blotter covers the period from one minute past midnight to midnight (0001 hours to 2400 hours). As noted in the example in Illustration 4–2, time recorded in the "time column" reflects the time for receipt of the information. The first daily entry on your blotter should always show "blotter opened," and the last entry on each blotter is always "blotter closed."

Illustration 4−2

EXAMPLE OF A
SECURITY DEPARTMENT BLOTTER

Security Department Blotter	Date:	Page No. 1
XYZ Industries Any City		No. of pages

Entry No.	Time	Summary of Event or Information	Action Taken

INVESTIGATION BEYOND CASE REPORTS

While the case report often contains enough information, certain events need follow-up investigations if only used as method of recording additional information. For example, after the police took custody of the two men who assaulted the warehouse employee used in the sample earlier, you need to continue recording information perhaps furnished by the police investigation. Whatever the need, you should create a standard investigative form. Always use the same control number and place investigative information or added documents in the same file as the original case report.

You may also use the investigative report to show action taken resulting from an event, such as an unexplained alarm activation found later by technicians to be a defective element within the system. The case report showed response to the alarm sounding by an officer who commented he or she could find no intruders or evidence of any intruder. You can use the investigative form to follow up to a conclusion and place it on file as a supplement to the case report.

The key point to remember about the investigative report is that it never has a separate control number. You must use a case report if only as a control document and cover for other activity that follows. For example, a company department manager might call you personally, asking that you examine a systematic pilferage problem in his or her department. The manager prefers to keep the matter low profile and doesn't want to involve security officers now. You agree and decide to conduct a discreet investigation of the complaint. You should fill out a case report, obtain a control number, and then proceed with your investigation. To prevent disclosure of a confidential investigation, have the blotter and control number log book showing the control number assigned to you (a blind number) with no further information. However, you should not permit others in your department to use that discretion without your express authorization. Although periodically, conducting a quiet inquiry might include a supervisor or officer, thereby developing a need to issue a "blind control number." Always ensure the issue of such numbers be to you and with your authorization the supervisor or officer can discreetly proceed but report directly to you for keeping a proper record of the activity. When the case must stay confidential, you can keep it in a separate control file; however, the number is logged and the accountability remains intact.

Illustration 4–3 provides an example of an investigation form you might consider using or developing your own from the format.

Illustration 4–3

EXAMPLE OF A
SECURITY DEPARTMENT INVESTIGATIVE REPORT

Security Department
HYZ Industries, Any City

Investigative Report

Case Control No. _____*00-00-0000*_____   Date: _____*June 27, 0000*_____

Page __*1*__ of __*1*__   Progress? ( )   Final Report? (**✗**)

George Wilson, Alarms International inspected the detection system in Warehouse 5 and found a defective element. He replaced the element and tested the system. No further problem expected.

QUICK REFERENCE REVIEW AND GUIDE
FOR
CREATING A CONTROLLED REPORTING SYSTEM

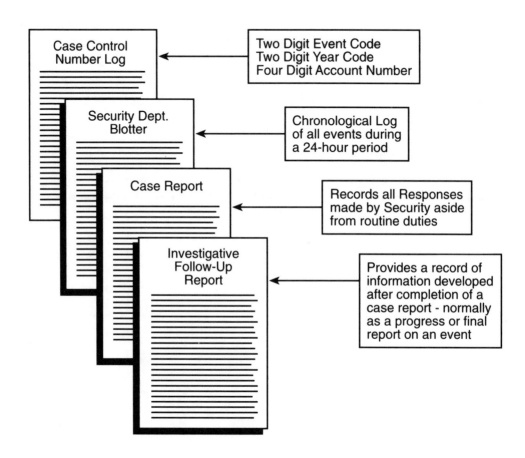

Case Control Number Log ← Two Digit Event Code / Two Digit Year Code / Four Digit Account Number

Security Dept. Blotter ← Chronological Log of all events during a 24-hour period

Case Report ← Records all Responses made by Security aside from routine duties

Investigative Follow-Up Report ← Provides a record of information developed after completion of a case report - normally as a progress or final report on an event

ADDITIONAL RECORDS TO CONSIDER

Additional types of records that help you manage the security department include the following suggestions depending on your specific situation, size of operations, and company policies.

● **Telephone Call Logs**

This type log works effectively for busy control centers or any central security facility that receives call-in reports from security post, complaints, and other business regularly. Using the telephone log system helps to keep control center staff alert and can help to track down information often months later when a crucial point involves a question about the receipt of a phone call and what action taken. While this is a good management tool, it does increase the administrative load for smaller security departments.

● **Radio and Communication Logs**

Like the telephone log, keeping radio and communication logs depends largely on the size and diversity of your department and amount of radio traffic involved. When you have static and mobile security positions, they should routinely make communication checks and let the central control know they are okay, especially at night, during storms, or, under other conditions when officers are working alone. A radio log can help a busy center manager to look back over the log and note which officer hasn't checked in and can dispatch a supervisor to ensure that he or she is okay.

● **Vehicle and Equipment Inspection Records**

When your department uses several vehicles, each operator needs to be attentive to the preventive maintenance benefits. This attention can be ensured by requiring routine preduty vehicle or equipment inspections. Often, damage or some other infraction surfaces through this measure that might not otherwise be reported and later create operational problems. These records also enable a current record of vehicle needs, condition, and serviceability that can be cost effective over the long term.

● **Duty Rosters**

Duty rosters have an inherent place in most security departments that operate on shifts. You should use a standardized duty roster and integrate that information regularly into your other record statistics. Doing so helps you to develop the need for more officers, find better ways to manage their duty time, develop training time, and serve other purposes that might be unique to your situation.

● Officer's Daily Activity Reports

At a minimum, supervisors should maintain a daily activity report, and depending on your situation, each officer should complete one and turn it in as he or she departs after working a shift. An activity report helps to keep people alert, supplies an opportunity for increased responsibility, and can help when a problem arises by having a record of what happened at a given time. For example, a company maintenance inspector sends a report through his channels complaining that the security department isn't checking a pumping station as agreed upon months earlier. The result, he claims, is a burned out system costing thousands of dollars and hindering a part of company production operations. You can check back to the rosters, identify the security officers working over the past weeks in that area, and verify from their activity reports that the pumping station checks were conducted and the results noted. With that documented defense, you can avoid being made the scapegoat and impress the company management of your competence.

● Vehicle Collision Reports

Most law enforcement agencies don't like to investigate vehicle collisions on private property and in many jurisdictions will not unless it involves a fatality or serious personal injury. In most states, there are reporting laws involving estimated monetary value of damage; however, that requirement normally involves "public ways" and not those on private property. When your security department responsibilities include large parking areas within the company property, your officers might need to investigate vehicle collisions. Coordinate with your local police and determine your requirements. When you do have this requirement, prepare and maintain records to ensure the company or others receive fair treatment in lawsuits or other actions that might arise from this type event.

● Industrial Accident Reports

Often, security departments become involved in the investigation of industrial accidents or witness them happen. Whatever your requirements, you might need to develop records that deal specifically with this type of event. Much of the tailoring of the reporting and investigation system stems from what the company or industry produces.

● Employee and Visitor Personal Injury Reports

Personal injury claims have a common place in any company, some legitimate and some not. Although normally a company has insurance and an insurance investigator will conduct his or her investigation, a security officer normally is on the scene soon after. You should always have a minimum of a case report and statements from the officer and witnesses for your records.

• **Other reports and records that benefit**

The list of record possibilities is long, and there is no substitute for documentation although most people try hard to avoid the task. However, when a form or file has a genuine need, and is well thought out to make each system interrelate and easy to manage, the cost-time-benefit outweighs the inconvenience or administrative work load.

CREATING CRIME REDUCTION RECORD SYSTEMS

The first and most important rule of your crime reduction records requires your crime reduction effort be focused on situations—not people. It is inappropriate to collect data and keep files on employees, vendors, or visitors that suggest, even by innuendo, they are dishonest. There is also a significant legal liability problem and perhaps, depending on the situation, criminal offenses involved in doing that. However, when you focus on collecting and recording information about criminal activity itself, you can better develop crime prevention measures by eliminating opportunities. When they persist in stealing, the perpetrators will at some point become clearly known or caught in the act through your enhanced security arrangements.

The sources of information that lead to effective crime reduction efforts come from your case reports that often identify a problem area within the company, from employees having knowledge of criminal enterprise and who don't condone it, and from security officer observation. Another source might stem from local law enforcement who discover through their sources that some criminal activity normally involving theft is happening at your company. Whatever your source, you need a way to establish retrievable working records and files. That process begins with a standardized reporting method or form.

Creating a Crime Reduction Report Form

Your first step in collecting and managing crime reduction information stems from a need for a standardized form that all security officers can use. It needs to be an easy form to complete, have little demand for administrative maintenance, and have information value. It can be either handwritten or typewritten. An example of a security department crime reduction report form is shown as Illustration 4–4.

Illustration 4–4

EXAMPLE OF A
CRIME REDUCTION REPORT

CRIME REDUCTION REPORT

Department – Area – Facility:

Warehouse 10

Description:

A shipping facility, 40,000 square feet, 5 employees including

one supervisor. Contains a mix of cameras, toasters and

small television sets. One security post to observe only.

Date: *Jan 10, 0000* Reporting Officer: *Sgt. John O'Hara*

Source of Information: *Any City PD – Lt. Adam Smith*

Summary of Information

Smith reported that the Any City Police Intelligence team learned from an informant that two of the employees at Warehouse 10, XYZ Industries are involved with at least five truck drivers and load extra cartons of cameras and television sets that are dropped off at one of the employee's home garage.

The shipping department manager contacted and will conduct a discreet, unannounced audit of Warehouse 10 and advise of the outcome.

Creating a Retrievable Crime Reduction System

The key word guiding a crime reduction reporting and records system is "retrieval." Having lots of reports and information that get lost in the files over the weeks, months, and years serves no purpose. In a corporate or industrial environment, filing reports by crime category tends to scatter, instead of focus, effort. Either you have to rely on memory or have an elaborate computer or manual system of referencing each report. The best, easiest, and least labor-intensive system involves dividing your company into areas, much as you do for developing and maintaining physical security. For example, if your company has 12 administrative departments, you should create a report and information file section for each department and place reports in the applicable file. Go a step further, with a file on facilities and areas probably keyed to your physical security areas such as warehouses and open storage. Although the separate areas probably are controlled by a department, your additional file further divides the departments, making them easier to monitor. Whenever a report on activity comes to you on that department, file it under that department. However, unless you want to go through the files, or try to remember, another step in your system is important. Illustration 4–5 supplies an example of an easy-to-use filing system for your crime reduction reports and information effort.

Illustration 4–5

EXAMPLE OF A CRIME REDUCTION REPORT FILING SYSTEM
DIVIDED INTO DEPARTMENTS, FACILITIES, AND SECTIONS

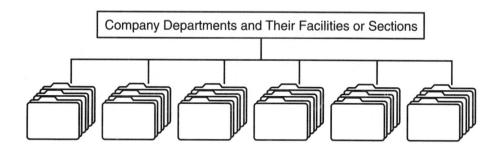

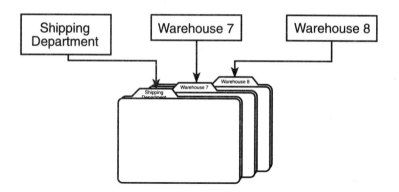

CREATING A REFERENCE CATALOG WITH A NOTEBOOK

For each file folder you create on departments, facilities, and areas, place a sheet in a three-ring notebook and tab it or arrange the sheets alphabetically, whatever is easier for you. When you put information into the corresponding file, for example, about pilferage at Warehouse 10, make a note on your notebook log for Warehouse 10. Beyond your memory, you can leaf through the notebook and spot problem areas quickly. The notebook also supplies an excellent tool if you have to brief your boss on what's happening in the security department. You have a record of your case reports, and the notebook catalog of information in the files covers both sides of your efforts beyond routine duty. Illustration 4–6 shows how you might set up your file reference catalog in a notebook.

Illustration 4–6

EXAMPLE OF A FILE REFERENCE NOTEBOOK

Crime Reduction File Catalog

Department:

Warehouse 10

Date	Item
Jan. 10. 000	*Report on pilferage at warehouse – 2 employees. and truck drivers. (Dept Mgr contacted.)*
Feb. 22. 0000	*Report on Dept Mgr audit – shows major shortages – wants investigation*

QUICK REFERENCE REVIEW AND GUIDE
FOR
CRIME REDUCTION REPORTS AND RECORDS

- Establish Easy to Use Crime Reduction Information Reports

- Establish a Department - Facility or Area Filing System

- Establish a "Notebook" File Catalog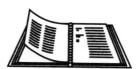

PART 2

The Basic Foundations of Security

The world of business offers many opportunities, not only for employment, production, and sales, but also for those who have other motives, not always dishonest in a legal sense, although questionable from a moral viewpoint. Your job, protecting corporate and industrial assets, like building a house, needs a solid foundation. In the security profession, a foundation builds through a variety of systems depending on your situation and circumstances. Part Two supplies you with the basics, equally important whether the company or area you protect is small or large. The key point to remember, but one that often gets lost in the high-tech deluge of security equipment and devices, remains consistent throughout your program—*layer your security systems*.

Since a company exists to do business, you cannot turn the building or complex into an armed camp that resembles a banana republic guerrilla base. However, using skill, you can create an effective mix of high-profile systems, followed by low-profile systems, and include some stumbling blocks that cannot be detected readily. That layering technique, using basic equipment and techniques, serves despite the weather, power source availability, or equipment breakdown. The basic systems also need less training to operate and have many cost-effective benefits.

IDENTIFY WHAT NEEDS PROTECTION

Within the concepts of corporate and industrial security, like most professions, a line of traditions exists. Many of the traditions or conventional viewpoints of security have solid merit and need to be preserved and have continued application. However, others need rethinking or discarding, and that's not always easy because your paycheck comes from business-oriented persons who either dislike security or want more than what is deemed necessary. Your first step is to evaluate what you need to protect in specific terms opposed to general concepts. For example, there is no valid reason to have a fence around an area that contains property requiring a huge crane and special trucks to move. Instead, use the funds for areas and systems that serve a genuine purpose. *Throw out the negative traditions, build on the positive traditions, and create some new ones in the process.*

One of the negative traditions in the security profession often resembles *one train of thought, to protect against theft.* Although that remains a primary threat, other problems involve a total security view, such as protecting your company assets from destruction or damage from fires, storms, inadvertent accidents, demonstrations by activists opposed to your company's business, and other problems that have no connection to theft of assets. Consider your priorities of protection and design your security systems accordingly. Your starting point begins with the control of the greatest problem—people.

5 Internal Security Management

Much of the problem of controlling people inside the company stems from perception. For example, a well-dressed person carrying a clipboard and looking "official" can move about in most companies with little challenge even when no one knows the person. Following that example, a person in coveralls, an equipment belt filled with tools, and a clipboard and maybe wearing a hard hat can probe in all the nooks and crannies, ask questions, and receive answers with great success. The key is look official and act as if you belong. The person with a mission can often move freely, albeit for the purpose of criminal enterprise reconnaissance, competitor representative snooping, or free-lance information collector.

DEVELOPING EFFECTIVE IDENTIFICATION SYSTEMS

Your first priority in controlling who enters or departs company property stems from having an effective way of issuing, maintaining, and recognizing identification. There's also a side benefit from each employee having an identification card. People like to identify with their employer, and the card supplies a way for each employee to feel a part of the company, plus using it when cashing a check, opening a credit line, or engaging in some other personal affair calling for positive identification. However, you need to develop an efficient, and effective way to issue cards and recover them from employees no longer working. You must also guard against duplication and forged versions, and the following techniques serve that purpose.

DESIGNING YOUR COMPANY IDENTIFICATION CARDS

Certain factors have importance when you consider the design or redesign of company identification cards. Control and recognition establish your priorities in design, with other side benefits pointed out throughout this section.

• Personalize the ID Card with a Photograph

Without a photograph on an identification card, the effort of supplying identification serves no purpose. An identification card or any identifying document without a laminated photograph of the authorized holder is easily duplicated or forged and another form of photograph ID must be presented. Added identification also creates a deficient control because, for example, sources not hard to find produce excellent forgeries of driver's licenses, and several legitimate sources in cities make photoidentification cards. They have no obligation to verify the information provided by the client, since the liability begins with the user, not the maker unless involved in some type of criminal conspiracy.

The best methods for taking photographs involve making two pictures simultaneously: one photograph affixed to the identification card and the other on a security file for reference. Should the employee lose or damage the card, never use the duplicate for replacement; take a new set of photographs but save the old copy. The reason you do that stems from possible use to breach security by a look-alike, or the card turns up in a police investigation or some other situation. When you have the duplicate photograph for a card reported lost, for example, it serves to verify a card found and turned in to ensure the authenticity of the document. When the card turns out to be a forgery, that alerts you to a new security problem of imposters trying to enter the company area with forged ID cards.

The best equipment for making photoidentification cards comes from Polaroid (IDenticard℠) or companies using Polaroid equipment. Most states use the system for driver's licenses, taking two photographs and a picture of the ID card forms simultaneously. The card is a composite photograph of the person and the card. The system features efficiency and portability that can help when your company has several locations within a reasonable geographical area and traveling to each site to make identification cards is economical. An example of this card design shown in Illustration 5–2 also applies to conventional identification cards shown in Illustration 5–1.

• Number Each Card and Account for the Numbers

Serial numbered cards serve two important purposes. The first involves control of the blanks and ensures a verification checkpoint for those issued, helping to prevent or detect counterfeit cards. You need a log book and inventory system for the numbering system to work. The serial number of a card issued should also be sent to the personnel department for entry on the employee's records. Guard against printer error and mishandling. Printers don't have the same interest in safeguarding each printed card or destroying slightly defective cards as you do. Also, ensure the plates, computer disks, and other methods used by the printer come to you with the printed cards. Although you might have tightly controlled security and issue accountability for the identification cards, a determined perpetrator can burglarize or otherwise obtain the proofs from the printer's place of business. With them, the person can run off "authentic" company identification cards that your security officers or other employees aren't likely to detect as fraudulent. Illustration 5–1 and 5–2 are examples of the numbering system.

● What Type of Information to Put on The Card

Your company logo needs to be the first piece of information appearing on the card. Also, you should include a brief statement, normally on the reverse side of the card, making it clear the card remains the property of the company. Include an address for the finder of lost card to send it or call. Next, ensure the employee's identification through a physical description and date of birth. Both have importance in verifying that the person holding the card is the right person. For example, when an employee loses a card or a perpetrator makes a counterfeit, one of the stumbling blocks for an impersonator might be the date of birth or physical characteristics. Illustrations 5–1 and 5–2 are examples of personal identification information to consider.

● Color Coding your Company ID Cards

Color coding your company ID cards makes it difficult for an impersonator to move about the company freely without challenge. For example, a person wanting to obtain mailing lists would need a card color-coded to allow access unchallenged in the marketing department. Assuming that the department safeguards its information in computers, on disks, and in files, the intruder would need time to move about and look for the information or normally would enter before quitting time so he or she could stay in the area after other employees left and appear to custodians or security officers to be working late.

If using conventional identification cards with a stick-on picture, have the cards printed on different colors of stock. If using a system such as the IDenticard by Polaroid, color code the background behind the employee's photograph. For example, you can use red for the computer center, blue for warehouse personnel, and green for the accounting department. Depending on the number of employees, cost factors, and other considerations, change the colors periodically. Illustrations 5–3 and 5–4 show examples of color-coding badge and control systems.

● Displaying the ID Card

The best security includes employees' wearing their identification cards to enable observation by security officers and other company employees. The best security for impostors or other suspicious activity, including that of employees, requires getting the company employees involved. Most cooperate readily when they understand the problems, and it is often surprising how protective they become when given the responsibility. The display issue depends on how many employees a company has in a location. For example, when 2,000 employees are within a complex, no one knows everyone else. However, when a company has only 200 employees, the chances of noticing an impostor or suspicious employee activity increases markedly. Whether employees wear their identification cards attached in plain view on clothing depends on your company needs for security restrictions, and often, that decision involves the number of employees. When you do require that, the best system to use is a "pin-on" clear plastic card holder. The card slips into the holder easily when the employee enters his or her workplace and worn through the day or night. When leaving, the card easily slides from the holder and is returned to a wallet or purse. Most employees prefer having the ID card available for other identification uses as noted earlier and can safeguard it with more success using this technique.

● The Exchange System

Although exchanging ID cards for badges, or badges for badges, increases the work load for security officers plus adds operational expense, the benefit of using the exchange clearly improves security. This technique dramatically lessens the possibility of impostors entering company areas. With this system, the employee presents his or her issued identification card at a gate or building entrance and the card is exchanged for a clip-on "badge," normally color-coded and showing a large number, letter, or both. When using this method, you need to control the badge printing or manufacture in the same way as noted earlier for the ID cards. Each employee is assigned a numbered badge that must never leave the security area where it's obtained and returned. The best method of control for efficient exchange includes a slotted rack to store badges when not in use. When the employee turns in an ID card, the security officer removes the assigned badge from the slot and replaces it with the ID card. When the employee leaves the area, a reverse exchange occurs, badge for ID card. Security officers must stay alert for impostors entering, and leaving the area after entering some other way. However, when your layered security designs work properly, the intruder cannot just hand over a badge and leave the area quickly while the security officer is looking for the ID card. More information about that control technique appears later in the book. Illustration 5–2 shows examples of how the card-badge exchange system works. Increased security needs can have multiple badge exchanges outside each high security area. For example, before an employee can enter a high-security storage area, he or she might have to exchange his or her badge for another "area badge" and return it for the original badge on leaving that area. The concept creates "stumbling blocks" and discourages people from trying to enter areas where they have no legitimate business. Illustration 5–3 and 5–4 show examples of how the badge exchange system works.

IN TOUCH WITH TECHNOLOGY

Sophisticated identification cards, including photographs and other identifying data unseen in a magnetic strip, now enhance the security systems, but the technology to produce them is costly to install and maintain. These systems and how they can work for you are discussed and illustrated in Part Three.

IDENTIFYING VENDORS

Most companies have a steady stream of salespersons and vendors servicing equipment and food service/beverage systems. Those who come to the company areas regularly need a special ID or badge that identifies the person as a vendor clearly. To obtain one, vendors need to complete an application and undergo the same process as employees, with photographs on file, their company authorization, the type vehicle they operate, and other easily identifiable data. Being complacent about vendors can result in impersonation or temptation of theft and information collection when opportunities afford that chance. The concept of dealing with vendors includes moving them in and out quickly (they're in business too) but limiting the opportunity for conducting any business except the one they are there to conduct. An example of a vendor badge shown in Illustration 5–5.

CONTROL OF VISITORS

Visitors do not normally call for much attention since most companies discourage employees' friends or relatives from coming into their workplace. While the problem of dishonesty is always a concern, the greatest problem companies have with allowing employee visitors stems from creating a distraction for the employee and his or her colleagues. However, when the visitor has authorization, the person they visit needs to be responsible for their actions, and they need to wear a security badge that clearly identifies them as "a visitor." It should be color coded, issued at the point where the employee is summoned to escort them. Have the employee sign a log book, showing the time of entry, time of departure, name of the visitor, address and telephone number, relationship to the employee, and the badge number issued. Making it a bit difficult serves as a strong deterrent for the visitor having any thoughts about breaching the company security of assets. An example of a visitor badge is shown in Illustration 5–5 and sign-in, checkout log in Illustration 5–6.

SOLVING THE PROBLEM OF TOUR GROUPS

Many companies offer tours of their facilities to various organizations, schools, and the general public. Control these groups by handling "adult" members of the group as you do visitors, with the detailed sign-in and checkout log and a required "Tour" color-coded badge, issued on arrival and turned in on departure. These types of visitors normally don't pose a threat; however, those wanting to enter the company area to conduct some type of surreptitious activity might use the tour group as a cover for gaining entry without suspicion. The identification log, badges, and other restrictions supply a solid deterrent; however, continue to monitor the tour discreetly. When a security officer knows 12 people entered with a company escort and now only observes 11, it is time to find the missing person. Tours might allow a person to slip away and return without notice. When a school group comes for a tour, security officers need to log in adults and count children. The adults pose the possible threat because of impostors noted earlier; the children can become lost and left behind.

Illustration 5–1

EXAMPLE OF A CONVENTIONAL EMPLOYEE IDENTIFICATION CARD

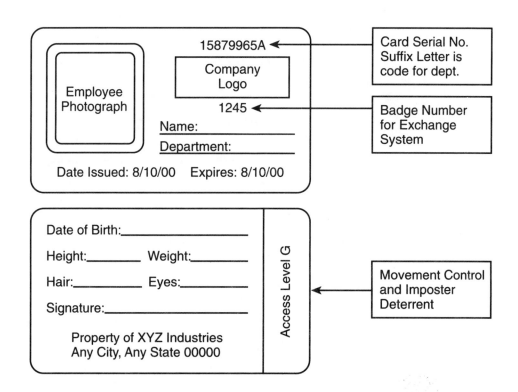

Illustration 5–2

EXAMPLE OF THE POLAROID IDENTICARD SYSTEM PROCESS

Employee Photograph	Name:_____
	Dept:_____
	Issue Date:_____
	Exp. Date:_____
	Access Code:_____
Company Logo	58975264B 8547

(optional) Employee Photograph Profile	Height:_____ Weight:_____
	Eyes:_____ Hair:_____
	Date of Birth:_____
	Signature:
	_____

Property of XYZ Industries, Any City, Any State 00000

Illustration 5-3

EXAMPLE OF A COLOR-CODED SECURITY BADGE SYSTEM

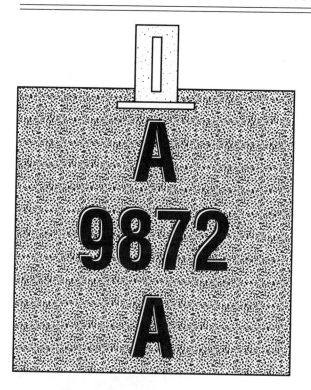

Color-coded security badge received from security personnel by surrendering issued company identification card at entrance. Badge should be clipped on outer clothing and be visible. The color and letter symbol, such as "A" designate the area the employee has authorization to enter and move about.

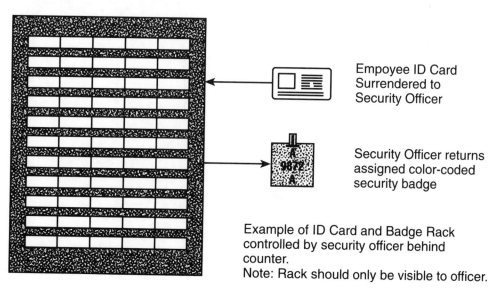

Empoyee ID Card Surrendered to Security Officer

Security Officer returns assigned color-coded security badge

Example of ID Card and Badge Rack controlled by security officer behind counter.
Note: Rack should only be visible to officer.

Illustration 5-4

EXAMPLE OF A SECURITY DEPARTMENT COLOR-CODED BADGE
CONTROL SYSTEM MAP

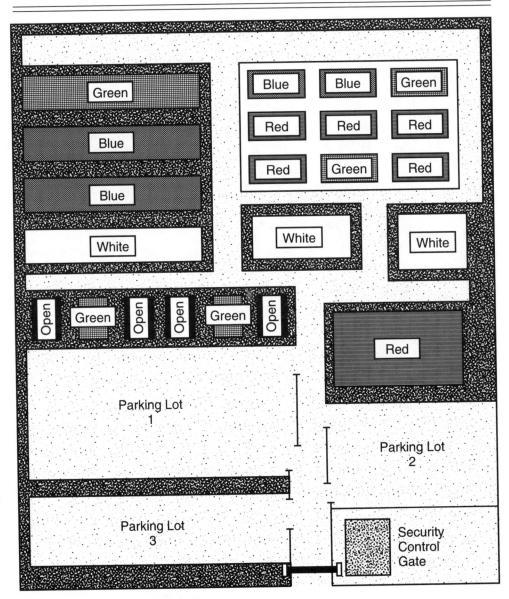

Color-coded diagram of industrial area supplied to security posts - but only visible to security officers.

Illustration 5–5

EXAMPLES OF TEMPORARY SECURITY BADGES ISSUED TO VENDORS, VISITORS, AND TOUR GROUP ADULTS

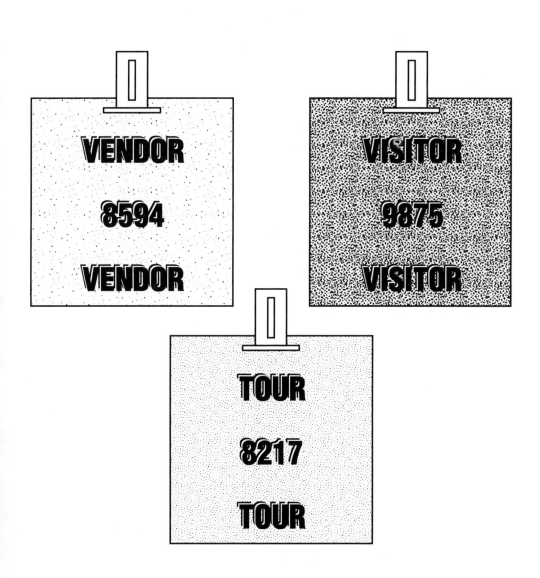

Illustration 5–6

EXAMPLE OF A SIGN-IN AND CHECKOUT LOG FOR NONEMPLOYEES

Vendor – Visitor – Tour Adults Sign-in and Checkout Log			
Date Time In	**Date Time Out**	**Name – Address – Tele Representing**	**Badge No.**
9 a.m.	*9:30 a.m.*	*John Smith* *7789 Elm St.* *Any City, Any State* *The Office Supply Center*	*8567*

CONTROLLING EXPENDABLE PILFERAGE—A PEOPLE PROBLEM

The problem of expendable item pilferage, the taking of company property normally used and not precisely accountable, for personal use, happens in three ways. First, is the systematic pilferer, who intentionally takes company property and converts it to personal use either at home, to supply a small personal business, or to help supply friends and relatives. Next, is the pilferer who takes advantage of an opportunity to convert company property from time to time. This person doesn't always see his or her theft as a crime; instead he or she rationalizes the act as a reward for diligent, but unappreciated work on behalf of the company; another rationalization common in this category involves the idea that the employee is poor and the company is rich and, therefore, that the small and occasional item taken for personal use won't matter in the scheme of things. Third, is the pilferer who doesn't take anything home directly, but uses the company computers, copy machines, postage, and facilities to further his or her personal interests. The conversion of company property and assets always poses difficult questions for company and security management. Many companies have grown so accustomed to it that they make no effort to prevent it.

What Does Employee Pilferage Really Cost?

In a bustling business environment, little or no thought goes to how much of the hard-won profits walk out the door or gate. After the year-end, when auditors pore over the books and find no embezzlement or fraud, they laud the company management for holding down expense accounts and making prudent buying and personnel decisions. The books are clean, but for some reason no one can fathom, there should be a few million dollars more in the coffers. Most charge off the mystery as a paper error; someone miscounted something or wrote down the wrong figures. In the course of day-to-day operations that can happen, and trying to find the mistake, often tiny in the beginning, would be a nightmare. So the company moves onward, sending out terse memos about using greater care in reporting figures, and the matter fades until the next audit. All those things mentioned, and more, can cause heavy "paper" losses, money the company never had. However, often it's the pilferage within that causes major losses, and few even in the security profession try to control it.

A company that employs 2,500 people can suffer "petty" pilferage losses in the millions. Most of it stems from opportunity or impulse pilferage, while others take advantage of the situation existing in most companies and grow wealthy. For example, if 2,500 employees work in an office environment and each takes home something, paper, pencils, paper clips, and other items worth $1.00 each day, five days a week, from the vast array of office supplies normally kept in well-stocked cabinets and not controlled or questioned, the company would lose $650,000 each year. Not all employees do that—some never take anything—but others make up the difference by taking more. The problem with this type pilferage, where the items stolen fall into an "expendable" category, is that there is no way to prove where a pencil or pad of paper comes from. Also, maybe the employee took it home to work on a company project. The question remains, How can you control the problem? We cannot be so naive to believe that all pilferage will end because of security measures we take; however, the reduction can be substantial.

Why Employees Find It Easy To Steal and How to Prevent It

Preventing pilferage begins with deciding why employees steal and then using that finding to develop ways of lessening the opportunity and increasing the risk. With the exception of people who steal out of desperation with little care about discovery and maybe jail, the majority of people use a simple formula before deciding to steal. They weigh the value and need for the item to be stolen against the probability of being caught, and then against the punishment likely if caught. Last, they normally consider a plausible excuse for having made the mistake of stealing an item, so an admission of intentional theft doesn't enter into the excuse. Normally, pilferage happens because there are few controls placed on employees, and of those in place, few are enforced. There is also a problem in the past decade or so with employees suing companies for nearly any reason and often winning. Accusing an employee of thievery, without absolute proof, invites a lawsuit that probably will cost the company more than the systematic stealing. Obtaining the proof, that includes showing "intent" to steal, is not an easy task, however the best way is to throw out the "catch 'em in the act" mentality and get to work "preventing" it from happening. There are several techniques you can apply.

● Work with Department Managers

Pilferage prevention begins with two key steps. First, develop a plan and then ask the department managers to cooperate and implement their part of your security plan. Don't try to implement this type plan from the top down, for example, a directive from the president of the company, because it won't have any effect. Corporations, like it or not, admitted or not, have a bureaucratic and political system that often rivals government agencies. Directives from the top that benefit a specific department, such as yours, and create a perceived burden on others won't get much, if any, genuine response or effort. However, when you present it to middle management yourself in an organized, illustrated way, a department manager would be foolish to say no. To say no or not to be enthusiastic about helping the company is the same thing as saying they don't care if employees steal. In your discussion, however, you must never tell a department manager that his or her employees are stealing company property. When you do that he or she will immediately become defensive and you've lost cooperation, probably never to be regained. That manager probably will try to even the score and talk to the right people, and your career could be in jeopardy. Trying to do the right thing and fulfill your security responsibilities to your company can ironically put you in the unemployment line. Maybe that's why pilferage goes largely unchecked and few discuss it in a concerned voice. You can safeguard your job and career, however, by doing something and later, continuing with the information developed by the corporate "bean counters," take credit for the savings.

● What to Ask the Department Managers

Don't ask the department managers to "tighten up on company property" and leave it at that. If they knew how to do that effectively, the pilferage wouldn't be a problem. Remember the politics of companies, and the struggles for recognition department managers need to climb the ladder. You are an outsider and not a threat to the business managers and that's an advantage when used properly. Instead, ask them specifically to implement your plan on "a test basis" to see over a few months if the administrative supply costs diminish. Ask them to

- Appoint one or two custodians of the supplies for each section or wherever the employees now get their supplies. Have the custodian inventory and record what's in stock.
- Then, lock the supply cabinet and require employees to ask the supplies custodian for whatever needed, such as paper, pens, paper clips, and so on.
- Establish an incoming and outgoing log of supplies. For example, a notebook or pad can serve the purpose, or a special form can be created to note received or restock supplies, and each time an employee comes to receive working supplies the custodian writes down what it is, who obtains it, the date, and other information to help control the items.
- When the person receives the requested items, the custodian has them sign for the issued items.
- Have the supplies custodians turn in the control sheets each week to the department manager or their administrative assistant. That removes them from the hands or desk of subordinates and takes the responsibility of last week from them.
- Periodically, review the control sheets and compare the cost information with last year's costs for the same period.

● Measuring the Results

When the department's appointed custodian performs these control steps routinely, the employee's opportunity, and often their desire, to steal supplies decreases dramatically. Note that it doesn't necessarily end, because the person can still take things, but it becomes difficult and limits them from the freedom of "shopping" regularly at the supply cabinet. For example, before the plan, an employee could stock up his or her desk over a period of a few days so not to appear carrying too much to the desk. Then, after filling the desk with supplies intended for personal use, he or she begins filtering it out in a handbag, briefcase, clothing, or some other imaginative way. With the plan in place, the same person has to ask for the items, knowing the custodian has information written down and then the employee must sign for it. It converts an expendable item into an accountable item. That system will reduce employee pilferage dramatically. Follow up your effort and continue to show the department managers you have profound interest, and your enthusiasm transfers to them. When the figures come in and have dramatic reductions, the department manager will begin to think it was his or her idea and that's okay; you can glean your credit in other ways, primarily through your planning and budget with support documents and historical information. It can include a copy of your pilferage reduction plan, how you enabled it to be implemented, and the results you achieved.

What to Do About the Conversion Factor

Converting company property to temporary use involves another type of theft that is harder to prove than outright pilferage. It's difficult because there's little hard evidence sufficient even to fire an employee. The conversion happens when an employee uses company equipment for their personal gain. For example, suppose two employees decide to start a business of some kind that will operate out of their homes on a part-time basis. They can obtain all the administrative supplies from the company supply cabinets, but they need to send advertising and that's developed on the company computer. Once printed, they make 5,000 copies on the company copier, stuff the envelopes and run them through the company postage machine. This may not be feasible all in one day or week. The skilled converter integrates the personal needs into the work needs and no one notices. The two entrepreneurs can even use company computers to establish and maintain their bookkeeping, mailing lists, mailing labels, and other uses. Depending on what the company business includes, other equipment might fade away from the office scene, piece by piece, and company vehicles used to deliver goods from a home business. There's also a subtle conversion that cannot be traced to the person directly, although it involves personal gain. For example, a friend not associated with the company has the small business and "barters" with the company employee offering something for using the company copier, postage machine, or computers to supply the friend with benefit.

How Do You Prevent Conversion Pilferage?

The first step involves "educating" business management about the possibilities. Much of the security posture in a corporate or industrial environment involves tactfully informing the various department managers that problems like these do exist. You have to remember they have pressures to produce, to sell, to manufacture, or to engage in whatever business the company conducts. Security professionals often shake their heads about the business-oriented managers being so lax; however, we must keep in mind their job is business, ours is security. Just as they might explain the mechanics of doing business to us, we need to explain the mechanics of security to them, however tactfully. The human ego has much to do with the way we perceive a situation, and business-oriented managers often bristle when an "outsider" tells them how to run their department.

Reduction or elimination of company property conversion for temporary personal gain can be achieved when department managers and their subordinate managers establish subtle, but effective, control measures. Some companies use a key or insert block on copy machines to keep a record of which section makes copies and how many made in a period. However, few think about comparing copies with actual need. For example, the two employees operating their home-based business wanted to send out direct-mail advertising, and over the period of a month, they copied flyers along with their genuine company business. The section will report a figure representing the copies made and the bean counters pour over the figures that really have no meaning. However, if each section manager, normally the controller of the key, needs to also "justify" copies are necessary, an awareness grows. Some also use a log sheet that shows how many copies a person makes and the section absorbing the cost each month.

Ask the department or division managers to implement a program of using a copier key, plus making subordinate managers the keeper of the keys. Also, when an employee comes to a custodian to get the key to make copies, ensure they make an entry in the new log, in front of the manager, about how many copies they intend to make and reference the project or subject the document to be copied pertains to. They can still fudge, but it's far more difficult, since the custodian can always ask their supervisor why 21 copies of a letter is necessary. With this system, you now have an effective deterrent in place. Also, you can be certain a low-level manager who probably wants to climb the corporate ladder will be skeptical and aware of what's happening instead of just handing over a key and not paying any attention to its use. Copies sound trivial; however, like the pencils and paper noted earlier, when multiplied by hundreds or thousands of employees, they can add up to high amounts. Add copier conversion to the costs of taking supplies and we can easily move into millions in a large company. Illustration 5–7 is an example of an effective copier control log; however, it can be effective only when using a key and the custodian of the key shows an interest. Remember the earlier discussion about the benefit, value, and risk that employees consider when doing something they know to be wrong. That principle applies to conversion of company property to temporary personal gain.

Whether company computers, copiers, vehicles, or supplies, consider "prevention and controls" instead of trying to catch pilfering employees in the act. A good rule to guide business managers who often jump to conclusions and overreact is that employees are a company investment. The hiring and training process, benefits, salary, and workspace costs are considerable. Catching an employee in the act of stealing supplies or converting property and firing them might be the normal course of action but also can be very expensive. It's easier and more effective to nudge business managers to awareness that simple, but efficient, controls will solve the problem and protect the company's investments and assets.

Illustration 5–7

EXAMPLE OF A REPRODUCTION CONTROL LOG

Marketing Department Reproduction Control Log			
Time Period: _10/20-10/30_ Custodian: _R Johnson_			
Date/Time	Section/Person	Project	No. Copies
10/30/00 4 p.m.	Sales/Person	Smith Letter	5

Note: Similar logs serve to prevent and control various types of equipment and vehicles that might be otherwise converted to temporary personal gain.

PROTECTING COMPANY INFORMATION

One of the most challenging tasks confronting security managers and officers involves protecting company information. Although any information a company possesses is technically property, taking it, stealing it, or using it rarely arouses criminal justice interest and probably constitutes little chance of being grounds for firing an employee. An exception might be deliberate taking of research and development information and selling that information to another company. Unless a credible value is determined for it, and a variety of other procedures are fulfilled, the taking or stealing information by an employee stands little chance of any disciplinary action.

Why Is Company Information Important?

Often, information is the most valuable asset of a corporation or industry. Some business-oriented managers understand that some information has value and importance, but they often overlook the items that can be of great value to a competitor or some other entity needing it. Competitor intelligence has developed to a huge business in itself during the past few years. Japanese companies use it so extensively that they seek information about personal preferences of executives—such as what foods they like; what magazines they read; what sports, hobbies, and clubs they enjoy—and they pay well for that data.

Other information of value to competitors includes company personnel rosters, salaries, experience levels, and nearly anything that when collected and analyzed by a skilled person, can develop a profile of the company and its people. The value of going to all this trouble helps to determine what the company is doing and what it plans on doing. Information in computers is often tightly controlled, including budgets, research and development, and other aspects. The problem lies in the easy collection of other information that can be just as valuable. For example, a skilled analyst can look at company rosters from different time periods and determine shifts in personnel, subtle increases in the marketing department, and other aspects that tell him or her something will happen, such as a new product line, a new aggressive marketing blitz, or some other event. With that information, a study of the executives, their historical decisions, and their likes and dislikes might add another clue as to the direction the company is heading. For example, three new marketing people were hired over the past seven months—who are they? A background search reveals that each has a solid track record in marketing certain kinds of items, and more research establishes a pattern of how they go about conducting the marketing. Added information from a mundane company roster can show an analyst who the research and development people are, their areas of expertise, what they've done formerly, and their pet projects or aspirations.

This is a brief look at only a few possibilities easily collected from a company because that information is considered "secret" by the business-oriented managers. A competitor can develop the data and create ways to diminish the value of a plan to introduce a new product or develop new clients and other aspects that may severely damage their competition in the marketplace.

How to Protect Your Company's Information

Your first step includes looking around the company at the information readily available, whether it is thrown in wastebaskets or is often publicized. Each observation has value if you think about how a competitor could use the information. It could be as simple as lists of clients, mailing lists, company rosters, and other mundane documents. Note how they are secured at the close of business. Consider yourself as a member of a cleaning team coming in after the close of business and being able to take items of information from the trash, copy documents from the files, or take photographs of items lying on desks and in unlocked desks and file cabinets, maybe even terminal instructional booklets that supply mainframe entry codes. When you've studied the problem in that manner, develop a plan to convince business-oriented managers and executives of the importance in controlling information.

Establish a series of education and awareness talks that you present to employees. It doesn't need to be hours of instruction, just a few brief minutes. That effort, coupled with increased awareness of department and subordinate managers, will cause the collection effort by a competitor to become difficult or maybe impossible. When talking to employees, do plant a seed by making collecting information seem lucrative. Explain that the collection process is systematic and is done by experts who feed on the employees' carelessness. Continue to tell them that what affects the bottom line of the company also affects their employment, salaries, benefits, and expense accounts. It affects the facilities and equipment the company provides them and more. Show them how each employee has a stake in the employer making larger profits and maintaining strong growth. When you can convince them of the importance, coupled with management support and controls, protecting the assets of the company takes another step toward effectiveness.

QUICK REFERENCE REVIEW AND GUIDE FOR CHAPTER FIVE

- Identify and Observe with Effective ID cards and Security Badges

- Control and Prevent Theft of Expendable Supplies

- Control and Prevent Conversion of Company Property to Temporary Personal Gain

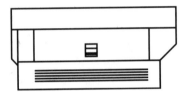

- Protect Company Information and Educate Employees and Company Management

- Important! Effective Internal Security Begins with the Cooperation of Corporation Managers

6 Managing Protective Barriers

Creating protective barriers incorporates three concepts of prevention. First, you want to prevent people from entering company property except in those places managed and controlled by security officers. Second, you want to prevent people from leaving the company property except through the same control points. Third, you need to prevent people from having access to certain buildings, places, and areas within the company property. You can achieve that goal with a system of barriers, in layers, some obvious and others not readily noticed.

Protective barriers do not always mean installing fences and other obstacles, since nature often provides us with better barriers than we can devise. For example, a natural protective barrier might include fields, rivers, mountains, deserts, and other terrain difficult for people and vehicles to cross. Structural barriers also come into consideration, such as a building joined by a fence.

CREATING YOUR FIRST PROTECTIVE BARRIER

The first type of barrier you need in your line of prevention and defense depends on what you need to protect. For example, a building in an urban environment differs significantly from a factory in the country. With that thought, next you'll need to determine the threat you're confronting. When your company has facilities in a high-crime area and has lucrative items to steal, you'll need more security than for a firm in a country setting with a low crime rate that produces massive steel structure beams. The following suggestions cover the normal minimum first barrier in suburban or rural areas, although elements can apply in an urban setting, depending on the area and geographical location of the city, the Southwest, East Coast, Midwest, and so forth. Also, even within a geographical area the needs differ such as security barriers applicable in Manhattan compared to those used in Queens or Long Island using New York as an example. You also need to think about the benefit you want from the barriers used or installed besides the three preventive concepts noted earlier.

FOUR KEY BENEFITS OF PROTECTIVE BARRIERS

1. Serve as *psychological deterrents* preventing entry through creation of an obstacle not easily breached. Only determined people climb over high fences topped with barbed wire knowing that security officers have the area under surveillance. The average person with theft or mischief in mind also stops at the protective barrier recognizing once inside, escape might not be feasible.

2. *Decrease need of security personnel* and enable their use in more important areas. A smaller security force also means a considerable saving to your company, not only from salaries and benefits, but also the costs of recruiting, hiring, training needed for each person to be effective.

3. *Channel people in and out of the company area*, causing people and vehicles to pass through security controlled and managed points of entry and departure.

4. *Confuse the intruder*; once inside the company area they become trapped when your protective barriers meet the confusion test. The chance of an intruder leaving the area without detection is low and especially when your barriers have enough complexity to confuse.

TWO IMPORTANT BARRIER DESIGNS

Size of the Area You Need to Protect

Your company or its facility might cover large amounts of land. The ideal barrier system might not be feasible depending on your budget restrictions. For example, the best fence barrier is always double fences set a few feet apart so an intruder must get through both to gain entry and risks observation in the open area between. That type barrier comes with a high price tag, and unless your company has extremely lucrative items to steal, the cost might not compare with the benefit.

The Vulnerability of Internal Areas

Often, you may avoid a costly perimeter barrier when interior buildings or areas have adequate protection. For example, instead of fencing the entire company perimeter, fence in vulnerable and smaller areas. This security technique, often called "compartmentalizing," develops by protecting several small areas within a large land area. A company might manufacture something made from ore mined near the plant facilities. Although the company property includes the mining area, and heavy equipment stays unattended overnight and on weekends, the vulnerability factor is low. Normally, the probability of theft or loss will not be enough, considering the items and terrain, to fence the entire company property. However, the plant, offices, warehouses, and manufactured items might be a lucrative target for thieves. Still your area might be too large, so you can economize and still protect the vulnerable areas by developing secured compartments or sections within it, leaving the other space open. Illustration 6–1 shows the concept of "compartmentalizing" a complex as opposed to enclosing the entire complex with a fence.

Illustration 6–1

AREAS REPRESENTING COMPARTMENTALIZED AND ENTIRE COMPLEX FENCES

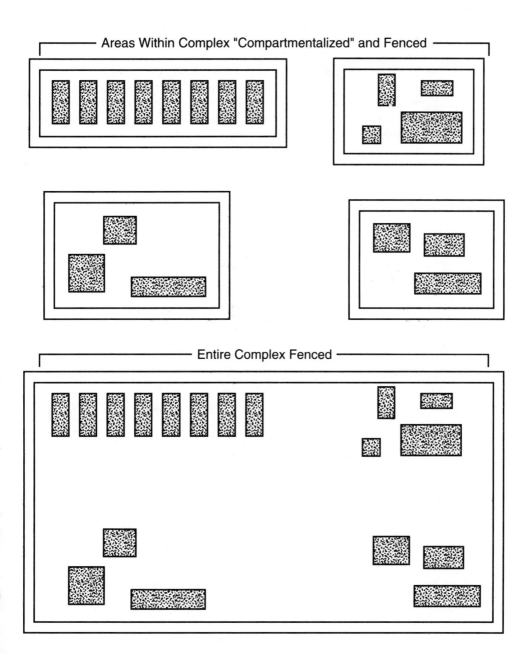

CHOOSING THE BEST FENCE BARRIER

Four types of fences proven effective over past years in suburban or rural areas or in high-crime urban environments are chain link, barbed wire, concertina, and barbed tape. Your choices depend primarily upon (1) permanence needed, (2) availability of materials, (3) location used, (4) time available for building the barrier fence, and (5) the type of threat confronting your security systems, for example, animals, people, vehicles, or a mix of each.

Generally, a cost-effective system chain-link fence is best for most applications. However, you need to think about all four types of fencing to strengthen, increase, or layer your security. For example, you might have a primary perimeter fence or double fences using chain-link; however, in key or vulnerable areas, you will harden the security with an added barrier line using barbed wire in various configurations. You might also use any of the types to heighten or harden the primary fence.

The Chain-Link Fence

Normally, chain-link fences, including applications at gates, provide the most cost-effective long-term systems. You need to build them about 7-feet in height for first-line perimeter fences. Second fences (in a double fence system) need a minimum height of about 6 feet. For long-term and cost-effective installation of chain-link fences, you should use 9–gauge or heavier wire, galvanized with mesh openings not larger than 2 inches. Your best choice will include a twisted and barbed selvage at top and bottom. (The selvage is the point where the woven part of the wire ends and can "unravel" a chain-link fence when cut unless protected.) Illustration 6–2 shows the selvage and how to protect it from intruders. When installing the fence, be sure that the wire is taut and securely fastened to rigid metal or reinforced concrete posts set in concrete. The bottom of your fence needs to reach within 2 inches of hard ground or paving to prevent lifting and keep small animals and people from digging under the fence. On soft ground, set the bottom of the fence below the surface of the ground, deeply enough to compensate for shifting soil or sand. For added resistance to people climbing the fence, and when you are not using barbed wire on top-supporting arms, omit the optional top rail or taut wire, leaving a jagged edge. The risk of someone cutting and unraveling the fence is less than enabling them to climb over easily. You need to consider painting the chain-link fencing with a non-reflective substance to reduce the glare of natural or artificial light. Reflection from shiny (especially new) fencing can create an effective hiding place for intruders who would otherwise be in plain sight. Weaknesses in the chain-link fence happen because of weather (oxidizing and rusting) and failure to keep fencing fastened to supporting posts and allowing the desired tightness to sag. Illustration 6–2 shows the application processes just discussed.

Illustration 6–2

EXAMPLES OF CHAIN-LINK FENCE INSTALLATION AND PROTECTION

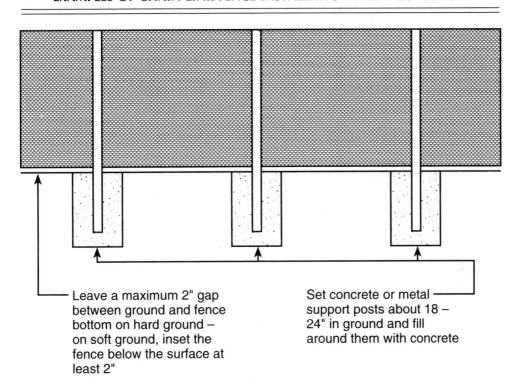

Leave a maximum 2" gap between ground and fence bottom on hard ground – on soft ground, inset the fence below the surface at least 2"

Set concrete or metal support posts about 18 – 24" in ground and fill around them with concrete

Unprotected Selvage

Protected Selvage with Brace Rail along top of fence

Protected Selvage with Barbed Wire Strands

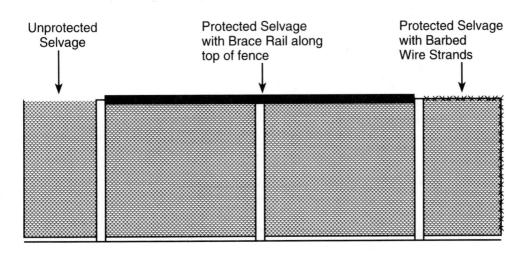

Barbed Wire Fences

You will receive the best service from this type fence choosing standard twisted barbed wire, double-strand, 12–gauge wire, with four-point barbs spaced an equal distance apart. Barbed-wire fencing, including gates, proves effective to prevent human or animal trespassing. Your barbed-wire fence needs a height of about 7 to 8 feet, excluding the top guard, and firmly affixed to wooden or metal posts not more than 6 feet apart. The distance between strands cannot exceed 6 inches and when practicable at least one wire interlaced vertically and midway between posts to add stability. The key to effective barbed-wire fences includes preventing people (or animals) from crawling under or through the fence line and forcing intruders to climb it. Most people understand the severe injuries possible from climbing a barbed wire fence and go elsewhere. Illustration 6–3 shows the correct installation of a barbed wire fence in a general application.

Tanglefoot and Concertina Barrier and Fence

Standard tanglefoot wire, barbed tape, or concertina wire is an excellent temporary or supplemental security technique. Some of the possibilities and explanations follow:

- Concertina wire is a coil of high-strength steel barbed wire, clipped together at intervals to form a cylinder. When opened, it is about 50–feet long and 3–feet in diameter. When you use concertina wire, as a temporary or supplemental perimeter barrier, it must be positioned between poles, one roll of wire placed on top of another with a minimum height of three rolls. Stagger the ends of the coils and fasten them with wire, making certain you picket the base wires to the ground. The reason for this process is to form a barrier as opposed to a mass of wire scattered over the ground. Although in a military setting, concertina wire is used that way, in time as weeds grow, rust sets in, the effectiveness decreases, and cleanup poses new problems. Keeping the concertina wire connected to form a high barrier serves your security problem effectively and it's easier to manage. Illustration 6–3 shows this application.

- Another effective technique, especially in high security environments, places barbed-wire fencing in a tanglefoot configuration. The concept of tanglefoot makes it impossible to walk through it quickly and the risk of tripping is great. Falling on barbed wire creates serious injuries. This technique serves you by an obvious psychological deterrent against intruders. A determined intruder must move through the maze of barbed wire very slowly, permitting security officers to observe the entry or departure. You might place the obstruction inside a single-perimeter fence or in the area between double fences to provide an added deterrent to intruders or unauthorized persons trying to leave the company area. When you use the tanglefoot technique, configure the system by crisscrossing barbed-wire fencing or barbed tape at irregular intervals on stakes about ankle level. Support the wire or tape on short metal or wooden stakes spaced at irregular intervals of about 3 to 5 feet and at heights about 4 to 8 inches. Extent of depth for your tanglefoot field involves the space available and specific security needs.

An added benefit of the tanglefoot systems is that you can build portable versions in small sections. When you need to counter a threat or protect an area involving a downed perimeter fence from an equipment mishap or a storm, you can load the prefabricated tanglefoot sections on a truck and place them (staked in place) in the areas needed. This technique allows their application in small to large areas and makes the system cost effective.

- Barbed tape is a system composed of two items: barbed tape and barbed-tape dispenser. Concertina tape is a variation of barbed tape that coils when dispensed. You may use this instead of conventional barbed wire; however, it is not as strong or lasting. Fabrication of barbed tape includes a steel strip with a minimum pressure breaking strength of 500 pounds. The width is $\frac{3}{4}$ of an inch, with $\frac{7}{16}$-inch barbs spaced at $\frac{1}{2}$-inch intervals along each side. There are 50 meters of tape on a plastic reel $8\frac{3}{4}$ inches in diameter and 1 inch wide. Illustration 6–4 show applications of barbed wire or tape.

Illustration 6–3

EXAMPLE OF A BARBED-WIRE FENCE AND TANGLEFOOT CONSTRUCTION

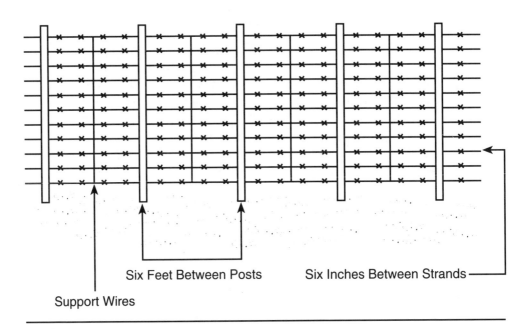

Six Feet Between Posts   Six Inches Between Strands

Support Wires

Tanglefoot Example

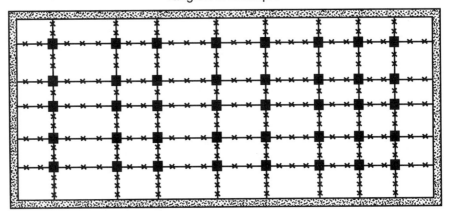

Barbed wire tacked on stacks ankle high and uneven spaced

Illustration 6–4

CONCERTINA WIRE USED AS PERIMETER BARRIER
OR
SUPPORTING BARRIER FOR PERIMETER FENCING

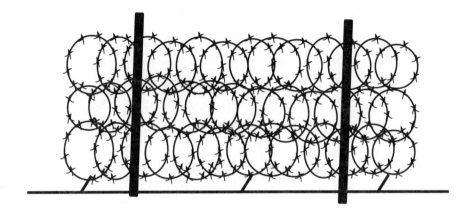

Top Guard Fencing

Increased security emerges from using top guard fencing supplements on your perimeter and interior fences or buildings. Top guard fencing provides an active deterrent to prevent or discourage people from trying to enter or leave the company property or internal areas by climbing over a fence or building. A "top guard" is an overhang of barbed wire or barbed tape along the top of a fence or building, facing outward and upward at a 45–degree angle. Top guard supporting arms need permanent attachment to the top of the fence posts or the outside edges of buildings. This application increases the height of your fence at least 1 foot. You should use a minimum of three strands of barbed wire or tape on the supporting arms; however, added strands supply better security. The top guard of fencing adjoining gates needs a minimum vertical height of 18-inches without the normal 45-degree outward slant. Slanting the top guard outward on a sliding gate prevents adequate gate operation while keeping it vertical in those areas along the fence enables opening the gates adequately. Do not install top and bottom fence rails where protection is of utmost importance. Top rails (those covering the selvage) will aid a person climbing. Bottom rails supporting the fence supply intruders with a foot step for climbing up or down. The purpose of the rails can be compensated for by setting the fence posts, (heavy metal or reinforced concrete) in concrete-filled holes. The top section of your fence needs to remain selvage, and better still weave barbed wire through the selvage. Illustration 6–5 shows this application. When top guard fencing is not practical, you can use fragments of broken glass set in an anchored masonry top coating. Illustration 6–6 shows masonry wall top guard applications.

Illustration 6–5

EXAMPLE OF FENCE AND BUILDING TOP GUARD PROTECTION

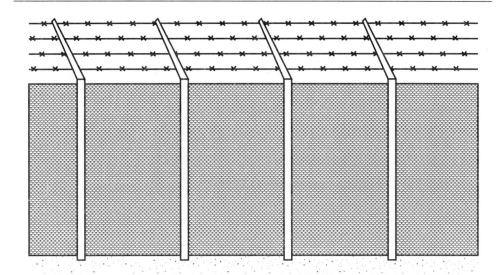

Example of a Fence Top Guard on a Chain-Link Perimeter Fence

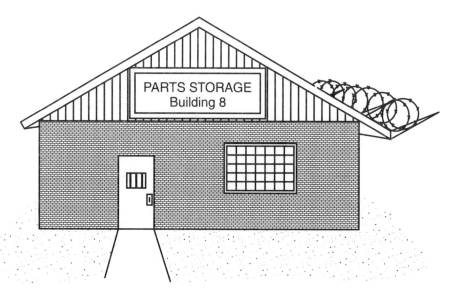

PARTS STORAGE
Building 8

Example of a Top Guard on Fence-Line Side of a Perimeter Building

Illustrtion 6−6

EXAMPLE OF BRICK AND MASONRY TOP GUARD PROTECTION

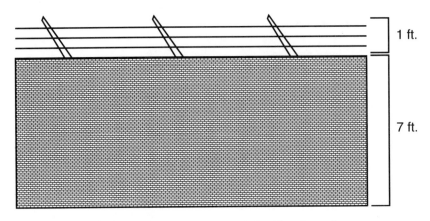

Brick or Masonry Wall with Barbed Wire Top Guard

Brick or Masonry Wall with Broken Glass Set in Masonry Top

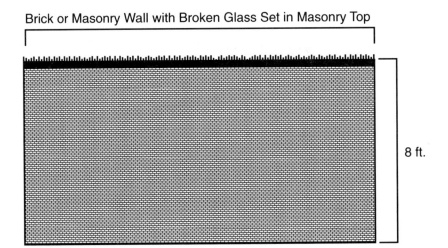

TECHNIQUES FOR ENTRANCE-EXIT BARRIERS

With a strong perimeter in place, your attention must turn to the your weakest perimeter points, entrances and exits. You need to provide easy access and departure routes for employees, visitors, and vendors yet maintain control to prevent intruders from entering or leaving unchallenged. You also need to supply a sound deterrent against employee, visitor, and vendor pilferage by making the apparent risk significant. Your entrances and exit problems increase beyond the normal perimeter safeguards because vehicles become an important consideration. Stopping an unauthorized person at an entrance or exit doesn't pose a great problem; however, stopping a vehicle becomes another matter.

Much of your security intensity depends on the company's need for security and how you manage the entrances and exits remains within that thinking. The suggested techniques here supply an average or minimum concept, and increasing or decreasing the security level involves adding or subtracting layers.

Active Perimeter Entrances and Exits

Your key elements of an active entrance or exit normally hinge on the presence of security officers and a gate operations center often perceived as a gatehouse. It can serve a variety of security functions, including issuing passes, verifying identification, and performing other tasks. During the heaviest traffic, both vehicle and pedestrian, be sure to post enough officers to keep control without hindering the flow of people and vehicles in and out of the company area. The best technique for controlling active gates includes "channeling" the people and vehicles through separate control points. Pedestrians, for example, may enter and exit passing through a turnstile with a security officer present to verify identification and authorization to enter or depart. That presence also supplies the added benefit of a deterrence against pilferage of company property. When your company doesn't have high security items and special policies, your security officers will not likely perform searches of employees or others as they leave. With that in mind, ensure the presence of an attentive security officer. That action serves primarily as a psychological deterrent, but normally proves effective to reduce theft by those tempted to but not intent on stealing. However, when pilferage or theft is apparent, the officer can take the proper action according to your policies and procedures dealing with that problem. When your company authorizes such action, it may include checking handbags and briefcases, packages, and other carried items. Although rarely will that action reveal thefts by determined pilferers, it often keeps employees and others honest.

Vehicle control poses the largest problem at gates. One technique for managing vehicles is equipping the entrance or exit with a crash beam that security officers control, allowing vehicles to pass or causing them to stop. Added to the control of vehicles, the crash beam and presence of security officers also create a deterrent against pilferage and theft if only from the psychological perception that maybe the officer will notice something or search the vehicle. Other measures include sliding gates added to crash bars, or in pairs so a vehicle must enter one gate and stop until it closes behind them. The second gate prevents entrance or exit until the security officer ensures the vehicle and occupants have authorization to do so. However, in most of your security applications that type of security takes too long to clear each vehicle. For example, the process would be too slow for a factory or other company operations where hundreds of vehicles enter or depart at the beginning and ending of a shift. When that includes your situation, you need to have other internal controls that help to create layered security before and after the onslaught of traffic at the gates, for example, security officers at entrances and exits of buildings, other pedestrian gates leading to parking lots, detached parking areas some distance from the workplace, and other techniques discussed in this book in other chapters. Illustrations 6–7 and 6–8 show gate control examples and the general type of crash beam that serves well under most applications.

Illustration 6-7

PRIMARY AND ALTERNATE ENTRANCE PLANS WITH CRASH BEAM

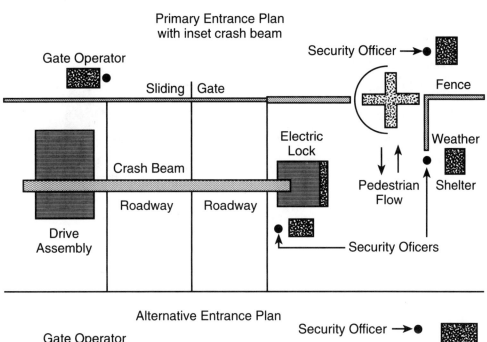

Primary Entrance Plan
with inset crash beam

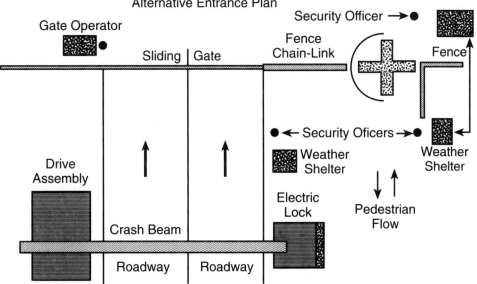

Alternative Entrance Plan

Illustration 6–8

EXAMPLE OF A GATE CRASH BEAM SYSTEM

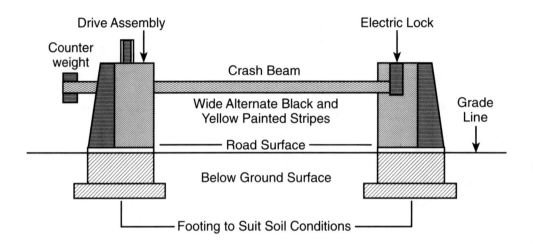

Inactive or Limited Active Gates

This category of entrance and exit points might include those opened only to allow a large volume of employees and vehicles entering or departing at the beginning and end of shifts, a railroad entrance-exit point, or special truck entrance-exit during limited hours. Having the constant presence of a security officer at these points is not cost effective so you need to have added barriers for times when the gate is closed. Vehicles pose the greatest problem with this type entrance and exit primarily because a road or street leads to and through the gate. A heavy truck, for example, can easily crash through most fence gates and crash bars. Often, the location of these gates will be in companies that have large land areas, and the gate can be remote from active security forces, especially after an area or facility closes for the day, such as noted in an earlier example about a plant having an adjacent mining operation. However, you can install effective vehicle blocking devices either permanently or used for portable applications as needed. When collapsed, or moved aside, traffic can pass over or past them with no restrictions. However, when raised, they have a capability of stopping most trucks and inflicting considerable damage to a vehicle trying to force entry with the device in place. Illustration 6–9 shows an example of this device produced by several different manufacturers in various sizes and capabilities.

Illustration 6−9

VEHICLE BLOCKING SYSTEM

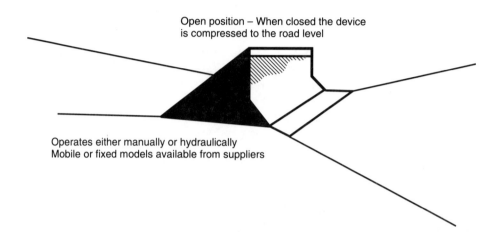

Open position – When closed the device
is compressed to the road level

Operates either manually or hydraulically
Mobile or fixed models available from suppliers

DON'T FORGET THE UTILITY OPENINGS

Depending on your specific location and company's operations, you might have an abundance of sewers, air and water intakes, storm drains, exhausts, and other utility openings that enter or exit the perimeter of company property. These types of openings also need your attention since they can, when large enough, enable a person of small stature to gain access to the interior parts of your company areas. In suburban and rural areas, and some urban environments, a variety of "critters" might decide to visit and create more problems, especially in some factory or plant situations. A good rule of thumb for screening or barring these openings is anything 10 inches or larger needs protection. If you have small-animal problems, screen all openings.

For openings that a small person can enter or exit through, you need welded bars, and for animal protection, a heavy screening or piece of chain-link fence welded or bolted in place. Drain intakes (storm sewers) might also be a problem, especially those outside a perimeter fence but connected by huge underground ducts to your company's drainage system. In some areas, drainage systems are massive and create an underground system of tunnels that lead throughout an area. Except for periods of rainy weather, they remain clear, and people can access the drain system walking or crawling through them to points under a building or area and exit through other drain intakes or sewer hole covers.

You can easily secure sewer hole covers inside your protected area with flat steel straps secured through slotted fixtures fastened to the roadway or ground. Illustration 6–10 shows that application. Large intake drains inside your company area can be secured by welding small pipes inside the intake area small enough to prevent a person or animal from crawling out or into the pipe. An example of how to do that appears in Illustration 6–10 also.

Illustration 6–10

EXAMPLES OF INLET AND OUTLET CONDUIT PROTECTION

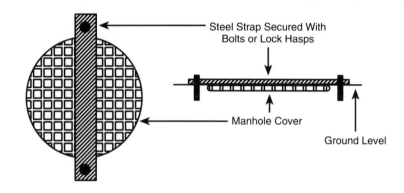

Steel Strap Secured With Bolts or Lock Hasps

Manhole Cover

Ground Level

Example of Drain Intake Security

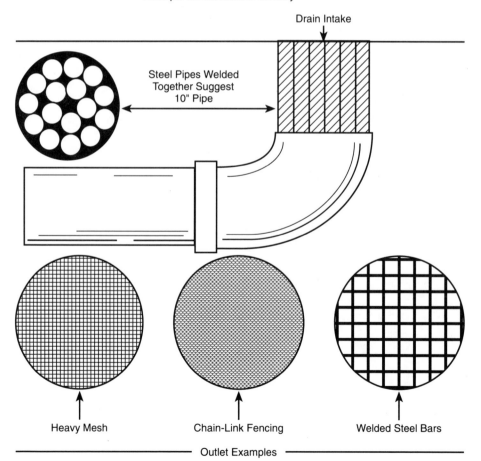

Drain Intake

Steel Pipes Welded Together Suggest 10" Pipe

Heavy Mesh

Chain-Link Fencing

Welded Steel Bars

Outlet Examples

IMPROVE PERIMETER SECURITY WITH CLEAR ZONES

Clear zones around perimeter fences and buildings must receive priority maintenance. They are important prevention factors. Often, perimeter fences, once in place, receive little attention and become overgrown with vegetation or serve as receptacles for trash, either thrown there or blown in by wind. Whatever the reason for their derelict condition, the deterrence of fences diminishes because determined intruders can benefit by having a place to hide until believed safe to climb over into the protected area. Patroling security officers will pass by the intruder hidden in the weeds or clutter without noticing his or her presence. Cluttered fence lines also supply pilferers an excellent place to toss over stolen items for retrieval later.

Your clear zone around fences should be about 20 feet on each side of the fence. When you have a double fence line, ensure the space between the fences also remains clear. When building double fences, you should ensure leaving enough space to drive a vehicle through and it needs to be graveled or paved when possible. Illustration 6–11 shows clear zones examples.

Illustration 6–11

EXAMPLES OF CLEAR ZONES FOR FENCES AND BUILDINGS

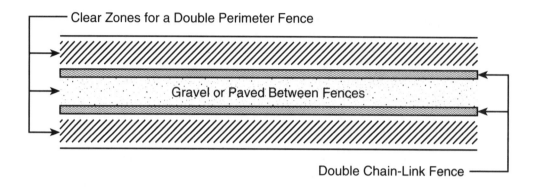

Clear Zones for a Double Perimeter Fence

Gravel or Paved Between Fences

Double Chain-Link Fence

Example of Clear Zone Around Buildings

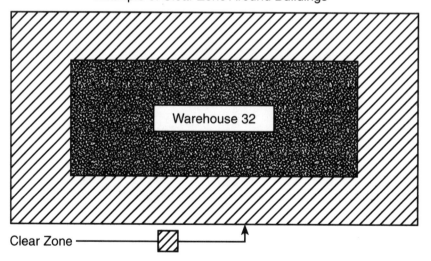

Warehouse 32

Clear Zone

THE SENTRY DOG CHOICES

One of the most economical security techniques of protection uses sentry dog teams. One security officer and one well-trained sentry dog can replace five to ten security officer positions, especially in large open areas. An added cost-effective benefit includes eliminating the need for extensive fences and lighting. Sentry dogs work best in near darkness, using only the natural light from the moon or light reflected from a distance. Instead of having a costly perimeter fence containing the entire company property, the sentry dog alternative enables you to fence only important buildings and areas as in the examples discussed and shown earlier in the chapter regarding "compartmentalizing" techniques.

Another economy realized from use of sentry dogs for primary security involves the lack of salary and benefits and other costs that affect only half the sentry dog team. The cost, including training, subsequent care, feeding, housing, and continued training, has little effect on your security budget, providing you design your uses to save money in other areas, such as fences, lighting, and conventional security officers. The first rule of effective sentry dog use includes assigning and working with only one handler. Any properly trained, effective sentry dog will not accept multiple masters, only one. Those who use multiple handlers for one dog should save their money and build fences because the dog teams cannot be effective. Having several masters for a dog creates confusion, just as human beings who try to please several bosses don't contribute to productivity, but rather to frustration. Those who claim effectiveness from one dog and several handlers don't know sentry dogs or have only an economic motive in mind.

Beyond the economical benefits of using sentry dog teams another important security advantage includes areas where fog and inclement weather restrict the vision of conventional security officers but do not escape the dog's attention. A well-trained sentry dog team can detect an intruder long before he or she reaches the company property because of the dog's ability to detect the slightest amount of scent. The dog can also distinguish differences in scent, for example, animal or human, and between multiple humans and animals approaching through the darkness. A skilled handler can learn to discern the dog's response (alert) and what the actions mean. A dog's hearing is also about 20 times as acute as that of humans, and dogs can detect movement 10 times better although they see no color and have no ability to focus on one specific object. For the intruder, knowing that out there in the dark lurks a 110-pound German shepherd and security officer creates a considerable psychological effect and deterrent. Few people try to outwit or tackle a large dog backed by a security officer, even when there might be multiple intruders.

HOW TO USE AND BENEFIT FROM SENTRY DOGS

Before making a decision to convert your security forces to sentry dog teams, you need to consider the pros and cons, plus the suitability of protected areas within your company, and the following rule of effective sentry dog use. *The effectiveness of sentry dog teams depends almost entirely on the degree to which their area of operations is free from external distractions.*

Strangeness is The Key

Sentry dogs rely on strange sights, sounds, and odors to detect the presence of intruders. Unfortunately, they are incapable of rational thought. Instead, they use their aggressive nature and well-developed senses of hearing and smell to augment the decision-making capability of their human counterpart, the security officer. You must ensure their use in a controlled environment. This means enough isolation so any strange sight, sound, or scents the animal perceives will come from an actual potential intruder. One danger of working dogs in busy areas or having regular distractions stems from the dog becoming so used to them he cannot distinguish the intruder from the authorized person. When that happen, the dog's value decreases only to a psychological deterrent.

Site Selection

Rarely will any sentry dog post be ideal in every respect. Your best applications of sentry dog teams include protection of the following sites:

- Supply centers and depots
- Open storage yards
- Perimeters when there are no adjacent distractions
- Docks and terminal facilities
- Railroad yards
- Warehouses
- Interior passages
- Entry ways to sensitive areas
- Areas like to those environments listed

Darkness and Reduced Visibility

Sentry dog teams are most effective when used at night (in darkness, not in lighted areas) or during periods of reduced visibility. Dogs are especially alert in darkness and rely heavily on their senses of hearing and smell to detect intruders. Security officers, too, are more watchful and tend to be attentive to their dog's actions.

Despite the advantages inherent to night operations, daylight-hour application of sentry dog teams might be feasible in certain circumstances. Although they are less effective from a technical standpoint, their psychological deterrent value is still substantial. When there is unavoidable need for dog teams working during daylight hours, or at night in a lighted area, they should patrol on a varied route, remain in the shadows, or stand in an obscure stationary position downwind of the areas protected.

Wind, Weather, and Terrain

Of all the natural elements you need to consider, wind is essential. The direction, speed, and consistency of prevailing wind conditions affect the manner in which a sentry dog team works. *A basic guideline includes using the sentry dog where he can use the wind to the best advantage.* Wind is critical because it affects optimum use of the dog's two more important senses: smell and hearing. A dog can detect an intruder and alert reliably at a distance of 250 yards downwind of the intruder if other conditions are suitable.

The terrain surrounding the protected area is important primarily because of how it affects the prevailing wind. Hills, valleys, trees, dense ground cover, and man-made objects affect the direction and speed of the wind. Terrain can also distort sound and diffuse scent so that pinpointing an intruder's location is extremely difficult, if not impossible.

Inclement weather, such as snow, rain, or high winds, tends to reduce the alerting range of a sentry dog. Despite this, the dog's ability to detect an intruder is still superior to that of a human security officer. During bad weather the use of alternate patrol routes is often prudent and length of duty time may need to be lessened. (Under good conditions, a sentry dog tires and loses interest within 6 hours. Four-hour shifts prove most effective.) It is reasonable, as a guideline, to assume that dogs can endure exposure to foul weather equal with their handler. In cold climates, there should be little difficulty in using sentry dog teams where temperatures fall as low as 40 degrees Fahrenheit below zero. However, the dog in these extreme conditions needs boots to prevent cutting their paws on frozen ground and ice and dog blankets to retain body heat.

A Search Bonus

One of the most difficult situations a security force confronts involves finding an intruder within a large protected area once observed or their presence known or suspected. Those problems are compounded at night and other times when no employees are working. However, a sentry dog can find any person in a warehouse, other buildings, or in an open area.

Illustration 6–12

EXAMPLE OF A SENTRY DOG TEAM WORKING OUTSIDE PERIMETER FENCE—WORKING WITHOUT A FENCE USES THE SAME TECHNIQUES

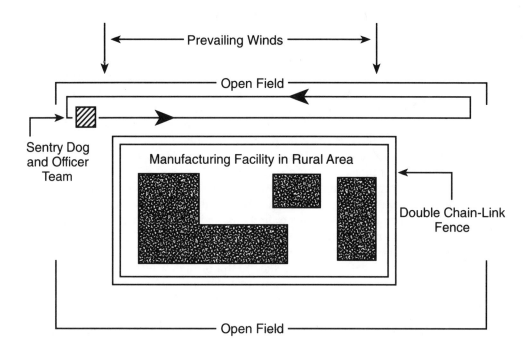

Illustration 6–13

EXAMPLE OF A SECURITY DOG AND OFFICER TEAM
WORKING AN OPEN AREA

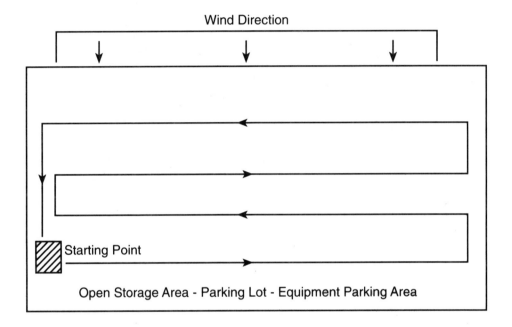

CREATING AN OVERVIEW CAPABILITY WITH TOWERS

The use of towers has long prevailed, especially for protection of industrial areas. The tower provides excellent visibility day or night; however visibility can be limited during inclement weather. At night, the tower, even in near darkness (without lights), provides a strong advantage for viewing the ground. That capability is greatly enhanced now with the improved night vision equipment. But as with everything, there are advantages and disadvantages. Cost creates the major problem with adding towers to your security system, including mobile tower systems. Although increasing security capability, the expense of construction and maintenance is often prohibitive, except for the largest companies. They are, however, worthy of your consideration in your security planning, especially the idea of mobile tower systems when you may need to move them from site to site periodically. Illustration 6–14 shows the ideal security tower, hardened and large enough to be a strong psychological deterrent for intruders and a key spotting element for security forces on the ground. However, the type tower you need or decide against depends on your situation—and your budget.

Illustration 6-14

BASIC SECURITY TOWER DESIGN

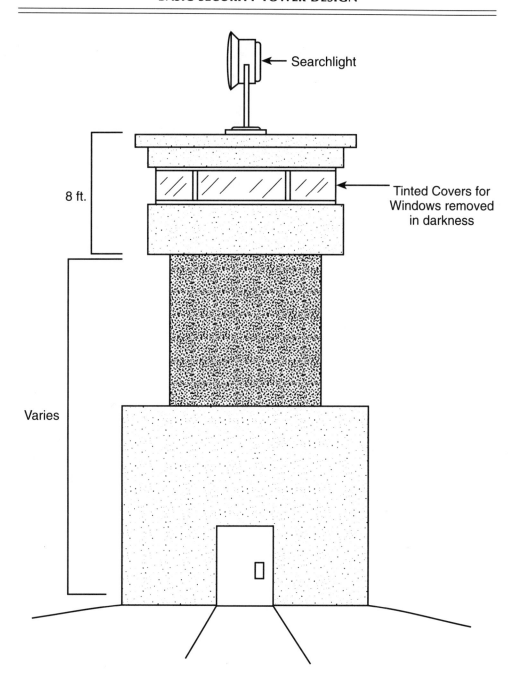

QUICK REFERENCE REVIEW AND GUIDE FOR CHAPTER SIX

- Protective Barriers Have Four Key Prevention Benefits

- Choose Cost-effective Designs That Serve Your Needs

- Choose the Best Fence Designs

- Use Top Guards to Increase Your Security Advantage

- Plan and Develop Efficient, Effective Entrance-Exit Control

- Don't Forget to Secure Utility Openings

- Make Clear Zones a Priority

- Consider Advantages of Sentry Dog Teams

- Think About Using Towers for Better Security

7 Protective Lighting Management

Much of the intrusion and pilferage problem corporations and industry experience traces directly to a lack of properly managed light. The lack of light is the best friend of a criminal enterprise. It's your security management responsibility to ensure adequate protective lighting during the hours of darkness and supply your security force with advantage. In this chapter, you will learn how protective lighting works, including its strengths and weaknesses.

Protective lighting enables your security systems to continue during hours of darkness and provides a level of protection for your company approaching that maintained during daylight hours. That capability also delivers an important deterrent value to discourage a criminal enterprise. Managed properly, effective protective lighting makes the task of an intruder difficult. Protective lighting is an essential element of your integrated physical security systems.

The management style of protective lighting at a corporate or industrial complex relies on your specific situation, combined with the type of environs you're responsible to protect. Each situation calls for attentive effort to provide the best visibility practicable. Corporate and industrial security management faces diverse responsibilities that increase during hours of darkness. For example, security officers need to verify security ID and badges, control people at gates, and inspect incoming and outgoing vehicles. Also, security officer responsibilities during hours of darkness include prevention of illegal entry and internal pilferage, detection of intruders, and a timely response to unusual or suspicious circumstances.

The absence of planned, effective protective lighting and its consequences are costly. Compensating for effective protective lighting deficiency calls for expensive added numbers of security officer posts, mobile patrols, sentry dog patrols, and a variety of other security techniques. Often, the deficiency of inadequate protective lighting results from flawed perceptions of benefit and advantage gained from effectively lighting corporate and industrial complexes during the hours of darkness. It is unusual for corporate executives to recognize that protective lighting serves any purpose beyond a psychological deterrent. It is your responsibility and obligation first to understand the mechanics and benefits of effective protective lighting. Then you must educate your company executives, convincing them that the cost of effective, efficient protective lighting converts to savings through prevention of possible staggering losses.

Protective lighting priorities begin with your company perimeters and sensitive areas or structures within the perimeter, for example, pier and dock areas, important buildings, storage areas, and vulnerable control points in communications, power, and water distribution systems. Interior areas also include those involving night production operations and others. Developing your skill to light priority areas adequately enables security officers to easily detect and prevent unauthorized persons (criminal enterprise) approaching or others attempting malicious acts within the area. Protective lighting is important to your security systems, and understanding the techniques begins through developing a clear understanding that effective lighting of an area is more than just throwing up floodlights.

IMPORTANT CHARACTERISTICS OF PROTECTIVE LIGHTING

Protective lighting is inexpensive comparable to the security advantage and it's cost effective to maintain. When properly planned, installed, and managed, lighting reduces the need for costly extensive security forces during hours of darkness. It also provides an important level of personal protection for security officers on duty by reducing advantages of criminal enterprise secrecy and surprise by a determined intruder. The conservation of security forces and equipment enabled through effective protective lighting adds another benefit, enabling you to assign officers to areas of better advantage.

Protective outside lighting usually calls for less intensity than interior working light, except for security tasks such as identification and inspection at authorized gateways and in emergency situations. Each area of your company or facility presents its particular problem based on its purpose, physical layout, terrain, atmospheric and climatic conditions, and the protective requirements. Other factors involve your company's operational commitments, for example, a 24-hour factory, presence of aircraft, explosives, and other elements that create unique problems.

YOUR KEY RESPONSIBILITIES OF PROTECTIVE LIGHTING MANAGEMENT

Your responsibility begins with assessing the protective lighting needs of your specific corporation or industrial complex. It's dependent upon the specific threats, perimeter extremities, surveillance capabilities, available security forces, and budget allotted to security operations.

The Three Key Elements

You must ensure that your design of protective lighting and its application serves to

1. Discourage unauthorized entry into the company areas

2. Simplify and ensure accurate detection of intruders approaching or trying to gain entry into protected areas

3. Prevent and detect internal pilferage or other like problems

Your protective lighting system must ensure continuous, effective, and efficient security operations during periods of reduced visibility. Your planning also needs integration techniques for standby lighting, maintenance, and periodic testing of all systems ensuring immediate options for emergencies.

CHARACTERISTICS OF LIGHTING—GUIDELINES IMPORTANT TO YOUR PLANNING AND APPLICATIONS

When you begin the task of planning for new protective lighting or evaluating systems already in place, the following key points supply immediate guidelines.

- Develop lists of descriptions, characteristics, and specifications of various incandescent, arc, and gaseous discharge lamps.

- Develop an understanding of lighting patterns supplied by the various luminaries.

- Develop layouts showing the most efficient height and spacing of lighting equipment needed to provide effective protective lighting.

- Define minimum protective lighting intensities needed for various applications within your areas of responsibility.

EIGHT ESSENTIAL PLANNING STEPS FOR PROTECTIVE LIGHTING

When you are designing or revising your protective lighting system, give specific consideration to the following important areas:

1. *Maintenance requirements*, including cleaning and replacement of lamps and luminaries. Determine the cost of maintenance including essential equipment, such as ladders, mechanical buckets, and others you'll need and those now available.

2. *Evaluate the advisability* of including mercury and photoelectric controls in your protective lighting systems. These may be desirable in normal circumstances, but undesirable during power failure or even brief interruptions.

3. *Determine how weather and climate* in your locale affect various types of lamps and luminaries.

4. *Investigate the threat* of fluctuating or erratic voltages in your primary power source.

5. *Decide the viability* of grounding lighting fixtures and feasibility for using a common ground on an entire line.

6. *Establish a working ledger* to provide you with a maintenance record of various lighting element burning times. Use a common average of 80% of the total expected element life. Record each element based on lamp life expectancy as supplied by manufacturers. Your working ledger needs the following minimum information:
   a. Type and wattage of each lamp used in your system
   b. The area, facility, or utility pole used within your lighting system (make a diagram).
   c. Date of placing each lamp or element into service
   d. Schedule date (based on life expectancy) for replacement (using the 80% factor)
   e. Current location of the lamp or element within your lighting system

7. *Provide protective lighting for all limited or exclusion areas* (highly controlled access) on a permanent basis at their perimeters and access control points. Position your lighting to accomplish the following points:
   a. Prevent glare that may temporarily cause security officers to have trouble seeing and provide advantage to an intruder.
   b. Avoid silhouetting or highlighting the working security officers, creating a danger to them or enhancing an intruder's effort by allowing him or her to know how many officers are present and their location.
   c. Ensure the working security officers control the lighting system in sensitive areas to prevent intentional or accidental extinguishing of essential protective lighting.

IMPORTANT SPECIFICATION TIPS

Your perimeter blend of lighting must provide a minimum intensity of 0.2 foot-candles (explained later), measured horizontally 6 inches above ground level, at least 30 feet outside the protected area barrier. Lighting inside protected areas or when directed on sensitive structures must have enough intensity to enable detection of persons in structure entrances. Protective lighting at entrance control points must have adequate intensity to enable security officers to compare accurately identification cards and badges with the actual appearance of employees or visitors seeking authorized entry.

8. *Interior and exterior areas* need intense protective lighting surrounding the facilities, for example, buildings that contain industrial materials, equipment storage areas, aircraft, and hangars including outdoor parking areas for vehicles or aircraft and others. Requirements you must consider for this type of effective lighting include

   a. During hours of darkness, direct part of your lighting to outside entrances of buildings, and others. You will need to ensure illumination achieving intensity of not less than 1.0 foot candle at any point to a height of 8 feet on their vertical surfaces and to a horizontal distance of 8 feet from the entrance.

   b. Your interior entrances need illumination of a minimum of 0.10 foot-candle at any point within a 20–foot radius of the entrance.

   c. When your company parks vehicles and aircraft outside you'll need illumination of 0.10 foot candle at any point within a 30–foot radius of the vehicle or aircraft.

   d. Ensure the lighting switch installations for outside lights deny access to unauthorized persons. Also, cover all vulnerable outside lights with wire mesh screen or other material to prevent breakage from thrown objects.

   e. You need to develop systematic programming for upgrading or downgrading lighting requirements on existing facilities to satisfy security needs.

TYPES AND PRINCIPLES OF PROTECTIVE LIGHT SOURCES

The object of your protective lighting is creating illumination needed for the specific security task. For instance, the glare projection method of protective lighting is well suited for perimeter security under average circumstances, whereas diffused light gives freedom from glare and is generally applicable when glare projection is objectionable. The principal types of lamps you can use in your protective lighting systems are as follows.

Incandescent Lamps

This is the common type of glass light bulb and the light it produces generates from the resistance of a filament to an electric current. Special-purpose incandescent bulbs feature (1) interior coating to reflect the light, (2) built-in lens to direct or diffuse the light, and (3) a naked bulb enclosed in a shade or fixture to achieve similar results.

Gaseous Discharge Lamps

Mercury vapor lamps emit a blue-green light made by an electric current passing through a tube of conducting and luminous gas. They are more efficient than incandescent lamps of comparable wattage and are in widespread use for interior and outside lighting, especially where people are working or moving about.

Sodium vapor lamps are similar to mercury vapor lamps but emit a golden-yellow glow. They are more efficient than the other type listed and are used where the color is acceptable, such as on streets, roads, and bridges.

Metal halide lamps emit a harsh yellow-colored light using sodium, thalium, indium, and mercury.

Fluorescent Lamps

These are large, elongated bulbs (to 9 inches long) which supply high light output with an average expected life of 7,500 hours. They have a higher initial cost than incandescent lamps, but provide a lower operating cost using less electricity to emit an equivalent amount of light.

FIVE IMPORTANT PRINCIPLES AND BENEFITS OF PROTECTIVE SECURITY LIGHTING

Ideally, your protective lighting system enables security officers to observe activities around or inside a complex without disclosing their presence to an observer. This type of managed lighting for approaches to your company area not only discourages unauthorized entry, but also enables surveillance and observation of persons within the area. Being capable of doing that and keeping others unsure of their concealment reduce the threat of pilferage, vandalism, or malicious acts against company property. However, effective protective lighting is only one ingredient for your total security system during hours of darkness. It is a tool that needs to be integrated with other measures such as fixed security posts (observation towers) or security patrols, perimeter fences, and alarm systems. You need to consider five important principles of protective lighting as you develop your protective lighting systems.

1. Your protective lighting achieves measurable security advantage when your lighting applications include (a) adequate, evenly dispersed light on areas bordering your company, (b) glaring light focusing on potential intruder approaches, and (c) dim light on security patrol routes. Besides enabling security officers to see long distances, they must be able to see low contrasts. Low contrasts include indistinct outlines of a person's silhouette. Security officers must be able to see an intruder who may be exposed to view for only a few seconds.

2. When you're planning effective protective lighting applications, ensure placement of high brightness contrast between a potential intruder and that background security officers observe. It must be your first consideration. When security officers are looking at mostly dark, dirty, or flat painted surfaces, you need more light intensity and brightness to produce the same effect around areas and buildings with clean concrete, light brick, white sand, or light-colored pea gravel. A security officer responsible for observation of the area depends on contrasts of light reflected. His or her skill to distinguish an intruder on a background of poor contrasts dramatically improves with increased illumination.

3. When an intruder is darker than his or her background, the observing security officer sees primarily an outline or silhouette. Intruders wearing and depending on dark clothing and even darkened face and hands to blend into the environs quickly find their effort foiled when you use correctly applied light focused on the lower parts of buildings and structures. Your lighting advantage dramatically increases with a couple of easy techniques. For example, stripes on walls have effective benefit. This technique supplies recognizable breaks, enabling a security officer quickly to detect outlines, silhouettes, and movement. Illustration 7–1 shows that technique.

Illustration 7–1

EXAMPLE OF STRIPING BUILDINGS OR STRUCTURES
TO CREATE SILHOUETTES IN PROTECTIVE LIGHTING

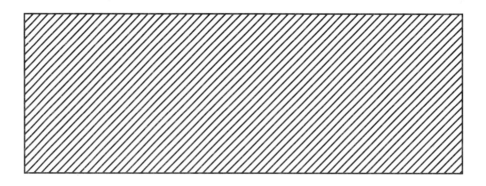

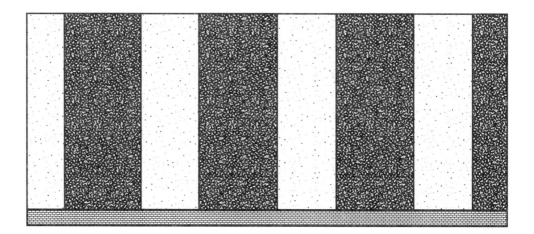

4. Two basic systems, or a combination of both, provide practical and effective protective lighting. The first method is lighting the company boundaries and gate approaches. The second is lighting areas and structures within the general boundaries of company property.

5. To achieve effective protective lighting design, you need to create an integrated lighting system that
   a. Discourages or deters surreptitious entries by intruders. Effective, managed illumination leads a potential intruder to believe detection is inevitable.
   b. Makes detection probable during surreptitious entry attempts.

ADDITIONAL BENEFITS OF CREATING EFFECTIVE BACKGROUNDS

Indirect interior lighting uses the ceilings and upper sidewalls of a room for redirecting and diffusing light given by lamps. This in part is the light-reflecting properties of colored surfaces. The same principle is true of outside lighting techniques. Dark areas become the ally of a potential intruder seeking ways to overcome your security systems. Illustration 7–1 points out the advantage of striping dark-colored walls for detection of persons moving along them. The same principle with different techniques creates a security advantage along perimeter fences at low cost. Security officers need to see an intruder approaching, climbing over, or cutting through a perimeter fence. You can create that advantage with an 8-foot strip of white sand or light-colored pea gravel outside the perimeter fence and another strip inside the fence. That technique, shown in Illustration 7–2, creates excellent visibility with less light intensity.

Illustration 7–2

EXAMPLE OF REFLECTING LIGHT ALONG PERIMETER FENCES

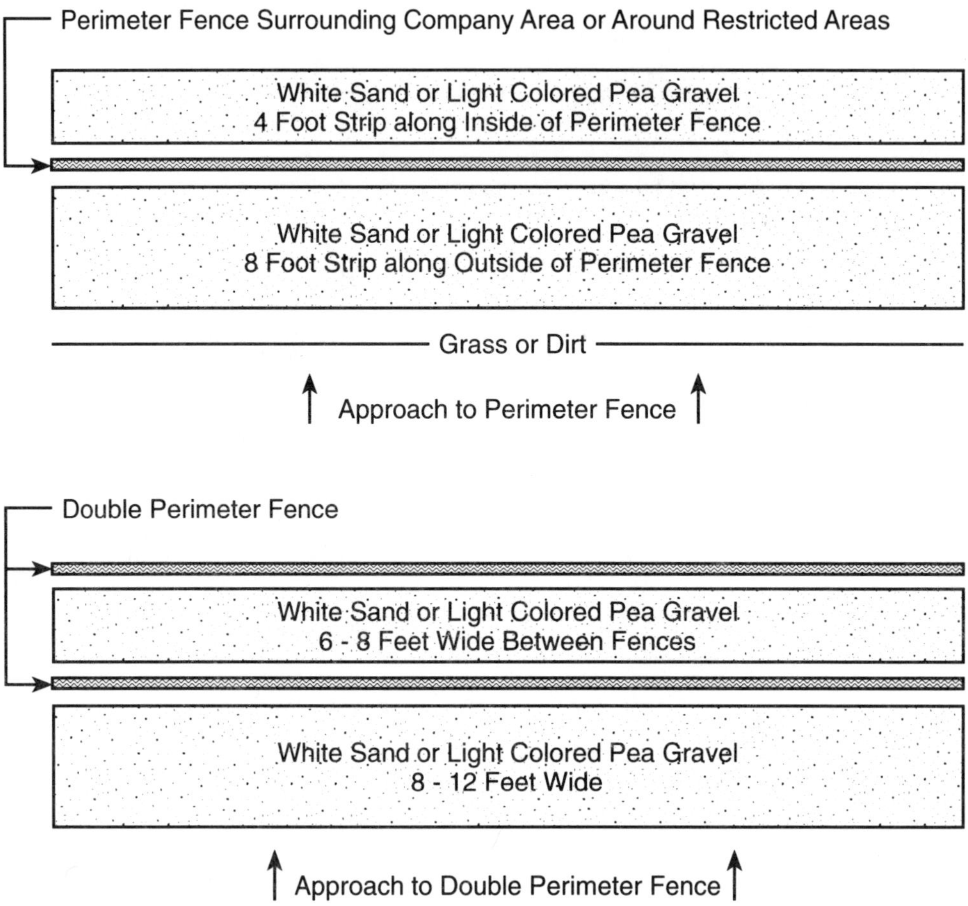

Perimeter Fence Surrounding Company Area or Around Restricted Areas

White Sand or Light Colored Pea Gravel
4 Foot Strip along Inside of Perimeter Fence

White Sand or Light Colored Pea Gravel
8 Foot Strip along Outside of Perimeter Fence

———————— Grass or Dirt ————————

↑ Approach to Perimeter Fence ↑

Double Perimeter Fence

White Sand or Light Colored Pea Gravel
6 - 8 Feet Wide Between Fences

White Sand or Light Colored Pea Gravel
8 - 12 Feet Wide

↑ Approach to Double Perimeter Fence ↑

CREATING EFFECTIVE ILLUMINATION ARRANGEMENTS

The cone of illumination from your lighting units needs direction downward projection and away from a structure or area protected and from the security officers you assign the various positions. Your lighting needs attentive organization creating a minimum of shadows and avoiding reflective glare in the eyes of security officers.

Positioning lighting units along perimeter fences calls for staying a reasonable distance within the interior of a protected area and above the fence. Often, a shortcoming of lighting is putting it too close to a chain-link fence, creating reflection from the wire. Correcting that problem happens by increasing the height or moving the fixture further inside, generally both techniques. Doing that creates a light pattern on the ground, on both sides of a fence. Generally, the light band needs to illuminate the barrier and extend deep into the approach area. Limiting factors, however, often prevent deep extensions of protective lighting outside your company perimeters. For example, limits happen when a fence borders waterways, highways, railroads, and residences or other reasons limiting the outside depth of your light band.

When you determine the best locations of illuminating fixtures along a perimeter fence, including internal restricted or exclusion areas or the company boundary perimeter fence, positioning guidelines prove helpful. Also important is placing the poles for mounting the lighting fixtures far enough behind the inner fence to ensure they don't become a climbing aid for an intruder breaching the perimeter fence.

FOUR IMPORTANT PHASES IN CHOOSING THE RIGHT HARDWARE (FIXTURES) FOR YOUR PROTECTIVE LIGHTING

Choosing the right hardware is as important as your illumination design. The following guidelines supply information to help you during planning or evaluating your company's protective lighting system.

1. *Consider the operating environment* you need to evaluate and determine your requirement for heavy-duty or general-purpose fixtures. The following list provides a general concept to follow.
   a. Subject to rough use—use heavy duty. Climate is an important factor in choosing lighting fixtures, especially when seasons bring extreme cold, heat, dusty, or wet conditions. Other reasons for choosing heavy-duty equipment include the impact caused by the company operation environment. For example, lighting alongside active railroad tracks or areas that have a regular presence of heavy equipment and fixtures receive consistent vibration.

b. Exposed to severe atmospheric or corrosive conditions—use heavy duty. High winds and saltwater spray create severe problems for lighting poles and fixtures. Besides using heavy-duty fixtures, you'll need to choose waterproof construction and ensure frequent performance of preventive maintenance.

c. Installation to be permanent—use heavy duty. Although more costly to install, heavy-duty fixtures save your company money in the long run when known to be permanent. There's also the consideration of having reliable protective lighting, and the best guidance rule is selecting equipment that goes well beyond requirements. When you do that, there's a benefit of compensating for future developments and errors during planning.

d. When a primary consideration calls for lightweight equipment—use general purpose. Lightweight lighting fixtures often become a matter of necessity instead of choice. For example, when your security situation requirements dictate, you need to place high-intensity lighting on a building or other structure. Although you might prefer heavy-duty equipment, it's often too heavy or cumbersome for this type of installation.

e. Located in a low priority area—use general purpose. Your company might have several areas infrequently used and only need security during times of use. Examples might be open storage or parking areas used during fulfillment of a manufacturing contract or temporary storage of incoming material. Other situations might include materials that have no criminal enterprise appeal or are too difficult to remove from company property easily.

2. *When you have chosen the fixtures needed*, you'll begin determining the quality and quantity of light needed. The following guidelines supply you with information to help you in planning and implementation. (Note: Iodine quartz is often called "tungsten halogen.")

a. To achieve a greater number of burning hours per year, use iodine quartz.

b. When your needs call for a lesser number of burning hours per year, incandescent lamps or elements serve you well.

c. For color clarity, use either incandescent, or iodine quartz lamps and elements.

d. To achieve low initial floodlight cost for limited budgets, iodine quartz elements provide the low-end value.

e. When your company location is subject to frequent power failures, use incandescent or iodine quartz lamps or elements.

f. For maintenance difficulty, limitations, or challenging inaccessibility because of hardware positioning, use long-term iodine quartz elements.

g. When you have protective lighting in a low priority or minimum threat area and rapid relight capability isn't critical, use gaseous lamps such as mercury vapor or fluorescent.

Although gaseous filament lamps can produce high light intensity, they do not have an instantaneous relight capability. Dependent on the type of lamp you choose, the relighting response may vary from 1 to 35 minutes. Also, weather affects this response time, including the inherent delay features of the illuminating material used in the lamp manufacture.

3. *A variety of lighting fixtures* manufactured provide adequate floodlighting. These fixtures involve either incandescent or iodine quartz lamps. Recent innovation in floodlighting design produces fixtures that feature an adjustable beam and use single-ended iodine quartz filament. Design of other fixture types include glare projection bulbs which are easily adaptable for use with single-ended iodine quartz lamps.

4. *The use of double-ended iodine quartz lamps* is discouraged. Fixture mounting is critical for this type filament. The fixture needs mounting with 4 degrees of absolute level. Any greater variation makes the light fail because the gaseous substance in the lamps will not provide an electrical bridge between the terminal poles of the filament. The failure to complete the circuit make the lamp blacken and burn out rapidly.

INSTALLATION TIPS AND MOUNTING GUIDANCE FOR HARDWARE AND ELEMENTS

A fixture (hardware) is mounted on poles singly or in clusters. A foot-candle chart supplies information needed for accurate mounting at various heights. The foot-candle values vary inversely as the square of the mounting height, and the scale varies according to the mounting height. The distance to your metering point varies according to the mounting height.

FUNDAMENTALS OF LIGHT MEASUREMENT AND CONTROL

The basis of lighting engineering involves a few simple principles of the physics of radiation. For example, a light source radiates light because part of its emitted radiation creates a particular sensation when it strikes the retina of the human eye. Outside the visible spectrum, radiation that does not create a sensation of light needs short wave lengths (i.e., ultraviolet radiation) or longer wave lengths (i.e., infrared radiation). The ultraviolet type serves to detect hidden marks on identification cards, or often spotting counterfeit ID cards or security badges.

Infrared systems serve for effective night vision equipment when standard lighting is not available or inoperable.

The name "light flux" describes the rate of emission from the light source. The unit of light flux is the lumen. The light output from lighting fixtures is expressed in lumens. For example, an ordinary wax candle emits about 13 lumens, a 100 watt filament lamp about 1,200 lumens, and a 5-foot fluorescent tube about 5,000 lumens.

UNDERSTANDING THE TERMINOLOGY: ILLUMINANCE AND REFLECTANCE

The lighting level, that is, light spread over the area receiving the light, is called the illuminance (or illumination) and is expressed in lumens per unit area. For example, 1 lumen per square foot is illuminance of a surface 1 foot from the light of one ordinary wax candle. Unobstructed daylight from a bright sky gives 1,000 lumens per square foot.

Light falling on a surface reflects off objects, depending on the ability of a surface to reflect light. That reflection factor, or reflectance, relates to the light falling on a surface as seen by the observer. A white surface has a reflectance of nearly 100% while a black surface has a reflectance of about 2% and a medium-gray surface about 40%. If the surface diffuses light equally in directions (e.g., a matte surface paint), the brightness of the surface will relate directly to the illumination falling upon it. The physicist and engineer use the word "luminance" to express the physical measure of brightness. The unit of luminance used in the United States is the foot-lambert. Luminance, illuminance, and reflectance relate with the equation; luminance (foot-lamberts) equals illuminance (foot-candles) times reflectance. For example, diffusing off a white surface of 50% reflectance, the surface receiving 10 foot-candles will have a luminance of 5 foot-lamberts. Illuminance of 100 foot-candles falling on a desk top with a reflectance of 30% and a sheet of white paper with a reflectance of 80% would give a luminance of 80 foot-lamberts to the paper and 30 foot-lamberts to the desk top.

A USEFUL GLOSSARY GUIDE OF LIGHTING

When you start planning or evaluating your security system's protective lighting, you'll often hear a variety of new terms surface calling for a source of information. You may talk to manufacturers, engineers, and others who freely use this new, strange terminology. The following glossary lists the terms you might hear in discussions with lighting engineers.

- **Candela.** The unit of luminous intensity.

- **Candle power.** One candle power is a measurement of light emitted by one international candle or one standard candle. That measurement is credible at the source of illumination. This is a standard characteristic of a lamp available from the manufacturer's descriptive data.

- **Foot-candle.** A light source of a given candle power rating will produce the same foot-candle rating only on surfaces equidistant from the light source. Since the quality of light received at a surface varies inversely as the square of the distance between the source and the surface, the foot-candle will decrease as distance is increased.

- **Horizontal illumination.** Horizontal illumination is the illumination expressed in foot-candles on a horizontal surface. The surface is always at ground level.

- **Vertical illumination.** Vertical illumination is the illumination expressed in foot-candles on a vertical surface.

- **Lumen.** A quantity of light needed to light an area of one square foot to one candle power.

- **Brightness.** The luminous intensity of any surface in a given direction. Brightness is one of the basic factors of seeing. Extreme brightness in the visual field causes glare and eye fatigue. When brightness values are low, seeing becomes difficult. To achieve acceptable conditions matching the visual task, and the immediate surroundings, the intensity needs three or less. A meter, known as the Luckiesh-Taylor brightness meter, enables direct measurement of brightness in foot-lambert.

- **Foot-lambert.** A unit of brightness obtained when diffusing surface of uniform brightness emitting one lumen per square foot viewed from a given direction.

- **Calculated illumination.** The estimated degree of illumination based on the results of photometric tests of separate units accurate within plus or minus 2%. A basis for the tests uses an average clean reflector and tests need rigidly controlled laboratory conditions with new lamps standardized for their rated lumen output. Calculated illumination is important for planning purposes. Effective management of field tests determines effectiveness of light patterns. Obtain separate fixture capabilities from the manufacturer's specification.

- **Photometer.** Instruments used to inspect protective lighting systems provide readable data and need large-scale deflections for reading the values, for example, the Macbeth Illuminometer and the G. E. Low Range Sensitive Meter with the 0–2, 0–6, and 0–20 candle scales.

    You cannot rely on the small meters used in photographic work. This accuracy of the meters is for measuring a single source of light entering the cell perpendicular to its face. The designs of protective lighting systems provide light from multiple sources. It is not practical to use a small meter for correcting angular deviation. This type meter cannot give you comparative readings along a given line of lighting fixtures.

For your corporate and industrial security protective lighting purposes, all light meter readings need observation from a horizontal plane at the ground level. In this configuration, keep the photoelectric cell of the meter at ground level, with the sensitive part of the meter facing upward. The light striking the meter in this position will produce the foot-candle intensity that is equated to the minimum standards shown in this manual. The readings in Illustration 7–3 are horizontal foot-candles.

Illustration 7–3

PRINCIPLES OF READING PROTECTIVE LIGHTING

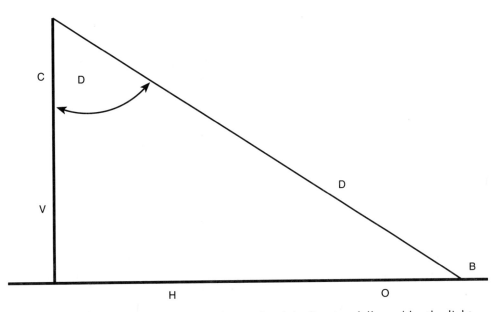

Point C is the light source. Line *D* is the angle of declination followed by the light pattern. Point O is the maximum point from the light source when to get a minimal reading. Item *B* is the photoelectric cell of the light meter positioned to reflect a true reading of the horizontal foot-candle. Line *V* is the vertical height of the mounted fixture light source to the point of taking the meter reading. Mathematically, this procedure is as follows:

$$\text{Horizontal foot-candles at point } O = \frac{\text{CP (candle power) of C} \times \text{cosine of angle } X}{V^2 \times H^2}$$

THE SEVEN PRIMARY TYPES OF PROTECTIVE LIGHTING

The type of protective lighting system you choose depends on the overall security requirements of your company or industrial complex. Lighting units are of seven general types: (1) continuous, (2) controlled, (3) area, (4) surface, (5) standby, (6) movable, and (7) emergency.

1. Continuous Lighting (Stationary Luminary)

This is the most common protective lighting system. It includes a series of fixed luminaries arranged to flood a given area continuously during the hours of darkness with overlapping cones of light. Often, a viable supplement for continuous lighting systems includes glare projection lighting, especially along boundary perimeter fences.

The glare projection lighting method is useful where the glare of lights directed across the surrounding territory won't be annoying or interfere with adjacent operations. It is a strong deterrent to a potential intruder because it creates difficulty for him or her to see within your company area. It also protects your security forces by keeping officers in comparative darkness, enabling them to observe intruders at considerable distance beyond the perimeter. A preferred technique is a light source that provides a band of light with an intensive horizontal angular dispersal and directs the glare while restricting the downward beam. In some companies, the perimeter security considerations against intruders might have a priority over principles of security against internal pilferage; however, the tightening of perimeter security in turn strengthens your other physical security efforts.

Illustrations 7–4 and 7–5 shows two systems of a typical continuous perimeter lighting system. Illustration 7–4 adds glare lighting and illustration 7–5 is continuous lighting without glare lighting.

Illustration 7–4

HIGH-PRESSURE SODIUM-TYPE FLOODLIGHT

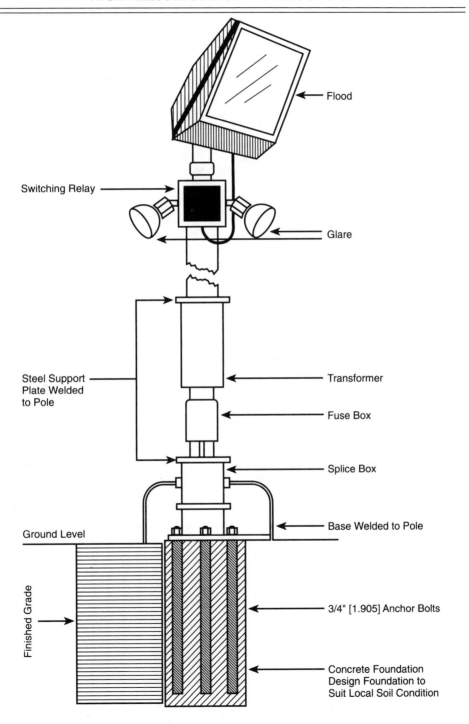

Flood

Switching Relay

Glare

Steel Support
Plate Welded
to Pole

Transformer

Fuse Box

Splice Box

Base Welded to Pole

Ground Level

Finished Grade

3/4" [1.905] Anchor Bolts

Concrete Foundation
Design Foundation to
Suit Local Soil Condition

Illustration 7–5

CONTINUOUS LIGHTING EXAMPLE

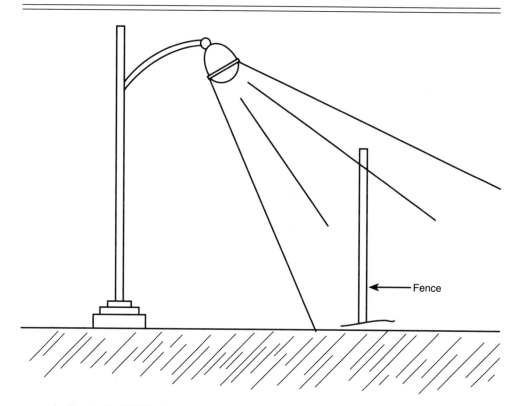

Fence

2. Controlled Lighting

Controlled lighting techniques become your best choice when you need to limit the width of the lighted strip outside the perimeter fence. Reasons of these restrictions include adjoining property because of nearby highways, railroads, navigable waters, or airports. Using controlled techniques, your lighting management adjusts the width of the lighted strip to fit the particular need. For example, you might illuminate a wide strip inside a fence and a narrow strip outside or floodlight a wall or roof depending on the situation. The disadvantage of this method of lighting is that it often illuminates or silhouettes security officers as they patrol their routes. Illustration 7–6 and 7–7 shows controlled lighting using different devices.

Illustration 7−6

EXAMPLE OF BOUNDARY LIGHTING NEAR ADJOINING PROPERTY

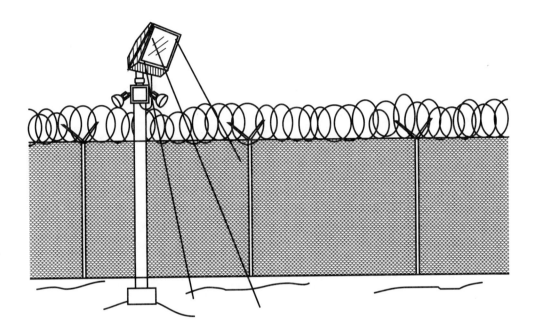

Illustration 7–7

CONTROLLED LIGHTING EXAMPLE

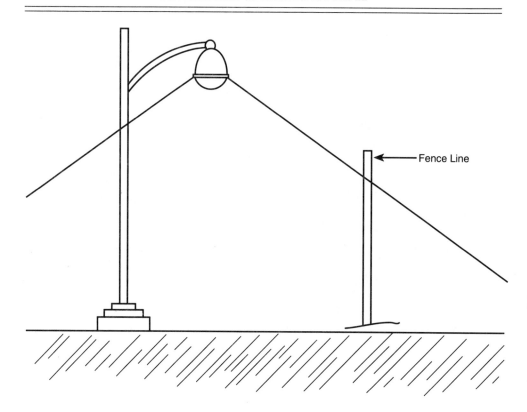

Fence Line

3. Area Lighting

This method provides illumination of open areas, including material storage yards, streets, and parking lots. You can also effectively light aisles, passageways, and recesses, diminishing shadowed areas where persons can hide.

4. Surface Lighting

This method needs application when it is desirable to illuminate the surfaces of important structures and buildings that can be most easily and seriously harmed at close range. Its usage needs consideration during the construction of important structures and buildings. For example, a building containing explosives, toxic chemicals, or other priority items needs added lighting to ensure the security of its contents. Flooding the building with surface light discourages intruders and enables security officers to maintain effective surveillance.

5. Standby Lighting (Stationary Luminary)

The layout of this system is similar to continuous lighting. However, standby lighting enables a supplemental system started automatically or manually, when security officers or alarm systems detect suspicious activity. You might use this technique in lower-priority areas and activate the lighting only when there's a need. It is an effective, efficient cost-saving technique to consider in your planning and implementation of protective lighting systems.

6. Movable Lighting (Stationary or Portable)

This manually operated type of system includes movable floodlights and search-lights. You can use either type during hours of darkness as a supplement, lighted only as needed. The system normally will supplement continuous or standby lighting. Often, mounting these types of lighting on trailers allow expedient uses during inclement weather, impending threats, or other situations needing flexibility.

7. Emergency Lighting

This system can duplicate any or all these systems. It's limited to periods of power failure or other emergencies that make your normal lighting systems inoperative. The system reliability depends on your choice of emergency lighting power sources. For example, portable gasoline-powered generators or high-output batteries generally serve your needs best. This system is most efficient when trailer or truck mounted for mobility.

EIGHT OTHER KEY CONSIDERATIONS AND LIGHTING SPECIFICATIONS

Your lighting assessments and evaluations normally reveal the most vulnerable sections in your perimeter sections, the perimeter or fence line being the company property boundary, unless the fence surrounds limited or exclusion areas inside the property line. The following examples provide general guidance for you to consider when designing or evaluating specifications for your protective lighting throughout the perimeter, also those vulnerable sections you identify. Fenced perimeters category and specification guidelines follow:

1. *Isolated fenced perimeters* are fence lines around areas where the fence is 100 feet or more from buildings or operating areas. The approach area is clear of obstruction for 100 to 300 feet outside the fence line and not used by other than security officers. Generally, both glare projection and controlled illumination are acceptable for these perimeters. In either situation,

patrol roads and paths need to remain unlighted. Where glare projection isn't objectionable, provide it as follows:

    a. *Width of lighted strip* needs 210 feet divided into two zones:

        1. Zone I—from 10 feet inside to 25 feet outside the fence line

        2. Zone II—from 25 feet inside to 200 feet outside the fence line

    b. *Minimum illuminations* within the lighted strip need no less than 0.15 foot-candle at any point measured on a vertical plane 3 feet above the ground and parallel to the fence line. Also, for Zone I, provide enough illumination to assure ready detection of persons as necessary.

2. *Semi-isolated fenced perimeters* are fence lines where the approach area is clear of obstruction for 70 to 100 feet outside the fence line and the general public or company employees seldom have reason to be in this area. Patrol roads and paths stay in relative darkness. The lighting for semi-isolated fenced perimeters needs the following specifications:

    a. *Width of lighted strip* needs 80 feet extending from 10 feet inside to 70 feet outside the fence line.

    b. *Minimum illumination* within the lighted strip is no less than 0.04 foot-candle at any given point.

3. *Non-isolated fenced perimeters* are fence lines immediately adjacent to company operating areas. They also include fenced areas within the complex such as limited or exclusion areas, other company operations or property lines, or public thoroughfares, where outsiders or company persons move freely in the approach area. The widths of the lighted strip in these situations depend on the relative clear zone inside and outside the fence line. It is not practical to keep the patrol area dark. The lighting for nonisolated fenced perimeters needs to be as follows:

    a. *Width of the lighted strip* next to the fence line needs 60 feet extending from 20 to 30 feet inside and from 40 to 30 feet outside the fence line.

    b. *Minimum illumination* within the lighted strip needs 0.08 foot-candle at any point if 40 feet outside the fence line and 0.10 foot-candle at any point if 30 feet outside the fence line.

    c. *Unfenced perimeters* where the property lines include more than 20 feet from buildings and there's no fence line or outdoor operating areas between buildings and property lines. The lighting for unfenced perimeters needs the following:

    (1) *Width of lighted strip* needs 80 feet outward from the building in the unobstructed area.

    (2) *Minimum illumination* within the lighted strip needs 0.04 foot-candle at any point.

4. *Building face perimeters* have faces of buildings on or within 20 feet of the fence line or area line protected and where the general public might ap-

proach the buildings. Security officers need post assignments inside or outside the buildings. Doorways or other insets in the building face perimeter need special attention for lighting to eliminate shadows. Lighting for building face perimeters needs the following:

    a. *Width of lighted strip* needs 50 feet extending from the building face.

    b. *Minimum illumination* within the lighted strip needs 0.10 foot-candle at any point.

5. *Active entrances, pedestrian and vehicle,* need two or more lighting units with adequate illumination for recognition of persons and examination of identification items. All vehicle entrances need two lighting units to simplify complete inspection of passenger cars, trucks, and freight cars, including their contents and passengers. Semiactive and quiescent entrances need the same degree of continuous lighting as the remainder of the fence line, with standby lighting of adequate illumination when the entrance becomes active. Gatehouses at entrances (control points) need a low level of indoor illumination (preferably dim red light) enabling security officers to see adequately while increasing their night vision adaptability. Also that type of lighting prevents making the officers a clear target for aggressive or hostile intruders. The lighting for active entrances needs the following:

    a. *Extent of lighted area* needs the width of the road or walkway extending 25 feet inside and outside the fence line gate for pedestrian entrances and the width of the roadway extending 50 feet inside and outside the fence line gate for vehicular entrances.

    b. *Minimum illumination* within the lighted area needs 2.0 foot-candle (pedestrian) or 1.0 foot-candle (vehicular) at any point.

6. *Areas and structures* within your company fence lines or unfenced perimeters have yards, storage spaces, large open working areas, piers and docks, and other sensitive areas and structures.

    a. *The illumination of open yards* (defined as unoccupied land only) and of outdoor storage spaces (defined as material storage areas, railroad sidings, and parking areas) needs the following:

    b. *Illumination of open yards* needs 0.02 foot-candle at any point.

    c. *Minimum illuminations* of outdoor storage spaces need 0.10 foot-candle at any point.

    d. *Lighting units need placing* to provide an adequate distribution of light in aisles, passageways, and recesses to reduce shadowed areas where unauthorized persons might hide themselves.

7. *Piers and docks* found within a company area or part of separate company facilities need safeguarding by illuminating both the water approaches and the pier area. Movable lighting capable of being directed as needed by the security officers is recommended as a part of the protective lighting system for piers and docks. The lighting cannot violate marine rules and regulations or be glaring to pilots. Consult the U.S. Coast Guard and obtain approval of your proposed protective lighting adjacent navigable waters. The lighting for piers and docks needs the following:

    a. *Minimum illumination* of land approaches needs the same guidance supplied in (b) and (c) following.

    b. *Minimum illumination of water approaches* (extending a distance of 100 feet from pier) needs 0.10 foot-candle horizontal out to 50 feet and 0.05 foot-candle vertical from 50 to 100 feet at any point.

    c. *Minimum illuminations of decks of piers* need 0.10 foot-candle at any point.

    d. *Minimum illumination beneath piers* (when pier construction makes it applicable) needs 0.04 foot-candle at any point.

8. *Critical structures and areas* need the first consideration in designing protective fencing and lighting. Power, heat, water, communications, explosive materials, sensitive material storage or production areas, and valuable finished products need special attention. Critical structures and areas most easily and seriously harmed at close range need lighting of an intensity of not less than 2.0 foot-candles at any point. Their vertical surface requirements include measurement to a height of 8 feet in the approach area immediately surrounding the structure. Critical structures or areas not determined vulnerable from a distance need no lighting although standby lighting is recommended.

Illustrations 7–8 and 7–9 supply you with a valuable guide to use during your planning, designing and evaluation stages of protective lighting.

Illustration 7–8

LIGHTING SPECIFICATION TABLE	
Location	**Foot-candles on Horizontal Plane at Ground Level**
Perimeter of outer area	0.15
Perimeter of restricted area	0.4
Vehicle entrances	1.0
Pedestrian entrances	2.0
Sensitive inner area	0.15
Sensitive inner structure	1.0
Entrances	0.1
Open yards	0.2
Decks on open piers	1.0

Illustration 7–9

LIGHTING SPECIFICATION TABLE			
Type of Area	**Type of Lighting**	**Width of Lighted Strip (ft)**	
		Inside Fence	**Outside Fence**
Isolated perimeter	Glare	25	200
Isolated perimeter	Controlled	10	70
Semi-isolated perimeter	Controlled	10	70
Nonisolated perimeter	Controlled	20–30	30–40
Building face perimeter	Controlled	50	
Vehicle entrance	Controlled	50	50
Pedestrian entrance	Controlled	25	25
Railroad entrances	Controlled	50	50
Important structures	Controlled	50	50

MANAGING YOUR PROTECTIVE LIGHTING WIRING SYSTEMS

Both multiple and series circuits create advantage in protective lighting systems. The role each plays depends on the type of luminary used and other design features of your system. Your arrangements of effective circuits ensure that a failure of one lamp or element won't leave a large part of the perimeter line or a major part of a critical or vulnerable section in darkness. Circuitry design needs to overcome or work around normal interruptions caused by overloads, industrial accidents, and building or brush fires. Also, feeder lines need underground conduits (or enough inside the perimeter for overhead wiring) to minimize the possibility of sabotage or vandalism from outside the perimeter. Your design must provide for simplicity and economy in the system maintenance and call for a minimum of shutdowns for routine repairs, cleaning, and lamp replacement. It is necessary sometimes to install a duplicate wiring system, particularly using a series circuit, to prevent loss of illumination because of a break in the primary line. Redundancy is an excellent rule for you to follow in your design and implementation.

PREVENTIVE MAINTENANCE OF LIGHTING SYSTEMS

Any security system needs diligent maintenance and lighting is a priority item. The following guidelines supply maintenance concepts important to your lighting systems.

1. Make periodic inspections of all electrical circuits to replace or repair worn parts, tighten connections, and check insulation. Keep luminaries clean and properly aimed.

2. Use the replaced lamps in less sensitive locations for cost-effective benefit. The actuating relays on emergency lines, which stay open when the system is in operation from the primary source, need to be cleaned often. Dust and lint collect on their contact points and can prevent their operation when closed.

3. The intensity of illumination and specification for protective lighting for fences or other antipersonnel barriers should meet the minimum requirements set forth in the lighting tables shown as Illustrations 7–6 and 7–7.

4. Lamps used in your protective lighting system need a schedule for replacement at 80 percent of their rated life. Use the old lamps in less sensitive lighting locations.

MAKING CERTAIN YOU HAVE RELIABLE POWER SOURCES

Usually, the primary power source at a company or industry is a local public utility. Since your security does not extend beyond the company perimeter, the interest of the security force begins at the points at which power feeder lines enter the company area. Provide an alternate source of power where the primary power source is subject to interruptions or failures. Standby batteries or gasoline-driven generators that start automatically upon the failure of outside power will ensure continuous light, but may be inadequate for sustained operations. Generator- or battery-powered, portable or stationary lights must be available at key control points for use of security officers if a complete failure makes even the alternate power supply ineffective.

Alternate power sources need preventive maintenance periodically to ensure they're operable and at full potential. The frequency and duration of test operations will be dependent on the type and condition of the equipment, weather (temperature affects batteries) and factors such as the company's purpose and operational situation.

Continual physical security calls for inspections of power sources to determine security measures and replacement of equipment (i.e., transformers, lines, and other critical elements).

QUICK REFERENCE GUIDE

- Primary power source: usually a public utility.
- Alternate power sources: provide the following:

Standby batteries, gasoline- or diesel-driven generators.

☐ If cost effective, a system should start automatically upon failure of outside power.

☐ Must ensure continuous lighting.

☐ May be inadequate for sustained operations, consider added security precautions.

☐ Tested to ensure efficiency and effectiveness. The frequency and duration of tests depend on
   - Purpose and operational factor
   - Location, type, and conditions of equipment
   - Weather (temperature affects batteries)

☐ Located within a controlled area for added security.

☐ Generator- or battery-powered, portable or stationary lights.
   - For use in a complete power failure
   - Include alternate power supply
   - Available at designated control points for security officers

☐ Security—a necessity.
   - Starts at the points where power feeder lines enter the company perimeter.
   - Security emphasis goes to sources of essential and vulnerable activity.
   - Continual physical security inspections of power sources determines security measures and replacement of equipment (transformer, lines, etc.)

8 Structural Security Management

Despite a long-term structural security problem, corporate and industrial building trends generally ignore security needs, opting instead for beauty, and focus on design for the business efficiency, operational functions, and investment. Corporate leadership rarely considers including built-in security, or if it does, eventually decides it is too costly. Management often forgets that no matter how great the business, there is no profit when criminal enterprise converts company property to personal gain. That fact is clear when we consider the staggering losses corporations experience each year.

Builders also bear responsibility for structural security problems, using attractive, but lower-quality materials, taking shortcuts, and making the facade appear as a fortress to the average person while actually providing opportunities for criminal enterprise. Whatever the reason, security professionals get stuck with protecting company property, and since you are unlikely to change the construction process without considerable effort, you need to have alternatives. There's also the problem of securing older structures, sheds, warehouses, and many other situations. This chapter supplies security possibilities on new and old buildings and focuses on the basics of security countermeasures.

In this age of high-tech security equipment, it is easy to inundate your corporate environment with gadgets in a desperate hope they deter and detect the criminal enterprise problems. Without arguing the pros and cons, I have only to point out the corporate and industrial losses of billions each year. That certainly makes clear that high-tech equipment, although useful and the subject of several later chapters in this book, is a security tool, enhancing your efforts but not a solution. High-tech equipment, like a building, needs a solid foundation, and in the security profession that begins with the basics. Your core security techniques need operational capability not reliant on electrical power, the skill of security officers to operate and interpret high-tech equipment, or being dependent on the electronic devices continuing to operate effectively and indefinitely without breaking down. In this chapter, you will review the basic structural security problems you are likely to encounter and consider viable, cost-effective solutions and techniques. When you tighten up your company's structures, you are adding another "layer" of security to your total security system. In the same way that fences, lighting, and locks create layers, each of them without the other leaves a gap in your security system.

Some years ago, a federal inspector told me that certain rural banks coming under the Federal Deposit Insurance Corporation program spent vast sums of money installing impressive vault doors. Their vaults passed initial inspection; however later, a series of bank vault burglaries (not publicized in fear of causing a massive problem) sparked added inspection and a startling discovery was made. The vaults presented nearly impregnable facades; however, a person with a 20-pound sledge hammer could easily enter the vault from the outside by knocking out the single brick wall and the light backing. Most rural banks occupy old freestanding brick buildings failing to consider the vulnerability a single layer of bricks and plastered walls create. In a sweeping effort, these banks installed an interior reinforced wall and floors covered with a steel liner to curb the problem of burglary. As you can see, you cannot rely on appearances; the criminal enterprise elements make it their business to find ways to overcome security measures and quickly recognize your structural weaknesses. You need creative solutions in your efforts to strengthen structural weaknesses and that begins with your attentive evaluation of threats and vulnerability in the buildings and areas you are responsible to protect.

CONSIDER YOUR SITUATION AND ACCURATELY ASSESS THE SECURITY THREAT

The diverse world of corporate and industrial business carries so many different problems and threats it is not possible to include every situation and solution. Instead, I hope to improve your awareness and provide ways to find the problems and offer suggestions about fixing them. Vulnerability often becomes a matter of what business your company does and has to offer to a criminal enterprise. For example, a company manufacturing clothing, computers, or other product easily sold on a blackmarket operation has appeal to a specific category of criminal enterprise. An insurance company has no tangible product to sell in a store or backstreet warehouse; however, it does possess confidential information on policyholders and other information. Another category of criminal enterprise might have a distinct interest in stealing segments of that information that can be marketed to competitors or used for other schemes. Companies that produce heavy equipment or steel or wood products might seem unlikely targets for theft;

however, there is always a threat. Not only is the product difficult to steal, it is more difficult to sell, especially without identification. However, a competitor might have considerable interest in company planning, budgets, projected pricing, sources, business deals, key employees, financial status, and research and development projects. The thief might, like the insurance company example, be looking for valuable competitor information that he or she can sell to the highest bidder or to a broker. Competitor intelligence has become a huge business, both legal and illegal, depending on the approach and the method used to obtain the information. Whatever your situation, whatever business your company is in, there is certainly a criminal enterprise who is interested in the commodities. Beyond the sophisticated conspiracies, there is the lesser thief who is looking for an opportunity to steal typewriters, television sets, video equipment, computers, or any other item commonly found in a corporate or industrial working environment.

Another threat involves disgruntled employees, vendettas of former employees, terroristic acts by groups, and actions by persons who perceive your company as an evil entity. The problem with this type of threat is that the person looks for ways to damage the company, often severely, and normally seeks publicity. Those intending on planting bombs, destroying equipment, or starting fires often hope for arrest to fulfill a desire of becoming a martyr for their cause. For example, early in 1991 an alert employee found bombs attached to huge fuel storage tanks in Virginia. Had they not been spotted and disarmed, the results might have been catastrophic to the company and certainly to the surrounding community. Unexplained fires, damaged equipment, and other examples happen often but receive little or no lasting or conclusive publicity.

These examples and many other situations increase when your company is active with hundreds or thousands of employees, visitors, vendors, and vehicle traffic. The problem multiplies if your company operates shifts of workers, and when there is a 24–hour operation to deal with 7 days a week. Even when your corporation or industrial situation closes after the business day and on weekends, you have to be attentive to "stay behind" employees or visitors. They are employees who are intent on helping some other person on the outside by delivering a product to them, or creating a breach for the other person to enter undetected, such as opening a door otherwise locked.

Your important first step is to recognize that whatever your company's business, there is always someone who wants to get in, and normally get out without being detected or caught. You need to decide what anyone might want to take from your company, and that entity or commodity leads you to solutions. However, your protection must be "layered," and when the intruder manages to bypass the perimeter, lighting, and security officers, your last line or layer is the structure housing the items he or she is targeting.

Another problem you have is safety requirements, such as a requirement of supplying easy exits for people in a building during a fire or other emergency. The emergency exit doors usually are "crash doors." These doors deny entry for persons outside the building, but are easily opened by persons inside by pressing a release handle running across the door and attached to the door latch. Employees may use these exits during nonemergency situations, but the door often does not securely latch upon closing unless it's pulled tight from the inside using the crash bar. However, a viable solution is available and discussed later in this chapter.

IDENTIFY, RECOGNIZE, AND EVALUATE YOUR REAL PROBLEMS

Physical security measures play an important role in preventing crime. Nationally, crimes against property (theft) from burglary represent over 90% of all reported crime and include at least 50% of corporate and industrial externally caused losses. By determining vulnerable points in your company structures, you can take effective action physically to secure or harden them. Statistics show that in most corporate and industrial burglaries, intruder entries happen through doors or windows. Your first goal, then, is to concentrate on evaluating your company's window and door weaknesses and develop ways to harden them. The following checklist (shown as Illustration 8–1) supplies comprehensive solutions and guidelines through recognizing the basic minimum standards for your evaluations.

Illustration 8–1

CORPORATE AND INDUSTRIAL DOOR AND WINDOW INSPECTION CHECKLIST

Doors:

☐ Are all doors lockable from the inside?

☐ Is there some type of control (or alarm) so that unauthorized entry is detectable?

☐ When doors need opening for ventilation, are they properly protected?

☐ Are doors, locks, and hardware in good repair?

☐ Are exterior doors as strong as aesthetically possible?

☐ What type of hardware used on exterior doors?

☐ Have you removed serial numbers from padlocks?

☐ Are padlocks adequate to secure the door?

☐ Are padlocks rotated often?

☐ How are keys to padlocks secured?

☐ Would the doors be more secure if faced with sheet metal?

☐ Are openings covered with heavy wire mesh or grillwork?

☐ Is the wire mesh or grillwork secured properly?

☐ Are vulnerable glass door surfaces covered with wire meshes or grillwork?

☐ Are door locks deadbolt type?

☐ Are auxiliary locks used?

☐ What is the door's thickness?

☐ Is the door hollow core?

☐ Is the door solid?

☐ Do doors have thin panels or ventilators?

☐ Do doors have a transom?

☐ Do doors have glass windows?

☐ Can door frames be readily pried loose from the door far enough to release the locking bolt?

☐ Are door frames constructed of metal?

☐ Is the metal door frame solid or filled metal?

☐ Is the metal door frame hollow and weak?

☐ Are door frames constructed of wood?

☐ Is the door frame hard wood or soft wood?

☐ Are all unused doors secured from the inside?

☐ Are the doors built so the lock cannot be reached by breaking out glass or a lightweight panel?

(continued)

Illustration 8–1 (continued)

☐ Are door hinges heavy duty?

☐ Are door hinges designed or installed in ways the intruders cannot remove the pins?

☐ Are door hinges welded or bradded?

☐ Is the lock bolt designed or protected to prevent being pushed back with a thin instrument?

☐ Is the lock designed or the door frame built to prevent release by spreading the frame?

☐ Is the lock bolt protected or built to prevent cutting?

☐ Is the lock firmly mounted to prevent it from being pried off by an intruder?

☐ Is the lock a cylinder type?

☐ Are all locks in good working order?

☐ Are the setscrews holding the lock cylinders firmly in place?

☐ Are padlocks in place when the door is unlocked?

☐ Are padlock hasps heavy enough?

☐ Are padlock hasps installed so screws cannot be removed by an intruder?

☐ Are the padlock hasps made of high-grade steel that is difficult to cut?

☐ Are the padlock hasps mounted in ways to prevent being pried or twisted off the door?

Windows:

☐ Are windows located a sufficient height from the ground to afford better than average protection?

☐ Is safety glass used in any windows?

☐ Are windows removable so large objects can be passed through them?

☐ Are windows permanently sealed?

☐ Can windows open enough to allow an intruder to open a window lock or other latch or opening device easily?

☐ Are windows covered with wire mesh grill or steel bars?

☐ Are steel bars or heavy wire mesh adequate to protect the windows and prevent entry?

☐ Are steel bars or heavy wire mesh secured with hardened steel bolts with round outside heads?

☐ Are steel bars or heavy wire mesh security with lag bolts running through the wall and fastened inside?

☐ Can the steel bars or heavy wire mesh be pried off allowing an intruder access?

☐ Are window protective bars no more than 5 inches apart?

☐ Are valuable items, equipment, or products visible through windows?

(continued)

Illustration 8–1 (continued)

☐ Are unused windows permanently closed?
☐ Are windows protected by alarms?
☐ Are window locks designed and installed properly to prevent opening by breaking the glass?
☐ Have you considered the use of glass brick in place of some windows?
☐ Are all windows locked when office, building, or area is closed?

Other Openings:
☐ Are needless skylights eliminated?
☐ Are accessible skylights protected with steel bars?
☐ Are accessible skylights protected with alarms?
☐ Are exposed roof hatches properly secured?
☐ Are doors to roofs strong and secured?
☐ Are elevators and their controls secured?
☐ Are exhaust or intake ventilator fan openings protected with heavy wire mesh or steel bars?

GUIDELINES, TIPS, AND SOLUTIONS

Door Frames

You need to ensure all door frames have a minimum of 2-inch-thick wood or metal with a rabbeted jamb or hollow metal with a rabbeted jamb filled with a solid material able to withstand spreading. For example, an intruder places a heavy pry bar between the door and the door frame just below the lock. When the material in the door and frame are inadequate, a created security gap happens. This burglary technique makes the door lock release and the door opens. An experienced intruder can open this type of door in seconds.

Doors

All doors in your security system need 2-inch-thick solid wood or covered with 16-gauge sheet steel if wood is $1\frac{3}{8}$ inch or less or 24–gauge steel bonded to kiln-dried wood core, minimum of 60–watt illumination above doors.

Door Locks

As noted in Chapter Nine, you need a minimum of a dead bolt or dead latch type with a 1-inch throw and antiwrenching collar or secondary dead bolt with a 1–inch throw or minimum $\frac{1}{2}$-inch throw for low-priority areas.

Windows

Large windows need burglary-resistant material. Smaller windows like those in warehouses, shops, and storage buildings need to be painted over when practical and protected by $\frac{1}{2}$-inch round steel bars 5 inches apart or 1-by-$\frac{1}{4}$-inch steel flat bars 5 inches apart, the bars being secured in 3 inches of masonry or $\frac{1}{8}$-inch steel wire meshes no larger than 2 inches square bolted over the window. When ventilation windows are not required, glass brick provides a secure choice. Also, secure windows to prevent lifting them out of the frame (This applies to windows below 18 feet above ground level or within 40 inches of an interior door handle.)

Window Locks

Use clam shell (crescent) thumbscrew pin in hole or as applicable to the type of window.

Other Doors

Sliding, garage, and loading dock doors need to be secured with the best possible hardware to make opening by intruders difficult.

Other Openings

Any opening larger than 96 square inches needs to be covered by steel bars or mesh screen.

Because statistics show doors and windows are the most frequent points of attack in a burglary, the standards on the following openings need your consideration. Any opening to a structure provides a probable or potential entry point and receives adequate protection. All openings of 96 square inches or larger need protection. Examples of these potential points of entry are skylights, hatchways, air ducts and vents, and elevators.

Skylights

The best protection is installation of metal bars, grills, or mesh. Bars should be steel not less than $\frac{3}{4}$ inch in diameter and not more than 5 inches apart. Mesh should be at least $\frac{1}{8}$ inch thick with spaces no larger than 2 inches, secured firmly by machine or use of round head bolts preventing removal from the outside. Otherwise, use special burglary-resistant glass.

Elevators

Where feasible use an elevator operator, CCTV, continuous open listening device connected to a security control station, or special keys or card limiting access to authorized persons.

Hatchways

Cover hatchways with 16-gauge steel screwed to wood, secure with slide bars or bolts from the inside or padlock.

Air Ducts and Vents, Transoms

Those more than 8 by 12 inches on roof side or rear should have round or flat iron or steel bars secured by nonremovable bolts.

Illustrations 8–2 through 8–4 provide you with solutions for increasing security of existing doors and windows.

Illustration 8–2

EXAMPLE OF TYPICAL OFFICE DOOR CONSTRUCTION

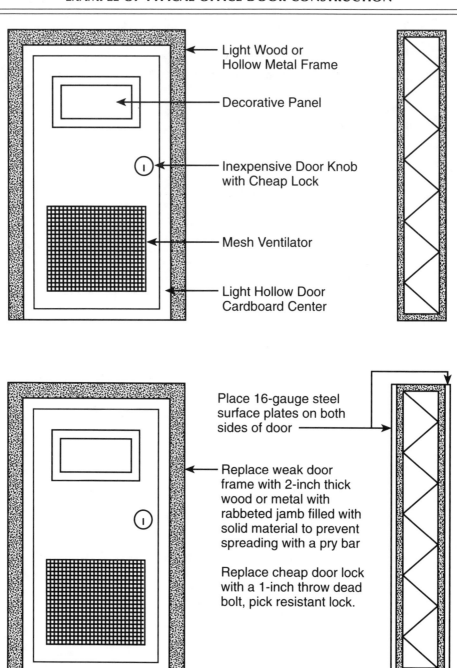

Light Wood or Hollow Metal Frame

Decorative Panel

Inexpensive Door Knob with Cheap Lock

Mesh Ventilator

Light Hollow Door Cardboard Center

Place 16-gauge steel surface plates on both sides of door

Replace weak door frame with 2-inch thick wood or metal with rabbeted jamb filled with solid material to prevent spreading with a pry bar

Replace cheap door lock with a 1-inch throw dead bolt, pick resistant lock.

Illustration 8–3

EXAMPLE OF TYPICAL WINDOW CONSTRUCTION

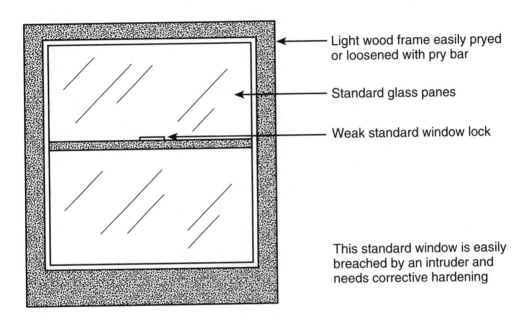

Light wood frame easily pryed or loosened with pry bar

Standard glass panes

Weak standard window lock

This standard window is easily breached by an intruder and needs corrective hardening

Illustration 8–4

HARDENING WINDOWS ON WAREHOUSES, SHOPS, AND OTHER AREAS REQUIRING INCREASED SECURITY ALLOWING VENTILATION

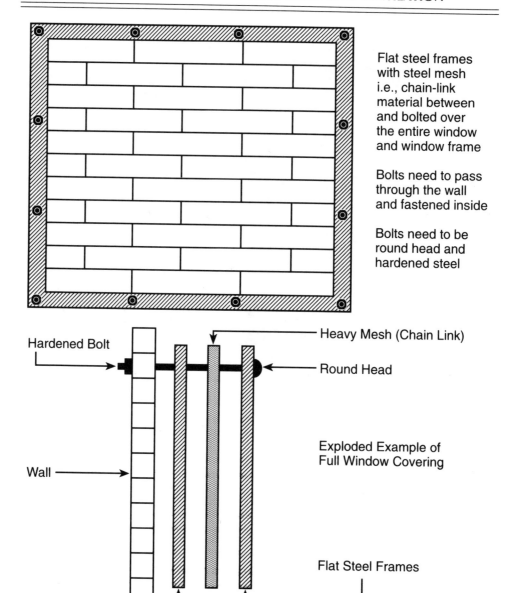

Flat steel frames with steel mesh i.e., chain-link material between and bolted over the entire window and window frame

Bolts need to pass through the wall and fastened inside

Bolts need to be round head and hardened steel

Hardened Bolt

Heavy Mesh (Chain Link)

Round Head

Wall

Exploded Example of Full Window Covering

Flat Steel Frames

SOLVING THE CRASH DOOR PROBLEM

In business workplace environments, federal, state, and local safety laws need your attention. Emergency exits may create a security problem since they must have crash bar doors. There normally will not be any requirement for gaining access from the outside; however, employees or others in a room or building must be able to escape quickly even when smoke or darkness makes seeing impossible. Even the need to turn a doorknob or unlocking a door can cost lives in many situations. The safety crash bar, however, enables anyone reaching the locked door to push forward the bar that immediately releases the locking mechanism.

Security problems spawn when employees or others use the door as a normal exit, maybe with good intentions, as a shortcut to another area. Often, crash bar doors do not relock unless pulled to latch from the inside. The result when an employee exits with this type door and it does not relock is a breach in your security system. It is also possible that an employee opens a crash bar door deliberately so that another unauthorized person can enter the area to carry out a criminal scheme. This type of door also allows unnoticed departure of either authorized or unauthorized persons and encourages a degree of safety for a criminal enterprise operation. Illustration 8–5 shows this type of door viewed from inside and outside. Notice the door needs reinforced steel construction when possible and leaves no opportunity for access from the outside. It is a door reserved for emergency exits only.

A solution for preventing intentional nonemergency use resulting in an unnoticed unlocked door allowing access to unauthorized persons is placing a self-contained alarm that activates when the crash bar is depressed. You may want to save money and buy available kits to install on existing crash bar doors. They have a strong steel alarm box that attaches to the door containing a loud alarm bell or other noise powered by ordinary flashlight batteries. The alarm box is secured with a special key, normally a round, pick-resistant lock to prevent disarming the alarm surreptitiously. A paddle extends tightly behind and below the crash bar so when it is depressed the alarm begins and continues to sound until reset with the special key and the door relocked. A sign needs to be placed on the door warning the alarm will sound when the crash bar is depressed. That discourages employees from using the door as an exit unless a true emergency exists and prevents unauthorized use for criminal enterprise purposes as discussed earlier. Illustration 8–6 shows that type alarm system. You can purchase the entire crash bar assembly with the alarm built in when establishing new installations.

Illustration 8–5

EMERGENCY EXIT CRASH BAR EXAMPLE

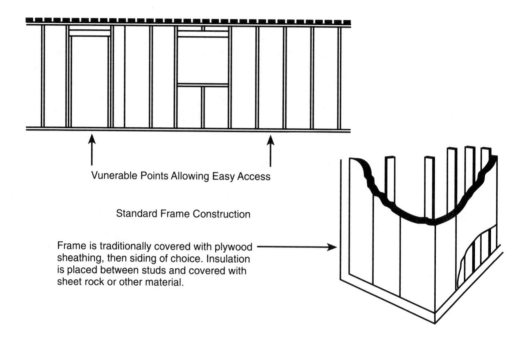

Vunerable Points Allowing Easy Access

Standard Frame Construction

Frame is traditionally covered with plywood
sheathing, then siding of choice. Insulation
is placed between studs and covered with
sheet rock or other material.

Illustration 8–6

VIABLE SECURITY SOLUTION TO CRASH BAR DOORS
SERVING AS EMERGENCY EXITS

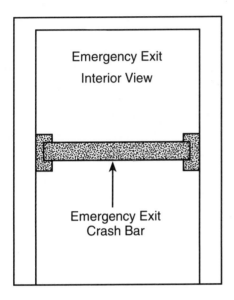

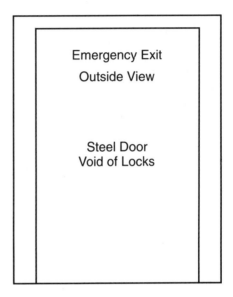

Crash Bar attaches to the locking device that releases when the bar is depressed.

Assessing and Hardening the Walls of Your Company's Structures

At the beginning of Chapter Eight was an example of vulnerability of brick walls. When your evaluation of threats and assessment of security determine a building housing sensitive or valuable property vulnerable through a brick or stone wall, you will need cost-effective solutions.

Wood frame buildings are equally vulnerable, maybe more so because of the ease of sawing or chopping through wood. In many areas, corporate or industrial buildings have a metal frame and thin sheet aluminum or steel. These facilities are popular because of their versatility and the fact that companies achieve large square footage space quickly and with less expense. Although many of these types of buildings serve as offices, a majority remains storage and manufacturing facilities.

Whatever type security challenges your company supplies you, the following guidance helps you to overcome the problem and harden vulnerable walls quickly and stay cost effective. Illustrations 8–7 through 8–12 show the techniques that can work for you.

Illustration 8–7

EXAMPLE OF TYPICAL FRAME CONSTRUCTION

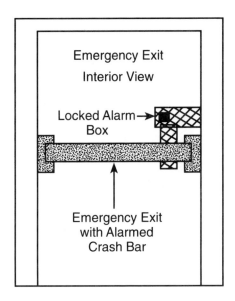

Emergency Exit
Interior View

Locked Alarm→
Box

Emergency Exit
with Alarmed
Crash Bar

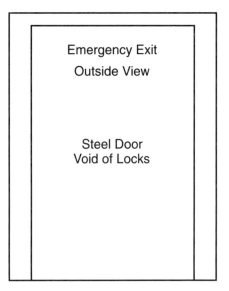

Emergency Exit
Outside View

Steel Door
Void of Locks

Entire crash bar kits with alarms or add-on alarms with a paddle arm are available from a variety of manufacturers in different configurations.

Each crash bar alarm system is self-contained with batteries and loud alarm.

The alarm sounds until turned off with a special key. It prevents either intentional or unintentional unlocking of the door and if that occurs, alarm sounds until turned off with a key and the locking latch returned to a locked position.

Illustration 8–8

STANDARD CONCRETE BLOCK STRUCTURE WALLS

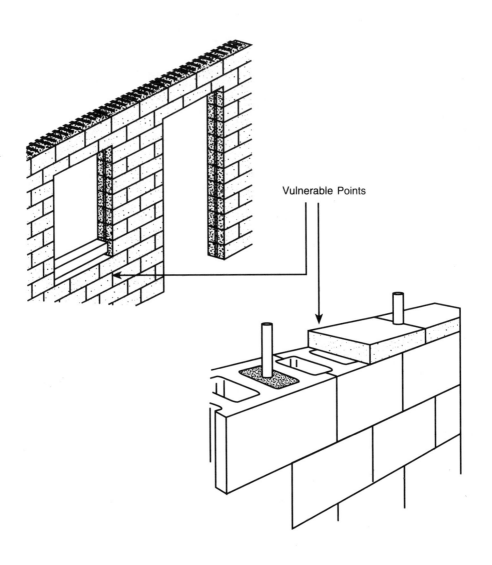

Vulnerable Points

Illustration 8–9

EXAMPLE OF STANDARD BRICK STRUCTURE CONSTRUCTION

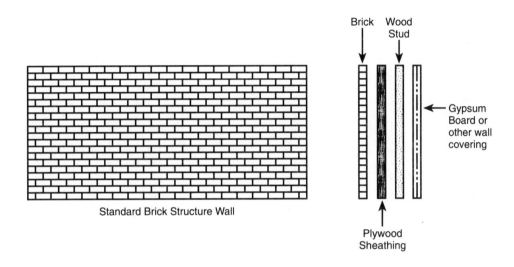

Brick   Wood Stud

Gypsum Board or other wall covering

Standard Brick Structure Wall

Plywood Sheathing

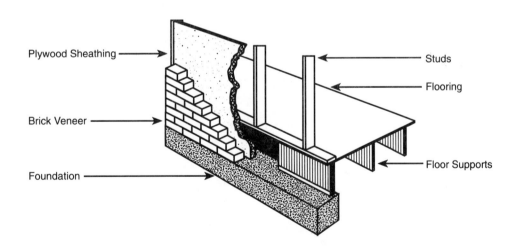

Plywood Sheathing

Brick Veneer

Foundation

Studs

Flooring

Floor Supports

Illustration 8–10

EXAMPLE OF REINFORCED BRICK STRUCTURE WALL CONSTRUCTION

Top of Brick Wall Reinforcement

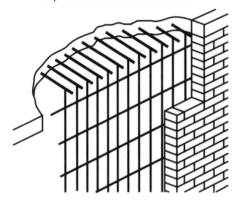

Double Reinforced Brick Wall

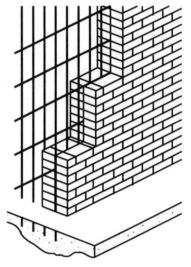

Illustration 8–11

EXAMPLE OF REINFORCED CONCRETE BLOCK WALL CONSTRUCTION

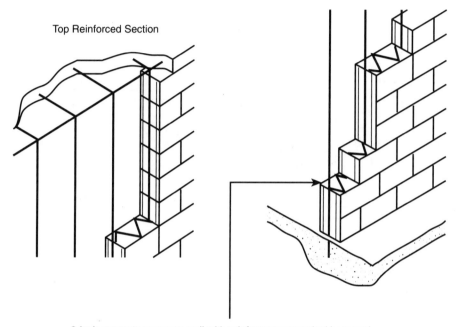

Top Reinforced Section

8-inch concrete masonry wall with reinforcement vertical bars and horizontal cross-rod trussed wire.

Illustration 8–12

VIABLE SOLUTION TO VULNERABLE STRUCTURE WALLS
WITH ADDED LAYER OF SECURITY FENCES

Protective Chain-Link Fence

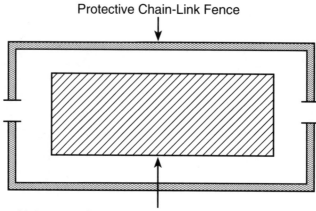

Vulnerable Structure Walls on Important Building

THE ROLE OF ENVIRONMENTAL SECURITY IN DEVELOPMENT OF CORPORATE AND INDUSTRIAL BUILDINGS

Despite the efforts of upgraded and expanded agencies of the criminal justice system, crime in the United States continues to rise both in numbers and in seriousness. Even the value of police as a crime deterrent for corporations and industrial complexes seems to be in question. The existing correctional practices aimed at rehabilitation of offenders are not producing significant achievements. To find approaches with high potential for success in the corporate and industrial crime problem, security professionals are turning to new technologies.

One approach develops through scientific research that affects crime prevention through adjustment of the corporate and industrial building design and environment. This embryonic field applies various technologies to build in a structural environment that discourages and prevents crime from happening. These techniques often involve placement of buildings on project sites, and myriad other environmental management approaches including the structure itself.

One approach that has gained attention throughout the country is called "crime prevention through environmental design" (CPTED). The basic aim of CPTED is forecasting and preventing crime through physical and structural construction planning. It needs the cooperation of security professionals working with corporate and industrial planners, architects, builders, and others to identify and eliminate vulnerable points in structures providing criminal opportunity before building them into the structures. CPTED seeks to identify positive structural and layout designs that can be merged into buildings and projects.

CPTED is many disciplines brought together under one new label, with their focus on crime prevention, largely through creating structures that harden the common weak points before building or during renovation projects.

THE QUESTION OF EXISTING BUILDING CODES AND BUILDING SECURITY CODES WITHIN CPTED

Crime prevention needs an identifiable role in revising existing or developing proposed regulatory building codes. Building, fire, and safety codes need cooperative review between regulatory bodies and security professionals to avoid conflict with implementation of effective crime prevention measures.

Throughout the 50 states there are myriad codes and regulations at the local, state, and national level covering fire, building, and safety. They explain the "do's and don'ts" that affect the lives of everyone. Often, provisions within building codes conflict; occasionally they complement one another. For example, some large cities now have four different electrical codes for alarm systems.

There are two very serious interests to consider when discussing the integration of security provisions into existing building codes. The first concern is the fear that crime prevention measures become a stepchild among the strong fire, electrical, and plumbing provisions, and security might be lost in the verbal foliage of the code. The second concern is the problem of conflict between crime prevention measures and fire, building, and safety codes. For example, security principles might clash with various safety code tenets, and many generate construction expenses more than estimated budgets and aesthetics that do not correspond to conventional building codes. Also, as most security professionals know, the principles of effective security often run counter to safety and fire regulations.

WHAT ROLE YOU CAN PLAY TO CORRECT THE SITUATION

Your participation begins with convincing your company leadership about the advantages and benefits of allowing you to provide your expertise in the construction or renovation planning. You will need to begin documenting your assessments and evaluations now and decide the best ways to enhance the corporate structures to meet excellent security principals. You also need to determine the cost-benefit factors of integrating the security principles at the beginning stages as opposed to the losses and added costs by adding necessary security measures after construction.

APPLICATION AND BENEFITS OF A CRIME IMPACT FORECAST

Becoming involved might be successful when you develop a crime impact forecast as an element of the environmental design approach to corporate and industrial crime prevention. Your forecast can become an effective, invaluable planning instrument used to determine what changes in crime patterns involving your company might result from including security measures in its building and development projects.

Your crime impact forecast is a written statement that projects expected security results of building in security at a new company building or renovation of an existing structure. Your forecasts need to include projections about your company's vulnerability to crime, its past history, and added statistics involving other corporation and industrial problems in the same business or local areas. A guide for drafting your report includes the following categories.

1. Type of crime
2. Time of crime
3. Target of crime

4. Place of crime

5. Tactics of crime

Your forecast might also include (1) the effect of inadequate structural security, creating a need for increased and more costly security forces; (2) the adequacy of the public infrastructure about crime prevention and security provided by police and community surrounding your company; (3) the current assessment of company buildings and facilities, including structural weaknesses and the cost of overcoming them; and (4) the cost, advantage, and benefit to the company for dollars spent on proper structural security built into new projects and renovations.

Eventually, with attentive persistence, your crime impact forecasts will become an important part of all new building and development projects involving your company. Your immediate efforts, coupled with effective liaison with local law enforcement agencies, architects, and other planners are necessary to achieve a goal of built-in structural security. Resolving the questions regarding content, applicability, controls, and other areas evolves through the cooperative efforts of all the professionals and involves convincing your company leadership of the advantages, benefits and cost reductions over the long term as opposed to immediate short-term construction savings by excluding built-in security.

DEVELOPING STRUCTURES WITHIN STRUCTURES

An important part of your involvement in CPTED and developing ongoing crime impact forecasts includes proper construction techniques to house high-security elements of your corporation's operational groups. These elements include structures within the building such as computer centers, vaults for storing information, research and development centers, your security offices, and others. The following information focuses on computer centers; however, the problems and techniques apply to other types of important company operational elements.

Computer centers are important to the corporate and industrial operations, often critical to the company's survival in the business world. Your physical security considerations include such elements as the physical location of the computer facility within corporate structures. Important elements you need to consider include the following:

Physical Access Control

You must determine how easy or difficult it is for an intruder to reach the computer center or other important operational area within the structure. You need to view both interior and exterior possibilities. For example, older buildings often have external fire escapes that essential but create a vulnerable breach in security. Other areas to consider include large heating and cooling ducts or thin walls separating the high-priority area from conventional offices that have no attentive security needs.

Fire Prevention and Procedures

Fires create hazards for human safety and serve as effective techniques for persons who want to do harm to the company. A computer center or other important operational element might easily be shut down or destroyed by fire caused by an intruder. Your security responsibilities include ensuring all possibilities within a structure contain adequate countermeasures to prevent entry or damage, with the threat of fire included in that plan.

Power Source Security

Power sources gain importance since computer centers and other elements do not function without electrical power. Beyond sudden power outages causing computer systems to lose data, you need to consider the failure might create an opportunity for an intruder to cause further damage. Often, companies rely on electronic equipment to ensure security, and the elimination of power not only jeopardizes the security of your computer center, it might allow intruders access otherwise denied.

Flood and Water Protection

Floods create problems each year, often in unlikely places. Your total security system needs to consider the possibility for all types of corporate or industrial security. However, water protection might include the threat of fire that triggers internal sprinkler systems. An entire computer center is easily destroyed by automatic sprinkler systems that may be set off by an intruder or disgruntled employee. You need procedures and fast response to sprinkler shut-off valves coupled with a sprinkler system not vulnerable to this type of problem.

The Handling and Storage of Magnetic Media

Theft of data generated by computers often happens intentionally and unintentionally when handling or storage brings disks or tapes in contact with metal or storage not well thought out is located near steel structural beams, columns, or other metal materials used and often hidden within the walls.

Disposal Procedures

Data theft can occur when data are determined to be of no further use and a disposal process takes place. A person determined to steal data or cause further problems might switch the data scheduled for disposal with important information, or when printed data are being removed from the center for disposal merely include current information that is separated later at another location.

The examples deal with data processing property and capital equipment and the physical threats to the continuing operation of the company's computer facility. The component parts of the facility need tight security calling for your creation of a "structure within a structure." Your security planning needs to identify the critical areas within the internal structure; each might require similar but different security techniques. Areas to consider include

1. The computer room.
2. The data control and conversion area.
3. The data file storage area.
4. The forms storage area.
5. The maintenance area.
6. The mechanical equipment room.
7. Plans and procedures supplying adequate physical protection and access control.

The controls you establish to protect the computer center and related elements include:

   a. Prevention and detection of theft
   b. Prevention of vandalism
   c. Prevention of employee, visitor, or intruder sabotage
   d. Corporate or industrial espionage (competitor intelligence)
   e. Civil disorder threats
   f. Forced intrusions
   g. Physical barriers at doors, windows, and other openings
   h. Security officer presence as appropriate

Your minimum access control measures need to include protection of the center with both conventional or electronic door locks, supervision by security officers over movement of people and materials, administrative procedures such as sign-in logs, identification cards or badges, property passes, shipping and receiving forms, and other regulations as needed.

For almost every data processing situation, including hardware, software, or data loss risk, there is an insurance policy available. Developing special policies to cover the complex environment surrounding a data processing facility enable compensation for your company when losses result from physical exposures such as fire, flood, and windstorm damage. Because each organization and its data processing facility usually has unique requirements and considerations, the appropriate insurance coverage needs negotiated coverage. However, important for that coverage, your company's negotiation leverage, and importantly the ultimate cost factors your company pays, often rely largely on your effective security procedures. Insurance coverage representatives apply a risk analysis formula to identify threats, countermeasures, and procedures involving the computer center's structure within the structure coupled with the other elements noted. When your security is inclusive and adequate response is programmed into the security response to threats, the risk factor is lower. When the risk factor is lower, insurance coverage is greater and cost is decreased.

THE IMPORTANCE OF THE COMPUTER CENTER LOCATION WITHIN CORPORATE OR INDUSTRIAL BUILDINGS

Your company's computer facility needs an area not congested with pedestrian, air, or truck traffic. It is preferable for the facility location either in a separate building designed for computers or within an existing building in a separate area. A dramatic reduction of damage risk comes from the proper location of the computer facility including avoidance of

1. Outside walks
2. Hazardous areas where fire can spread
3. Low ground subject to flooding
4. Ground floors making the computer center visible from the outside and allowing easier intrusions

To prevent damage from external fires or explosions or from weather and intruders, your company's computer room and storage libraries must not be close to outer walls of a building. Avoid locating the computer center near boiler rooms or other potentially dangerous areas or near sources of electromagnetic radiation such as large transformers or generators.

Controlling Access Effectively

Access to your company computer center needs restrictive procedures limited to employees needed to operate the equipment, supervise the operation, deliver and pick up material in the area, and perform maintenance on the equipment. User personnel, programmers, analysts, clerical personnel, and visitors need to stay outside the actual machine operating areas unless authorized by an appropriate supervisor of operations or the person in charge of production control. Areas where these persons work may be within the computer center but in separate areas. These factors need consideration in the design planning for your company's computer center, or the "structure within a structure."

The computer facility must be a restricted access area with admittance through a single entrance with other doors used only as emergency exits. Earlier in this chapter, I discussed effective security measures for controlling emergency exits with protected crash bar doors; the same method applies to your company's computer facility. Employees must wear security badges while working in the computer center. The best security includes different colored and distinct badges for each of the areas within the center. With compartmentalization, the center becomes far easier to control, keeping employees in the areas they are supposed to be in and enables fast identification of unauthorized employees in the various sections within the center. When employees working in the computer center no longer require access to the area, change from one section to another, or leave employment, ensure you recover all badges, keys, identification cards. Visitors who need temporary identification should have badges that differ significantly in appearance from employee badges. Their distinctive badge and color readily tells employees in the center that the person is a visitor and must be escorted. Visitors also need your control with a requirement they sign in on a log showing time in, time out, and purpose of visit coupled with the security officer's signature having authorizing entry.

CONSTRUCTION CONSIDERATIONS FOR THE COMPANY COMPUTER CENTER

The walls enclosing the computer center need to extend from the structural floor to the true ceiling and the doors kept closed to provide added protection. The area needs to exclude windows when possible with all ducts for air conditioning, heat, and ventilation secured to prevent intrusions. Walls, floors, ceiling, and doors need reinforced hardening to prevent opening that might be used by determined intruders.

Another access control technique is called the "person trap." This is a small room or passageway between two doors that contains only one person at a time. When a person entering a restricted area such as the computer center, goes through the outer door, it locks behind him or her, and must be locked before the second door will unlock. Identification and verification of authorization of the person entering the "person trap" is made by employees or security officers through a glass window or on a closed-circuit television monitor. After making positive identification, the inner door is opened from inside by the authorizing person permitting entry to the computer center. When identification of a person in the "person trap" is questioned, both doors remain locked until security officers determine the identity and purpose surrounding the attempted entry.

To determine that your security for the company's computer center is sufficient, you will need to develop a checklist to review this structure within a structure. Illustration 8–13 provides a ready-to-use checklist you might consider for your computer center physical security test.

Illustration 8–13

COMPUTER CENTER OR FACILITY PHYSICAL SECURITY SURVEY

Yes	No	N/A	Item Surveyed
☐	☐	☐	Is the physical location of the computer center adequate and secured effectively?
			Do minimum security procedures include
☐	☐	☐	Security officer posts?
☐	☐	☐	Door controls (alarms, locks, other)?
☐	☐	☐	Is surveillance of the area adequate?
☐	☐	☐	Are security procedures adequate to prevent unauthorized entry by visitors, disgruntled employees, or militants?
☐	☐	☐	Are all employees or visitors entering the center required to wear a security badge issued and controlled by the security department?
☐	☐	☐	Are procedures for issuance, modification, and retrieval of identification badges in place and followed rigidly?
☐	☐	☐	Do company policies exist for determining level of access badges issued to persons?
☐	☐	☐	Are procedures in place to handle lost, stolen, or forgotten security badges?
☐	☐	☐	Are all visitors logged in and out by a security officer?
☐	☐	☐	Are access controls in the building housing the computer center effective as a preemptive barrier before reaching the computer center?
☐	☐	☐	Are there adequate controls over the removal of materials from the computer center?
☐	☐	☐	Do procedures exist for disposal of confidential printed materials and are the procedures enforced?
☐	☐	☐	Are procedures in place to prevent unauthorized entry to the tape and disk library?
☐	☐	☐	Are there a telephone and a list of emergency numbers convenient to the security officer and supervisors in the computer center?
☐	☐	☐	Are assigned security officers aware of emergency responsibilities and procedures?
☐	☐	☐	Do you routinely review the computer center security system and plan for adequacy to meet changing conditions?
☐	☐	☐	Does your company consult with you when planning changes to the physical facilities affecting the computer center?

Illustration 8–13 (continued)

☐ ☐ ☐ Is there a procedure to follow to protect the integrity of your security system if an employee loses a key or badge?

☐ ☐ ☐ Is compliance with security standards, procedures, and guidelines readily acceptable?

☐ ☐ ☐ Is the computer center designated by the company as a "restricted area"?

☐ ☐ ☐ Is there a security officer on duty at the entrance to the computer center to monitor access during working hours?

☐ ☐ ☐ Are visitors prevented from entering the computer center after business hours?

☐ ☐ ☐ Are employees prevented from entering the computer center after business hours without special written and verified written authorization from an authorized person?

☐ ☐ ☐ Are employees issued and required to wear security badges showing which area of the computer center they are authorized to enter?

☐ ☐ ☐ Are locks and encoding equipment at entrances changed periodically?

☐ ☐ ☐ Are pass-through windows used in the computer center input and output areas instead of allowing outsiders into these areas?

☐ ☐ ☐ Is a log maintained of all deliveries to and pickups from the computer center?

☐ ☐ ☐ If so, do the logs show the date, time, description of materials, employee name, and name of authorizing person?

☐ ☐ ☐ Are all service entrances to the computer center locked always and opened only by a security officer from the inside?

☐ ☐ ☐ Are computer operations effectively supervised to ensure that operators do not use computer equipment and time to run jobs without authorization?

☐ ☐ ☐ Have you developed procedures to cope with fire, flooding, bomb threats, loss or compromise of sensitive information, or unauthorized intrusions?

☐ ☐ ☐ Do security officers have a procedural checklist at their computer center post?

Does the Security Officer Procedural Checklist for Emergencies Include

☐ ☐ ☐ Shut down of electricity, gas, and water?

Illustration 8–13 (continued)

☐ ☐ ☐ Closing fire doors, locking cabinets, using fire extinguishers, and evacuating the computer center and the building?

☐ ☐ ☐ Securing data and equipment when necessary?

☐ ☐ ☐ Procedures for handling security checks at the close of a business day?

☐ ☐ ☐ Procedures for verifying that a genuine emergency situation exists?

YOUR SECURITY DEPARTMENT—ANOTHER STRUCTURE WITHIN A STRUCTURE

The location of your security department or offices depends on the size and layout of the corporate or industrial complex you are protecting. The objective is efficient control of the security force and adequate security of its important activities. Your security headquarters needs to be the control point for matters about physical security of the company and its facilities. It is also the center for monitoring protective alarm and communication systems. Illustration 8–14 provides you with a general concept of how your security center needs to be constructed either in a separate building or within another structure. Since the security headquarters is the center of protection for company property and personnel, its security needs to be hardened to the maximum extent possible.

Illustration 8–14

GENERAL CONCEPT DIAGRAM OF A CORPORATE OR INDUSTRIAL SECURITY DEPARTMENT LAYOUT

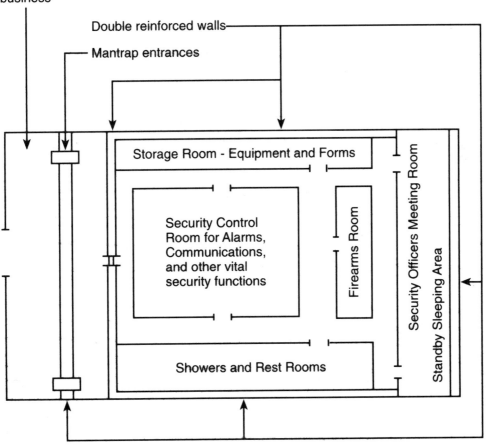

Entry point for company employees, i.e., ID cards security badges and other business

Double reinforced walls

Mantrap entrances

Storage Room - Equipment and Forms

Security Control Room for Alarms, Communications, and other vital security functions

Firearms Room

Security Officers Meeting Room

Standby Sleeping Area

Showers and Rest Rooms

QUICK REFERENCE REVIEW AND GUIDE

- Consider Your Situation and Accurately Access the Security Threat

- Identify, Recognize, and Evaluate Your Real Problems

- Develop and Use Checklists for Analyzing Your Company's Structural Strengths and Weaknesses

- Harden Structural Security on Vulnerable Buildings with Creative Solutions

- Layer Your Structural Security

- Get Involved in Environmental Security for Your Company's New Construction or Renovation of Older Buildings

- Use Effective Techniques of Crime Prevention Through Environmental Design Whenever Possible to Enhance Your Company's Structural Security

- Integrate CPTED in Your Local Building Codes

- Apply Principles of Crime Impact Forecasts to Your CPTED Efforts

- Develop Structures Within Structures Effectively

9 Lock and Key Systems Management

The lock originated in the Near East. The oldest known example comes from the ruins of the palace of Khorsabad near Nineveh. Possibly 4,000 years old, it is similar to the modern-day pin tumbler lock.

Despite their quality or cost, locks remain delay devices and not positive bars to entry. Many ingenious lock systems continue to be developed, but equally ingenious techniques have been developed to open them. Some locks need considerable time and expert manipulation for covert opening, but all succumb to force and the proper tools.

The important factors of locks in your security system provide you with a "layer" of protection. Locks are vulnerable to criminal enterprise just as are other security safeguards. However, when you view them as a "layer" as opposed to a "total solution," you will perceive and apply the use of locks with considerable advantage within your security system.

SEVEN COMMON TYPES OF LOCKING DEVICES

The measured protection afforded by a well-built lock depends on the resistance of the locking mechanism to picking, manipulation, or drilling. The types of locks you choose for your corporate or industrial security needs depend on the security level needed, including what must be locked and your budget. The following concepts provide a starting point in the discussion of locks. There are seven common types of locking devices.

1. Key Locks

The design of a basic cylinder lock provides you with a measure of adequate security. It is the most used lock for most corporate and industrial security roles, and choosing the ones supplying the best protection on a cost-benefit basis is often difficult. Each manufacturer claims that its design is best, and many boldly say theirs withstand the most ingenious techniques of opening without the proper key. Brass or steel is the average construction of a cylinder lock with five pin sets and springs, although some later models use six pin sets to make picking efforts difficult.

The easiest locks to defeat include the most commonly available and used locks. The primary reasons begin with reducing expenses and standardization. Locks and keys represent a considerable investment in a corporation or industrial complex. One common error in choosing locks is a perception that a costly lock offers greater protection. However, placing an expensive, pick-resistant lock in a door needs your examination of how easy the intruder can breach door, not the lock. There is also consideration of other ways of entry to a building, room, or area, allowing the intruder to bypass the costly, difficult lock. When you find other ways to enter, spending significant amounts of company money for expensive locks makes little sense.

The time needed to defeat most locks can vary from a few seconds to an hour or more for the nonprofessional not adept at picking locks. Experts pick most key locks in a few minutes. The possibility of the loss and compromise of a key and the prospect of making an impression should also play a role when you are determining the security value of a key-type lock. One problem experienced with corporate and industrial key locks is routine issuance of keys to authorized persons. The person understandably thinks about a possibility of losing the key and obtains a duplicate. Often that person considers he or she might forget the key when coming to work and makes another copy to place in a car used to commute each day. Maybe after losing one of the keys, the person makes another duplicate key to replace the one lost. It is not uncommon for issued keys to multiply and equally common for criminal enterprise to exploit that problem. Many illegal entries happen with keys that leaves suspicion of theft squarely on an employee instead of the real intruder. Criminals also might find ways to make an impression from a key as the one left in a car being repaired. Not only can the person obtain a copy from an impression, but an experienced lock-picker can use it to determine how to gain fast entry using picks gaining knowledge about how the lock operates from the impression.

2. Conventional Combination Locks

A skillful manipulator can open this type lock quickly. He or she can determine the settings of the tumblers on a common three-position dial-type combination lock through the sense of touch and hearing. Although the manipulations of some combination locks call for several hours, a skillful manipulator can open an average conventional combination lock in a few minutes.

Combination locks have merit, but like a key lock also poses many security problems. For example, like making duplicate keys, the user writes down the lock combination in several places to avoid the embarrassment of forgetting the code. Another problem results from an observer watching an authorized person open a combination lock and remembering the numbers.

3. Manipulation-Resistant Combination Locks

The design of a manipulation-resistant lock stems from a concept that prevents the opening lever from contact with the tumblers until setting the correct combination. This lock furnishes a high degree of protection for corporate or industrial information and sensitive areas not regularly in constant surveillance by security officers. Its primary weakness is the security of the combination.

4. Other Combination Locks

Combination locks with four or more tumblers probably need your consideration for most unobserved corporate and industrial environments. Remembering that locks are primarily a delaying device, not absolute security, a thought to consider when choosing a lock is how long a delay it provides. The delay allows your other security techniques, for example, walking or mobile security patrols, lighting, sentry dog patrols and others, to play a role.

5. Relocking Devices

A relocking device on a safe or vault door furnishes an added degree of security against forcible entry. The device appreciably increases the difficulty of opening a combination lock container calling for cumbersome punching, drilling, or blocking the lock or its parts. It is the type recommended for heavy safes and vaults. An intruder needs equipment, makes noise, and creates betraying odors detected by security officers. As noted earlier, this type lock provides excellent means of delaying intruders while other techniques reveal his or her presence.

6. Interchangeable Cores

The interchangeable core system uses a lock with a core removed and replaced by another core using a different key. Its main features include

- Fast replacement of cores when necessary, instantly changing the matching of locks and keys. This valuable feature minimizes compromise of your company's security.
- Keying of all locks to a general locking system.
- Economy, because of reduction in maintenance costs and new lock expense.

- Flexibility and tailoring to the company's needs.
- Simplified record keeping.

Your choice of core locks provides excellent security management with long-term cost-benefit advantages. A tip for choosing a core lock system offering greater layered protection includes those keyed for maximum key controls. Some lock manufacturers have designed locks that have special internal mechanics making picking or other techniques difficult and time consuming. These models also have specially engineered keys that cannot be duplicated by anyone other than the manufacturer. Even having an impression is of little use because of the engineering process. Although the initial cost is significant, you will save money and enhance security in the years to come.

7. Cypher Locks

A cypher lock is a digital (push buttons numbered from 1 through 9) combination door locking device used to deny area access to any person not authorized or cleared for entry into a specific company area. This type lock operates on the same principle as a combination lock, except that it is more difficult to overcome. Its weaknesses remain primarily with the person controlling the combination.

UNDERSTANDING THE PROS AND CONS OF LOCK SECURITY

In the competitive marketplace of security equipment, each manufacturer strives to develop a better product supplying greater security and stronger sales to security managers. However, as I've noted earlier, a lock is only a part of your "layered" system, not the ultimate solution as it's often portrayed. Often, a cheap lock serves you with the same amount of protection as a costly high-tech lock, depending on your company environment. For example, placing costly locks on doors that can be kicked or easily pried open does not increase security and raises eyebrows about your security management skill. Much of your security management development to make wise, cost-benefit, and protection-enhanced choices includes understanding or rethinking the role locks play in your total security system. The following information provides you with many key elements needed to make prudent choices.

1. Combination Locks

This popular type of lock works effectively in padlocks, vaults, and door locks. The combination lock evolved from the "letter lock" used in England at the beginning of the seventeenth century. Originally, use of the letter locks served only for padlocks and trick boxes. In the last half of the nineteenth century, their use developed for safes and strong-room doors, and they proved to be the most secure protection. The added security happens from the possible combinations of letters or numbers, almost infinite, and the absence of keyholes into which an explosive charge might be placed.

The operating principle of most combination locks is a simple one. The operator uses numbers (or other symbols) as reference points to enable him or her to align tumblers so that the locking parts of the lock can move to an unlocked position.

Illustration 9–1 represents a three-tumbler combination lock mechanism. (A combination lock has the same number tumblers as there are numbers in the combination. Therefore, a lock having three numbers in the combination has three tumblers; four numbers, four tumblers; and so on.) In Illustration 9–1, "A" represents the dial, which is firmly fixed to the shaft "E." Any movement of the dial is directly imparted to the shaft. Letters "B," "C," and "D" identify the tumblers.

Illustration 9–1

EXAMPLES OF THREE-TUMBLER COMBINATION LOCK SYSTEMS

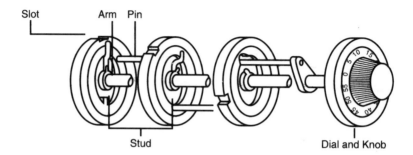

Three-Tumbler Combination Safe Lock

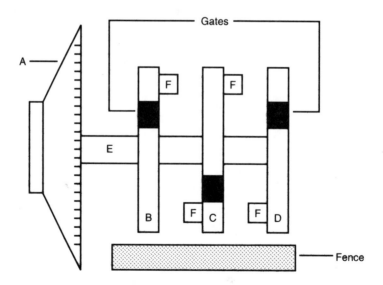

How a Three-Tumbler Combination Lock Works

Each tumbler resembles a disc with a notch cut into its circumference. The technical term for this notch is a gate. "D" represents the driver tumbler. The driver, like the dial, is firmly fixed to the shaft so that, when the dial moves, the driver tumbler also moves. "B" and "C" are called rider tumblers. They merely rotate around the shaft. The movement of the dial cannot immediately cause corresponding movement to the rider tumblers.

To operate the lock, you must align the gates with the fence; when the fence is free to move into the space made by the gates, the lock will operate. First, rotate the dial in one direction several times. The driver follows the dial and within a 360–degree turn, and the drive pin "F" on the driver comes into contact with the drive pin on rider "C," making "C" rotate in the same direction. As the dial continues to turn in the same direction, the drive pin on "C" contacts the drive pin on "B, and then all the tumblers are nested (that is, all tumblers are going in the same direction).

You then stop the dial when the first number of the combination comes into alignment with the index mark on the front of the lock. This will align the gate on tumbler "B" with the fence. You then reverse direction and rotate the dial one less turn to the next number of the combination. This allows "B" to stay in alignment while "C" comes into alignment. Changing direction and turning the dial one less turn again bring "D" into alignment and the lock will now open. Illustration 9–2 shows gates and fence in open position.

Illustration 9–3 shows improper alignment of all gates and fence. That happens by applying the wrong combination, preventing operation of the lock.

Illustration 9–2

EXAMPLE OF COMBINATION LOCK GATES ALIGNED AND FENCE IN OPEN POSITION

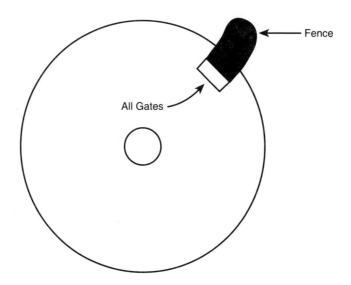

Example of Combination Lock Gates Aligned and Fence in Open Position

Illustration 9–3

EXAMPLE OF COMBINATION LOCK WITH GATES NOT ALIGNED

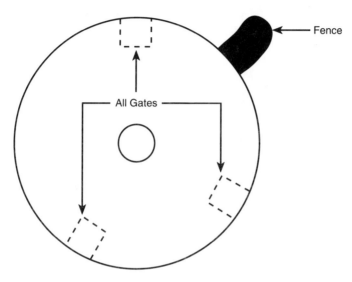

Example of Combination Lock with Gates Not Aligned

To determine possible combinations on a lock, raise the total number of reference points on the dial to the power equal to tumblers. For example, consider a lock that has 40 numbers on the dial and a three-number combination. The three-number combination indicates there are three tumblers in the lock. Therefore, combinations possible is 40^3 or 64,000. How can someone find one combination out of 64,000 in less than an hour?

On inexpensive combination padlocks you will find a serial number stamped on the back. Code books (available from locksmith supply houses) have the lock serial number, and you find the combination for that lock. This is one easy technique an intruder uses to neutralize the combination lock. Incidentally, a code for some Master brand combination padlocks is available at low cost from major lock suppliers. A primary weakness of inexpensive locks is tolerance between the widths of the gates and the widths of the fence. That tolerance allows some leeway for the combination numbers. For example, you can open the lock with manipulation and applying the exact combination is not critical. If the exact combination is 1-3-8, for example, the lock might also open on 2-4-7 or 1-4-9. Therefore, manipulation calls for the intruder to try every other combination instead of every combination. This cuts the intruder's time to overcome the lock greatly.

There are still other ways to neutralize small combination padlocks. The bolt (that part engaging the shackle) is spring loaded in most models. A sharp blow on part of the lock will make the bolt to jump to the blow. When done properly, the bolt disengages from the shackle and the lock will open. A common term for that technique is "rapping." The combination padlock with the spring-operated bolt also opens by shimming with a small piece of thin metal known as a sneaker. This technique is a quiet, simple, and fast operation.

Manipulation of a combination safe lock is possible, often with the same success experienced on simple locks. However, it is not as easy as it appears on TV and in the movies. Most big combination locks use very close tolerances between gates and fences, balanced tumblers, and false gates to foil surreptitious burglary attempts unless the intruder has the proper skill, knowledge, and equipment.

Combination locks and padlocks with changeable combinations are your best cost-benefit technique of using combination locks. However, all good systems need attentive management to sustain the advantage. Changing lock combinations needs to stay under your strict control and be managed with accurate record keeping. Combinations need changing regularly on a routine basis, and each time there is a change in employee status. You must retain the change keys in the security office and keep a log of changes. The best security occurs when the lock changes happen without the authorized user knowing the time or date of change. In situations especially concerning competitor intelligence, another unauthorized employee might have obtained the combination to a container with sensitive information. If an employee interested in or intending to steal information knows when the lock combination is scheduled for change, an unauthorized person, although an employee, can copy valuable information on a weekend or at night under the guise of working on company business. He or she then delivers or sells the information to a competitor under a prior arrangement. Unannounced lock combination changes might prevent the loss of information or other valuable items.

2. Warded Locks

While combination locks are popular, key-operated locks are even more popular, primarily because they are often cheaper and easier to maintain from a business point of view. One type of key-operated lock is called the warded lock. Wards serve as obstructions in the key way (keyhole) and inside the lock to prevent all except the properly cut key from entering or working the lock shown in Illustration 9–4. The key must have the proper ward cuts to bypass the wards in the key way or in the lock. There are keys made to bypass most wards in any warded lock. These will commonly be called skeleton keys. However, a skeleton key is not absolutely necessary to bypass a warded lock. A piece of wire bent to the right shape bypasses the wards and makes contact with the bolt of the lock.

You will see warded locks and padlocks in older buildings and storage sheds. The locks are more for show and offer very little security. Specifications of most ward locks include laminated metal, and to the unaware might appear strong and secure. Their mechanical operation becomes identifiable by a free-turning key way. An object, such as a nail file inserted into the free-turning key way will turn the key way but not operate the lock. The key way is simply a guide for the key, not a functional part of the lock. However, when you insert it too far into the lock, the tool will no longer turn the key way.

Illustration 9–5 shows a warded padlock. Characteristics of this type of lock include the shackle being secured not by a bolt but by a flat spring. The leaves of the spring compress on the sides of the shackle and engage a notch on each side of the shackle. To open the lock, you need only to spread the leaves of the spring. You do that with the proper key, or use a specially designed key, or use an ingeniously bent paper clip.

Any lock relying entirely on wards for a delay factor is not a good lock for security purposes. Most modern locks use wards to curtail insertion of unauthorized keys; however, the locks have other security features besides the wards.

Illustration 9–4

EXAMPLES OF INTERIOR WARD AND MATCHING WARD CUTS IN KEYS

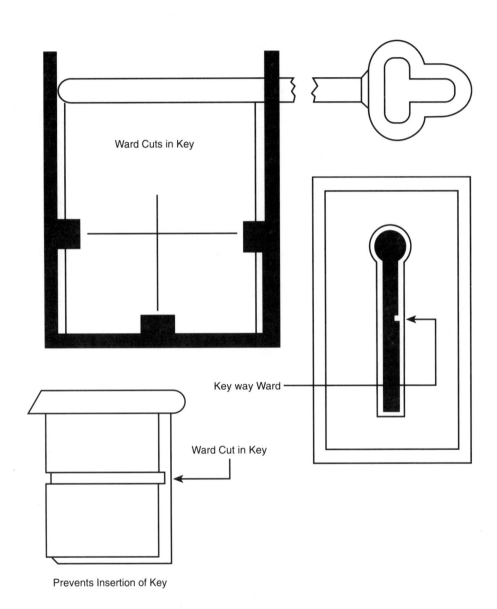

Ward Cuts in Key

Key way Ward

Ward Cut in Key

Prevents Insertion of Key

Illustration 9–5

WARDED PADLOCK WITH SPRING SECURED SHACKLE

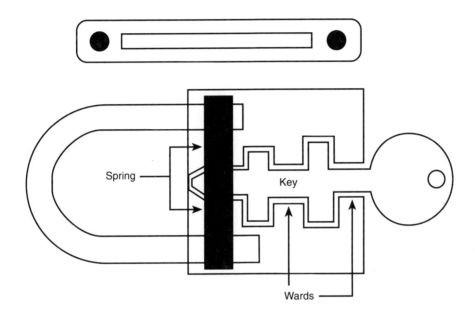

Open View of Spring with Key Inserted

3. Key Operated Wafer or Disc Tumbler Locks

Generally, these devices provide more security than warded locks. You will find wafer locks on most automobiles, desks, and file cabinets and in some padlocks. The description of the operation principle for a wafer or disc tumbler lock follows. This lock includes several wafers in the core or plug of the lock (the part that turns). The wafers are under spring tension and protrude outside the diameter of the plug into a shell formed by the body of the lock (see Illustration 9–6, locked), keeping the plug from turning and keeping the lock locked. Insertion of the proper key makes the wafers to be withdrawn from the shell into the diameter of the plug, allowing the plug to turn (Illustration 9–6, unlocked). A wafer lock in a door or a desk, has an easily shimmed spring-operated bolt.

If used in a padlock and has a spring-operated bolt, it is easily rapped open. When used in a vehicle or if it contains a dead bolt (a bolt that operates only when the key plug turns) it is opened easily by picking.

Illustration 9–6

EXAMPLE OF WAFER LOCK OPERATIONS

Wafer Clear of Shell; Lock Unlocked

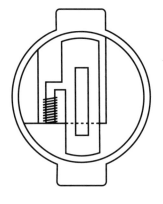

Wafer Locked in Shell, Lock Locked

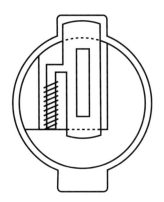

4. Pin Tumbler Locks

This lock has widespread application and is used extensively in commercial, corporate, and industrial security. The pin tumbler lock generally has greater security than do warded or wafer tumbler locks. The pin tumbler lock mechanism uses pins, moved by a key. It opens using a shear line obtained when the key turns the plug (see Illustration 9–7).

You can use pin tumbler locks in a variety of applications such as padlocks, door locks, switches, machinery, and so on. The padlocks are overcome when the bolts are spring operated by rapping or shimming open. In other devices, such as door locks, when the pin tumbler lock operates a spring-operated bolt, the bolt is easily shimmed open. Shimming a door lock open is often called "loiding," derived from the word "celluloid," a material commonly used in this technique.

Illustration 9-7

EXAMPLE OF PIN TUMBLER LOCK OPERATION

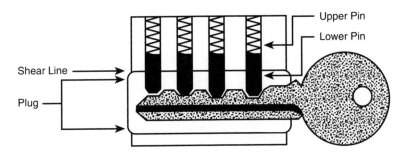

Pin Tumbler Lock – Wrong Key

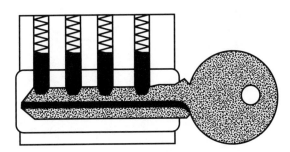

Pin Tumbler Lock – Correct Key

The dead bolt, as used within wafer locks in a pin tumbler lock, prevents rapping or shimming. The plug of the lock must turn to operate the dead bolt. When a deadbolt feature is present the lock must be picked to open or overcome. Some locks feature a secondary deadlocking latch bolt (Illustration 9-8). When properly adjusted so when the door is closed the bolt is fully extended into the strike (recess for the bolt in the door frame), and the secondary bolt is fully depressed, the secondary deadlocking latch bolt prevents loiding or shimming. You can effectively use this type of lock on office doors of nonsensitive corporate or industrial areas—it is low-cost security.

Illustration 9–8

EXAMPLE OF A SECONDARY DEAD LOCKING LATCHBOLT

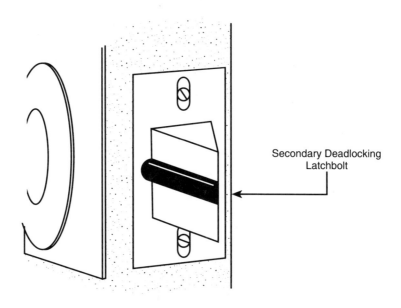

Secondary Deadlocking
Latchbolt

The principal operations of pin tumbler locks enable the technique of mastering. Mastering allows the use of several differently cut keys to operate the same lock. In mastering (except for one or two makes of pin tumbler locks), the pins are segmented by splits that allow several possible pin alignments at the lock's shear line (see Illustration 9–9). Because of this feature, mastering makes picking easier for the intruder.

Illustration 9–9

DIAGRAM OF MASTER SPLIT IN PIN TUMBLER LOCK

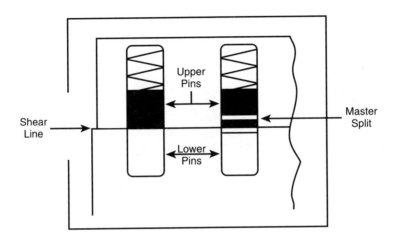

To counter master lock susceptibility to picking, a mushroom or spool tumbler or pin is available for use in the lock. This pin feature makes picking more difficult because picking tools tend to cant the tumbler sideways and bind it at the shear line (Illustration 9–10). Effective use of the mushroom-type pin applies also to nonmastered locks.

Illustration 9–10

EXAMPLE OF MUSHROOM TUMBLER ACTION DURING PICKING

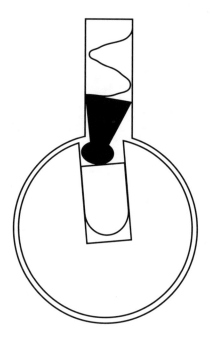

5. Lever Locks

Some locks use a system of levers under spring tension to provide security. The properly cut key moves levers so the gates will align with the fence, allowing movement of the bolt (see Illustration 9–11). You can use lever locks on some door locks and padlocks. One advantage of large lever locks includes a pick-resistant quality since construction of the lock includes internal springs of considerable pressure to resist picking. However, with knowledge and skill, the lever lock is susceptible to picking. When the lever lock contains a spring-operated bolt, it is surreptitiously opened by either shimming or rapping.

Illustration 9–11

EXAMPLE OF LEVER LOCK MECHANISM

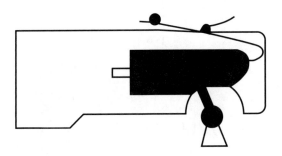

THE ART AND SCIENCE OF LOCK PICKING

People create locks; other people defeat them. So it is foolish to state a lock is pickproof. A lock might be termed pick resistant, and that is a relative term. In reality, picking locks is a simple task, based on a few principles, including the construction characteristics of the lock. Picks provide a common means of opening locks surreptitiously. Purchase of lock picks is not restricted; they are easily available from locksmith supply houses and a variety of mail-order catalogs. There is no requirement for credentials to buy professional quality lock picks. With a few materials easily found, lock picks can be created at home or fashioned out of materials at work. Many locks, as those found in office desks, file cabinets, and others will open quickly using lock picks fashioned from ordinary paper clips. After completing the theft, an intruder can also relock the breached lock with lock picks, including the paper clip version.

Illustration 9–12 shows a typical professional lock picking kit. The basic picking tools include the tension wrench and the pick. Both are necessary. The tension wrench enables light pressure in a rotary motion to the key plug of the lock. The tension tools aid in finding the bindings or locking tumblers of the lock and hold them in place as the pick moves each tumbler to the shear line. The pick will move the tumblers, one at a time, to the shear line. When all tumblers are aligned properly with the shear line, the lock opens. Closing the lock with picks involves the same process.

Illustration 9–12

EXAMPLE OF A PROFESSIONAL LOCK PICKING SET

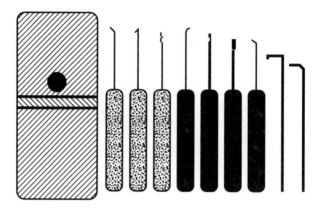

Picking a lock takes practice, skill, and a little luck. However, despite the ease in picking most locks, intruders normally use other methods to bypass locks. Traditionally, they cut locks, pull them apart, blast them with light explosive charges, or pry them off the door. In some doors, an intruder simply spreads the door frame away from the door to release the bolt from the strike. You can discourage that action using locks with long bolts (to 1 inch) and by using grouting around the door frame (this holds the frame rigidly).

Sometimes intruders saw the bolts of padlocks or door locks by putting a saw blade in the space between the door and the frame or sawing the padlock shank. Some door lock bolts and good quality padlocks have hardened steel in the middle of the bolts. This foils the saw attack because the saw cannot get a bite. Intruders often breach padlock hasps because of improper installation, allowing easy removal of the screws holding them on the door.

ADVANTAGES OF DEAD BOLT LATCHES

The dead bolt latch is available for use on almost any door lock. It is easy to install and inexpensive and increases the security posture of your facility. For most effective application, the bolt of the door latch needs application so the bolt slides into the door casing from or into a keeper firmly attached to the frame (not the door facing). Look at the examples of best dead bolt installation in Illustration 9–13. The dead bolt latch is recommended for use in offices or storage rooms, as an effective security measure in your company crime prevention program.

Illustration 9–13

DOUBLE CYLINDER DEADLOCK EXAMPLES

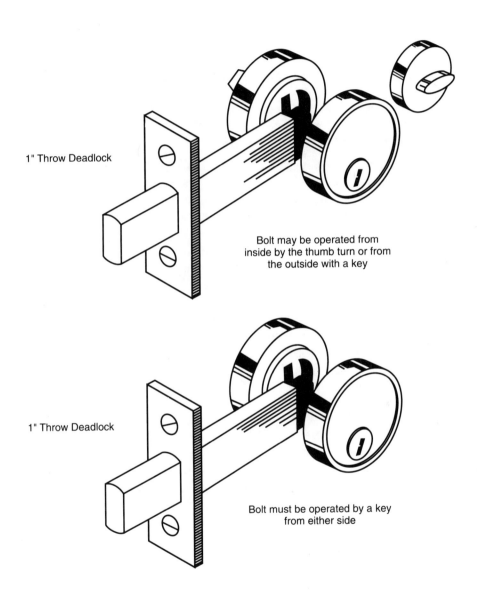

1" Throw Deadlock

Bolt may be operated from
inside by the thumb turn or from
the outside with a key

1" Throw Deadlock

Bolt must be operated by a key
from either side

ISSUE AND CONTROL OF LOCKS AND KEYS (GENERAL)

Of primary importance in safeguarding property and company information and preventing criminal activity in your corporate and industrial environment is an effective lock and key issue control system. The system includes control of combination locks. The firm control procedures become another beneficial "layer" in your total security system. The following steps are the minimum effort you need to make. Your action depends on the specific security needs and company environment. You can easily expand them as appropriate to meet the security requirements.

For effective lock and key control, you will need accurate lock and key control records. Also, you need to make periodic physical inspections and inventories to ensure accuracy of your system.

1. Combinations or keys to locks must be accessible only to persons you or your company authorizes to access offices, storage areas, and other facilities. Normally, you need to maintain control yourself or appoint a reliable security officer as the lock and key control officer.

2. Combinations to company safe locks and combination padlocks securing containers for sensitive company information need changing at least once during each 12-month period. Other types of locks need regular rotation or core changes. Circumstances might call for changing combinations before scheduled dates. The following examples are situations that prompt immediate combination or other types of lock changes.
   a. Loss or possible compromise of the combination or key
   b. Discharge, suspension, or reassignment of any person having knowledge of the combination or assigned a key
   c. Receipt of a container with built-in combination lock

3. Frequent rotation of key padlocks in certain instances is recommended practice in security situations.

4. When choosing combination lock numbers, avoid multiples and simple ascending or descending arithmetical series.

5. When padlocks with fixed combinations include use with bar locks as supplemental locking devices, keep an adequate supply to enable frequent interchange of locks among users. This type of lock does not provide adequate security unless used in large numbers over extensive areas, enabling a successful interchange without compromise. Never use fixed combination locks for the protection of sensitive company information.

6. Records containing combinations need the same security levels as the highest sensitive level of the material authorized for storage in the container the lock secures.

7. A viable basis for use of keys applies the same general concept as those controlling safe combinations. Issuing keys need minimum limits, and your responsibility calls for constant key control supervision. Generally, the security key system needs the control of the company security manager. However, when your control is not feasible, you need to retain staff supervision over the system. The following measures are recommended for control of keys to warehouses and other company structures.

    a. Keys must be stored in a locked, fireproof container when not in use. Keep the key container in the security office under supervision.

    b. Access lists for persons authorized to draw keys to sensitive storage facilities must be maintained in your key storage container.

    c. Your best company security procedure prevents keys issued for personal retention or removal from the company areas.

    d. Key containers need supervisory inspection ending each shift and all keys accounted for. A log sheet for security supervisors to sign for keys and records of locks and keys must be a part of your administrative process.

    e. Key controls records must be maintained on all key systems. Accountability concepts include records, key cards, and key control registers. Each record must include at least the following information:

        (1) Total number of keys and blanks in the system

        (2) Total number of keys by each key way code

        (3) Number of keys issued

        (4) Number of keys available

        (5) Number of blanks in stock for each key way code

        (6) Persons issued keys

You need personally to inventory your company key systems at least annually. Requests for issuance of new, duplicate, or replacement keys from employees need approval of the appropriate company official and must be reviewed by the security manager.

A key depository in the security officer is best at companies where keys need securing during nonoperational hours. Company department or division supervisors need to sign a register for the keys at the beginning of each working day and to turn in keys ending the working day. Security officers need to check the key storage container and register regularly to ensure accountability for keys.

Your key control systems need attentive planning to provide maximum security with a minimum interference with the business operations of the company. Basic requirements for designing your effective key control systems are as follows:

1. Use high-security pin tumbler cylinder locks specified for use in sensitive company areas. These areas might include research and development, high-

value item storage areas, information libraries, computer sections, and others.

2. Develop key control systems to ensure against usable keys left in possession of a contractor or other unauthorized person. Achieving that assurance stems from using locks with restricted key ways and issuing new keys on blank stock that is not readily available to commercial key makers.

3. Prevent master keying except in rare minimum security cases. When pin tumbler systems are master keyed, the use of several shorter pins reduces the security afforded when using a maximum number of pins in a non-master-keyed lock. One or more mushroom-type pins or variations of this type pin need application in each lock.

4. Number all locks (lock cylinders when appropriate) and keys in a master keyed system according to an unrelated number system. Imprint the words "Property of XYZ Corporation—Do Not Duplicate" on all master and high-level security control keys.

PRUDENT SECURITY MANAGEMENT INCLUDES APPOINTING A KEY CONTROL OFFICER

You need to appoint a security officer in your department to a full time or added duty position to key control officer. The security officer manages the following functions under your supervision. The lock and key control officer manages the following duties:

1. Stores the locks and keys.
2. Manages keys.
3. Maintains records of locks and keys.
4. Investigates loss of keys reported or discovered.
5. Conducts inventories of locks and keys.
6. Makes inspections of company keys and locks.
7. Manages master keys and control keys.
8. Ensures compliance with your regulations about locks and keys within the company and its facilities.
9. Conducts maintenance and operation of the company's key depository (where keys to certain areas are checked out and turned into the security office).

The lock and key control officer needs to maintain a permanent record of the following:

1. Locks by number, showing
    a. Location of each lock
    b. Key combination (e.g., pin lengths and positions)
    c. Date of last key change
2. Keys by number, showing
    a. Location of each key
    b. Type and key combination of each key
    c. Record of all keys not accounted for

Your key control officer needs to assist you in responsibility for the purchase of locks and keys. Based on determined requirements, you will need to coordinate purchasing with the appropriate corporate department and know the availability of improved locks and keys.

MECHANICS OF IMPLEMENTATION

Since each company or industry experiences conditions and requirements peculiar to its business activity, your key control systems will vary. Before you establish a lock and key control system, conduct a vulnerability survey to determine actual requirements. You will need to identify all warehouses, shops, storage areas, safes, filing cabinets, and so on that need added protection afforded by lock and security of keys. When you make that decision, add an annex to your physical security system plan. Include the following information.

1. Location of key depositories (when applicable)
2. Keys (by building, area, or cabinet number) turned into each depository
3. Method of marking or tagging keys for ready identification
4. Method of control for issue and receipt of keys to include maintenance of register and identification of persons authorized possession of company keys.
5. Action called for when keys are lost, stolen, or misplaced
6. Frequency and method of lock rotation
7. Assignment of responsibility for keys by job or position title and department
8. Emergency keys, readily available to the security forces
9. Other controls as thought necessary

CHOOSING THE KEYS AND LOCKS FOR SENSITIVE INFORMATION AND PROPERTY

All corporations and industrial complexes have special areas requiring added security measures, for example, a computer center where access is controlled and information stored there has vital importance to the business operations. Depending on the business your company conducts, you might secure microchips, computer components, or any other type of valuable or fragile products and supplies. Whatever the reason, added security ranging from vaults to special storage rooms need layered security and high security locks that make entry difficult for the determined intruder and prevent the casual pilferer. The following guidelines help you to decide the proper approach to effective high security protection.

All doors used for access to sensitive item storage rooms must be locked with high-security locking devices. On storage facilities, the locking devices used on the most secure doors must be a high security padlock and hasp. The best method is using a steel door with two $\frac{1}{4}$-inch or stronger steel bars running across the door. The bars can be separate, with a slot at each end slipping over a heavy hasp that is welded to the reinforced steel door casing. Or the bars may have their own welded hinges on one side and slipped over a welded hasp on only one side. The secondary padlock needs to be of good quality, preferably also a high security lock. One lock should be a high-security key-operated padlock; the secondary lock should be a high-security changeable combination lock. That technique is baffling to the most determined intruder, having to overcome two different types of locks. Added protection comes from a double-door arrangement or a triple door system, depending on the importance placed on the contents of the room, building, or area you are protecting. Using double doors calls for the same protective measures for the first door or layer, with a single bar on the second door also secured with a high-security lock. On triple-door arrangements, you need only add another layer, using the same techniques as the second door on a double door system. You might also use or add a cylinder high-security lock in the opening handle section of the door. It needs to be supplemental to the other padlocks cited.

Illustrations 9–14 and 9–15 show the single-, double-, and triple-door systems. Your high-security locks must meet the following specifications depending on their application:

1. Be a key-operated mortise or rim-mounted dead bolt lock for door handle security.

2. Have a dead bolt throw of 1 inch.

3. Be of double cylinder design.

4. Have a cylinder with five-pin tumblers; two must include mushroom- or spool-type drive pin designs.

5. Have 10,000 key changes.

6. Permit no master keying of lock.

7. Contain hardened saw-resistant inserts or be made of steel if bolt is visible when locked.

8. Have padlocks with high security rating.

9. Have changeable combinations and be rated as high security in the case of combination locks.

Illustration 9–14

EXAMPLE OF HIGH-SECURITY STORAGE—SINGLE DOOR
WITH DOUBLE LOCKS

Note: High Security Changeable Combination Locks also acceptable

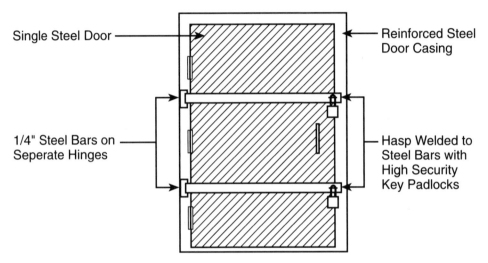

Example of High Security Storage - Single Door with Double Locks

Illustration 9–15

OUTER STEEL DOOR WITH DOUBLE LOCKS—INNER DOORS WITH SINGLE HIGH-SECURITY LOCKS

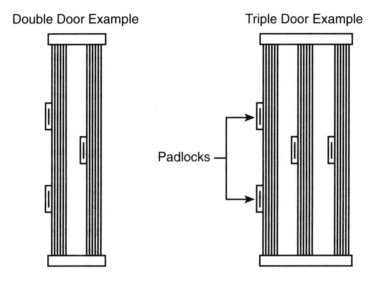

Double Door Example   Triple Door Example

Padlocks —

Outer Steel Door with Double Locks - Inner Doors with Single High Security Locks

At least two locks must secure the first door and one lock secure each subsequent door in the triple barrier system. Vehicles and storage facilities in which items are stored must be secured by approved secondary padlocks. Doors that cannot be secured from the inside with locking bars or dead bolts need securing on the inside with secondary padlocks. Illustrations 9–16 through 9–19 show examples of high-security door cylinder locks. High-security key padlocks operate in the same manner.

Illustration 9–16

EXAMPLE OF HIGH-SECURITY KEY FOR CYLINDER OR PADLOCK

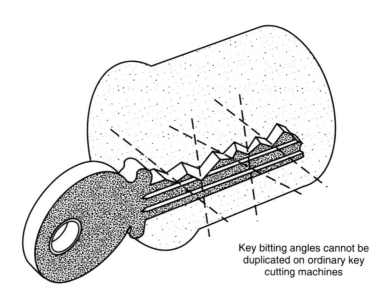

Key bitting angles cannot be
duplicated on ordinary key
cutting machines

Illustration 9–17

EXAMPLE OF HIGH-SECURITY CYLINDER OR PADLOCK MECHANISM

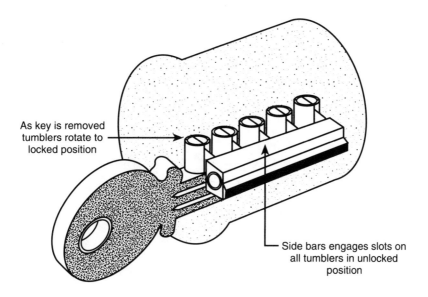

As key is removed tumblers rotate to locked position

Side bars engages slots on all tumblers in unlocked position

All tumblers must be at specific heights and angles for unlocking

Illustration 9–18

DIAGRAMS OF HIGH-SECURITY CYLINDER OR PADLOCK INTERIOR AND OPERATING MECHANISMS

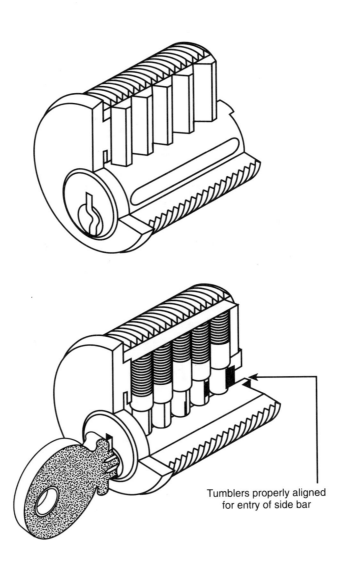

Tumblers properly aligned
for entry of side bar

Illustration 9–19

EXAMPLE OF A HIGH-SECURITY LOCK MULTIPIN STAGGERED MECHANISM
(One of the most effective pick resistance locks)

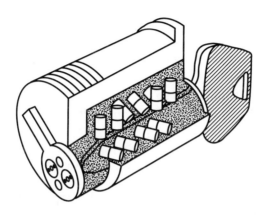

Keys to high-security storage rooms, buildings, and containers need to be kept separate from other keys and be accessible only to persons whose company positions require access to them. A current roster of persons authorized for keys, combinations, and entry must stay within the security office and be protected from public view. Custody of keys remains a problem unless controlled effectively. Most companies have regular turnover of employees resulting from retirements, terminations, and transfers to other divisions or facilities. When keys transfer between authorized persons, ensure that the transfer happens after both parties conduct a visual inventory of the sensitive storage items. The change of custody and physical inventory needs documentation and record in your security records.

Keys secured in your security office need a locked container built of at least 20–gauge steel or material of an equivalent strength. Never leave keys unattended or unsecured. Keys to sensitive buildings, rooms, and containers need a second container in your security office to prevent mistaken issue to unauthorized persons or their leaving the company area. Do not use master key systems in high-security areas. When high-security keys are lost, misplaced, or stolen, you must ensure the immediate exchange of the affected locks or lock cores. Replacement or reserve locks, cores, and keys need enough security to prevent them from ready access to unauthorized persons.

When your company circumstances dictate control of high-security keys and locks to a specific division or facility not directly within your control, special arrangements must be made. You must

   1. Appoint a key and lock custodian in that division or facility with clearly defined duties, including ensuring the proper custody and handling of keys and locks.

2. Establish a division or facility key control register to ensure administrative accountability for keys.

3. Keep a key control register that contains the signature of each person receiving the key from the appointed division or facility custodian, including the date, hour of issuance, serial number of key, initials of person issuing the key, date and hour of return, and signature of the person receiving the returned key.

4. Retain division and facility key control registers in your files for one year. An additional copy needs to be in security office files for five years or more.

You must provide clear instructions and procedures, including emphasis that high-security padlocks remain locked to the staple or hasp after opening an area or container to prevent theft, loss, or substitution of the lock.

Combinations to locks on vault doors or other sensitive item containers need changing semiannually and the combinations safeguarded. Padlocks used to secure entrances to sensitive storage facilities need rotation at least semiannually and a record maintained reflecting the date of rotation. The lock rotation plan needs to include preventing use of the same locks within an area where the doors, or containers protect sensitive items, or within the same storage facility. A sound preventive measure and effective rotation program includes exchange of locks among other areas in the company.

Your security office needs to maintain available backup sets of locks amounting to 15% of company locks in use. That technique enables fast replacement when needed and makes a viable rotation program possible. Keys to locks brought temporarily out of service (within the 15%) must be inventoried and checked when rotated. The loss or inability to account for any key to a lock makes that lock ineffective for securing sensitive items. It needs transfer to locks you use in a nonsensitive area. Lock rotation or combinations need change in the following circumstances.

1. When placed in use after purchasing

2. At least semiannually

3. On transfer, reassignment, resignation, or termination of any person having the combination

4. When there is a compromise of the combination or the lock found unlocked and unattended

DEVELOPING AN INSPECTION PROCEDURE FOR DEFECTIVE LOCKS

You or your designated lock and key security officer need to conduct a periodic inspection of all company locks to determine their serviceability and condition. The inspection determines the locking mechanism's effectiveness, detects previous tampering, and makes necessary replacements. You can test the locks by inserting a test key (any comparable key other than the correct key) no more than $\frac{1}{4}$ inch into key way. Turn the test key carefully, using the normal amount of force needed to open the lock. If the lock opens during the test inspection, replace it immediately. Take care during inspection to prevent jamming your test key into the key recess. Jamming will cause severe damage to locking levers and may prevent you from removing the test key.

Besides regular inspections you or the lock and key officer need to perform periodic preventive maintenance on company locks to ensure adequate lubrication, apply rust preventive on outer surfaces, and clear dust and moisture from key ways.

A QUICK REFERENCE REVIEW AND GUIDE CHECKLIST
FOR
A LOCK AND KEY SYSTEM

☐ Are all company entrances equipped with secure devices?

☐ Are they always locked when not in active use?

☐ Are hinge pins to all locked entrance doors spot welded or bradded?

☐ Have you appointed a lock and key control officer?

☐ Are locks and keys to all buildings and entrances supervised and controlled?

☐ Are authority and responsibility for issuance and replacement of locks and keys clear within your company?

☐ Are keys issued only to authorized employees?

☐ Do you have a clear policy about removal of keys from the company premises?

☐ Are backup keys properly secured in a locked cabinet in the security office?

☐ Are records maintained showing buildings and entrances for which keys are issued?

☐ Are records maintained showing location and number of master keys?

☐ Are records maintained indicating location and number of duplicate keys?

☐ Are records maintained indicating issue and turn-in of keys?

☐ Are records maintained showing location of locks and keys held in reserve?

☐ Is a current company key control policy in effect?

☐ Are locks changed immediately upon loss or theft of keys?

☐ Are lock and key inventory inspections conducted at least once each year?

☐ If you use master keys, are they without marking identifying them?

☐ Are losses or thefts of keys promptly investigated?

☐ Are all requests for reproduction or duplication of keys approved by you or the key control officer?

☐ Are locks on inactive gates and storage facilities under seal?

☐ Are they checked periodically by security officers?

☐ Are locks rotated within the company at least semiannually?

☐ Where applicable, is manufacturer's serial number on combination locks obliterated?

☐ Are measures in effect to prevent the unauthorized removal of locks on open cabinets, gates or buildings?

☐ Are company policies in effect ensuring all doors are locked at the close of the business day?

PART 3

In Touch with Technology

Technology for the security profession grows daily in a high-competition marketplace. This constitutes a problem for the security professional stemming from an inundation of high-tech equipment and the perplexing problem of which system to choose. Throughout Part Three, we cut through the marketing terms and claims of manufacturers to show you important concepts. When you think about concepts, finding the right technology for your security application becomes effective. Consider, for example, that motor vehicles come in a variety of sizes, shapes, models, and price ranges. The many added features appear to make the vehicle have greater advantage; however, the concept of basic transportation remains the same. When choosing technology-based tools for layers improving your security plan, you need to be concerned, first, that the system meets the basic concept of security advantage. Second, you must ensure that the system you choose effectively satisfies the application requirements in your company and provides cost-benefit value. For example, when you buy a car featuring air conditioning, it costs more than an automobile without that option. When you live and drive in a hot climate, the air conditioning is a cost-effective benefit. However, when you live in a climate with an average high temperature of 70 degrees Fahrenheit, the air conditioning is a feature you will probably not need or use. When you buy and install high-tech security equipment, ensure you *need* and *effectively use* the total system. Buying and installing equipment with features you cannot use because of the application environment limitations is not advantageous or cost effective. Do not throw the dice and hope you come up with a winner, or be persuaded by a skilled marketing person who overwhelms you with technical terms. Many technical terms we hear today originated as a creation of the equipment manufacturer. In reality, the concept remains the same but has an impressive name that implies advantage.

Because security technologies have become an irreplaceable tool in crime prevention and detection, you need to develop specific standards applied to the situational requirements for your company. For example, instead of allowing a high-tech security firm to tell you about your company needs, you decide the standards and results you are seeking. The best rule to observe is caveat emptor (buy at your own risk). Clearly, most manufacturers of high-tech security equipment have integrity and express well-meaning advice. However, they are not unlike your own company. They are in business, and they need sales and profits to stay in business. Many security professionals place the security decisions for their company and professional responsibilities in the hands of high-tech "consultants" who need to earn their keep. Their integrity for the quality and operational dependability of equipment they make, sell, or install is not the primary question. Instead, the question becomes Do you need it?

Moreover, you must develop your own standards, not accepting or relying on those others offer. Throughout Part Three, you will find the concepts, applications, and standards to use as a guide in developing your standards and planning for applications of high-tech security systems.

10 Intrusion Detection System Management

The use of intrusion detection systems dates back to 390 B.C. and the Roman Empire when squawking geese alerted the Romans to surprise attack by the Gauls.

The basic electronic security systems for corporate or industrial application have three integral elements, including a sensor (integrated by data transmission and links) that detects the intrusion and signals a monitored annunciator console that is backed by a security response force. Intrusion detection systems are an inherent element of corporate and industrial security and play an important part in the total protection efforts of companies, their activities, information, equipment, and material assets. The systems detect intrusions through sound, vibration, motion, electrostatic means, light beams, and broken circuits. For an effective security effort, the system you choose must focus on detecting unauthorized persons at the vulnerable entry point (gate, door, fence, etc.), in the important area (building, etc.), and at the specific object (vault, file, safe, etc.). Remember, however, that the intrusion detection system can tell you only that an intrusion into a protected area occurred. It cannot do anything about it. Whatever system you choose always depends on your capability to react positively to the alarm. Ensuring the systems you install as part of your total security system remain within your performance standards, you will also need sufficient security officer response to be totally effective. With that factor in mind, the following information helps you develop some concepts aided by increased awareness of advantages and limitations.

FOUR IMPORTANT PARTS OF MODERN INTRUSION DETECTION SYSTEMS

Adapting the historical example of the geese used by the Romans into contemporary physiological analogy brings you the following four important basic parts of the intrusion detection system.

1. Sensors

The sensor involves the first function of the intrusion detection system. It detects or senses a condition that exists or changes, be it authorized or unauthorized. That action relates directly to the human senses of touch, hearing, sight, smell, and taste. It includes all actions that happen since, separately, your senses have no means of distinguishing authorized or unauthorized actions. That feature emerges in common and simplest of sensory devices, such as the magnetic contact on a door. That device activates with an alarm each time the door is operated. However, the sensor alone has no means of determining whether the person opening a protected door is authorized or unauthorized.

2. Controls

The control function receives the information from a sensor, evaluates the information, and transmits it to the annunciation function. The control function provides the power and relates to our physiological functions, including the brain, nervous system, and the circulatory system of our body. The nervous system collects and evaluates information from the various senses (sensors) and transmits signals to the muscles for appropriate action. The circulatory system then supplies the power source (i.e., nutrients and oxygen from the blood) to enable the system to function.

3. Annunciation

This part of the system alerts a human monitor to initiate a response that results in an investigation of the sensor environment. It can be a bell, buzzer, light flashing, and so on. This function is similar to the squawking of geese, barking of dogs, or person calling for help.

4. Security Officer Response

Combining the three basic parts into a complete system, your protective alarm detects an intrusion and transmits and articulates a message for help. However, the fourth element requires that the human factor respond to the call for help.

THE BASIC CONCEPTS AND DEVICES OF SENSORS FOR AN INTRUSION DETECTION SYSTEM

Devices for the sensor function of an alarm system provide a broad range of choices from simple magnetic switches to sensitive ultrasonic Doppler, light beams, sound systems, and others. The following list includes most of the systems now available:

- *Alarm Glass.* Glass contains small wires molded into the glass that form an electrical circuit that triggers an alarm if the glass is cut or broken.

- *Alarm Screens.* Screens placed in front of windows or other areas contain thin metal wires that activate an alarm if the screen is cut and electrical circuits interrupted.

- *Capacitance Proximity Detectors.* These sensors respond to a change in the electrical capacitance of a protected metallic item or area induced by the approach of an intruder. Their uses include metallic screens, doors, safes, cabinets, and similar items.

- *Duress Alarms.* These devices activate manually and alert security officers to a situation needing their response.

- *Metallic Foil Sensors.* Used on glass or other breakable material, windows, walls, or doors to detect the breaking of the glass or other material, the thin foil breaks with the material cutting an electrical circuit and activating an alarm.

- *Photoelectric Controls.* These devices sense a change in available light either from a light source or from the general area.

- *Photoelectric Sensors.* These sensors project a light beam or invisible infrared beam triggering an alarm when an object or person passes through and interrupts the beam.

- *Pressure Mat Sensors.* Uses for this sensor include placing them under interior or exterior carpets or under grass and other materials. The sensor triggers an alarm when an intruder satisfies the prescribed level of pressure. For example, the alarm system activates when an intruder walks on the pressure mat within a protected area.

- *Pull-Trip Switches.* These mechanical sensors respond to the pulling of a wire connected to a protected object. For example, a thin wire or maze of wires placed across a particular area can activate the switch when an intruder walks into it or the wire is pulled while attached to a door or other object opened. It works best for doorways and other entrance points.

- *Stress Detectors.* These sensitive instruments connect to a floor beam, stairs, or other structural components. They activate an alarm by sensing a slight stress placed on the particular structural component.

- *Switch Sensors.* This sensor detects opening doors and windows. The various types of these sensors include:

  - *Magnetic Switches.* These switches are used where the contacts of the switch open and close in response to the movement of a magnet mounted on it.

  - *Mechanical Switches.* These switches have contacts that open and close by spring action in response to opening and closing a door or window.

  - *Mercury Switch Sensors.* The contacts in these switches open or close when the device tilts. Highly sensitive, they work in many applications for protecting doors, windows, transoms, or skylights.

- *Vibration Sensors.* These sensors detect the vibrations of structural components of a building, wall, or other structural feature and trigger when force is used to penetrate the area protected.

- *Infrared Motion Sensors.* These devices sense a source of heat that moves into their field of sensitivity. The body heat of an intruder is enough to trigger an alarm.

- *Microwave Motion Sensors.* Microwave sensors detect motion in the protected area and trigger an alarm.

- *Sound Monitoring Sensors.* These devices trigger alarms from sharp noise sounds and also serve as a listening device for security officers manning a control station.

- *Ultrasonic Motion Sensors.* The sensors generate a high-frequency sound that is above the usual hearing range. Motion in the protected area triggers an alarm.

- *Laser System Sensors.* Similar to photoelectric sensors, here laser beams replace regular light beams.

- *Wafer Switch Sensors.* These sensor switches are small negative-pressure switches. However, instead of signaling an alarm under pressure, they operate when the pressure is released. They are used to protect objects that an intruder might pick up as part of a theft or to protect against illegal entry to collect competitive intelligence.

- *Doppler Sensors.* These sensors utilize the effect of compression of expanding sound or radio frequencies reflected from or originating from a moving object.

EVALUATING THE COMPATIBILITY OF SENSORS

Before ensuring your system sensors function properly, you must carefully study the environment you intend to protect. Overlooking certain environmental factors at the time of installation can render the system useless. For example, installing vibration detectors in a bank vault located above a subway would be futile. Factors such as the state of repair of a building and the type of heating (i.e., radiators and air currents) can affect the successful operation of sensory equipment. You must ensure the sensor devices are operationally compatible with the area in which the systems are located and provide the results you need from them.

OVER-EXTENSION OF INTRUSION DETECTION SENSOR EQUIPMENT

This problem develops when a system works effectively under ideal conditions, but in the environment you need to protect, the ideal factor is unlikely. This situation normally develops when you try to economize or allow a manufacturer or supplier tell you what you want or need. Your solution is attentive evaluation of the system offered and reducing the claimed protection benefit about 30% to ensure it can perform well in your company situation.

THREE KEY BENEFITS OF MODERN IDS APPLICATIONS

Buying, installing and using intrusion detection systems (IDS), as part of your total security system begins with a clear understanding of why they create benefit and advantage for your corporation or industrial complex. Intrusion detection systems accomplish one or more of the following benefits.

A key benefit of effective intrusion detection applications enables an efficient use of your security force. With a solid nontechnological security system in place (i.e., barriers, lighting, structural hardening), intrusion detection devices add greater capability of protection with fewer security officers, smaller numbers of mobile patrols, and often a reduction in protective lighting.

Often, safety regulations, operational requirements, appearance factors, layout of a company area, cost limits, or other reasons prevent adequate conventional security measures. The application of effective intrusion detection systems in those situations often solves protection problems that meet otherwise prohibitive conditions.

Applications of intrusion detection systems often provide added controls at critical points or areas.

TWELVE NECESSITY AND FEASIBILITY FACTORS AFFECTING YOUR IDS DECISIONS

Deciding to increase your security system layers with intrusion detection system applications often becomes a problem, especially justifying the cost. The 12 factors that follow will help you to create a cost-benefit formula that removes doubt and justifies your decision or enables you to decide on alternatives.

1. The Business Your Company Conducts

All companies need security; however, the decision of how much and what type relies largely on the business or mission. For example, a company producing massive steel construction beams (hard to pilfer) might need less security protection than a company producing laptop computers (easy to pilfer). In the first company, you need to protect company information and small operating tools, supplies, and equipment. It is unlikely that people have an interest in stealing the manufactured product, steel beams. The latter company however, has all the security problems of the first, plus the theft of the product (lap-top computers) itself becomes lucrative.

2. Vulnerability of the Company Facilities

Location plays an important role in this factor when making your decisions. For example, when your company's business includes a lucrative product for employee pilferage or external motivated theft, coupled with the standard problem of pilfering office supplies and other problems, the first inclination might include heavy security efforts with intrusion detection equipment. However, you need to consider the prospect of intrusions before making your decision. For example, companies in the rural Midwest need less security protection than does a similar company in or near a large metropolitan area, such as New York or Los Angeles or any city that traditionally experiences higher levels of crime.

3. Accessibility of Your Company to Intruders

Crimes against companies call for access to the vulnerable areas within the company, involving outside theft intrusions, employee pilferage, or efforts to sabotage the business operations with explosions or fire. There is also a threat from competitive intelligence intrusions by unscrupulous collectors of information who are not particular how they gather it. Your intrusion detection and basic security programs need to assess the accessibility of your company to intruders and design your total system consistent with the need.

4. Location of Your Company (Location), Its Areas, and Facilities

This factor is akin to vulnerability; however, your company might be scattered over a geographic area, having various facilities throughout the country. For example, you might protect the corporate headquarters complex in South Dakota where the crime rate, population and probability of theft are minimal. However, your company also may have a facility in northern New Jersey, another near Chicago, and others in or close to other large cities with high crime rates. Each facility location requires your consideration and effective level of protection needed or enhanced by prudent application of intrusion detection devices.

5. Structure Construction Factor

Older buildings will provide you with more problems than new buildings as a rule. Building construction before air conditioning became a standard feature put in many large windows for ventilation, coupled with other features that did not consider security. Another element affecting older structures is that crime rates, threats, and vulnerabilities of that era were far lower than they are today. On the other hand, many new buildings have structures designed for beauty, accessibility, and other features that create many security problems in this era of increasing crime. Plan your intrusion detection systems according to the strengths and weakness of your company's structures.

6. Hours of Operation

This important factor not only plays an important role in deciding the need and feasibility of intrusion detection application, but also what type serves your company best. For example, when your company operates 24 hours a day, 7 days a week, obviously your primary security concern is not burglary. However, pilferage remains high on your list, and maybe your company has several unmanned storage warehouses. Look the company operational factors and plug that into your decision process.

7. Availability of Other Forms of Protection

Depending on the type of company and the protection level needed, you might decide no intrusion detection applications need to be within your total security system. Do not make the mistake that many security professionals do about high-tech equipment and install it for the sake of having it on site. When you cannot clearly envision the need and feasibility, probably you do not need it in your total system.

8. Initial and Recurring Cost

Consider, first, the adequacies of your basic security system; then, determine the losses sustained by your company each year for the past five years; then, figure the cost of the intrusion detection systems you are considering, including

(1) equipment cost, (2) installation cost, and (3) maintenance cost. For example, if your company losses total an average of $300,000 each year with your conventional system and the high-tech costs show equipment and installation costing $500,000 with a $100,000 per year maintenance cost, you might want to consider less costly ways of increasing security. It is important to recognize that the presence of intrusion detection equipment does not guarantee elimination or reduction in losses. It is always possible that no decrease occurs; however, your system expense saps profits, and most companies view that as incompetent security management.

9. Design and Salvage Value

Consider the feasibility of the intrusion detection system for your needed application, coupled with efficient operation of the equipment by members of your security force. Consider, for example, (1) how difficult the system is to operate, (2) the tendencies for false alarms, (3) the requirement for constant monitoring, and (4) number of officers needed to manage the system. Another factor includes the salvage value at later dates when you decide to upgrade your security systems. Do the systems you are considering have any value later? Suppose your company designs and builds a new complex. Consider if you can transfer the intrusion detection systems to other locations or exchange them for others suited better for the new applications.

10. Response Time by Your Security Force

An important factor for effective intrusion detection systems includes the capability to respond by your security forces. That normally equates to how many security officers you have available at the time of system activation. The benefit of an intrusion detection system depends on capability of response, and when that cannot happen quickly, the system is not beneficial. A person with intent to steal company property might trigger the alarm and then watch from a secure position to time the response. When an intruder notices slow security response, he or she perceives an advantage and might complete a theft despite the system being operational.

11. Saving in Security Force Requirements and Company Money

Depending on your protective responsibilities, the configuration of company facilities, and business your company conducts, intrusion detection systems might enable smaller security forces than otherwise needed. Whenever you determine the systems work for your situation, you will also need to evaluate the feasibility of reducing the security force to save company money.

12. Intruder Time Requirement

Evaluate the need and feasibility of the intrusion detection system regarding difficulty an intruder might experience entering a protected area. Without question, silent alarms at the site often provide the best choice when you can ensure a fast and adequate response to the alarm. However, in some situations, a loud siren or bell also provides a way of causing the intruder to flee instead of steal and probably will not return later.

Seven Important Elements When Choosing an Intrusion Detection System

Each type of intrusion detection system must meet a specific type of problem. Factors you need to consider in choosing the best components or systems for your protection effort include, but are not limited, to the following seven points.

1. Location and response time capability of the security force
2. Value of the protected company facility or material or sensitivity of contents
3. Area environment including building construction, sound levers inside and outside, climate, and other similar factors
4. Radio and electrical interference
5. Operational hours of the company or facility
6. Specific facility, area or site protected
7. Availability of security officers and security force

A consideration of these factors readily shows the advisability of researching all the possibilities in making a wise choice. Often, more than one type of sensor or system is necessary to give adequate protection for an area or structure.

THE PROBLEMS OF INTRUSION DETECTION SYSTEMS

Although intrusion detection systems have proven effective in deterring and apprehending intruders, they are subject to certain inherent problems. A traditional problem is that of false alarms. The high percentages of false alarms normally trace to three key factors:

1. User error or negligence, including lack of preventive maintenance
2. Poor installation or placing the system in a location incompatible with that area
3. Faulty or poor quality equipment

THREE KEY PROBLEMS OF IDS DEPENDENCE

Statistics collected throughout the years show that more than half the intrusion system false alarms result from user error or negligence. Users often do not understand how to operate their systems properly. Commonly, false alarms result from actions of employees who do not lock doors or windows or enter a secured area without regard to an engaged system. Alarm system problems also activate accidentally by workers, cleaning crews, and outside noise and vibrations.

The second factor leading to false alarms is poor installation or servicing. To function as intended, installation and maintenance of an intrusion detection system play a key role. Equipment installed in an inappropriate environment or improperly positioned, set, or wired produces false alarms. Also, if equipment is not adequately maintained, the chances of false alarms increase. Too often installers and service persons lack the necessary skills and knowledge for sophisticated equipment.

The third common cause of false alarms is faulty or poor-quality equipment. When intrusion detection equipment is electrically or mechanically defective, the alarm may activate when, for example, the equipment breaks or shorts out the circuit. The use of substandard equipment that is especially vulnerable to breakdown or that can be easily set off by a variety of extraneous conditions leads to frequent false alarms.

Besides false alarms that trace to the three causal factors, there are a certain number of undetermined reasons for false alarms. Various studies conducted over the years show an average of 25% of intrusion detection system false alarms fall into this unknown category. It is possible that they may be the result of user error. Faced with probable sanctions, a security officer or other company employee may deny responsibility for a false alarm. Another possibility is that an intruder or other unauthorized intrusion by an employee of the company into a specific secured area might have been successfully prevented, leaving no visible evidence of intrusion or attempted entry.

The frequency of false alarms, whatever the cause, often leads to other problems. In the use of automatic telephone dialer alarm systems, many storm-related false alarms happening simultaneously may tie up security center lines and seriously hamper your security forces' capacity to respond to genuine situations. Malfunction of the systems can lock in communications systems for considerable periods of time. Although telephone dialers offer effective, low-cost protection, these problems have created negative security offer reaction to their use.

Another problem involves security officer attitudes toward intrusion alarm systems generally. Often, the security officers, faced with repeated false alarms, tend to give alarms a low priority for response. The resulting important response delays reduce the likelihood of apprehension and limit the value of your company's intrusion detection systems. Further, security officers, lulled by the high incidence of false alarms, may not conduct thorough on-the-scene investigations or be alert to the risks of valid alarms.

To solve the problems of an intrusion detection system, you need to recognize the interrelationship of all factors involving the application of this security tool. You also need a clear understanding about the roles of intrusion detection system manufacturers, dealers, sales and service persons, company employees, security officers, and maybe local law enforcement officers who respond to the alarms. Deciding and defining the interdependence and interaction important to increased reliability and effectiveness of the systems is important.

STEPS HELPING YOU FIND SOLUTIONS TO IDS PROBLEMS AND ADD BENEFITS

To ensure your protection layer involving intrusion detection systems stays or becomes effective, there are certain factors to consider. As I noted earlier, intrusion detection systems provide you a valuable advantage of complete security. Their effectiveness in reducing corporate and industrial crime provides a reasonable advantage and benefit. They help your company by offering added protection at a cost lower than salaried security officers and often reduce high insurance premiums associated with high rates of crime. Another benefit you cannot overlook stems from the formula of reduced losses equaling increased company profits. Considering the benefits and advantages, the solution becomes a cooperative effort of persons involved in the system to overcome existing problems leading to improvement of their efficiency and reliability.

First, intrusion detection system manufacturers need to develop dependable equipment. Performance standards for separate components and installed systems need constant improvement and you can help with recommendations and documented problems. When you document problems and share the experience with the manufacturer, improvement of weaknesses is possible. You can also help by working closely with manufacturers to test their improvements in real circumstances. Often, you can not only help evaluate systems but save your company significant sums of money. Another factor includes developing more reliable human-discriminating sensors, and you can play a helpful role with your suggestions.

Assuming that you are using dependable equipment installed in a compatible environment by well-trained and well-qualified persons, there is another factor you need to consider: user error or negligence. Your remedy becomes effective cooperation with the manufacturer to train security officers and educate company employees about systems installed in specific areas. Often, users of intrusion detection systems assume meaningful responsibility for proper operation and total effectiveness, yet are unaware of essential operating procedures or the effect of false alarms.

Ensure that you arrange effective backup power sources for your intrusion detection systems. An important problem for power sources involves severe weather that interrupts power from a few seconds to several hours. Others include heavy drains or breakdown of power stations, motor vehicle accidents that involve striking a pole and downing wires, and fires and other causes that effectively shut down many of your security systems, including intrusion detection systems. Two backup power sources need your consideration, preferably using both of them to ensure adequate protection. They are batteries and portable or stationary generators. Batteries provide instant continuance of operation for several hours. However, you need to provide for continued protection beyond batteries and that includes emergency generators. Generators are costly when you need significant amounts of power over long periods of time. It is a good idea to develop backup power through cooperating and sharing it with other company operations, for example, the important computer center and other elements that cause major business operation problems without power to continue their functions. Your security lighting, intrusion detection systems, and other heavy power needs happen normally during the hours of darkness. Other business operation element requirements happen during the day, when your needs are smallest or can function on work-around measures not dependent on electrical power. With that concept in view, your company management probably will agree with you that costly backup systems supplying electricity for essential company operations during the day and enabling effective protection of company assets at night is a good investment.

TYPES OF COMMON ECONOMICAL AND EFFECTIVE INTRUSION DETECTION SYSTEMS

A simple, inexpensive, and easy means of protecting points of entry into your company's buildings or enclosures involves using electrically sensitized strips of metallic foil or wire. Any action that breaks the foil or wire also breaks an electrical circuit and activates an alarm. Metallic foil works effectively on glass surfaces and protective screening. Doors and windows equipped with magnetic contact switches sound an alarm when the door or window opens. Metallic wires running unseen through wooden dowels or between panels or walls, doors, and ceilings also provide adequate protection in many situations.

ADVANTAGES, DISADVANTAGES AND APPLICATIONS OF ELECTRICAL CIRCUIT SYSTEMS

Advantages

Electrical circuit systems consistently provide you the most trouble-free service. They cause few, if any, nuisance alarms, and provide adequate protection in low-risk environments. They are often used for the economy and reliability of effective operation.

Disadvantages

Electric circuit systems might constitute a complicated installation problem when a protected area has many openings. The system is also susceptible to compromise in some circumstances, especially when used in unprotected soft walls or ceilings that can be penetrated in ways to bypass the system. Defeating the system by bridging the electrical circuits might become a problem when confronting a skilled intruder. The system uses magnetic contact switches recoverable for use elsewhere. It cannot detect "stay behind" persons unless they try to depart the area or building after securing.

Suggested Applications

This system serves you best when protecting a building or area that does not have high-value items or that functions as a redundant system supporting other types of systems. For example, a combination of visible and hidden electrical circuit systems serve as both a prevention feature and detection feature. A skilled burglar bridges the circuit to gain entry; however, unseen elements have the same effect as used by magicians creating an illusion. The entertainer makes certain things clearly visible and draws a viewer's attention to that element while using the unseen elements to create the illusion. When you use clearly visible systems, the effect might prevent many burglars, especially amateurs lacking practical skill about the system. Redundancy becomes effective when a skilled intruder carefully bypasses the obvious system and is detected from a concealed redundant system that he or she is unaware is present. Illustrations 10–1 through 10–3 show this type system.

Illustration 10–1

EXAMPLES OF MAGNETIC CONTACT SWITCHES

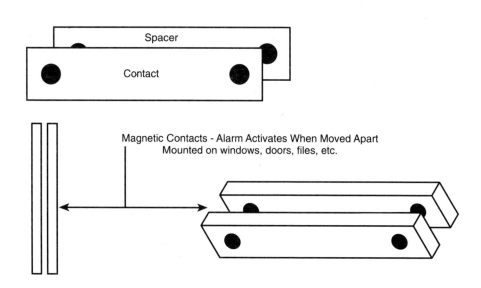

Spacer

Contact

Magnetic Contacts - Alarm Activates When Moved Apart
Mounted on windows, doors, files, etc.

Illustration 10–2

EXAMPLE OF MAGNETIC CONTACT SWITCH APPLICATION

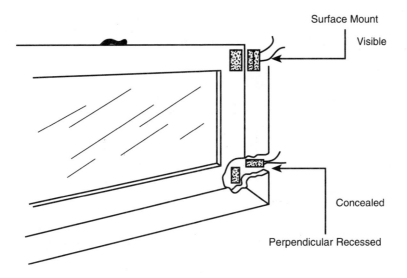

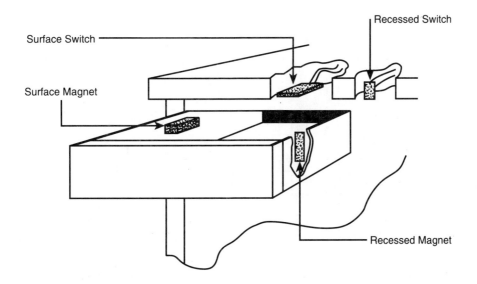

Illustration 10–3

EXAMPLES OF METALLIC FOIL ON GLASS WINDOW

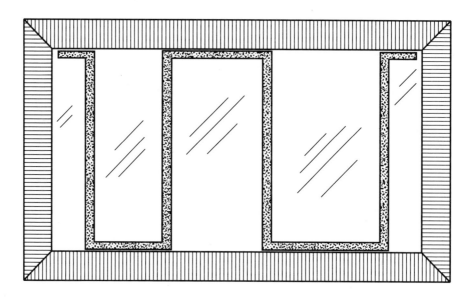

Metallic Foil on Window Coupled with Protective Mesh Screen

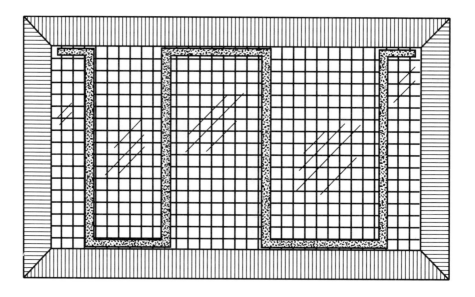

LIGHT BEAM TECHNIQUES

The photoelectric (electric eye) type of intrusion detection gets its name from the technique of using a light-sensitive cell and a projected light source. Characteristics of this type of protection include the following:

1. A light beam is transmitted at a frequency of several thousand vibrations per second. An infrared filter over the light source makes the beam invisible to intruders.

2. A light beam with a different frequency (such as a flashlight) cannot be substituted for this beam. The beam projects from a hidden source and crisscrosses in protected areas using hidden mirrors until it contacts a light-sensitive cell.

3. Wires connect this device to the control station. When an intruder crosses the light beam, he or she breaks contact with the photoelectric cell, and that activates an alarm.

4. A projected beam of invisible light can be effective for about 500 feet indoors and will cover an area of about 1,000 feet outdoors. The effectiveness of the beam decreases from 10 to 30% for each mirror used.

ADVANTAGES AND DISADVANTAGES OF A PHOTOELECTRIC INTRUSION SYSTEM

ADVANTAGES

1. When properly applied, the system yields effective, reliable notice of intrusion.

2. The system works well in open portals or driveways with no possible use of obstructions.

3. This type of system detects "stay behind" persons.

4. The system increases in value because it can be recovered and used elsewhere.

5. This system can actuate other security systems including cameras, and lighting.

6. The system may detect fires through smoke interruption of the beam.

DISADVANTAGES

1. Application limitations include those locations where it is not possible to bypass the beam by crawling under or climbing over it.

2. The system needs some type of permanent installation.

3. Other factors, such as fog, smoke, dust, and rain, in enough density will create an interruption of the light beam and trigger the alarm.

4. This system calls for frequent inspections and maintenance of light-producing components to detect deterioration.

5. You need to ensure that the ground beneath the light beam used outside is free from tall grass, weeds, drifting snow, and sand.

Illustrations 10–4 and 10–5 provide examples of application for a photoelectric intrusion system.

Illustration 10–4

EXAMPLE OF PHOTOELECTRIC BEAM INTERIOR APPLICATION
HALLWAY, ENTRANCE, OR ROOM

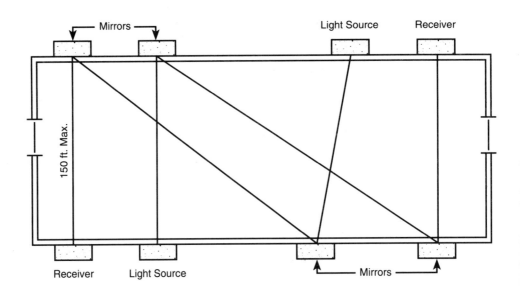

Illustration 10–5

EXAMPLE OF EXTERIOR PHOTOELECTRIC BEAM APPLICATION

Double Chain-Link Fence with Protective Lighting

Gate

Light Beams

Loading Dock

Warehouse
Palletized Products

◄─── Truck Entrance and Loading

This facility contains high-value products requiring truck assisted theft. It is well-protected but located in a remote area and without constant security surveillance. Mobile security patrols check periodically.

TECHNIQUES OF DETECTING SOUND

Sound-activated intrusion detection systems effectively safeguard enclosed areas, vaults, warehouses, and similar enclosures. Supersensitive microphone speaker sensors installed on walls, ceilings, and floors enable the system to detect sounds made by forced entry by an intruder. The sensitivity of this system is adjustable regarding amounts of sound needed to trigger the alarm.

CHARACTERISTICS OF THE SOUND DETECTION SYSTEM

Advantages

The system is economical and easily installed and you can recover the components from one location and install the system in another building or area as needed.

Disadvantages

Your greatest limitation with this system is noise. It is usable only in enclosed areas where a minimum of extraneous sound exists. It is not satisfactory where high noise levels are encountered. You cannot use it, for example, in areas close to aircraft and railroad or truck traffic. The system does not work in outdoor areas and has a problem normally of false and nuisance alarms. You might consider using this system as a clandestine listening device for other intrusion detection systems. For example, when a sound triggers the alarm in an area where other systems also should respond but do not, security officers in a control center can listen to determine whether the alarm is false or actual. An intruder might find ways to bypass other systems without knowledge a sound detection and listening system is present. It is an excellent "layer" or redundant system to consider.

Detecting Vibration

This system works well with the sound detection system. It is effective in closed areas and activates from the vibrations made by an intruder forcing entry or moving about. Installation includes placing vibration-sensitive sensors to walls, ceilings, and floor of the protected area. Any vibration made by an intruder triggers the alarm system.

CHARACTERISTICS OF THE VIBRATION DETECTION SYSTEM

Advantages

The system is economical and easily installed. Components are recoverable and installed in other locations. The applications are flexible and provide an independent or supporting system for other layers of your security.

Disadvantages

You can only use this system in areas where a minimum of vibration exists. It is not satisfactory or reliable where high vibrations are encountered, especially in nearness to heavy construction, railroads or automobile and truck traffic. The system cannot work effectively outdoors.

Illustration 10–6 shows a vibration sensor application in a company building.

Illustration 10–6

EXAMPLE OF A VIBRATION SENSOR APPLICATION

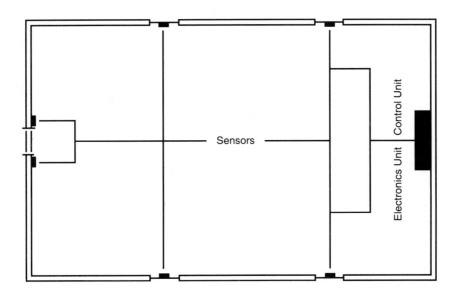

DETECTING MOTION

Intrusion detection systems using ultrasonic or microwave motion sensors can be very effective for the protection of interior areas. Such systems flood the protected area with acoustic or microwave energy and detect the Doppler shift in transmitted and received frequencies when motion happens within the area.

Ultrasonic systems have a transceiver (single unit containing a transmitter and receiver or separate transmitters and receivers), an electronic unit (amplifier), and a control unit. Key elements include the following:

1. The transmitter generates a pattern of acoustic energy that fills the enclosed area.

2. The receiver, connected to the electronic unit, picks up the standing sound patterns.

3. If they are of the same frequency as the waves emitted by the transmitter, the system will not alarm.

4. Any motion within the protected area sends back a reflected wave differing in frequency from the original transmission. The change in frequency is detected, and amplified, and the alarm signal activated.

5. Multiple transceivers of a transmitter and multiple receivers operate effectively from the same control unit for more effective coverage of large or broken areas. This system works only indoors.

ADVANTAGES

1. Provides effective security protection against intruders hidden within the premises.

2. Has high salvage value. The systems have an advantage of recovery used in other locations.

3. Has invisible protective field. Therefore, it is difficult to detect the presence of or to compromise the system.

DISADVANTAGES

1. May need reduced sensitivity to overcome possible disturbance factors in the enclosed area (such as telephones, machines, and clocks).

2. Can be set off by loud external sounds.

Illustration 10–7 shows you the concept of this type of intrusion detection system.

Illustration 10–7

EXAMPLE OF HOW ULTRASONIC MOTION SENSOR WORKS

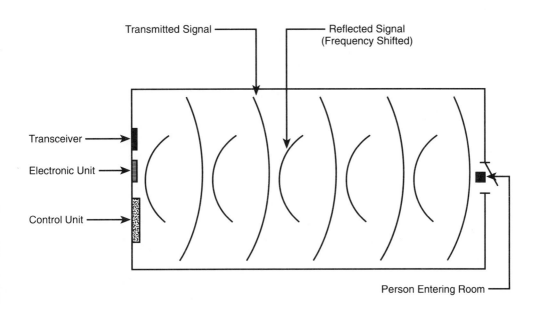

MICROWAVE SYSTEMS USED TO DETECT MOTION

Microwave motion detection systems closely parallel the operation of ultrasonic systems. A pattern of radio waves transmits back to an antenna. If all objects within the range of the radio waves are stationary, the reflected waves return at the same frequency. If they strike a moving object, they return at a different frequency. The detected difference in the transmitted and received frequency triggers an alarm signal.

ADVANTAGES OF THE MICROWAVE SYSTEM

1. Good coverage is supplied if antennas are properly placed.
2. System is not affected by air currents, noise, or sounds.
3. System can be recovered from one location and installed in another.

DISADVANTAGES

1. Coverage is not confined to a desired security area. It penetrates thin wooden partitions and windows and may be accidentally activated by persons or vehicles outside the protected area.

2. Fluorescent light bulbs will activate the microwave sensor.

DETECTING CAPACITANCE CHANGES IN AN ELECTROSTATIC FIELD

The capacitance or electrostatic intrusion detection system performs effectively when installed on a safe, wall, or opening to establish an electrostatic field around the protected object. The field tuning happens from a balance between the electric capacitance and the electric inductance. The body capacitance of an intruder entering the field unbalances the electrostatic energy of the field. The imbalance of energy activates the alarm system.

ADVANTAGES

1. An extremely flexible type of system, its uses include protection of safes, file cabinets, windows, doors, partitions, and any unguarded metallic object within maximum tuning range.

2. It is a simple system to install and operate.

3. The system provides an invisible protective field, making it difficult for an intruder to determine when the system has been set off.

4. It can easily be dismantled and reinstalled at a different location.

5. The equipment is compact.

6. The system provides a high level of protection.

DISADVANTAGES

1. The system applies only to ungrounded equipment.

2. Housekeeping of protected area needs careful attention.

3. Accidental alarms can happen if protected area or object is carelessly approached, especially by cleaning crews or others when working when office or building is not in normal business operation.

Illustration 10–8 shows you an example of how this system operates and the applications possible.

Illustration 10–8

EXAMPLE OF CAPACITANCE PROXIMITY SENSOR SYSTEM

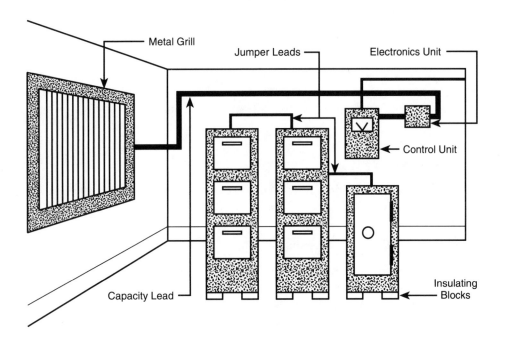

INTRUSION DETECTION PENETRATION SENSORS

Modern penetration alarm sensors serve well at any company location for an added security layer. Their versatility lends to use on windows, interior or exterior doors, ceilings, walls, and other potential entry areas. Examples of applications include the following:

Exterior Doors

To guard against unauthorized entry, equip the door with balanced magnetic switches. The surface of an interior door or wall covered with a grid wire sensor or any type system using the principle of breaking an electrical circuit warns of intrusion.

Interior Doors

These sensors are subject to the same considerations that govern the choice of systems for exterior doors.

Solid Walls, Floors, and Ceilings

To monitor attempts of penetration for solid walls, floors, and ceilings, cover the interior surface with a grid wire sensor, or they equip the protected room with a passive ultrasonic sensor. Sound detection systems and vibration detection systems work effectively to detect penetration through such areas.

Open Walls and Ceilings

Wire cage walls and ceilings present distinct problems. To protect this type of construction, certain modifications are necessary. The wall and ceiling may be enclosed with building material on the surface outside the cage. This permits use of passive ultrasonic or grid wire sensors.

Windows

Wherever possible, eliminate windows and other openings providing lucrative entry points for intruders. Where windows are necessary, consider using interior metal shutters which can be closed and locked. This allows use of passive ultrasonic sensors. If the character of the room does not allow the use of a passive ultrasonic sensor, a vibration sensor or capacitance proximity sensor suffices. Also, you need to consider a system using the principle of breaking an electrical circuit.

Ventilation Openings

These are any openings in the ceiling, walls, or doors to allow the free passage of air. They need a covering using steel bars, mesh, or louvered barriers. For maximum protection, you should consider eliminating ventilators. Where it is not possible to seal ventilators, consider the use of locked metal shutters. Then, detected intrusion through the ventilators becomes effective using the passive ultrasonic sensor or the vibration sensor. When ventilators are open continually, place a metal grill over the ventilator opening and attach a capacitance proximity sensor to protect it.

Construction Openings

These are unsecured openings from unfinished construction. Cover the opening with a grid wire sensor installed on plywood. Where the opening must stay open, use a capacitance proximity sensor within the opening.

Air Conditioners

To monitor for intrusion through an air conditioner aperture, attach a capacitance proximity sensor to a metal grill extending into the room in front of the unit.

Illustrations 10–9 through 10–11 provide you with examples of balanced magnetic switches placed on exterior doors, with the grid wire sensors used on interior surfaces. Also, see the illustrated example of passive ultrasonic sensor applications.

Illustration 10–9

EXAMPLE OF BALANCED MAGNETIC SWITCHES
PLACED ON INSIDE OF EXTERIOR DOORS

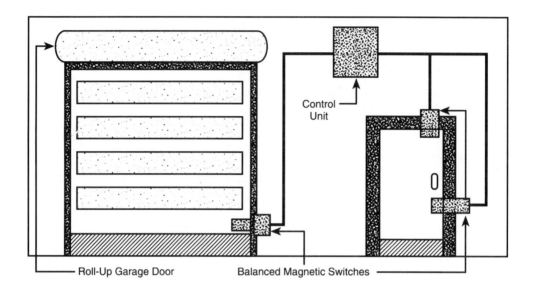

Control Unit

Roll-Up Garage Door   Balanced Magnetic Switches

Illustration 10–10

EXAMPLE OF GRID WIRE SENSORS USED ON INTERIOR SURFACES

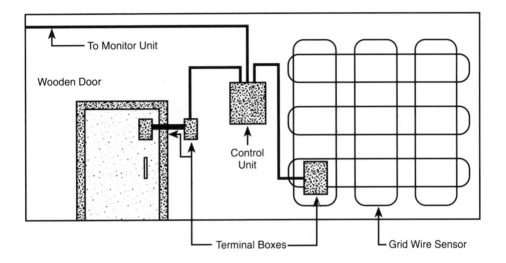

Illustration 10–11

EXAMPLES OF PASSIVE ULTRASONIC SENSOR SYSTEM APPLICATIONS

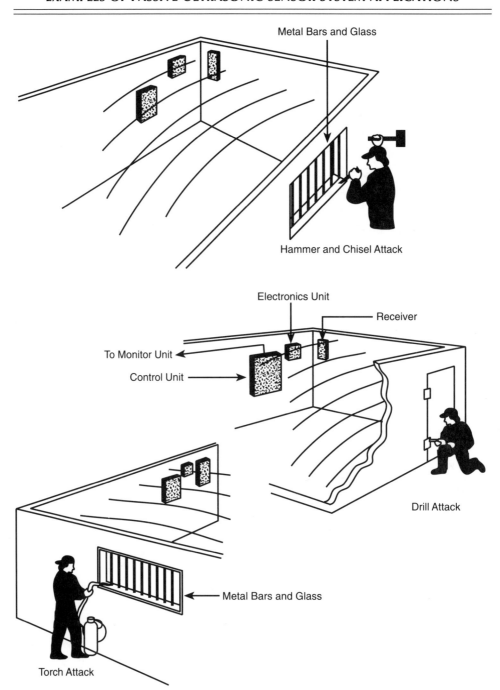

Metal Bars and Glass

Hammer and Chisel Attack

Electronics Unit

Receiver

To Monitor Unit

Control Unit

Drill Attack

Metal Bars and Glass

Torch Attack

QUICK REFERENCE GUIDE AND REVIEW

Motion Sensor

To detect the motion of an intruder inside a protected area, an ultrasonic motion sensor works when there is the smallest flow of air from heating units, air conditioners, cracks in the protected area, or any other possible source of air turbulence, as this may reduce the effectiveness of the sensor or cause nuisance alarms. A microwave system might provide adequate protection within an enclosed area.

Duress Sensor Considerations

Fixed

This sensor alerts security officers about an employee requesting immediate help. It activates from a foot- or hand-operated switch in a position most likely occupied by employees working in the protected area.

Portable

An alternate to the fixed duress sensor, the portable duress sensor is an ultrahigh frequency transmitter that can send an alarm to a receiver at the control unit. The restricted effective range depends on whether it is used inside a building or outside in an open area.

Point Sensors Considerations

Storage Cabinets and Safes

To detect movement near to or discover contact with any part of a storage cabinet or safe, you need to use a capacitance proximity sensor.

Control Unit

Place one control unit in each secure area to receive signals from the sensors and transmit signals to the monitor unit and local audible alarm.

Monitor Unit

Each control unit must report to a separate monitor unit status indicator module. Each monitor unit needs to contain one signal and power status indicator module.

Local Audible Alarm

Install a local audible alarm outside the protected area. This alarm serves two purposes. First, it may scare the intruder away. Second, it alerts security officers in the area. This alarm has limited value for areas where there are no security officer response teams. A local audible alarm supplies the best advantage when used with a remote monitor unit.

Telephone Dialer

A telephone dialer might serve your needs where it is not possible to install a monitor unit. This device telephones an alarm to several preselected phones. Use telephone dialers only for low-security applications. Telephone dialer lines can tie up when systems continue to call the number receiving the alarm notification message. They are subject to other tampering and interruption and do not alarm when out of order, cut, or grounded.

Data Transmission System

The data transmission system works wherever there are segments of the signal transmission line accessible to tampering or wherever the transmitted signal sends over commercial conductors. One data transmission system needs installation in each security zone covered by a control unit connected to such a line.

Intrusion Detection Alarm Report

Alarm and communications detection systems become closely allied in any comprehensive protection system. Telephone and radio communications are so common in everyday usage that their adaptation to a protective system poses few new problems. An alarm detection system is simply a manual or automatic means of communicating a warning of potential or present danger. Types of alarm detection systems include the following:

Local Alarm System

In a local alarm system the protective circuits or devices actuate a visual or audible signa. in the immediate vicinity of the object of protection. Response is by the security force within sight or hearing. The light or sound device needs installation outside the building and is protected against weather or willful tampering. The component connects to the control element with a tamperproof cable and is kept visible or audible for a distance of at least 400 feet. This system can work with a proprietary system.

Auxiliary System

An auxiliary system is one in which the company-owned system is a direct extension of the civil police and fire alarm systems. This is the least effective system because of dual responsibilities for maintenance.

Central Station System

A commercial agency may contract to provide electric protective services to its clients by use of a central station system. The agency designs, installs, maintains, and operates underwriter-approved systems to safeguard against fire, theft, and intrusion and monitors industrial processes. Alarms transmit to a central station outside the corporate or industrial complex where appropriate action might include notifying local police or fire departments.

Proprietary System

A proprietary system is similar to the central station system except owned by, and located on, the company property. Control and receiving equipment located in the company security department. This type of system normally connects with the local law enforcement and fire departments through a commercial central station.

Illustrations 10–12 through 10–17 show the systems discussed.

Illustration 10–12

EXAMPLES OF FIXED DURESS SENSOR PLACEMENT

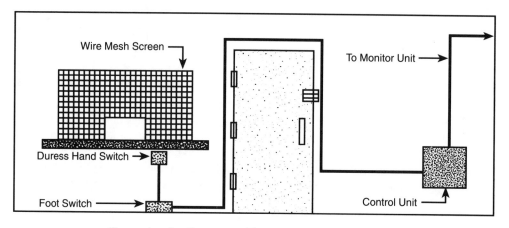

Example of a Company Financial Dispersal Center

Illustration 10–13

EXAMPLE OF AN INTRUSION DETECTION SYSTEM CONTROL UNIT

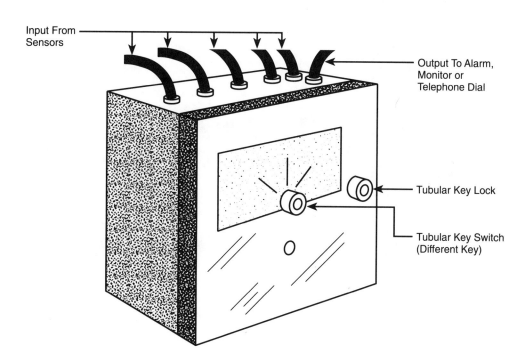

Input From Sensors

Output To Alarm, Monitor or Telephone Dial

Tubular Key Lock

Tubular Key Switch (Different Key)

Illustration 10–14

EXAMPLES OF MONITOR UNIT FOR INTRUSION DETECTION SYSTEMS

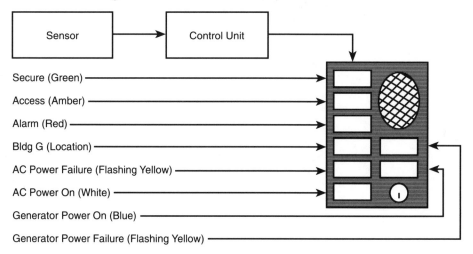

Twenty-Five Zone

Six-Zone

One-Zone

Signal Indicator Module and Signal
Signal and Power Status Indicator Module

Sensor → Control Unit

Secure (Green)

Access (Amber)

Alarm (Red)

Bldg G (Location)

AC Power Failure (Flashing Yellow)

AC Power On (White)

Generator Power On (Blue)

Generator Power Failure (Flashing Yellow)

Illustration 10–15

EXAMPLE OF AN AUDIBLE ALARM

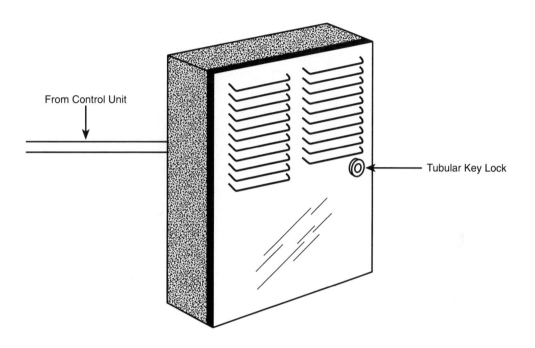

From Control Unit

Tubular Key Lock

Illustration 10–16

EXAMPLE OF A TELEPHONE DIALER SYSTEM

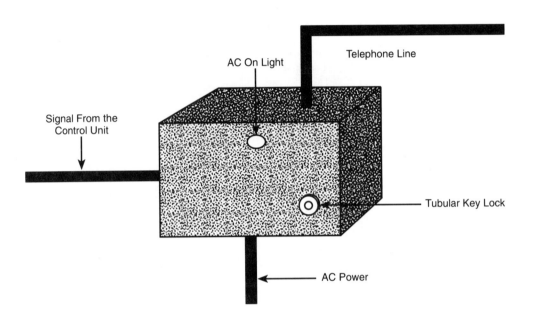

Illustration 10–17

EXAMPLE OF DATA TRANSMISSION SYSTEM

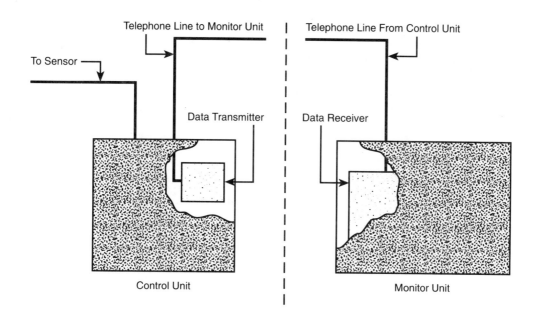

SIGNAL TRANSMISSION LINES

An intrusion detection system is no better than the security of the conductors that transmit the alarm signal to the monitor unit. These conductors must be sensitive enough to cause an alarm in the event of tampering.

Defeating an intrusion detection system happens despite the effectiveness of its sensor when a signal transmission line does not function properly or is damaged by a skilled intruder. Conductors easily become ineffective by an intruder who has enough knowledge of electricity and the necessary equipment to adjust the resistance in the signal transmission lines.

Signal transmission lines need management in a variety of ways, according to the location of the lines and the security called for. The management processes include the following:

1. Monitoring a break in the electrical circuit which may be grounded or shorted.

2. Monitoring to see if a predetermined variation in an electrical current has occurred. For example, an alarm light shows a possible 30-milliampere current increase or maybe decreased 5%.

3. Monitoring two or more features of a complex signal, such as current and frequency. If the signal changes on a random basis, the likelihood of the signal being recorded and replayed successfully is very remote.

4. Monitoring a digital- or tone-type signal transmitted through a telephone system. An investigation and replies scheme is ordinarily used. Since an electrical current is not being monitored here, the distance limit (a few miles) of the other types does not apply.

The needs for constant electronic or other type surveillance of signal transmission lines require emphasis to ensure security officers recognize this is often the weakest link in the intrusion detection system. Emphasis must also include the necessity of maintaining records of nuisance alarms and scheduled or unscheduled maintenance to ensure proper evaluation about continuing operation of the system.

The best protections of signal transmission lines result from locating them on high overhead poles, burying them underground, leading into buildings as high as possible, using locked terminal cabinets, and other such measures.

Manufacturers of the best intrusion detection equipment incorporate in their annunciator panels two relays, designated as the underload and overload relays. The underload relay detects any appreciable drop in line current while the overload relay detects a large increase in current. However, careful installations of the signal lines prevent defeating techniques mentioned earlier, and attempts to tamper with the line will not disturb either of the two relays.

Signal line tampering detection becomes assured when your circuits have low line tolerance. For example, an alarm may operate on 20 milliamperes of line current. If the overload relay is set to drop out when the line current exceeds 30 milliamperes and the underload relay will drop out at 10 milliamperes, the line becomes 20 milliamperes. Most standard alarm circuits have line tolerances ranging from 3 milliamperes (for storage vault applications) to 30 milliamperes (for window foil and door switch protected areas). Systems having line management on tolerance in the milliampere range can be defeated with little difficulty. To be effective, line management must not exceed 25 microamperes.

If your signal lines for company alarm systems installed at important facilities extend outside protected areas, you need to determine their vulnerability to tampering and, where feasible, provide microampere line sensitivity.

THE IMPORTANT ELEMENTS OF INTRUSION DETECTION SYSTEM MAINTENANCE

Intrusion detection systems should stay in continuous operation during nonoperational hours of the protected activity if they are to be effective security aids. In some situations it may be necessary to have continuous 24–hour operation. Therefore, the rule includes properly performed preventive and corrective maintenance. Each system should be capable of operating from a standby power source to compensate for the vulnerability of power sources outside the company. The time requirement for such capability needs evaluation for each application dependent upon such factors as alternate power supplies, maintenance support, hours of active operation, and so forth.

Maintenance is not a problem if proper care is routinely exercised. Most malfunctions, when using the correct system, precisely installed and adjusted, result from improper maintenance. To prevent malfunctions, regularly inspect all component parts and have qualified security personnel perform tests as often as recommended by manufacturers. Keep spare parts, such as fuses, condensers, relays, and other parts as recommended by the manufacturer, in the security department inventory.

Normally, the manufacturer will train and inform security personnel on maintenance of their equipment. To ensure proper operation of detection systems, observe the following steps:

1. Designated security offers should be available and capable of effecting immediate minor repairs, including replacement of burned-out bulbs, replacement of fuses, maintenance and replacement of the auxiliary power unit, and correction of obvious causes of malfunctions and invalid alarms. Other types of replacement parts should be provided and repairs should be made by specially trained security officers.

2. When you cannot train maintenance officers, a service contract needs to

be negotiated with the manufacturer. Therefore, maintenance service must be available on a 24-hour basis. Maintenance response time to critical areas should be no more than 3 hours.

The alarm receiving area needs designation to give adequate protection to monitoring security officers since it might otherwise provide a prime target for aggressive intruders. Provisions for emergency help to these areas need a prominent place in your corporate or industrial security plan.

Security officers on duty at monitor units need to maintain a daily record of all systems including alarms and any malfunctions experienced. Operations records need to reflect the following information.

1. Date, time, and prevailing weather
2. Identity of officer recording alarm signal
3. Identity of area where alarm signal originates
4. Action taken in response to alarm signal received
5. Total time needed by responding officers to arrive at the scene of an alarm
6. Cause for alarm signal to be activated
7. Tests of alarms
8. Malfunctions, including nuisance alarms
9. Servicing or maintenance of detection systems

WIRING, INSPECTION, AND TESTING THE SYSTEMS

Whenever practicable, ensure that your wiring of protective alarm and communication systems includes separate poles and conduits for company intrusion detection and lighting systems. Include tamper-resistant wire and cable, with sheaths of foil that transmit an alarm signal when penetrated or cut, as that will provide your systems with added protection.

All your company intrusion detection equipment and component elements, including communication circuits, need performance testing at least once during each shift (8 hours) by specific security officers. All intrusion detection equipment needs detailed inspection periodically by security officers or technical maintenance representatives from the manufacturer. Repairs or replacement of worn or failing parts within these systems need to happen on a regular schedule.

The following Quick Reference Guide contains definitions and tables useful during your planning, evaluating or troubleshooting intrusion detection systems and their component elements.

QUICK REFERENCE REVIEW AND GUIDE

Definitions

The following definitions provide a common understanding of intrusion detection systems and their component parts.

Actuator. A component element of the system that makes the alarm activate.

Annunciator (monitor). A visual or audible signaling device that shows conditions of associated circuits. Usually accomplished by the activation of a signal lamp and audible sound.

Antenna. A conductor or system of conductors for radiating or receiving electromagnetic waves.

Balanced magnetic switch. A magnetically operated switch designed to detect the opening of a secured door, window, or other closure. It also detects attempts to defeat the switch by substituting a magnetic field and may have provisions for internal adjustments and detection of tampering attempts.

Capacitance. The property of two or more objects that enables them to store electrical energy in an electrostatic field between them.

Capacitance proximity sensor. Records a change in capacitance or electrostatic fields to detect penetration through windows, ventilators, and other openings. Also effective in detecting attempted penetration into safes or storage cabinets.

Conductor. Material that transmits electric current. Wire and cable are conductors (also called signal transmission lines).

Contacts. The parts of a switch or relay that when touching or being separated permit electric current to flow or cease to flow. Often, used improperly to designate an entire magnetic switch or balance magnetic switch component.

Control unit. The terminal box for sensors that receives alarm and tamper signals and transmits the signals to the local audible alarm or monitor unit. The control unit supplies the primary and the backup power for sensors and both activates and deactivates the system.

Data transmission system. A component consisting of a data transmitter located in the control unit and a data receiver located in the monitor unit and is the communication link used to pass alarm and equipment status signals from the control unit to the monitor unit over a via-wire transmission line via RF.

Doppler. The effect of compression of expanding sound or radio frequencies reflected from or originating from a moving object.

Fail-safe. A term applied to a system so designed that during a failure of some component of it to function properly, the system will, by a signal or otherwise, show its incapacity.

(continued)

Fixed duress sensor. An emergency notification device, switch, or button manually operated by employees needing security officer assistance.

Grid wire sensor. Detects forced entry through walls, floors, ceilings, doors, and other barriers by the break wire method.

Intrusion detection system. The total of all intrusion detection components, including sensors, control units, transmission lines, monitor units, and cell-associated function integrated to perform as needed.

Intrusion detection sensors. Devices that initiate alarm signals because of sensing a stimulus or change or because they react to a condition for which they are designed.

Local audible alarm. An electronic screamer or bell for outdoor or indoor use near the protected area.

Magnetic contact—simple magnetic switch. Has two separate items, a magnetically actuated switch and a magnet. The switch normally works best when mounted in a fixed position (door frame or safe) opposing the magnet that is fastened to a hinged or sliding door. When the movable barrier opens, the magnet moves with it and the switch opens. Magnetic contacts need connection, so that the switch remains closed while the magnet is near. This allows the electric current to flow. When the door or window opens, the magnetic contact opens. This stops the electric current flow, causing an alarm.

Microwave sensor. A radio/radar frequency (RF) transceiver having a frequency range of gigahertz (GHz) (billion cycles per second) that detects motion through the Doppler shift effect.

Monitor. A device that senses and reports on the condition of a system commonly used interchangeably with the terms, monitor unit, monitor panel, status indicator module, annunciator, and other similar terms.

Monitor unit. The primary notification or reporting device. Commonly used interchangeably with the terms monitor, monitor console, monitor panel board, monitor display, and other similar terms.

Motion sensor. Detects movement inside the protected area.

Nuisance alarm. The result of a sensor activation caused by accident, neglect, malfunction, or natural causes such as wind, lightning, or thunder. Often called a false alarm.

Overload. A load greater than the rated load of an electrical device.

Passive ultrasonic sensor. An ultrasonic sensor used to detect the sounds of forced entry through walls, ceilings, and doors.

Penetration sensor. A sensor that detects entry through doors, windows, walls, or any other openings into the protected area.

Photoelectric system. Usually supplied as two separate units, a transmitter and receiver. Transmission of a light beam to the receiver. Any interruption of this light beam causes an alarm.

Point sensor. Detects the removal or attempted removal of an object from its storage container.

(continued)

Portable duress sensor. An emergency notification device having an UHF transmitter carried by a person and separately enclosed receiver at the control unit.

Radar. Radio frequency transceiver having a frequency range of 100 MHz to 1 GHz.

Sonic. Having a frequency within the audibility range of the human ear.

Managed line. A conductor, which, if cut, broken, or shorted, or if any other feature of the current that is being monitored exceeds limits set, will alarm indicating a problem at a monitoring unit (also called supervised line).

Telephone dialer. A device normally installed within the protected area that automatically dials preselected telephone numbers upon sensor activation and provides a prerecorded message notifying of intrusion.

Ultrasonic. The frequency range of sound that is above the capabilities of normal human hearing. In intrusion detection systems it usually varies between 21,500 and 26,000 Hz (cycles per second and higher).

Ultrasonic motion sensor. An ultrasonic Doppler or frequency shift sensor used to detect the motion of an intruder inside the protected area.

Vibration sensor. A disturbance sensor used to detect forced entry through metal barriers placed over windows and ventilators or attempts to drill, saw, or cut through walls, ceiling, floors, or doors.

The following checklist helps you to determine need and evaluate existing intrusion detection systems in your company.

CHECKLIST FOR EVALUATING YOUR COMPANY'S INTRUSION DETECTION SYSTEMS

Yes	No	Evaluation Item
☐	☐	Are intrusion detection systems installed at key facilities and activities within your company?
☐	☐	If not, have you requested these systems?
☐	☐	Do you believe there is a need for the systems?
☐	☐	If yes, do you have a standard operating procedure as a guide for your security officers?

Does your standard operating procedure include

Yes	No	Evaluation Item
☐	☐	Instruction for daily testing, activation and deactivation and response to alarms?
☐	☐	Requirement that a log be maintained indicating alarm activations by date, time, and type of activation (actual or false)?
☐	☐	If the IDS has proven unreliable (excessive false alarms), is the system at fault or is it the result of faulty installation?
☐	☐	According to your evaluation, are the systems adequate?
☐	☐	At the time of this inspection or evaluation, is your system functioning properly?
☐	☐	Is your system suitable for its present location and environment? If not, explain in remarks.
☐	☐	Is your system capable of accomplishing the job that your company management expects?
☐	☐	Do security officers and company management understand that intrusion detection systems are designed to detect, not necessarily prevent, unauthorized or unlawful intrusion into the protected area? Also, is there an understanding the system is not effective beyond a predetermined point of approach to a protected object or area?

Is security of the IDS provided with other measures built into the system, such as

Yes	No	Evaluation Item
☐	☐	Height of alarm signal reporting lines on poles?
☐	☐	Depth that alarm signal reporting lines are buried in the ground?
☐	☐	Use of shielded transmission and power lines?
☐	☐	Control of access to system equipment?
☐	☐	Use of seals on controls and exposed adjustment mechanisms?
☐	☐	Placement of transmission and power lines inside walls or metal conduit?
☐	☐	If local annunciator is used and is displayed on exterior of a building, is it protected from the weather or willful tampering?
☐	☐	Is your system underwriter approved?
☐	☐	Is your system installed by underwriter-approved, qualified persons?
☐	☐	Is your system equipped with a two-position lock switch for on and off operation?
☐	☐	Are there at least two keys available?

(continued)

☐ ☐ Are adequate key controls exercised?

☐ ☐ Can the system be turned on and off from outside?

☐ ☐ In addition to the on and off switch, is the system equipped with electrical shunt-type switches for testing?

☐ ☐ Is it a multiple-purpose system (smoke, water, heat or other elements)?

☐ ☐ Is the system equipped with a pilot light or with any other type of operational readiness indicator?

☐ ☐ If an AC power supply is used, is the system designed to operate by automatic switching to DC power when necessary to provide continuous protection? (standby battery in place?)

☐ ☐ Is the system designed to make an uninterrupted and silent protective circuit transfer with only a local visible indicator to signal when the transfer takes place?

☐ ☐ Can activating devices be unobtrusively operated?

☐ ☐ Are properly qualified officers or others used to maintain the systems?

Is the alarm system properly maintained by

☐ ☐ Trained security officers or other maintenance persons?

☐ ☐ Readily available trained persons from outside the company?

☐ ☐ An appropriate service contract?

Are records kept of all alarm signals received, to include

☐ ☐ Time?

☐ ☐ Date?

☐ ☐ Location?

☐ ☐ Action taken?

☐ ☐ Cause for alarm?

☐ ☐ Is your system tested prior to activating it for nonoperational periods?

☐ ☐ Are frequent tests conducted to determine the adequacy and promptness of response to alarm signals?

☐ ☐ Is there any inherent weakness in the system itself?

☐ ☐ Is it connected to a capable response element?

☐ ☐ Are activating devices appropriately located and sufficient in number?

☐ ☐ Is the equipment visible to public view?

☐ ☐ When system is activated, is it audible on the premises?

☐ ☐ Are independent transmission lines used?
Are adequate spare parts, such as fuses and bulbs, readily available to users?
Are security officers capable of conducting minor maintenance and installing fuses and bulbs as required?

☐ ☐ Is a duress capability built into the system when an authorized person deactivates the system under duress?

11 Electronic Countermeasures

The same advances in electronics technology that improved the quality of television and radio have made significant impact on the security profession. The progression from vacuum tubes to transistors to today's subminiaturization age of hybrid integrated circuit technology has played a major role in the growth and sophistication of security management. The dramatic advances reduced component cost and size, leading to the introduction of security measures now commonly in use, such as low-light-level, closed-circuit television cameras and electronic article surveillance devices. Several recent technological advances in electronics and communications engineering will soon find important applications in the development of security products and systems. Electronic security will probably become more prevalent as applications develop and become cost effective. For many companies, however, the sheer magnitude of corporate or industrial assets often calls for highly sophisticated security measures despite cost.

DEVELOPING YOUR STRATEGY FOR SUCCESS

Well-rounded security management knowledge is important, but it is not the only thing that separates the winners from the losers in the security business. What makes the difference is the winner's ability to recognize potential weaknesses from the start and compensate for them. Often, the security weaknesses stay hidden within a maze of electronic countermeasures designed to create an impregnable environment—until skilled intruders prove it is not. The presence of technology-based security equipment does not assure anything beyond the costly acquisition, installation, and maintenance, unless you properly layer and manage the technology-based equipment and systems built on the foundation of nontechnology-based techniques.

AUDIT YOUR SECURITY EFFECTIVENESS IN EIGHT STEPS

The best way to assess and evaluate your protection efforts and know what you need to add, move, or enhance starts with never becoming content with performance your security equipment appears to provide. Instead, stand back and plan how you would get into or out of the company to pilfer, commit major theft, destroy property, or steal information for a competitor. You have the advantage of knowing the systems; however, using this unique approach, you will probably be surprised at holes you will find in the systems viewing them from the skilled intruder's perspective. As a skilled security manager, you should try to overcome each system you have or install. When you can no longer overcome your company security systems, chances for a skilled intruder doing that becomes unlikely.

As you work through the techniques that follow, remember to take detailed notes. They will prove valuable later and provide a foundation for continued assessment of your security systems and deciding what technology-based systems will genuinely enhance your current systems.

1. Begin at the perimeter boundaries of your company. You may be protecting an industrial complex or a single building in an urban environment; however, the problems of security begin at the perimeter. Envision yourself as the aggressive, determined intruder and decide after placing yourself in that role how you would breach the existing security measures.

2. Start with the basics, discussed in earlier chapters, and work your way inside (e.g., fences, lighting, security patrols, sentry dogs, or other barriers and supporting elements).

3. Use penetration techniques when employees are coming for work, when they are leaving, and when your company closes for the day, night, or weekends. The skilled intruder chooses the best time advantage for his or her approach, and what appears favorable at one time may appear unfavorable at another time. You need to use the same reasoning during your penetration assessment.

4. Set priority targets and avoid aimless penetration efforts. Know exactly what area you want to reach undetected, remembering the determined intruder will surely know exactly what he or she is after. Using that concept will show you a probable motive and target an intruder will probably consider as the best items to steal compared to the risk involved. The benefit of assessing the threat provides you the advantage of deciding effective ways to layer your protective security.

5. Also, consider the intruder who does not steal company property, but instead inflicts property and operational damage. Examples include an activist who disagrees with your company's business and believes he or she can cause a downfall of operations or wants to create attention; terrorists seeking publicity for their cause that may have nothing to do with the business of your company; and the disgruntled employee or former employee, vendor, or others formerly associated with your company who are set on exacting retribution for what he or she perceives as an injustice. It is important to remember you are often dealing with intense people who probably know they are committing illegal acts, but rationalize that in a variety of ways. This intruder category might want to be detected and arrested after committing the crime and can be a dangerous threat to both your company and security officers.

6. When you reach the target areas or the general area inside your protective barriers without detection, improvements clearly need consideration. Depending on how you breached the security barriers, you are supplied with the information on how to harden it with technology-based equipment.

7. After doing that, assuming your efforts proved successful, determine how to extract yourself undetected, escaping in ways to avoid identification or arrest. This technique helps you assess the threat and countermeasures to protect against "stay behind" people and maybe an employee deciding to pilfer company property.

8. Assess your findings objectively and use them to determine exactly how to harden your current security systems, where added layers can help, and the best technology-based equipment to install.

FIVE IMPORTANT STEPS FOR EFFECTIVELY AUDITING INTERNAL SECURITY

When intrusion or departure security meets your satisfaction, look to the internal problem. According to research conducted by government and private agencies regarding crime problems within corporate and industrial environments, including financial institutions, about 80% of the losses happen from within. One reason attributed this problem stems from much security attention focused on intruders as noted and little attention given security threats posed by employees, vendors, maintenance workers, cleaning teams, and visitors who might have plans for stealing, damaging, or retribution. When a company employs several thousand workers, the percentage of those who have criminal enterprises might add to an impressive figure. There is also the factor of opportunity to consider, since many people decide to steal to ease perceived economic pressures, others steal just to be stealing.

Your internal security audit needs to address the fact that you need to protect your company's assets from people authorized to be there as opposed to intruders. Although your protective security effort needs to begin with basic nontechnology security measures, using technology-based security systems may also play an important role within the company with proper applications. It might enable better control, prevention, detection, and identification of the authorized persons breaching your company's internal security integrity to steal assets or create damage. The following steps supply you with an effective guide to determine the strengths and weaknesses of your current internal security systems. As noted earlier, place yourself in the role of a person intending theft, damage, or other act, not only in committing it, but escaping unidentified.

1. Determine probability factors involving accessibility to areas within the company without attracting suspicion of security officers or other employees. Most company environments permit "wandering" throughout the company. If challenged, and the person is a bona fide employee, who offers a reasonable spontaneous excuse or purpose for being there, he or she will usually be overlooked as a potential threat. When you are unable to control "wandering" because of company policy authorizing the practice, you will need to develop other means of controlling access to specific areas.

2. Determine what the specific priority target areas include, such as supply and file rooms, computer centers, research and development areas, or others depending on your company's business. Remember, the perpetrator might be seeking information for competitors; for blackmail based on misfeasance, malfeasance, or nonfeasance, real or imagined; or for any of a number of other reasons. Other reasons may include purely personal motives, such as learning the salary of another person, how much another employee spends traveling, or other data the company prefers to keep confidential to protect privacy and avoid damaging morale problems or internal disruptions. There is also another important reason for keeping certain records and files of employees protected. Often, competing companies can learn through information what your company is doing or planning (e.g., travel expenses), salaries so possible recruiting offers can be effective, and other competitive intelligence reasons.

3. Determine access and regress from the lucrative target areas and audit the area itself. For example, acts or crimes often stem from impulse that result from opportunity. An employee with a particular grievance with an executive or other employee might walk into a file room containing records and shred documents about the intended victim or photograph documents that show the company's planning, research and development, marketing plans or any number of information types. Note here that there is no theft of tangible property only destroyed or photographed records that result because opportunity helps the activity to remain undetected.

4. When you have assessed the weaknesses, choose the technology-based equipment that will prevent access, and take other steps to eliminate the opportunities. For example installing a closed circuit television system, alarms, ID lock systems, and many others discussed throughout this chapter and the book often offers the deterrent needed to prevent internal crimes or indiscretions. Consider ways of layering the systems internally, so that when one system is bypassed with ingenuity, another layer is not, and detection becomes immediate. High technology provides a spectrum of devices, and it is clearly not possible to note each one since they fill catalogs. However, concepts become the focus of this chapter to supply you with guidelines as opposed to a specific item of equipment and its specifications. Once the formulation of security layering, using only applications as needed, is in place, coupled with confidence that you have developed techniques for protecting company assets, your security will be effective and will continue improving with flexibility to meet any challenge.

5. Few things stay the same for long, and that is especially true in the corporate and industrial business environments. You need to make continuing assessments of your security systems. Also, an important tip in layering any security system, especially high-tech equipment, includes making some of it obvious and some of it covert. The first objective of security layering is prevention; the second is eliminating opportunity, and the third is detection when the first two points fail. Remember, determined ingenuity can always overcome a security system, especially when it is visible. However, in the complexities you might encounter, your security systems need applications similar to the performing illusionist (magician). Allow the observer to see what you want him or her to see, to provide the prevention and elimination of opportunity, while concealing other hidden elements that back up or harden the system for detection. Layering or redundancy remains the only way to provide your company with effective protective security. Illustrations 11–1 through 11–3 supply you with examples of layering security using technology-based equipment.

Illustration 11–1

EXAMPLE OF LAYERED TECHNOLOGY-BASED SECURITY MANAGEMENT

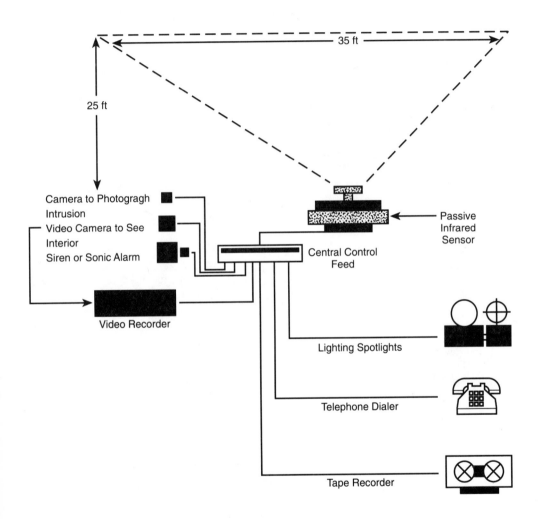

Illustration 11–2

EXAMPLE OF RECEPTION AREA LEADING TO A HIGH-SECURITY CORPORATE OR INDUSTRIAL OFFICE SUITE

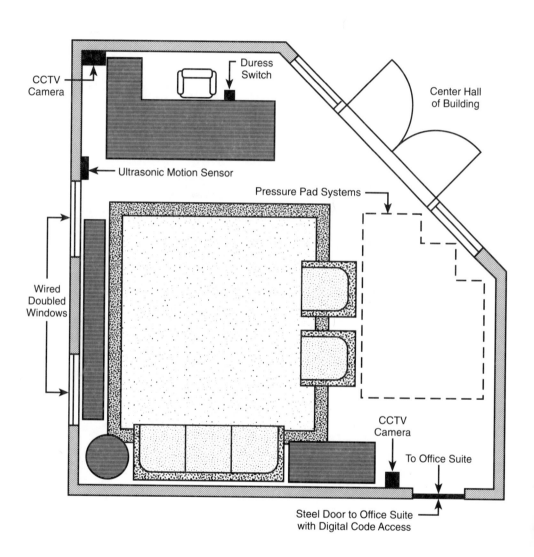

Illustration 11–3

CORPORATE OR INDUSTRIAL HIGH-SECURITY OFFICE SUITE

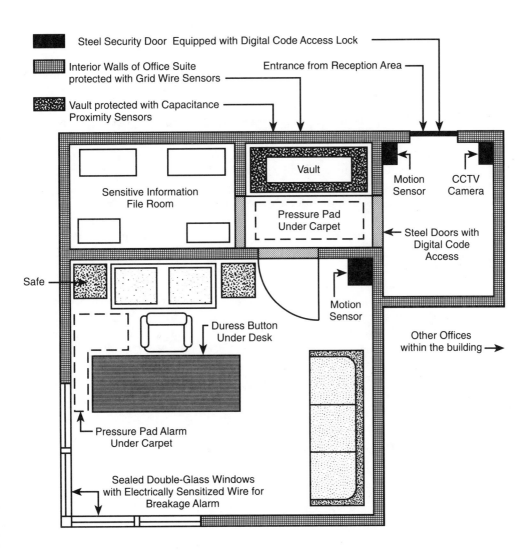

EFFECTIVE MANAGEMENT OF CLOSED-CIRCUIT TELEVISION SECURITY SYSTEMS

Closed-circuit television is a versatile surveillance method that has become widely used by corporate and industrial security managers. From a central location, security officers can monitor events at one or several remote locations. Installation of cameras includes fixed positions or setting to enable oscillation for viewing a large area.

Low-light-level devices have greatly extended passive optical surveillance capabilities. Practical low-light-level television systems are manufactured for optical surveillance operations under light intensities as low as 10^{-8} lumens per square yard or virtual darkness. Night vision adaptations also available, provide enhanced applications for your closed-circuit television surveillance systems.

Other corporate and industrial closed-circuit television applications include electronic photo imaging, effective when verifying identifies by comparing immediate identification of a person seeking access to company areas. This system works by using a standard video camera (normally color) combined with computer hardware and software. Security officers monitoring the system and controlling access to the company or specific areas can view the person seeking entry and compare it instantly with a video identification photo on the computer's database file.

In security applications, closed-circuit television (CCTV) serves a limited audience, that is, the security manager and security officers. A CCTV system installation supplies effective surveillance technique for any building or outdoor area in the interest of enhanced security by providing the three key elements, prevention, elimination of opportunity, and detection. Remember, however, for your protective systems to remain effective during power failures, you need to ensure an effective basic, nontechnology-reliant system continues to supply protection of company assets.

SEVEN BEGINNING STEPS OF EFFECTIVE CCTV APPLICATIONS

For effective selection and conceptual use of CCTV, you need the essential knowledge of component parts, camera movement capability, types of shots, and other aspects that make the system viable.

1. Characteristics of CCTV

The television camera you choose for CCTV applications needs to operate under any marginal light conditions and provide adequate security surveillance of the low-light-level type.

2. Component Parts of CCTV

The following components create a CCTV system:

- Television camera
- Automatic zoom lens
- Manual control override
- Mounting equipment

3. Camera Movement Capabilities

Detecting pilferage, theft, or intruders in directions (360 degrees), the camera movement needs a capability of

- Pan—turning horizontally, left to right, or right to left.
- Tilt—aiming the camera up or down.
- Zoom—changing the camera's field of view from wide angle to close up while the camera is in stationary position (through automatic changing of the focal length of the lens).

4. Operational Capability of CCTV

CCTV operation capability needs to include the following:

- Operation by remote control with monitoring security officers at a central location
- A camera that provides routine and continuous monitoring of a specific activity
- Preplanned monitor and automatic zoom of activity at specified intervals

Illustration 11–4 shows a possible CCTV monitoring application for outside activities at a warehouse loading and receiving facility.

Illustration 11–4

CONCEPT OF CCTV APPLICATION FOR AN INDUSTRIAL WAREHOUSE

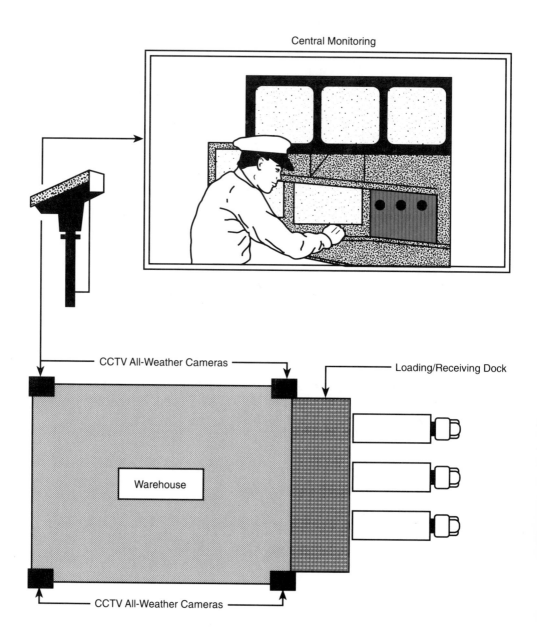

5. Central Security Monitoring and Control Room

Location of the central monitoring and control room at your security head-quarters enables fast response of security officers when needed. The essential factors to consider include the following:

- Control room monitor equipment is connected by secure cables to remote cameras (multiple) throughout protected company areas for conducting protective security surveillance.
- Security officers occupying the monitoring and control facilities have adequate protective access security to prevent interruptions.
- Your monitoring and control room needs efficient and effective communications capability with internal security forces and to other emergency agencies outside the company area, such as fire and police departments, paramedical services and so on.
- Your CCTV system needs a push-button capability to enable security officers to select different operational areas randomly for monitoring, depending on shipping, receiving, and potential intrusion or other observed threats to company assets.
- The system needs a videotaping capability, either triggered automatically, with a time-delay device, or by the monitoring security officer.

6. Camera Shot Classification

Understanding equipment capability and limits is an important element of effective application for CCTV. Illustration 11–5 provides a guide to consider when assessing your CCTV equipment application and location requirements. Determine the essential video capability for each area of protection including

- Extreme closeup
- Closeup
- Bust shot
- Medium closeup
- Midshot
- Three quarter length
- Full length
- Long shot
- Wide angle

Illustration 11–5

CCTV CAMERA SHOT CLASSIFICATIONS (LENS LENGTHS)

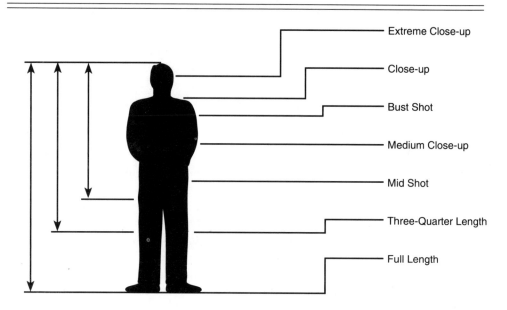

7. Applications of CCTV

Applications of your CCTV systems need the following minimum essential factors:

- The monitoring security officer should be able to speak to persons at the camera location (in most situations) and to hear people or noises at the camera location. This involves implementing a two-way communication system.
- Signal communication lines between the monitor panel and the control or surveillance points must be secured.
- Applications are for monitoring electrically operated gate locks or other areas where no security officers are present or for added protection in some situations when security officers are present.
- The CCTV system should allow a person at the monitor panel to converse with the person wanting entry to a protected area.
- The camera should show a person on the monitor accurately and clearly so monitoring security officers can verify identity and accurately determine to provide or deny permission to enter.

- The gate lock monitored by CCTV can be remotely released by the monitoring security officer to allow entry after verifying the person or vehicle identity and authorization to have access to the company area.
- The system allows effective observation of security cages, high-value goods in warehouses, fence lines, parking lots, banks, ports, ships, and other corporate or industrial areas.

APPLICATIONS OF CLOSED-CIRCUIT TELEVISION FOR TOUGH SECURITY PROBLEMS

The problem and advantage of closed-circuit television systems remain its visibility to people nearby. Prevention and elimination of opportunity supply the advantage. When employees or intruders believe security officers will detect and record their illicit acts, a strong deterrent exists. Advantage also includes detection of intruders and pilferage, fires, and other activities that need early assessment. Problems or weaknesses of CCTV systems include the same visibility providing advantage to the skilled and determined intruder. Also, it's often a problem for preventing or detecting employee pilferage after time passes and the employee fear of detection yields to finding ways to defeat the system. However, technology provides us with viable layers that enable your security management to defeat the problems. Doing that, however, requires an assessment of how people might defeat the CCTV systems you have and then determine how to harden those existing systems.

WEAKNESSES OF CCTV SURVEILLANCE APPLICATIONS

Three major problems of CCTV surveillance include darkness that disables the system and creates a diversion.

Most CCTV applications need adequate lighting to ensure effective operations. However, cameras now available need little light, and night vision attachments can provide enhanced security applications. A clever intruder or pilfering employee knows the CCTV surveillance is only as good as what the security officer monitoring the area on CCTV can see. Defeating the system for a specific area might be as simple as flicking a light switch in a hallway at one end, and after passing out of the camera's view, turning the lights back on. An attentive security officer might dispatch a response team, but the identification opportunity is lost and finding the intruder within an office or industrial complex might prove an exercise in futility. Often, the person might use this technique only as a ploy to see what the security response brings or to toy with the security force, having no other intent.

Visible CCTV cameras often sweep an area, leaving other areas unmonitored. The determined intruder waits out of view until the camera passes and then slips by it undetected by the monitoring security officer. Other means of defeating the CCTV system include cutting lead-in or feed-out wires, using smoke bomb devices to fill the area with intense smoke (available at any marine equipment store), and other ways limited only to the ingenuity of a person who can find ways around a visible CCTV camera.

The most effective way an intruder can overcome CCTV systems stems from creating a diversion. He or she creates a situation making the monitoring security officer focus attention on a specific area. Because security officers often must view several CCTV monitors, and when they note on one of them what they perceive as a crisis or emergency, their attention diverts to that activity. An example of diverting attention and creating a false emergency would be using the smoke bomb technique mentioned earlier. For example, a targeted area for the intruder is in area "D" and he or she wants the security officer monitoring the CCTV to concentrate attention on area "A" for about five minutes or more. The intruder also wants to direct a security response team away from area "D" so alarm systems backing up a CCTV system, when activated, will need a longer response time.

Smoke bombs are manufactured for vessels at sea that need to signal location or for help. The smoke devices designed for use in open outdoor areas can with some ingenuity be triggered from a remote location, enabling prepositioning during normal business hours. The security officer monitoring Area "A" on CCTV understandably perceives the dense smoke suddenly obvious on the viewing screen as a fire and starts to notify response teams, the fire department, and others on his or her notification list. The intruder waits until the flurry of activity is proceeding, including hearing sirens of fire trucks arriving at Area "A," and makes his or her move into area "D." Other diversions might include fast or remote control diversionary action to trigger other alarm systems in areas "B" and "C" so that one in area "D" is ignored or becomes less obvious. Until found otherwise, the perceived fire might also cause security officers to believe there is a malfunction in the security system alarms. The confusion normally helps an intruder to complete the illicit task and escape with little risk, using the CCTV and alarm systems to commit a crime unopposed.

You must alert your security officers about the advantages of CCTV and other systems, but caution them about ways they might easily be deceived.

TECHNIQUES OF CONVERTING WEAKNESSES OF CCTV TO STRENGTHS

The first step is clear procedural training for CCTV monitoring security officers. Alert them to the diversion possibilities, and although responding to perceptions, ensure their recognition that the situation might be other than what it seems.

The second step is developing effective redundant CCTV systems that include secondary viewing from different perspectives within the same area and using nonvisible CCTV devices to harden the visible systems.

Several manufacturers offer micro closed-circuit television systems (most connect to standard CCTV cameras and equipment) easily hidden as a successive layer in your primary system. Some clandestine cameras or lens connected to conventional cameras are clocks, fire extinguishers, and within dropped ceilings. Illustrations 11–6 through 11–9 show possibilities to consider depending on your company's needs. Several manufacturers specialize in CCTV applications, both conventional and clandestine versions.

Illustration 11–6

EXAMPLES OF COVERT CCTV SYSTEMS

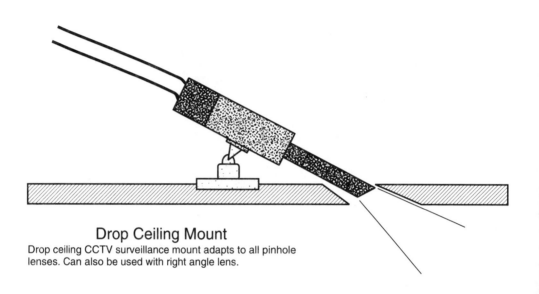

Drop Ceiling Mount

Drop ceiling CCTV surveillance mount adapts to all pinhole lenses. Can also be used with right angle lens.

Need picture to scan?

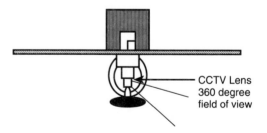

CCTV Lens
360 degree
field of view

Covert Lens System

Illustration 11−7

EXAMPLE OF PORTABLE MINIATURE CCTV CAMERA AND MONITOR (PROVIDES ENHANCED SECURITY FOR SPECIAL APPLICATIONS)

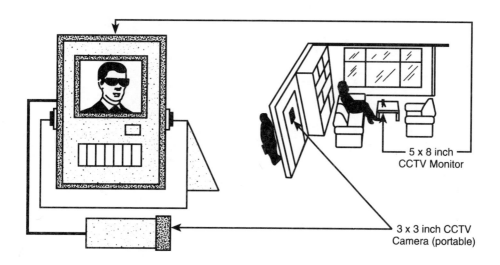

5 x 8 inch CCTV Monitor

3 x 3 inch CCTV Camera (portable)

Illustration 11−8

EXAMPLE OF CCTV FOR RECEPTIONIST IN A SECURE OR RESTRICTED AREA

Illustration 11–9

EXAMPLE OF DOOR-MOUNTED CAMERA FOR SENSITIVE AREAS
(REFERENCED TO ILLUSTRATION 11–8)

PROTECTING YOUR COMPANY FROM DANGEROUS MAIL, PARCELS AND PEOPLE WITH FIREARMS

Technology provides you with another advantage for protecting your company from incoming dangerous mail, parcels, and people. Depending on the company's business or circumstances emerging from decisions within the company, the threat of letter and parcel bombs needs your consideration. There are also threats involving people with firearms entering a corporate or industrial environment determined to injure or kill management executives. Whatever the threat, preventing these types of situations is a priority in most companies.

Protection Techniques from Explosive Mail and Parcels

There is only one way to ensure that mail and parcels do not contain explosives and that is to put each item through a variety of tests. Effective technology-based equipment needs a prominent place on your security planning agenda. One incident prevented far exceeds the cost of acquisition and installation of this valuable equipment.

After installing equipment to screen and detect dangerous incoming mail you must determine the scope of the screening effort. If a company receives more mail than is feasible to search, you need to decide, in concert with your company's management team, what mail is to be screened. When mail screening is limited, you need to develop priorities according to the perceived threat. For example, if one manufacturer is shipping in loads of parcels in its trucks, the threat is less than incoming piece mail or parcels through postal or other delivery services. The latter calls for priority searches since that is historically how mail bombs might arrive at the company. Do not be fooled by incoming mail or parcels that appear innocent because they appear to come from familiar sources. Studies show that persons sending explosive devices through the mails often conceal them by learning what sources the targeted company or person views as nonthreatening. Forging or counterfeiting labels and letterhead envelopes and even ensuring the postmark is correct is all part of the preparation a perpetrator might make before mailing the bomb.

The Threat of Firearms Entering Your Company and What to Do About It

Three types of threats create your toughest security problem regarding firearms: (1) persons seeking revenge against an executive or other employee including domestic problems, (2) persons intent on committing a crime using firearms as a method of force, and (3) terrorists or quasi-terroristic acts. (Terroristic acts can be any crime of violence intended on creating fear or coercion although the target selected is not necessarily associated with the purpose. For example, terrorists shoot up an airport terminal and kill dozens of people only to attract attention, not because they have a perceived grievance with the people or airport.)

Although the threats of violence within corporate or industrial areas are not a common event, whenever it happens, the results are tragic. Responsible security management includes preparedness for threats to company assets, preventing or eliminating opportunities for the criminal activity being the priority task, with detection as the third factor. Regarding firearms, all the factors apply; however, in this category of protective security, detection also can both prevent and eliminate the opportunity. Often, we fall into a trap set by pranksters, or people who intend on violent activity and change their mind, or those who test the security systems by observing reactions to their threats. Regularly, the reaction to specific threats is thorough and after a period of intense security, the effort wanes and returns to routine, having other matters to deal with and thinking the threat is past. The perpetrator, now having knowledge gained by casually observing security reaction during the intense time, uses the lull in security to strike with some success. Effective protective security management calls for your systems to be integrated and steady, not running in cycles of intensity and then relaxed efforts. When you ensure consistent security operations that provide consistent daily precautions and countermeasures, threats creating problems for others pose no great alarm at your company because your systems are already in place and effective. Cycles of visible intensity and relaxed security encourage instead of prevent crimes of violence.

There are several types of equipment available to screen persons entering the company areas, including handheld, portable, and walk-through portals. The latter is best applied as a permanently installed element within a door frame or hallway. Deciding whether to make the efforts visible depends on the type of company you protect and circumstances coupled with company policy on security intensity.

Illustration 11–10 shows two examples of common techniques for effectively screening mail and persons. However, there are dozens of specialized systems available from manufacturers, and your choices need to rely on the factors encompassing your company.

Illustration 11–10

EXAMPLES OF EXPLOSIVE AND FIREARMS COUNTERMEASURES

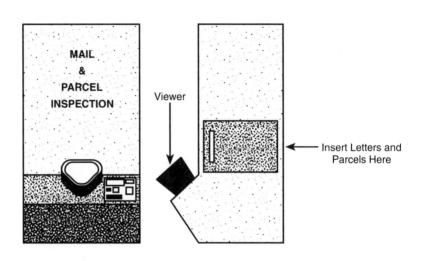

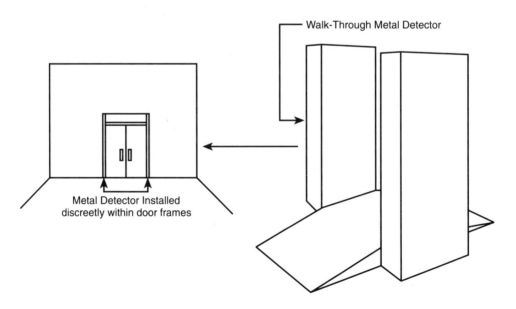

ELECTRONIC SYSTEMS TO CONTROL ACCESS

Applications of electronic systems controlling access in corporate and industrial environments base identification judgment on a remote capability through a routine discriminating electronic reading device for positive ID. That technology application replaces the manual system involving a security officer to verify identification based on access rosters, photo ID cards, and badges and personal recognition.

In a technology-based electronic reader identification, the following actions happen within the automated machine:

1. The machine receives physical identification data from the person seeking access to a specific area or building when he or she inserts a special card or performs other requirements.

2. Upon receipt of the information normally contained on a magnetic strip on a card, the device reads and encodes the data for its evaluation.

3. The machine compares data from the card, often coupled with numbers or letters entered on a keyboard (similar to a bank ATM machine) with information stored within the machine data base.

4. The machine makes a decision based on the comparison of the entered and stored data.

5. It then translates the results of the comparison into readable form and directs the proper response or action, for example, releasing a lock, signaling verification on a monitor, or sounding an alarm.

Several mechanical devices that add to your security posture are now commonplace in most corporate and industrial environments that use progressive security management techniques. Most systems use the following:

1. Magnetic coding

2. Embossing

3. Optical characters

4. Dielectric coding

Specialized systems are ideal for highly sensitive company areas because the systems use verified initial information created in a controlled environment to establish the data base. However, they are not infallible, and like a bank ATM machine, if an unauthorized person obtains the bank card and corresponding code number the machine cannot distinguish the difference. However, certain equipment that cannot be fooled so easily is included here:

1. One innovative technique with effective application to identification and admittance procedures involves dimension comparisons. A comparison of

a person's full hand dimensions compared to verified data in a computer linked to the reader determines identity and entry authorization.

2. Another specialized machine reader can scan a single fingerprint and provide positive identification of anyone trying to gain entry.

3. Voiceprints enable a reliable identification technique and feature rapid processing with accuracy.

Note: Items 1 through 3 are the best security measure, difficult or impossible to breach when operated properly.

4. An inexpensive application uses signatures of authorized persons. The device stores an employee's authentic signature within its data base. When seeking access to a company area, the employee signs his or her signature on an electronic pad, and the device compares it with the one on file. When matched, access is allowed and when the machine cannot make a positive match, access is denied.

The advantage of an inclusive automated identification and access control system reinforces the security depth through its easy and rapid change capability. The computer system controlling the devices operates through its memory, stored on magnetic tape or disk. Changes or instructions to the system originate from the remote entering or deletion of specific code numbers. The big advantage of these systems stems from making immediate changes without making wiring or media changes.

The security marketplace has a wide, constantly improved and enhanced array of mechanized and automated hardware and software security systems, often interfacing with each other for enhancing of your security posture. Assessments of your security needs and use of the planning, programming, and budgeting procedures outlined earlier will greatly help you in improving your complete security posture.

Illustrations 11–11 through 11–14 are examples of electronic identification system concepts you need to consider for your requirements.

Illustration 11−11

EXAMPLE OF ELECTRONIC CARD ACCESS AND DEPARTURE PERSON TRAP SYSTEM

A card is inserted into the electronic reader and the information is compared with information in the database. When the card is rejected, the person is trapped between two closed doors until arrival of security officers now alerted to a possible intrusion attempt by the machine.

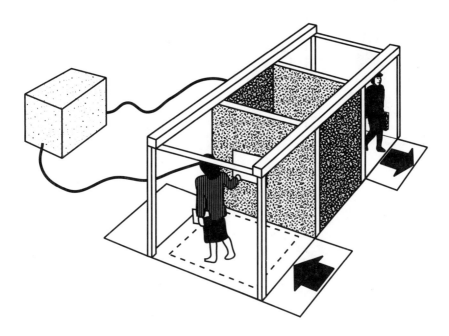

Illustration 11–12

EXAMPLE OF AN ELECTRONIC CARD READER APPLICATION FOR CORPORATE AND INDUSTRIAL SENSITIVE AREAS

Magnetic Strip with Data

The Electric Card Reader System operates much like a bank ATM system or credit card verifier used in retail stores. When an employee inserts the card in the reader, data on a magnetic strip on the reverse side is scanned and when verified, the door lock is released. The card should also be colored and received by the authorized employee who is assigned the card only after exchange of regular ID card is carried out.

Illustration 11–13

EXAMPLE OF PALM PRINT READER

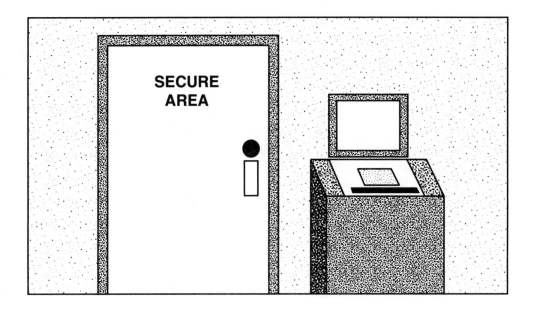

Illustration 11–14

EXAMPLE OF DIGITAL CODE ACCESS CONTROL APPLICATION

The person seeking access must know the proper sequence of numbers to enter.
When a person enters the correct sequence of numbers the machine releases the
lock and wrong entries cause the machine to stay inactive.

HARDENING CORPORATE AND INDUSTRIAL PERIMETER FENCES AND OTHER AREAS WITH ELECTRONIC SENSORS

Perimeter boundary fences or internal limited access areas can be hardened using buried pressure pads and vibration-triggered wires woven into sections of fences, or within top bars. This technique works well in remote areas or adding protection to high-priority protected areas and to improve security when visibility is limited due to fog, rain, or low light.

The buried pressure pad system triggers when a preset amount of weight presses down on the pad. Weight adjustment settings prevent false alarms by compensating for areas where small animals frequent the areas. The pads work best when placed under a thin layer of grass, gravel, or sand and cannot be readily detected by the determined intruder either during entry or while trying to escape from the area.

Vibration systems are less reliable in protected areas where small nocturnal animals roam around the fences or the area is prone to windy weather that shakes the fence. Another problem with vibration devices stems from heavy truck traffic nearby, trains, or other heavy equipment that might cause vibrations in the perimeter fencing. However, in certain applications this system works well, especially in internal limited-access areas where security officer observation can only be minimal and there are lighting restrictions. Also, the system provides added protection when inclement weather or fog limits visibility, especially during hours of darkness.

Illustration 11–15 shows examples of electronic hardening techniques for perimeter fence barriers.

Illustration 11–15

EXAMPLES OF ELECTRONIC PERIMETER FENCE SENSORS
BURIED PRESSURE PADS AND FENCE-MOUNTED VIBRATION SENSORS

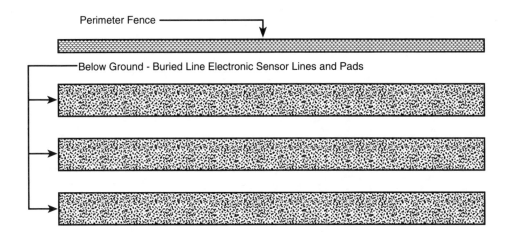

Perimeter Fence

Below Ground - Buried Line Electronic Sensor Lines and Pads

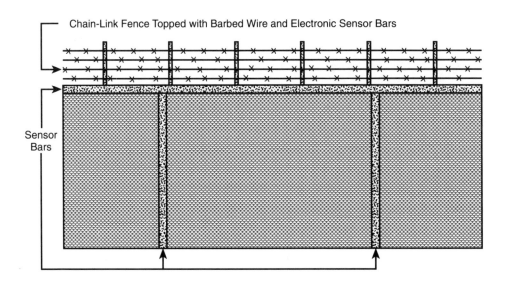

Chain-Link Fence Topped with Barbed Wire and Electronic Sensor Bars

Sensor
Bars

COMMUNICATIONS SECURITY FOR THE CORPORATE OR INDUSTRIAL ENVIRONMENTS

A major threat to your security protection includes the spectrum of communications within and outside the corporate and industrial environments. The communication threat involves the lines carrying signals from sensors from alarm systems, telephone systems, mail and personal conversations between executives and supervisors, and management conferences.

Security of Protective Systems Communication Lines (Alarms)

Protective communication systems vary in size and type with the importance, vulnerability, size, location, radio receptivity, and other factors affecting a specific corporate or industrial environment and create specific problems for you to solve.

Three Elements of Primary Signal Communication Systems

In many situations, the regular communication system of a company is inadequate for protective security purposes. It is desirable for security forces to have their own communication system with direct lines and an auxiliary power supply. Although principal communication is dependent on the telephone, interior and exterior radio communications also play an important role in the protective net of large corporations and industrial complexes.

Any of the following means of communication need consideration for your protective security system:

1. Telephone service
2. Intraplant, interplant, and interoffice telephone systems, not connected to normal telephone service
3. Radio systems with multichannels

Alternate Communications Systems

Provisions must be made for reliable alternate communication systems for use in emergencies. The flood of inquiries that follow emergency conditions added to the normal flow of messages may overload the existing system when communication is important. The most efficient emergency reporting system has direct connection to the security or communications center from telephones strategically placed throughout the company. The use of these telephones needs tight restrictions reserved for emergencies and security officer reporting only. The wires of alternate communication systems need separation from other communication lines and whenever possible in underground or protected conduits.

For emergency communication with agencies outside the company, alternate wires or a radio system adjustable to police and fire department frequencies need a place in your security department inventory.

Wiring, Inspection, and Testing

Whenever possible, conduct regular inspection of signal transmission lines of communications. These systems need separate poles or in separate conduits from the standard company communication and lighting systems. Added protection includes tamper-resistant wire and cables, with a sheath of foil that transmits an alarm signal when penetrated or cut.

All communication circuits need a routine testing procedure at least once during each tour of duty by the supervising security officer. Some systems have self-testing features; however, you need to inspect them periodically or delegate the responsibility to a security patrol or supervisory officers. Also, communications equipment needs inspection periodically by the technical maintenance persons who normally repair or replace worn or failing parts.

DOES YOUR COMPANY SEND CONFIDENTIAL DOCUMENTS DIRECTLY TO COMPETITORS?

The facsimile (fax) has become as common as telephones in the corporate and industrial environment. Within large office complexes, the fax machine saves time and steps between departments when needing fast and accurate information. However, when you use facsimile to transmit data, your competitor may be getting the information directly from your fax terminal. Unlike telex, facsimile uses normal telephone lines making data transmissions easy prey to outsiders. Transmission speeds of under 15 seconds per page and the growing uses of portable facsimile terminals make detection impossible.

Recent equipment, however, secures data transmission before it passes through the telephone network. All data are encrypted at the source using a sophisticated encryption algorithm without any change made to the fax machine itself and the data are transmitted at normal rates. However, the receiver must also have the same comparable equipment that decodes the document at its destination. Since most company information considered trade secrets communicates between subsidiaries or divisions separated geographically, or to law firms, accountants, and others handling confidential information, the safeguards might become costly, needing your cost-benefit assessment before installation.

Often, computers contain fax capability or transmit data from the computer data files to another computer through standard telephone lines. That information is easily tapped and intercepted without interfering with the transmission. The same or similar encryption and decryption equipment safeguards these data transfers. The expense of such equipment is far outweighed by the benefit and assurance of effective security.

Illustration 11–16 shows an example of how secure transmissions from fax and computer systems can happen.

Illustration 11–16

EXAMPLE OF PROTECTING DOCUMENT TRANSMISSION

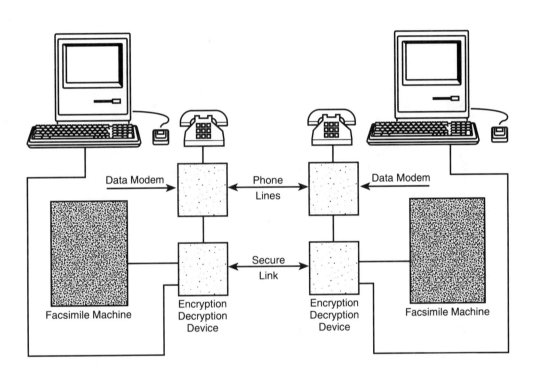

SECURITY OF PERSONAL AND BUSINESS CONVERSATIONS

Communications include telephone conversations and internal discussions and meetings. Within the highly competitive world of business, bits and pieces of information create patterns that help a competitor gain advantage. Although we like to view business conduct as honorable and fair competition, it is not so clean and responsible.

Call it "competitive intelligence" or flat-out spying, it is on the increase in American and international business. If your company is not taking part, look over your shoulder—the competition probably is. According to a study, almost each of the *Fortune* 500 companies surveyed will spend record amounts during the 1990s on competitive intelligence. Many big international companies already have such programs in operation, particularly Japanese and some European firms.

Although information rarely receives the perception by security professionals as corporate or industrial assets, it might rank among the most valuable assets in your company. With specific pieces of information, a competing company can cost your company millions, maybe billions, of dollars in research and development, marketing, and other costs when it comes out with a similar product or uses your information to make a better product. The result is security of assets and preventing valuable information from theft either legally or illegally.

Listening in on Portable Telephones

Technology in recent years brought us the portable telephone, enabling busy executives and subordinates to stay in touch or wander about the office without restriction as when using a conventional telephone. The portable telephone system is really a radio, transmitting back to the central base with radio waves instead of through a wire. When that type transmission happens, a scanner set on the proper frequency levels can easily pick up the conversation albeit one-sided.

Cellular (automobile) telephones also became an essential item in the business inventory; however, the same techniques of scanning on the levels of transmission frequencies can monitor and record the conversation. When the calls are between cellular telephones, both sides can be monitored when the effort is intense and placed together by technicians to provide a two-sided conversation.

Wire taps provide a greater challenge. Although they have the added risk of detection, they remain the most informative because the intruders can hear and record a two-sided discussion using conventional telephone systems. Bugging devices can also be planted in your company's telephones easily, and without proper security, not detected by the users.

BUGS EVERYWHERE AND THE THREAT THEY BRING TO YOUR COMPANY

Listening devices as tiny as a quarter can inundate your company boardrooms, offices, or other areas to listen in and record business conversations. The infamous "bug" is available from a variety of sources, and it is not illegal to manufacture or buy them. The legal question comes into play on their use. For example, the bug might help to listen in on children in a nursery while the mother goes about other household chores. Or bugs might be placed in a security post (with full knowledge of the security officers) as a clandestine duress device in situations where the officer cannot communicate by radio or telephone. There are many legal and logical uses for listening devices; however, competitive intelligence collection might also use them to collect valuable information your board of directors discusses at a meeting. Cleaning persons can easily saturate your company with the devices, as can nonloyal or pressured employees, vendors, service personnel, and others. Without proper security techniques on a routine basis, company profits can easily tumble, although there is no visible theft or management loss.

Listening to Conversations Within Your Company from the Outside

Several techniques invade corporate and industrial conversations hoping to pick up trade secrets or other important bits of information. In this category are parabolic microphones, laser systems, shotgun microphones, and others. Many can listen to conversations inside the building using windows as a weak point to pick up the vibrations resulting from speaking within a room. Open windows enhance the capability of eavesdropping; however, in modern office buildings, sophisticated equipment often works effectively from positions nearby and in a direct line with the targeted window.

Concealed Tape Recorders and Video Cameras

Sound or remote activated tape recorders and miniature low-light-level video cameras are easily hidden within an office or boardrooms. Video cameras, for example, are easily hidden within wall and desk clocks, fire extinguishers, and other accessories within a company environment. Their installation can include placement within an item common to the officer that might be duplicated and replaced, except the replacement contains a tape recorder or video camera or both.

EFFECTIVE COUNTERMEASURES TO ELIMINATE COMMUNICATIONS THREATS

Dozens of electronic devices are available to you to prevent the threats just discussed, some expensive and sophisticated, others inexpensive and simple to install. Much of the decision about what equipment you need to secure communications, from telephone, portable and cellular phones, or bugs within your company depends on the business your company conducts. Areas within your company also play a role in your decisions about how to protect the corporate or industrial information. The beginning point in communications security remains prevention through not discussing anything important or valuable to a competitor except when security is assured. Assuring that security is your responsibility and the following guidelines help you to begin that effort effectively.

Protecting Conventional Telephones from Taps

Your first technique needs to stem from electronic devices installed into the telephone or telephone system itself that monitor the lines and alert you to anyone tapping into the line or system. A device does that by alarming when there is a change in parameters caused by transmitters, tape recorders, extension phones, and other unauthorized uses. A sudden drop in voltage within the telephone line system indicates unauthorized eavesdropping and normally provides your telephone systems with effective protection. Study the manufacturer's specifications and tests before making a decision on the type of antitap countermeasure because there is a large selection available.

Protecting the Cordless and Cellular Telephone Systems

This type countermeasure poses a challenge and greater expense than conventional telephone antitap systems. Since the communications are picked up on a scanner, there is no way to detect the intrusion. Electronic scrambling equipment is the only way to safeguard this type transmission; however, both the caller and receiver need compatible or matched equipment to make the system operate. The scramblers also vary in effectiveness, and that is important in your decision process because a skilled technician might be able to unscramble the conversation especially when using less expensive systems. Some systems, although costly, change frequencies automatically, so often a scanner cannot follow the transmission coherently and record or descramble the conversation. However, added to your specialized equipment comes another security problem. Make certain the equipment itself is secured to prevent others from learning the frequencies and systems of operation.

DEBUGGING YOUR COMPANY ENVIRONMENT

A variety of electronic equipment is available and effective in sweeping areas of your company for planted listening devices. A listening device, also electronic, emits a radio-type transmission signal and the countermeasure equipment detects that emission. According to the sensitivity of the equipment, you will not only learn a listening device is present, but trace it to where the perpetrator placed it. The countermeasure devices come in various sizes and shapes and have a range of capabilities and costs. Remember, however, that sanitizing a room from bugs makes it secure only at that moment and the assurance of continued communication security calls for constant sweeps, especially in key areas and before any confidential discussions happen in those areas.

With each countermeasure, a new technique emerges. Some listening devices operate on a voice- or noise-activated system. For example, if you enter the carpeted room with your debugging equipment and move about trying to detect the presence of a transmitter sending out signals and finding none announce the room is clear, you might not detect anything. What you should do is arrange to have other people in the room with you and ask them to have a conversation about anything, but keep talking. The voice- and sound-activated systems will begin transmitting and you will be able to find them.

You can effectively guard against parabolic, laser, or other types of external listening devices with noise and window coverings that absorb sound. Examples of effective countermeasures include heavy closed drapes coupled with low music playing in the background.

Overcoming the communications threat of hidden tape and video cameras involves other types of electronic technology designed to detect and find these problems. One of the best safeguards for tape recorders and bugs in rooms and within a telephone instrument stems from eavesdropping nullifiers emitting signals that neutralize recording and listening devices.

QUICK REFERENCE GUIDE
FOR
SECURITY ELECTRONIC COUNTERMEASURES

- Develop your strategy for success by trying to defeat your own security systems.
- Enhance your existing security systems with new and carefully planned applications of
  - Closed-circuit television systems, both visible and hidden
  - Systems to detect and protect from mail bombs and firearms
  - Use of electronic technology to control access
  - Hardened perimeter fences with hidden sensors
  - A complete communications security system

PART 4

How to Implement Specialized
Protection

The major components of security techniques, equipment, and management discussed in previous chapters have application throughout the guidelines provided in Part Four. Corporations and industrial complexes use varying combinations of proprietary and contractual personnel, services, and hardware depending on their individual characteristics or security needs. Part Four presents you with an overview of selected areas to demonstrate both the prevalent uses of security in specialized areas and the diversity of security problems encountered and solutions found through understanding, planning, and implementation of effective security measures. The areas discussed throughout Part Four, although specific, bring techniques adaptable to any similar situation.

Many of your specific requirements begin to evolve when you conduct an attentive study of your situation. That technique supplies a usable "crime impact forecast" stemming from the environmental design approach to crime prevention, for example, considering not only the immediate area, but the entire community. This planning mechanism helps you to develop a clear focus on your problems and accurately determine what changes in crime patterns may result from your existing and future building and development projects. For example, the framework of your company areas might encourage or discourage criminal enterprise activities. Your crime impact forecast needs to include the following projections, coupled with the effect they have or will have on your company's profits and operations.

1. Types of crimes prevalent in your geographical area and the types predominant to the business your company conducts.

2. Time crime events happen. When do the types of crimes you identify in (1) above normally happen, including time of day and time of year?

3. Target of the crimes—viewing the crimes you identified in (1) above coupled with your company and its vulnerability of like targets. For example, in an office building, what items might a criminal enterprise target in your company based on crimes at other companies?

4. Tactics of the crime. During your study, determine how the crimes identified in (1) happen. When a consistent method becomes apparent, you have a sound basis for deciding effective uses of your security applications to prevent becoming a victim.

Remember in your planning and application process that crime is committed by humans, not laboratory specimens under controlled environmental conditions. It is not possible always to accurately predict which person will commit what crime and when. But knowing enough about criminal enterprise elements targeting corporate and industrial targets will provide you with information needed to make competent projections and decide how to safeguard against them effectively. Always remember that your crime impact forecast is just that—a forecast.

Your crime impact forecast needs to serve as your planning tool and may provide accurate use by your corporation or industry business planning, including where, when, and how they can expand and reduce the opportunity of criminal activity. It also serves to assure the proper measures and the best effort for the safety of the company employees and protection of the business's profits and inventories.

Security Management for Corporations and Financial Institutions

12

Most security forces perform a range of security functions at thousands of corporate and industrial office buildings throughout the country. Besides the need for security at manufacturing and distribution centers and other areas, corporations must also protect company assets and the lives and personal property of their employees and ensure a safe working environment in leased or owned office buildings.

The second part of this chapter addresses security of financial institutions or facilities. Although your security management responsibilities may or may not include financial institutions in a strict definition sense, the security measures and applications will easily adapt to high-security areas within other corporate and industrial settings.

CREATING EFFECTIVE SECURITY FOR CORPORATE OFFICE BUILDINGS

Some companies must establish and maintain specific levels of security in their offices and buildings to meet the requirements stipulated for certain government contracts. Similar security applications also work for nongovernment-related situations when your company must protect highly sensitive information, such as trade secrets.

Inner-city office buildings or commercial industrial parks (usually suburban office complexes that include nonmanufacturing businesses, such as research laboratories, sales facilities, medical buildings, and other professional and technical offices) are often built and owned by a private developer and leased by corporations. Corporations leasing in these areas often sublease to smaller, often related or subsidiary companies and may assume the responsibility of supplying security for buildings and tenants within the complex.

The major security problems encountered in corporate office buildings include

1. After-hours burglaries and theft
2. Theft from a tenant by another tenant's employees
3. Theft by service, maintenance, and custodial employees
4. Assaults
5. Rapes and other crimes against persons
6. Regulation and control of visitor traffic
7. Bomb threats
8. Threats against executive officers and personnel
9. Fires

The items most often stolen from office buildings include

1. Small office equipment such as
   a. Typewriters
   b. Computers
   c. Calculators
2. Photocopying machines
3. Office furnishings
4. Securities
5. Valuable documents and competitive information
6. Blank payroll checks and other blank documents, such as ID cards, forms, and other similar items
7. Check writing machines

DEVELOPING SECURITY TECHNIQUES FOR OFFICE BUILDINGS

The key to protecting office buildings is access control beginning with the first floor. The building above the first floor is a labyrinth that can easily become a security manager's nightmare. For example, when several unauthorized people go up into the building, there is no effective way to find them or control their actions in the short term. You can, however, create advantage through a series of systems that prevents easy access and enables a central security control station to monitor much of the high-rise maze.

Security techniques for general office space protection include card key readers and closed-circuit television (CCTV) coupled with other high-tech equipment albeit vulnerable to neutralization or deception by skilled intruders.

WHERE TO BEGIN—LOOKING FOR SECURITY ADVANTAGES

Large commercial office buildings typically have elevator banks in lobby areas where access-control measures are essential to monitor visitor access. People cannot get above the first floor without using an elevator or the stairs. Since fire regulations call for access to the stairwells, you cannot seal them off, except on the first floor. The stairwell doors on the first floor must open from the inside with a crash bar system to allow escape from the upper floors and building during a fire or other emergency; however, since in a fire no one is going up the stairs (except emergency crews), you can have the first floor entrance doors key locked from the outside. That allows emergency crews access to the stairwells from the first floor but prevents other persons from having access. Having that access problem controlled, you need to develop ways of controlling access to upper floors via elevators or, in some situations, escalators. On the surface, it sounds simple, however when several hundred or thousand of people enter the building in a short time frame, the problem seems hopeless. Once the building fills, another problem occurs at the close of business involving stay-behind persons, either working late or having intentions of committing a crime. However, there are solutions, especially using the card reader systems, connected to large computer control systems equipped with backup power equipment. The backup power needs to operate the entire card reader system to remain effective.

This system uses a card that looks much like a credit card or those used on a bank ATM machine. The magnetic strip contains programming information that allows security management to void the card and the access it allows with a few keyboard entries. The system also maintains a record each time a person uses the card, and the record tells you when a person is not present in a building or office. When all authorized personnel are issued the programmed card, you can establish systems to ensure the employee uses the card upon entry into the building and upon departure. When you develop your system by zones, you will have an instant reference to tell you how many people are in the building at any time, who they are, and where they are. You can program the system to take cards from people no longer authorized access but try to use a card they were issued. That action eliminates the need to collect the cards when an employee quits, retires, or is fired. At the close of business, the console operation can ask the computer system who remains in the building, where they are, and who they are. That information can be cross-checked with a telephone call to verify their presence, and at certain later times, security officers need to go to the location and verify the presence and that the person is okay. Also, once you have an after-business-hours fix on people in the building, your security officers can focus on watching the applicable CCTV monitor in that zone carefully.

HOW DO YOU GET A FEW THOUSAND PEOPLE TO USE THEIR CARDS?

The first consideration deals with channeling people into the building according to the configuration of the entrances and lobbies. The entrance control points need to have the presence of a security officer (several at peak times) to ensure that each person entering the building uses his or her card inserted into a machine. Like supermarkets, you need to have many entrance machines and portals to handle the flow of incoming persons. Visitors and vendors need to be channeled to a separate entrance where they are logged in and issued temporary passes to specific areas and then logged out and the passes collected when they leave. The logs and passes need to be filed and maintained for a minimum of one year, more if possible.

The card entry system should also replace conventional locks for offices. Each card can be programmed to allow entry into the building, into the elevator, and into specific offices. An authorized person trying to use his or her card to enter an office or area not authorized will lose the card to the reader which takes it and alarms the console of the incident It also records the breach, and it is left to the employee to explain why the breach happened.

Although some people might balk at the system, you can overcome most or all opposition by explaining how it creates benefit for them. That benefit includes protecting them while they are in the building during nonbusiness hours and eliminates them as suspects of a crime because they are proven not to be present when it happened. The system also helps solve crimes by knowing who is in the building and where they are when the crime occurs. The system, coupled with CCTV coverage (which should have recorder capability when needed or activated by the console operator or automatically when an alarm is noted in a specific zone) and the presence of a skilled, trained security officer force provides excellent security for your office building.

There are many added techniques, many discussed earlier in the book, and with the continuing growth of technology, newly available systems might be considered. The key, however, is control. When you have that, your problems decrease.

Many newer office buildings use construction techniques embracing the core concept design, which places all elevators, restrooms, and service facilities at the center of the building. The concept increases security control and permits more flexible use of office space. It clearly contributes to more effective control of lobby areas and visitor access by limiting entrances and exits in the building.

AFTER HOURS CONTROL OF LOBBIES, ELEVATORS AND OTHER AREAS

Security measures designed to protect lobby areas and elevator banks may include the use of CCTV, security officer presence, and receptionists who manage visitor pass systems. After normal business hours, elevator control techniques include key switches or programmable card key readers, allowing only authorized personnel to operate the elevators or to reach specified floors. The system reads information programmed on the card's magnetic strip and prevents the elevator from stopping at any other floor or the door from opening on any other floor.

MAXIMUM APPLICATION OF SECURITY OFFICERS

Where security officers perform patrol functions besides access control, they generally follow programmed watch clock stations routes while on duty, during the day and evening. Besides CCTV, access-control systems, and the annunciation of intrusion and fire alarms, many newer and larger office buildings use central consoles to monitor heating, ventilating, and air-condition systems. These reduce personnel requirements, increase monitoring and detection capabilities, and permit faster response by security officers.

Securities, cash, and valuable records and documents normally receive special attention storage in vaults equipped with closed-circuit television or time-lapse cameras. In large companies, records on payroll, accounts payable and receivable, sales mailing lists, product information, customer lists, and other important information generally is stored in computer systems. Protection of computer processing centers, remote terminals, and the information in machine-readable form is a major security concern. Physical security measures, that is special access-control and locking systems, CCTV, and security officer posts, are normally applications designed to protect computer areas. Data base security involves the design of program verification and usage procedures by computer specialists.

CORPORATE FINANCIAL INSTITUTIONS

The security and stability of financial institutions—banks and other types of financial centers—are critical to a lasting and healthy economy of the nation and the corporations that operate these businesses either exclusively or as a part of the total conglomerate. A wide variance in the number and types of security measures used by financial institutions has caused great concern to government agencies that regulate federally insured or controlled institutions, with surveys by the FBI disclosing that many banks had totally inadequate protective and preventive measures against most crimes that target the financial institutions. Their findings led Congress to enact the Bank Protection Act of 1968 calling for federally insured banks and financial institutions to have specific minimum security standards throughout the country. The law required such institutions to

1. Develop a written security plan meeting nine minimum requirements
2. Appoint a security officer (manager)
3. File a formal report with the proper regulatory agency on current security measures at bank facilities
4. Install and maintain vault-area lighting systems, taper-resistant exterior doors, and window locks and alarm systems.

The net effect of the Bank Protection Act was a mandated increase in security services and hardware used by most financial institutions. Despite the expanded security measures, violations of bank robbery statutes, which the act hoped to reduce, increased significantly in both numbers and dollar losses. Crime involving financial institutions that have government oversight has tripled since the act.

The Bank Protection Act did not address forgeries, fraud, and embezzlement, although losses to financial institutions from these actions far exceed losses from robberies and burglaries. Enormous losses result each year from fraudulent use of credit cards and checks, plus theft of stock certificates and government bonds. Even greater losses result from internal fraud and embezzlement. According to the FBI monitoring financial institutions having government oversight, a full 80% of losses results from internal theft.

Although the foregoing information addresses banks primarily, all financial institutions have generally the same types of problems, beginning with physical or intrusion security and then internal protective controls to reduce or eliminate the threat to the institution's assets and safety of employees, customers, and others in the area. The following checklist provides you with a credible guide for assessing your current security measures and concepts for increases as needed.

INSPECTION AND ASSESSMENT GUIDELINES FOR FINANCIAL INSTITUTIONS OR CORPORATE HIGH-SECURITY AREAS

The following text includes requirements established by the Bank Protection Act of 1968 plus other recommended physical and internal security techniques. Although your security needs may not involve a financial institution in the strict definition, many or all the applications in this checklist may apply to or be adapted to other high-security needs.

1. **Surveillance systems**—General surveillance systems should be:

(a) Equipped with any photographic, recording, monitoring, or like devices capable of reproducing images of persons in the banking office (or other corporate facility) with sufficient clarity to facilitate (through photographs capable of being enlarged to produce a 1–inch vertical head size of persons whose images have been reproduced) the identification and apprehension of robbers or other suspicious persons.

(b) Silent in operation.

(c) Designed and constructed so necessary services, repairs, or inspections can readily happen.

Any camera used in such a system should be capable of taking at least one picture each 2 seconds and, if it uses film, should contain enough unexposed film always to be capable of operation for not less than 3 minutes, and the film should be a least 16mm. . . .

(ii) Installation, maintenance, and operation of surveillance systems providing surveillance of other than walk-up or drive-in teller's stations or windows. Surveillance devices for other than walk-up or drive-in teller's stations or windows should be:

(a) Located to reproduce identifiable images of persons either leaving the banking office or positioned to transact business at each such station or window.

(b) Capable of activation by initiating devices at each teller's station or window.

(iii) Installation, maintenance, and operation of surveillance systems providing surveillance of walk-up or drive-in teller's stations or windows. Surveillance devices for walk-up and drive-in tellers' stations or windows located properly to reproduce identifiable images of persons transacting business at each station and area vulnerable to robbery or larceny. Such devices should be capable of activation by any initiating devices located within or in close proximity to such station or window. Consider omission of the devices at a walk-up or drive-in teller's station or window when the teller is protected by a bullet-resistant barrier from persons outside the station or window, but if the teller is vulnerable to larceny or robbery by members of the public who enters the banking officer, the teller should have access to a device to activate a surveillance system that covers vulnerable areas or the exits to the banking office.

(2) Robbery Alarm Systems.

A robbery alarm at each banking office where the police ordinarily can arrive within five minutes after an alarm activates. Robbery alarm systems should be:

(i) Designed to transmit to the police, either directly or through an intermediary, a signal (not detectable by unauthorized persons) indicating that a crime against the banking office has happened or is in progress.

(ii) Capable of activation by initiating devices at each teller's station or window (except walk-up or drive-in teller's stations or windows where teller protection includes a bullet-resistant barrier and isolated from persons, other than fellow employees, inside a banking office where the station or window may be a part).

(iii) Safeguarded against accidental transmission of an alarm.

(iv) Equipped with a visual and audible signal capable of showing improper functioning of or tampering with the system.

(v) Equipped with an independent source of power (such as a battery) sufficient to assure continuously reliable operation of the system for at least 24 hours during failure of the usual source of power.

(3) Burglar Alarm Systems.

Burglar alarm systems should be:

(i) Capable of detecting promptly an attack on the outer door, walls, floor, or ceiling of each vault, and each safe not stored in a vault, in which currency, negotiable securities, or similar valuables are stored when the office is closed, and any attempt to move any such safe.

(ii) Designed to transmit to the police, either directly or through an intermediary, a signal (not detectable by unauthorized persons) indicating that any such attempt is in progress; and at a banking office where the police ordinarily cannot arrive within 5 minutes after an alarm is activated, designed to activate a loud sounding bell or other device that is audible inside the banking office and for a distance of about 500 feet outside the banking office.

(iii) Safeguarded against accidental transmission of an alarm.

(iv) Equipped with a visual and audible signal capable of showing improper functioning of or tampering with the system.

(v) Equipped with an independent source of power (such as a battery) sufficient to assure continuously reliable operation of the system for at least 80 hours during failure of the usual source of power.

(4) Walk-up and Drive-in Teller's Stations or Windows.

Walk-up and drive-in teller's stations or windows need construction so tellers have protection from robbery or larceny by bullet-resistant barriers. Such barriers should be of glass at least $1\frac{3}{16}$ inches thick or of material of at least equivalent bullet resistance. Pass-through devices designed and constructed to prevent a person outside the station or window having a direct line of fire at a person inside the station or window. Remember, the factor emphasized about this technique stems from the thickness that is merely bullet resistant and not bullet-proof.

(5) Vaults, Safes, and Night Depositories.

Vaults and safes (if not placed in a vault) intended as safe storage for currency, negotiable securities, or similar valuables when the office is closed, and night depositories need to satisfy or exceed the following standards:

(a) Vaults. Vault walls, roof, and floor made of steel-reinforced concrete, at least 16 inches thick, vault doors made of steel or other drill and torch-resistant material, at least $3\frac{1}{2}$ inches thick, and be equipped with a dial combination lock and a time lock and a formidable, lockable day-gate; or vaults and vault doors built of materials that afford at least equivalent burglary-resistance.

(b) Safes. Safes should weigh at least 750 pounds empty or be securely anchored to the premises. The door needs a combination lock and relocking device that will effectively lock the door if the combination lock is punched. The steel body with at least 1 inch in thickness, with a tensile strength of 50,000 pounds per square inch, either cast or fabricated, and fastened in a manner equal to a continuous $\frac{1}{4}$ inch penetration weld having a tensile strength of 50,000 pounds per square inch. One hole not exceeding $\frac{3}{16}$-inch diameter provided in the body to permit insertion of electrical conductors but not allowing a direct view of the door or locking mechanism. The door made of steel that is at least $1\frac{1}{2}$ inches thick and at least equivalent in strength to that specified for the body, or safes built of materials that afforded at least equivalent burglary resistance.

(c) Night depositories. Night depositories (excluding envelope drops not used to receive large amounts of currency) should have a receptacle chest with cast or welded steel walls, top and bottom at least 1 inch thick; a combination locked steel door at least $1\frac{1}{2}$ inches thick; and a chute, made of steel that is at least 1 inch thick, security bolted or welded to the receptacle and to a depository entrance of strength similar to the chute; or night depositories should be constructed of materials that afford at least equivalent burglary resistance. The depository entrance needs security served with magnetic card lock. Night depository needs a burglar alarm and designed to protect against the "fishing" of a deposit from the deposit receptacle and to protect against the "trapping" of a deposit for extraction.

Note: Each device mentioned in this section needs installation and regular inspections, tests, and servicing by competent persons to assure realization of its maximum performance capabilities.

PHYSICAL SECURITY CHECKLIST FOR HIGH-SECURITY AND FINANCIAL CENTERS

1. Are enough security officers assigned to protect the high-security area or financial office?

2. Have you taken adequate precautions to prevent unauthorized entrance after normal business hours?

3. Have security measures been coordinated with local police?

4. Is the facility equipped with adequate facilities for the storing and safeguarding of company funds and documents?

5. Do the safeguards used during normal operations prevent loss, substitution, or pilferage of company funds and documents?

6. Are vaults or safes accessible to unauthorized persons?

7. Are unauthorized persons excluded from the working areas of the office with a railing or counter?

8. Are money exchanging windows situated to prevent unauthorized access to funds?

9. Is cash in excess of that currently disbursed promptly secured?

10. Are internal office procedures established to provide controls on all undelivered and returned checks?

11. Is there a central point for their receipt, holding, and final disposition, with responsibility therefore charged to a specific person?

12. Is the cashier or teller supplied with a separate working space or properly enclosed cage or room with a window for paying and receiving?

13. Is a cash drawer with key locks, or a safe, provided for safeguarding funds and vouchers during temporary absence of clerks or tellers?

14. If more than one person in the office has cash in possession, is each person supplied with a separate and secure receptacle for such monies?

15. Are receipts taken for money entrusted to the cashier and receipts given the cashier for money returned or valid vouchers accepted?

16. Is there a procedure for unannounced verification of cash on hand?

17. Do current records show verifications made on an unannounced basis at least once each quarter?

18. Is a detailed record maintained of daily settlement of cash transaction between managers and cashiers?

19. Is positive identification of the payee made before any cash payments?

20. Is the cashier furnished with a list of known impostors, forgers, or other scam artists?

21. Is the cashier furnished with a current list of lost or stolen financial data folders?

22. Is the cash in possession of the cashier verified daily by management?

23. Is cash entrusted to a cashier always kept within the limits of his or her bond or company policy?

24. Has authority to amounts of cash available in specific amounts been approved by the proper management person?

25. Are blank cashier or other forms of checks, when not in use, kept under lock and key in a safe supervised by the management?

26. Upon receipt of shipments of blank checks or other instruments are the cartons examined and the serial numbers checked?

27. Do at least two members of the management inspect the blank checks in current use at the beginning and end of each day's business to see that no blanks have been extracted?

28. Are cartons bearing evidence of tampering opened and checks counted separately?

29. Does management maintain a daily record of instruments released, written, and returned for safekeeping?

30. Are spoiled instruments voided and properly safeguarded?

31. When checks or other instruments are voided or spoiled, are they properly marked and reported?

32. Do cashiers make up receipts for cash received for each day's business?

33. What personnel are authorized access to keys within the facility?

34. Are keys to the locking devices of meters and check signing machines kept in custody of management always?

35. Are there keys or combinations to safes and cash drawers in the hands of any person other than the applicable cashier?

36. Are locks replaced when keys are lost or stolen?

37. Has the cashier sealed one key and the combination to his or her safe in an envelope suitably marked so that unauthorized opening may be detected?

38. Is that envelope secured in a safe controlled only by management?

39. Is the combination to the vault or primary safes known only by the management?

40. Is a copy of the combinations, sealed in an envelope, suitably marked so its unauthorized opening may be detected, delivered to a central officer outside the facility for use in emergencies?

41. Are procedures established to provide two disinterested persons to witness the opening of the cashier's or management safes when the responsible persons are not present?

42. Is there a requirement that the witnesses execute an affidavit regarding the contents of the safes when opened?

43. When authorized persons open vaults or safes, do they shield the dial during the operation of the combination to prevent observation by others?

44. Are the combinations of vaults and safes changed at least every six months?

45. Are safe and vault combinations changed when newly appointed management takes charge of the office or facility?

46. Is there a security officer post established at, in, or near the facility or office?

47. Is there a plan establishing security requirements for funds in transit?

48. Is the plan coordinated with the local police?

49. Does the plan provide for proper security escort?

50. Does the plan prescribe armament, communications, transportation, and equipment for security officers?

51. Does the plan provide for using various routes?

52. How is the plan and route information safeguarded?

53. Is an intrusion detection system installed?

Security
Management for
13 Port, Harbor, and
River Terminals

Port, harbor, river, and inlet security creates problems different from land-based corporate and industrial complexes. However, large companies involved in surface (water) transportation of goods and receiving materials by surface (water) craft often have both land-based and port and harbor terminals you need to protect. Many elements of port and harbor (water terminal) security are similar to security elements found in other situations involving corporate and industrial security operations. Physical protection requirements are the same in some areas of port and harbor as in warehouse and open storage areas. The need for personnel identification and control is, if anything, greater, and many of the problems encountered and physical security techniques and procedures used in storage and intransit security arise in port and harbor situations.

PORTS AND HARBORS POSE NEW PROBLEMS OF SECURITY

There are, however, some different and often more demanding aspects of physical security of a port or harbor, particularly in high-crime areas. The exposure to pilferage and sabotage intensifies and broadens because ports and harbors are prime targets for criminal activities and the perimeter areas of these activities are more vulnerable because of extensive distance and often exposed adjacent beach or pier areas. Theft and pilferage of cargo are extremely serious problems in terminal operations because it is not possible to surround the environment with perimeter fences. A seemingly trivial bit of laxness in security operations and procedures may provide a clever thief or a large criminal enterprise with an opening to steal systematically or to make off with an entire loaded container. (*Note: The description in this chapter of a container refers to the large steel containers often nearly the size of a trailer on a tractor-trailer truck used to ship products around the world. Many ships today are container ships that provide faster loading and unloading and greater security for the cargo. However, the containers are also easier to steal and involve huge losses when stolen.)*

YOUR PORT AND HARBOR OPERATING ENVIRONMENT

Managing the protective security operations for a port and harbor terminal operation might include only a part of your total responsibilities or be your only obligation to the company. Whatever your situation, it includes interesting challenges apart from your corporate or industrial landlocked area.

TERMINAL SECURITY OPERATIONS

A terminal has several, distinct, although correlated, areas, such as storage areas (covered and open), piers (land and water sides), shore areas, entrances and exits, anchorage areas, and ships tied up at piers. It also can include petroleum discharge points, pipelines, and storage areas.

Terminal areas are vulnerable to all the security hazards discussed earlier in the book. Also, the measures of physical protection, personnel identification and movement control, intrusion detection, locks, and other techniques coupled with storage security discussed earlier apply in port and harbor terminal areas.

YOUR SECURITY FORCE—THE KEY TO SUCCESSFUL TERMINAL SECURITY

Your security officers are the key to successful security in port and harbor terminals. Security posts you need to create include motorized, stationary, or walking, depending on the type of supplies and cargo on the wharves, the types of ships, size of the area, and threats to the company assets.

Security officers assigned to watercraft and water patrol operations must also receive special training in water survival, small-boat operations, and expedient methods of operation. Extensive practical work is needed to develop the necessary skills.

The importance of security officers increases in this environment over that in landlocked complexes because use of high-tech equipment is severely limited. One reason for the limitation includes the activity of shipping and receiving normally operating on a 24-hour basis and the constant number of people entering and departing, often contracted labor opposed to employees of the corporation or industry. Another problem is the sharing of the port and harbor terminal environment. Your company may have its separate area; however, often the areas merge with areas operated by other companies.

Identification and Movement Control

A major effort needs to focus security officers on checking passes and badges of all persons entering or leaving your terminal facilities; searching bundles and packages taken from the areas; examining documentation of cargo vehicles (trucks); controlling vehicle, railroad, and pedestrian traffic; and directing persons without proper passes to the identification section.

Pier and Wharf Security Officers

Pier and wharf security officers need to check passes and badges, observe dock workers, and stay attentive for evidence for indications of pilferage or tampering and identify intruders. One of the key duties includes watching for small boats approaching the wharves. They need to check for proper identification of persons on board who want to enter the pier or to board any vessel docked at the pier. Your security officers need training in and have access to fire-fighting equipment and should maintain constant vigilance for fires under piers and heavy accumulations of oil next to pilings. They should not, however, fight fires at the expense of their security duties, but take only emergency measures while awaiting fire-fighting crews. Fires often serve as an effective diversion to distract security officers.

Offshore Security Officers

Your security techniques need to include off-shore security officers who focus on watching the harbor or water entrances for trespassers in boats. They also watch for incoming vessels and alert the security officer so gangplank and ship security are ready immediately after it docks.

Gangplank Security Officers

Your gangplank security officers control dock workers, terminal personnel, crew, and ship handlers boarding and leaving a vessel.

Hatch Security Officers

Your hatch security officers maintain security in cargo hatches where dock workers load or unload cargo. Requirement for this activity depends on the type, value, or sensitivity of the cargo. Hatch security officers stay on the same level as workers when possible and make reports on damaged cargo and evidence of pilferage and deliberate damage. They need to be alert to any attempts to divert or "frustrate" cargo by changing the destination marking. Damaged cargo needs immediate security, setting it aside and having it watched until delivered to the terminal recooperage section for repair. Hatch security officers must also coordinate with security officer on deck to prevent the dropping of cargo overside from the ship.

Pier Security Officers

You can protect the landward side of a pier with fencing and pass control. However, you cannot protect the part of the pier that protrudes over the water with a perimeter fence. Not only is this part of the pier accessible from the sides and end, but also from the underside. Techniques for securing the pier along its water boundaries include

Water Patrols

Water patrol security officers patrol in small boats in pier areas to prevent unauthorized small craft from operating in adjacent waters and to recover jettisoned cargo. Patrol boats need to be narrow of beam to enable passage between the pilings when inspecting the underside of the piers.

Walking Patrols

Security officers assigned to walking patrols serve as a land-based coordinating factor with the patrol boats. Often, either the pier-based or water-based security officer can spot debris, small boats, or jettisoned cargo and coordinate the interception effectively.

Protective Lighting

The protective lighting of working areas on piers needs adaptation to the particular style of construction and work needs. The slips and under-pier areas need sufficient lighting to supply adequate night protection. Lights under a pier normally require being affixed to the piling close to the pier flooring. Wiring and fixtures in these areas must be waterproof to ensure safety in the event of unusually high tides.

Booms

Under certain circumstances it may be prudent to close the water side of a pier area using booms. A floating boom will prevent the entry of small boats. To deny underwater access, a cable net must be suspended from the boom.

Illustration 13–1 shows a narrow-beam security patrol boat and how it may work around under piers.

Illustration 13–1

EXAMPLE OF NARROW-BEAM SECURITY PATROL BOAT

Patrol boats need a narrow beam to enable passage between the pilings
when inspecting the underside of piers.

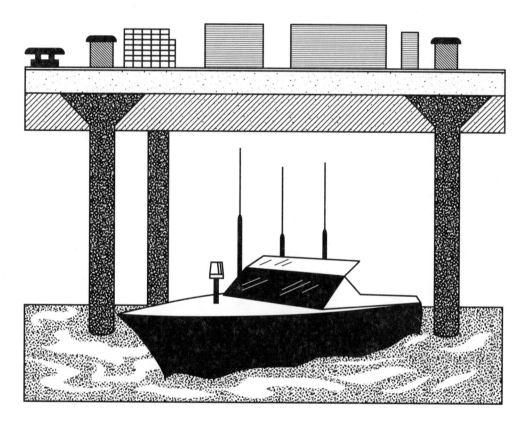

ANCHORAGE SECURITY

When a port lacks pier space to accommodate traffic, ships may anchor, or even load and unload, offshore. Positions of the ships in anchorage are assigned by local port authorities. Cargo is loaded or unloaded with lighters, which also transport the stevedores to the ship. This type of operation has advantages and disadvantages for security of the ships and the property on board. The trips to and from anchored ships give added time for the inspection or surveillance of laborers, but it is difficult to control the movements of small boats that bring provisions to the ships. Such crafts serve criminal enterprise in pilfering the cargo.

Security Officers Assigned Shipboard

Besides hatch security officers, other security officers need assignment, where proper to the decks of ships at anchorage. The officers may also serve security needs through either stationary or walking patrols. Besides cooperating with hatch security officers, their duties include

1. Security of cargo stowed on deck
2. Security of cargo being unloaded into lighters
3. Observation of small craft near the ships at anchor
4. Observation of surrounding waters to detect any attempted approach by swimmer thieves

Deck security officers must be able to communicate, preferably by radio, with your harbor patrol boats either directly or though the central security control. Ensure the deck security officers have proper equipment including foul weather clothing, binoculars, and portable lighting.

CONTAINER OPERATIONS

Cargo intransit is vulnerable to overt hazards (such as pilferage and other criminal enterprise operations). As one measure to provide additional security for supplies and equipment, the use of containers during shipment continues to increase.

Containers must receive close security emphasis during

- Filling
- Sealing
- Storage (shipper or receiver)
- Shipment (onloading and offloading)

Areas where security measures for containers must be stringent are

- On board ship
- Shoreline transitions
- Container marshaling area

Knowledge is the keynote to security during container operations. It is important that security personnel be aware of the following to detect pilferage and theft:

- Packaging, labeling, and placarding requirements
- Cargo compatibility characteristics and segregation requirements
- Container and cargo handling and safety measures
- Actions to be initiated when they observe suspected pilferage and theft operations
- Special storage, identification, and movement requirements
- Pertinent regulations and publications.

Some basic measures for increasing security are as follows:

- Control vehicular and pedestrian traffic entering and leaving the marshaling yard:
  - Establish a single control point for each.
  - Ensure security officers have training for document and cargo inspection.
- At the vehicular control point,
  - Prevent entry of unauthorized vehicles (only transporter and material handling equipment, maintenance, and essential administrative vehicles may enter).
  - Inspect inbound and outbound containers for
    - Evidence of damage or unserviceability.
    - Presence and condition of container seal and lock.
    - Evidence of illegal entry into container (such as tampering with or removal of door hinges).
    - Stolen items, particularly with outbound containers (look on top and under container, and inspect transporter cab).
  - Verify documentation for correctness, completeness, and legibility (check that the transporter number, container number, and container seal number match those shown on the control and movement document, CMD).
  - Prohibit container (inbound or outbound) from passing through the control point without a valid CMD.
- At the pedestrian control point,

- Permit only authorized personnel to enter container marshaling area.
- Establish, maintain, control, and safeguard a pass system for persons authorized to be in the area:
  - A photo-bearing, serially numbered, plastic-enclosed pass can be prepared for each person authorized to be in the yard. The person picks up the pass when entering through the gate and returns it to the security office upon leaving.
  - Further refinement of the pass system includes color coding to show the specific area of the yard in which the person is authorized. Enhance color coding and make identification easier and more visible by calling for hard hats that reflect the same color as the pass.

PERIMETER SECURITY OF MARSHALING YARDS

Your perimeter security of company marshaling yards reinforces gate security in keeping unauthorized people out of the area. Unauthorized people may engage in small- to large-scale theft or property diversion schemes. Collusion might develop with contacts between criminal enterprise operations and people working in the yard. Your perimeter security measures may include any of the following techniques:

1. Chain-link fencing topped by strands of barbed wire. Inspect your fences daily to assure there are not holes or breaks.
2. Concertina wire.
3. Protective lighting.
4. When feasible enhance security with use of sensors and IDS systems.
5. Sentry dog team patrols have large success in protecting this type area.

SECURITY CARGO PROTECTIVE TECHNIQUES

Although you may not be able to fence the entire yard, the security cargo (that is, sensitive, classified, and high-dollar-value cargo) area should, as a minimum, be fenced with its own security gate and security officer patrols. An added security measure is the stacking of containers door to door or with the door against a wall. The break-bulk point and damaged cargo storage area is also potential high-loss areas and needs close supervision and adequate perimeter barriers and lighting. Also, whenever possible, security cargo should be unloaded from the ship during daylight hours. Observation of unloading operations by security officers is highly desirable.

CARGO DOCUMENTATION—THE CONTROL AND MOVEMENT DOCUMEMT

Cargo moving through terminals needs to be documented with a control and movement document. Your form needs to be in multiple copies and serial numbered. Best control includes issuing the document by the security element at the shipping point (i.e., marshalling yard or terminal warehouse) for each shipment, for example, a truckload. Each form (CMD) needs to contain the following characteristics and information:

1. The form needs to show the cargo (type, number of packages, etc.), the consignee to whom it is being delivered, names of the cargo checker and truck driver, and the time the cargo left the shipping point.

2. The form provides you with an accurate record of company property and its movement, coupled with ensuring prompt delivery of the cargo, reducing the risk of loss, theft, or pilferage. It also provides an effective enforcement tracking device.

Your security officers need training about the CMD, since they must check the document against the load on a truck leaving the terminal, unless the load is sealed and wired or locked, such as a van or steel container. Otherwise, the security officer must check the itemized CMD, verify the types and number of packages, and check the security of the load by company security policy.

When the document and load are in order, the security officer writes his or her name on the CMD and stamps it with date and time stamp in spaces supplied on the form for that purpose. He or she also needs to record the date, time, and CMD number on a security gate log and returns the CMD to the driver for presentation at later security points and delivery.

When the security officer does not find the shipment in order (for example, less or more packages than listed on the CMD or load security requirements not met), he or she must hold the vehicle and report the circumstances immediately so that a supervisor can respond and investigate, resolving the differences that might be a paper error. The supervisor should know and be able to verify by a signature on the CMD, the person authorized to release the cargo. Signature cards or coded templates serve this purpose effectively.

Another instance of security office concern with the CMD is a report from a consignee that the shipment did not arrive at its destination or that there was a difference between the cargo as described on the CMD and that received. Either case will probably call for a security investigation, using the CMD as a starting point.

Two physical aspects of the cargo checking activity may be worthy of consideration:

1. When the cargo vehicle gates include use by other traffic, provide a turnout

where security officers direct cargo vehicles for inspection. This turnout eliminates congestion and confusion at the gate.

2. To simplify checking cargo shipments, you need to build a wooden platform at the checking areas. The platform should be the length as the vehicles inspected (e.g., tractor-trailer) and provide a deck at, or slightly higher than, the truck bed. Such a platform provides for easier and faster checking since it permits better observation of the cargo.

Security officers assigned to terminal and gate inspection points should receive specialized training in the processes and documents used for movement of company property.

Safeguarding and Controlling CMDs

Normally, CMDs are not accountable documents. However, ensure your CMDs have serial numbers to aid in your control and to discourage pilferage of the form for illegal use. Despite other measures, blank CMDs should be secured with one person responsible for their safeguarding and issue. Store completed CMDs in a vault file to prevent unauthorized changes or destruction to remove evidence of cargo diversions and pilferage.

SAFEGUARDING AND CONTROLLING CONTAINER SEALS

A container seal is a device applied to the container door fastening to show whether the door was opened or tampered with and, if so, at what point in the movement system it happened. Seals are serial numbered to help identify the person who applied the seal and to provide control. Unless your seals are strictly accounted for from receipt to application, their purpose (to pinpoint unauthorized entry into the container) is defeated. Container seal control and accountability are enhanced by the following techniques:

1. Maintain a record by serial number of seal to determine
   a. Received by the port operations officer.
   b. Issued to authorized persons for application to containers.
2. Store seals under lock.
3. Designate one person to be responsible for safekeeping, issue, and record keeping of seals applied at the port facilities.
4. Designate specific persons on each shift to apply seals (keep number of persons to a minimum).
5. Enter serial number of seal on your CMD.
6. Conduct periodic inventory of seals.

7. Apply seals:

a. Immediately after the container has been loaded with cargo.

b. Immediately after loading but still unsealed or detection of an improperly sealed container.

8. Conduct an inventory of contents when enough evidence exists that cargo has been pilfered. In any case make proper entries on the CMD to identify any change in seals.

9. Supervise application of seals. Failure to supervise or allowing a yard worker to move an unsealed container to the staking areas offers opportunity to
   a. Pilfer cargo before applying the seal
   b. Apply a bogus seal, break the seal later, remove cargo, and then apply the legitimate seal.

SECURITY OFFICER WATER PATROL OPERATIONS

River, inlet, harbor,and ports security operations require continuous coordination and liaison with several agencies, including

1. Local law enforcement agencies

2. The U.S. Coast Guard (in some areas)

3. The U.S. Navy (in some areas)

4. Other agencies having jurisdiction or control of harbor, port, rivers, and inlets

The extent and nature of coordination necessary for the effective use of this security support operation will vary with the company activity and facility supported. Waterborne security patrols provide the only practical means available to protect arterial and smaller waterways and pier facilities to include sensitive areas such as tank farms, pumping stations, cargo storage areas near the water, terminals, and other types of company operations on or near the water. Water security patrol operations should be conducted as an extension of and a supplement to shore based security operations.

Water patrol activity includes all the dangers normally encountered onshore plus the possibility of encounters with dangerous waterfront criminals in watercraft. A thorough and continuous consideration of safety, communications, support, and reserve factors is a necessity in water patrol operations.

Harbor, River and Inlet Water Patrols

Your port and harbor security need the use of patrol boats, not only for the open harbor area but for the water sides of piers and dock areas and patrol of inland waterways and beach areas nearby that serve for pilferage pickup points.

Assignments to security water patrols may include the following:

IN PORT AREAS

1. Enforce port policies, procedures, rules, and regulations.
2. Suppress criminal activity.
3. Provide offshore security for quays, piers, moorages, and anchorages.
4. Provide offshore security for communications facilities, port security devices, and aids to navigation.
5. Provide security for incoming and outgoing craft, moored or anchored craft, and lighter operations.
6. Assist in circulation and control of persons and small boats.

IN BEACH, RIVER SHORE OR INLET AREAS

1. Undertake any of the activities listed previously.
2. Support control and direction of watercraft near the shore or in restricted areas.
3. Guide cargo carrying small craft between larger craft and shore points.
4. Guide and escort and provide security for small craft engaged in high priority movements of sensitive cargo.
5. Provide security for cargo ships that can easily be boarded and pilfered in congested areas, rivers, and inlets.

Prevention of Waterfront Crimes with Water Patrols

Prevention of waterfront criminal activity includes adequate physical security measures to provide protection for company supplies and equipment and cargo. Physical security measures may be supplemented effectively by water patrols that perform the following:

1. Observe activities of watercraft and persons about watercraft.
2. Observe activities of persons on the waterfront and shoreline.
3. Suppress trafficking in controlled and pilfered items between the shore and watercraft and between watercraft.
4. Investigate and report any suspicious actions among persons or watercraft.
5. Enforce regulations and policies and provide offshore security for com-

munications facilities, port security devices, aids to navigation, dock facilities, moorages, and anchorages.

INLAND WATERWAY TERMINALS

An inland waterway terminal normally includes facilities for mooring, cargo loading and unloading, dispatch and control, and the repair and service of all watercraft capable of navigating the waterway. Intermediate transfer points may be along the waterway whenever a changing in transportation mode happens (e.g., ship to land transport, transfer from large smaller craft because of water depth, ship to barge, or land to barge).

Two advantages of using inland waterways as transportation modes are the ability to move large quantities of volume cargo and the relative ease of movement of large, heavy, or outsize loads. Disadvantages include the slow movement of the carrier (i.e., a barge, coupled with the vulnerability of pilferage), weather, and seasonal interruptions such as flooding and freezing, location restrictions on direct movement of materials either forward or laterally, and requirements for rehandling at a terminal or at a transfer point because of shipment diversions. For these reasons, inland waterway capability is incorporated into the transportation service only when enough transport capabilities cannot be supplied by the other modes.

Documentation for Cargo Movement on Inland Waterways

Cargo moving through inland terminals is documented in the same manner as cargo moving through other terminals as discussed earlier. Security officers assigned to inland waterway terminals will perform, generally, the same duties as discussed earlier.

COMMUNICATIONS FOR WATER-BASED SECURITY PATROLS

Water patrol operations require communications between patrol boats, patrol boats and other craft, patrol boats and shore-based security elements, and patrol boats and the various marine law enforcement agencies. Means, facilities, and devices that your water patrol officers need include

1. Radios netted with security and law enforcement agencies
2. Visual and sound signaling devices (blinkers, horns, and flags)
3. Megaphones or public address systems

4. Cellular or radio telephone systems

5. Pyrotechnics (flare guns and other types of flares)

CREATING AN OFFSHORE OPERATIONS BASE

Depending on your situation and operating environment, you might consider establishing a security base offshore, especially when a sizable amount of your company property is loaded and unloaded in an anchorage situation and transported to shore terminals by lighters. Another application might include protecting offshore petroleum equipment for loading and unloading petroleum products.

The offshore bases created by some companies work well and involve converting a salvage or transportation barge into a houseboat. The barge is anchored in a suitable and secure location off shore and is staffed by a security crew. The crew may live on board much as firefighters do in a fire house, for 24 or 48 hours. The houseboat, about 40 feet long and 12 feet wide, is divided into two parts. One side serves as an operations room; the other side is a combination bunk room and cooking and dining area.

In the proper circumstances the houseboat provides an offshore rendezvous point for the small security patrol boats and their crews. It may also provide a rapid response base for a call for assistance and serve as an added point for constant surveillance.

QUICK REFERENCE GUIDE
FOR
PORT, HARBOR, AND RIVER TERMINAL SECURITY OPERATIONS

- Terminals
- Special identification and movement controls
- Increased entrance and exit responsibilities
- Pier and wharf security
- Offshore security officers
- Gangplank security officers
- Hatch security officers
- Pier security officers
- Anchorage security
- Security officers shipboard
- Container operations
- Perimeter security of marshaling yards
- Safeguarding and controlling CMD documents
- Safeguarding and controlling container seals
- River and inlet patrols
- Prevention is the key element of water patrols
- Specialized training needs

14

Intransit Shipments and Cargo Security Management

Movement of goods and merchandise by the nation's transportation system—air, rail, motor, and marine carriers—represents one of the largest industries in the United States. That industry also supports the largest corporations and industries producing the goods and merchandise they transport. Manufacturing and industrial operations depend on the transportation industry to supply them with raw materials for production, including distribution and delivery of merchandise to customers. Most transportation of these materials and goods by common carriers instead of company-owned transportation fleets. However, many companies use their own fleets, and many own those viewed as common carriers. The term "cargo" commonly applies to anything that enters and is moved by the transportation system—beginning at the shipper's loading platform and ending at the consignee's receiving dock.

GETTING A HANDLE ON THE PROBLEM

The term "cargo theft" refers to the theft of entire shipments, containers, and cartons, including pilferage of smaller amounts of goods or contents. Annual loss estimates of $15 to 25 billion result from cargo theft involving all modes of transportation according to government figures. It is a difficult amount to pinpoint because of perceptions and failure to report the thefts, instead choosing to write off the amount as a business loss. According to the Office of Transportation Security of the U.S. Department of Transportation, the percentages of known losses include

1. Hijacking, 5%

2. Breaking and entering and external theft, 10%

3. Internal theft, collusive theft, and unexplained shortages, 85%.

Cargo theft happens throughout points of the distribution system, including warehouses, receiving and shipping platforms, storage areas, deports, distribution centers, terminals, and piers.

Estimates show that organized crime activities account for 15 to 20% of the value of all cargo theft. Organized crime involvement in actual theft and redistribution of stolen goods includes the consumption of goods in the businesses it controls or owns.

The remainder of the theft happens primarily as the result of employee collusion among themselves or with persons outside the transportation system and organized fences. Transportation security experts point to the large dollar amount and size of cargo thefts as indications of employee collusion. Fences (persons buying and selling stolen merchandise) often organize within geographic areas and product lines. Their operations range from very small, with a single person acting as a broker, or large with several persons having cash readily available for the purchase of stolen goods. Thieves can generally expect to receive from fences anywhere from one-third of retail value to 10 cents on the wholesale dollar depending on the type of goods and the prevailing market.

Most stolen cargo returns to the transportation system and legitimate businesses, and dealers are often the recipients, either knowingly through collusion, or unknowingly through forged or altered shipping invoices. Examples of legitimate dealers as receivers of stolen cargo include discount houses, wholesalers, salvage companies, and meat and food distributors.

The precise amount of direct financial loss to the transportation industry resulting from cargo theft is questioned because the figures cited are largely estimates. Some problems in arriving at accurate statistics include the reporting goods as stolen and then later found; the resolution of many claims shortly after reported; and the variances in assigning wholesale, retail, or invoice values to the reported losses. However, the figures shown include a composite of statistics averaged through collection of known figures over several years.

Transportation security officials point out that argument over statistics only downplays the true effect of cargo theft on the transportation industry and those they support. For example, losses generally portray a ratio of insurance claims to gross operating revenue, and, at an average of 1 to 2%, many firms view the losses as a simple cost of doing business. But officials point to the high indirect losses that result from cargo theft, for example, higher insurance premiums and increased deductible rates for insurance claims and difficulty in obtaining insurance coverage. Other disadvantages include lost time on cargo theft claims, delayed and lost sales by consignees, lost business by carriers, and increases in the price of goods and freight rates to absorb the loss in operating expenses.

Security measures undertaken by the transportation industry include the use of security officers in shipping, receiving, and storage areas; access-control systems and perimeter fencing and lighting; closed-circuit television systems and alarms; and special security seals and alarms on trucks. Some high-value shipment monitoring includes transmitters placed on the vehicle and a directional monitoring receiver in a helicopter.

Others use a system that monitors truck movements through electronic signposts in selected areas. High-security storage bins or areas used by various modes of carriers for high-value and high-loss classes of commodities enhance security. Also, security officers, electronic surveillance, and intrusion detection systems help prevent crimes in high-security areas. Because of the high incidence of employee involvement in cargo theft, you need to obtain criminal history information on applicants for employment in cargo areas, essential to screen out potential thieves, although that only serves well when the employee has a criminal record.

LOGISTICS MANAGEMENT CONCEPTS IN YOUR SECURITY OPERATIONS

It is important that your security forces assigned to intransit security have at least a basic understanding of some considerations that affect the company management and those responsible to manage movement of cargoes. They are, first, concerned with delivering the cargo, when, where, and in the quantities needed, using the best available and suitable mode of transportation.

You need to advise the logistics and movements managers encouraging them to adopt the use of the "inventory in motion" method of supply. With this type concept, your company's cargo and merchandise are delivered directly from the source to the ultimate user instead of movement to a storage depot for further breakdown and shipment. Depots cannot be eliminated, but through that concept, reductions happen both in number and in size. Continued and expanded utilization of this concept will lead to both reductions of requirements for storage security and an increase in requirements for intransit security. It not only saves money in both those areas; it also saves money in the dramatic reduction or elimination of intransit losses.

There may be situations where a risk needs expectation of some loss of cargoes in transit so that at least a part of shipment reaches its destination. It is then the task of your company to determine what, if any, rate of loss is acceptable, that is, an acceptable percentage delivered to the consignee from the total amount shipped by your company. Considerations of such a rate of loss would depend on the sensitivity and criticality of the cargoes. It is not a sound perspective; however, until losses become effectively controlled and eliminated, the expectation often proves accurate regarding the reality of cargo theft.

MODES OF TRANSPORTATION

Although your corporate management chooses the mode of transportation used to ship (sometimes receive) products, your interest evolves when security becomes necessary. The following guidelines provide insight into the modes of transportation and their advantages and disadvantages, important when management requests for you to know about your views about security. Normally, the following basic considerations help to define the categories of selection.

1. *Provide service according to need.* The need results from established priorities and type of the shipment. About the latter, an evaluation emerges from the effect of shipment characteristics and other factors, such as security requirements.

2. *Use the most economical mode for the complete movement.* When possible, from an economical point of view, use that mode's available capability as far as possible. The modes of transportation, their characters, and most effecting use are outlined later in this chapter.

3. *Whenever practicable, minimize or eliminate rehandling of cargo during transportation and avoid cross-haul and back-haul.* When available, mode combination services, such as trailer-on-flatcar, afford an effective technique of accomplishing this objective.

The following guide provides further insight into the selection of cargo shipment modes of transportation.

Motor Transport (Truck)

Most effectively used as a supplementary mode for supplying the connecting link that makes possible an integrated transportation system. It can also find effective application in scheduled line haul operations by the trailer relay system.

Capabilities:

It is the most flexible mode in nearly all weather. It increases flexibility of other modes of transportation. It can transport nearly any commodity with a variety of specialized equipment for movement by road.

Limitations:

Over-the-road operations are affected by route interferences (construction), terrain (mountains), and obstacles created by weather (e.g., snow, ice).

Rail

Most effectively used as inland modes for maintaining a sustained flow of large quantities of cargo over long distances. Also an effective mode for movement of oversized and heavy cargo.

Capabilities:

Rail transportation has all-weather capability, with any commodity. It is often the most economical continuous-line-haul mode. It has the greatest sustained ton-mile capability with a variety of specialized equipment and services.

Limitations:

Rail systems have flexibility limited by fixed routes.

Water

Most effectively used as overocean mode. It provides a supplementary inland surface mode for movement of large quantities of cargo in bulk and heavy and oversize material.

Capabilities:

All-weather capability is an advantage, including any commodity and economical over long distances.

Limitations:

Water or surface transportation by water is slow. Its flexibility is limited by adequacy of terminals, waterways facilities, and channels.

Air

Most effectively used as a complementary mode for proving expedited movement of cargo. It is a primary or major supplementary mode when terrain conditions reduce effectiveness of surface modes. The scheduled operation is the most economical method and produces greatest sustained ton-mile capability.

Capabilities:

It offers the greatest potential speed of delivery and most flexible for terrain obstacle.

Limitations:

Operations capabilities and effectiveness are limited by climate factors and trafficability of take-off and landing areas. In addition, ton-mile operating costs are relatively high.

TRANSPORTATION SECURITY TECHNIQUES

The concept of transportation security has evolved to include all security measures taken to protect shipments from criminal and possible terrorist activity. There are no universal or one-time solutions to the problems of cargo security, because each mode of transportation and type of shipment in each shipping and receiving terminal and each transfer point is unique. However, certain basic principles of cargo security are adaptable to accommodate any mode of transportation of any facility, large or small.

When developing your security systems for transportation security evolving from your specific situations, consider the following guidelines:

1. Exercise your security management obligation directly or through the company manager responsible for the shipment.

2. Determine the threat, sensitivity of cargo, vulnerability, and mode of transportation that dictate security needed during storage and in transit.

DECIDING THE LEVELS OR TYPE OF SECURITY YOU NEED

This evolves from

1. Facility size and location
2. Complexity of storage or shipment
3. Volume and value of items
4. Economic and geographical situation
5. Available crime statistics
6. Security forces available
7. Law enforcement
8. Transit shipments

Your development of an effective cargo security system depends on

1. Experiences of company management responsible for shipments and storage of cargo

2. Loss potential based on a risk analysis
3. Established security standards and policy

THE PROBLEMS OF PILFERAGE AND TECHNIQUES OF PREVENTION

The following characteristics apply to pilferage in the transportation environment:

1. Pilferage is difficult to detect because pilferers usually operate alone or in collusion with others outside the company parameters.
2. Evidence is hard to obtain because of the complexity in the shipment and storage system.
3. Pilferage is unsystematic.
4. Pilferage commonly happens in a terminal while cargo is awaiting movement from one vehicle or mode of transportation to another.
5. Pilferage is often committed by employees of a carrier service.

Prevention Techniques

To prevent transportation pilferage, apply these steps:

1. Analyze existing conditions.
2. Control personnel movement.
3. Use a parcel check system.
4. Exclude privately owned motor vehicles from parcel checkpoints.
5. Stress the moral wrong of pilferage in education programs.
6. Apply stringent accountability procedures.
7. Develop respect between security officers and employees.
8. Incorporate active security measures in a security in depth configuration.
9. Use other preventive measures discussed earlier in the book.

KEY ELEMENTS OF FINDING SOLUTIONS TO CARGO THEFT PROBLEMS DURING SHIPMENT AND STORAGE

Theft prevention is your first responsibility. A systematic and planned theft or other crime is often committed with accomplices and usually involves

- An available market for the stolen items

- Goods profitable and easily disposed of

Areas and Functions Vulnerable to Manipulation

The following points include areas and functions with high theft potential:

1. Terminal operation areas.
2. Truck drivers.
3. Facility employees.
4. False invoice shipments and receipts.

Management Controls

To minimize exposure to persons who display a motive to steal, you should work with your company management to ensure their cooperation with the security effort. Encourage and assist them to

1. Illustrate and use countermeasures.
2. Screen employees and applicants who will work in applicable areas.
3. Eliminate in-facility gambling among employees.
4. Eliminate the get-even attitude among employees.
5. Reduce exposure of cargo to theft and pilferage.
6. Ensure close coordination between packaging, shipping, and receiving personnel.
7. Increase the probability of detection when thefts do happen.
8. Discipline those persons apprehended for theft and pilferage.
9. Obtain feedback to determine implementation of cargo theft countermeasures and whether properly followed by operating personnel.

Shipping Department Awareness

You also need to coordinate your security effort with the company shipping department and managers, asking them to be attentive to

1. Packing requirements and procedures
2. Receipt procedures at destinations
3. Providing notice of shipments to receivers
4. Arrival and departure time of all cargo shipments
5. Specific routes of travel planning for the cargo

CREATING COOPERATION FROM YOUR COMPANY'S MANAGEMENT

Most company management groups listen when you can show them how to save money and increase profits. Enhancement of your security effort happens dramatically when company managers cooperate with you. Explain to them that cargo theft and pilferage losses in today's multimodel transportation system are ever present through the less visible impact of

- Insurance claims
- Administration of cargo theft claims
- Delayed or lost sales for customers
- Added cost created by the loss and the cost of replacing the stolen cargo and reshipping it to customers
- Lost time when raw materials expected do not arrive because of theft
- Lost business by carriers
- Interference with the flow of commerce
- Diversion of cargo needed to complete a project
- Higher prices and freight rates increase
- Reduced operations and production profit.

SECURITY EDUCATION FOR CORPORATE SHIPPING AND TRANSPORTATION MANAGERS

Your encouragement of security for corporate shipping and transportation management needs to include the following points. The areas also serve as your guide for training security officers and supervisors working in areas where cargo is shipped and received.

As practicable, insist on piece counts when cargo moves to and from vehicles and in and out of storage areas, vessels, rail cars, aircraft, and so on. Insist on clear identification of those who conduct such counts (i.e., driver, checker, receiving personnel, terminal cargo handler, or others involved). The two parties involved in a cargo transfer should not take one another's word regarding the count. When they do, accountability becomes blurred.

Negotiate with carriers for what might be called "signature security service" for certain kinds of shipments. This means obtaining a signature and tally from each person handling the shipment at each stage of its transit, from point of origin to destination (a type of "custody chain" document).

Prelodged deliveries or pickup orders need safeguarding from theft or unauthorized observation. Verify identity of carrier and carrier employee before releasing a prelodged pickup order. A large terminal operation needs to use prelodging. Truckers should bring their documentation to the terminal the day before they deliver cargo. The terminal prepares receiving documents from the trucker's papers and when trucks arrive; they give priority in handing the loads involving the advanced documentation. Cargo handling is expedited, checking is more precise, and the documents themselves are more accurate.

Restrict access to cargo documentation to a need-to-know basis. Systems assuring strict accountability for documentation are as important as those designed for the cargo itself. For example, after several thefts in a terminal involving stolen documentation, including its cargo, an internal release order was divided as follows. The cargo handler who is to retrieve a shipment in the terminal receives the release order, which describes the cargo and its location. Source documents remain in the order. The clerk retains a copy of the release that he or she records at the time of preparation and name of the cargo handler. The cargo handler takes the shipment to his or her control supervisor who verifies the identity of the cargo handler and description and quantity of cargo to be delivered. The supervisor requests the signature of the trucker after recording date and time of release. Finally, the release order returns to the clerk who prepared it.

An integral part of terminal security is a workable, accurate cargo location system. Delays in, or confusion over, removing cargo from storage increase the risk of theft or pilferage. Among other things, a good locator system does not give cargo handlers the excuse to wander throughout the terminal when looking for a shipment.

Devise procedures to minimize terminal congestion and poor housekeeping that lead to obstructed visibility of cargo, misplaced cargo, less efficient checking and handling, and other situations promoting theft and pilferage. The real enemy is congestion. When goods pile up, a loss of control happens.

When strikes hit other modes or carriers, some terminals need emergency plans to handle in an orderly fashion the expected extra flow of cargo (such as through a pickup and delivery appointment system for shippers and consignees).

SECURITY MANAGEMENT AND INVESTIGATIVE AUDIT TRAILS

Your security efforts cannot ensure the elimination of theft or diversion of company cargo shipments. However, another strong deterrent involves prompt and decisive investigation of thefts and prosecution of offenders. When your company uses a well-designed system of accountability for intransit goods, you can trace the shipment and normally find the point of theft through the audit trail. When you have found the point of theft, your investigation can expand and lead to arrest and prosecution, and often recovery of company property. When your security systems discourage a theft and when a determined thief does steal, he or she is promptly identified and prosecuted, your deterrent or crime prevention effort is effective.

Illustration 14–1 show a basic audit trail that guides your investigation to determine the point of theft. The system shown can be adapted to any situation your company might use.

Illustration 14–1

EXAMPLE OF CARGO MOVEMENT CONTROL AUDIT TRAIL

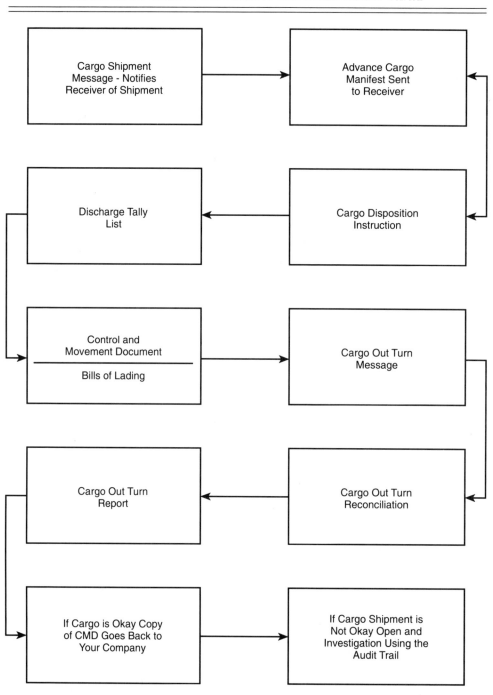

PROTECTIVE SECURITY TECHNIQUES COMMENSURATE WITH THE THREAT

Your protective measures for shipments must be compatible with the threat. Types of protective measures are

1. Physical protection (containers, storage warehouses)
2. Personnel involvement (security officers, screened employees)
3. Procedural techniques (accounting, shipping, receiving)

Levels of cargo control are

1. Minimum—provided all cargo
2. Medium—provided to
   a. High-value cargo with a ready resale
   b. Others as designated
3. Maximum—provided to
   a. Classified material
   b. Sensitive items (e.g., government contract items)
   c. Other materials needing strict control

Passive Security Measures for Cargo and Shipments

Identification Marking

Identification marking is used on containers, railroad cars and trucks to show the supplies they contain.

Locks and Seals

Locks and numbered seals are placed on railroad cars, vans, and some types of shipping cases to deny easy access and to disclose tampering or damage.

Tarpaulin Covering

Some supplies or equipment shipped by railway flatcar or by open truck may need protection against either weather or possible pilferage. They may need the added security of rope or wire cable crisscrossed from one side to the other across the top of the load.

Containerization and Banding

The most desirable technique of securing small boxes or packages of sensitive items is consolidating them in a steel shipping container. When containers are not available, large wooden boxes or crates will serve your security purposes. They need to be metal-banded when completely filled. Another alternative is to palletize small containers and band the entire pallet load. In any case, the most sensitive items should be placed in the center of the load to prevent easy access. Where practicable and desirable, use requisition voucher numbers for identification instead of item descriptions. You may use other identification marking that prevents identification of the materials by potential pilfers. Often, it is not desirable to allow vehicle operators or other cargo handling or transport personnel to know the contents of a shipment.

Special Security Techniques—Applications of Alarm Devices During Cargo Shipments

Alarm devices have the basic function of supplying a warning when a shipment moves from its proper location or when the security provided by the container or vehicle holding the shipment has been breached (such as opening container doors, or tampering with the shipment). The alarm devices you might use should

1. Augment other security measures
2. Provide protection under unusual circumstances
3. Conserve security resources

Your alarm devices are only that part of an intrusion detection system that sounds the alarm. There are three basic parts:

1. Sensor to detect noise, presence, or movement
2. Wire or transmitter to send the sensor signal to a receiver and annunciator
3. Receiver and annunciator to display or emit a notification (as a light, sounds, or switch to trigger another device), indicating the situation detected by the sensor.

Most intrusion detection systems have a design suitable for fixed applications and do not lend themselves to shipments. A few have the primary purpose of detecting anyone moving a shipment or entering a transport container or vehicle. Alarm devices appropriate for shipment use and available from several sources include:

- *Entry alarms.* Similar to the common burglar alarm, the system design enables it to operate on a small battery and emit a mind-wrenching sound that is felt and heard.

- *Movement alarms.* These operate on the principle of a radio, that is, transmitter and a receiver.

- *Small-motion sensors.* These devices easily attached to a container or vehicle door transmit a coded radio frequency signal when the door opens or the container moves. The signal transmits to a receiver, which notifies a security officer.

- *A tarpaulin.* Constructed of heavy waterproof fabric with built-in motion sensors, a tarpaulin detects movement of materials from under its cover and causes transmission of a radio signal.

Effective Use of Seals with Cargo Shipments

Effective users of seals—be they seal-locks or cable seals (a lock is not necessarily a seal, and a seal is not necessarily a lock)—in transportation security need to follow these guidelines:

- A compromise in the integrity of a shipment must be shown.
- Unless money and time are unlimited, there is no particular seal, lock, or combination suitable for every situation. For example, a high-grade lock on a weak container hasp is a waste of money, and a high-grade seal provides a false sense of security when the door is easily removed.
- Strict seal accountability is necessary, and accountability should be constant.
- Accountability starts with the manufacturer and ends with seal destruction.
- To be effective, seals must meet two basic requirements: construction specifications and accountability.

Seal Construction Specifications

Durability. A seal must be strong enough to prevent accidental breakage during normal use.

Design. The design must be sufficiently complex to make unauthorized manufacture of a replacement seal difficult.

Tamperproof. The seal should provide readily visible evidence of tampering and prevent reconstruction after that seal is closed; that is, a seal needs construction to make simulated locking difficult.

Individually identifiable. Identification best accomplished by embossing serial numbers and owner identification on each seal.

Seal Accountability Procedures

Record of Application. Seal numbers are entered on the designated place on pertinent transportation documents such as bills of lading, manifests, and gate passes and in users' seal application logs.

Time of Application. Trailers must be sealed immediately after the load is closed out (complete). Roll-up-type doors must be sealed by the checker at the loading dock. Swing-out doors must be sealed by the person pulling the unit away from the dock immediately after the unit is far enough away for the doors to be closed.

Verification. Seal examination and verification at every stop, such as terminal exits and entrances, docks, transfer points, and road stops for truck and driver services.

1. Security officers at gates must check the seal number against the gate pass and shipping documents and note seal numbers, including the trailer and tractor number on his or her gate log.

2. Persons receiving sealed shipments or equipment must examine the seal and record the number on the receipt.

3. Whenever removal of a seal or the seal is broken, or suspected of compromise, the following actions must happen:

   a. Record pertinent information:
      (1) Date and time of seal removal, broken or discovered broken, and so on
      (2) By whom, name
      (3) Circumstances and justification for breaking the seal
      (4) New seal number, if applied (new seal must be same type)
      (5) Person resealing
      (6) Witnesses

   b. Make proper disposition of broken seals:
      (1) Retain until determined whether the shipment contained discrepancies.
      (2) When there were none, destroy the seal
      (3) When differences are found, the broken seal must be sent to the security manager.
      (4) If shipment contains classified information, material, or equipment, the following actions, as a minimum, must be immediately started:
         (a) Secure the area.
         (b) Position security officers.
         (c) Notify the security supervisors.
         (d) Conduct immediate inventory.

Breaking Seals and the Law

Title 18, US Code, Section 2117, states that: "Whoever breaks the seal or lock of any railway car, vessel, aircraft, motor truck, wagon or other vehicle . . . containing interstate or foreign shipments of freight or express, or other property, or enters any such vehicle . . . with intent in either case to commit larceny therein, shall be fined not more than $5,000, or imprisoned not more than 10 years, or both."

LEGAL CONSIDERATIONS FOR YOUR SECURITY DEPARTMENT AND OFFICERS

The duty of a common carrier of property is to provide all reasonable and necessary facilities for safe and efficient transportation of such goods as it holds itself out to the public as engaged in carrying. This includes the duty to carry such goods safely and to exercise the care needed to protect them from loss or injury during transportation.

These duties are imposed by the common law and statute. So, from the release of goods to a carrier for transportation until final delivery made, a carrier's liability is an insurer, with certain exceptions (act of God, act of the public enemy, act of the shipper, etc.).

In keeping with the duties and liabilities imposed by law, a carrier, as a bailee of goods, will necessarily exercise full control and custody over the lading. Accordingly, while the goods are in transit, the carrier, not the shipper, is responsible for proper care of the goods.

Simultaneously, the shipper retains the legal right during the time the goods are in transit to have his consignment interrupted, withheld, reconsigned, or diverted at any intermediate point. While this is a right afforded the shippers under law, the services made by the carrier about it are supplementary services that the carrier is obligated to provide and may collect for. These services and charges, including the terms and conditions under which the shipper's right to be exercised, are, in effect, a contractual matter to be established and governed by the carrier's tariff or tender.

It is the right of the shipper to have the consignment interrupted, diverted, or rerouted. It is the right of the carrier to carry escorts or security officers approved by shippers to accompany shipments and, where authorized, is a matter of contract to be explained in the carrier's tariff or tender. In this connection, the inclusion of annotations on bills of lading setting forth a requirement for escorts and stating their responsibilities would be ineffective unless provisions are first described in the carrier's tariff or tender.

A carrier used by a shipper for transportation of special cargo needing an escort may be a contract carrier or a common carrier supplying services under a commercial tariff or a Section 22 tender. The Section 22 tender, as a commercial tariff, sets forth services the carrier will perform, applicable charges, and conditions of shipment. In effect, it is the governing contract. It usually contains the following provisions about armed security officers.

When requested by the shipper, an armed security officer (furnished by the company, accompanying the shipment), will be permitted to ride in the carrier's vehicle. This security officer will be responsible for the security of the shipment from origin to final destination but will not be responsible in any way for the operation of the vehicle or the route to follow.

Transfer of authority to direct or otherwise control movement of the cargo becomes a responsibility of the security officer escort, after placing appropriate provisions in the carrier's tariff or tender, and the escort is duly appointed to act as the company's transportation representative.

Instructions Needed for Security Officer Shipment Escorts

Specific written instructions and operating procedures must be furnished your security officers escorting shipments and include, but are not necessarily limited to, the following guidelines:

1. General outline of the escort responsibilities
2. Name and address of company to which the shipment is to be delivered
3. Receipting procedures on arrival at the destination
4. Means of transportation and route to use
5. Duties of each escorting security officer during the shipment movement, stops authorized, and during loading and unloading operations
6. Emergency and communication procedures

Specify the Shipment Escort Functions

Your security officer shipment escorts assigned for the protection of company assets must adhere to the following guidelines:

1. Conduct themselves in such a manner that the security of the shipment entrusted to them will not be prejudiced through carelessness, inadvertence, or lack of vigilance. Intoxicants that may impair their judgment cannot be ingested by security officer escorts while assigned to a security shipment.
2. Possess identification cards and carry them always while having custody of security shipments. These cards must be safeguarded, and the loss of a card reported immediately to the company security manager.
3. Carry packages on his or her person, or in hand-carried containers, until delivered to the consignee whenever practicable.
4. Provide continuous observation of the shipment, vehicle, or container and be in physical position to exercise direct security controls over the shipment.
5. Maintain liaison, as required, with train crews, airport, and other transportation personnel, special police and law enforcement agencies as appropriate.
6. Maintain continuous vigilance when escorting security shipments for the presence of conditions or situations that might threaten the security of the cargo, act as circumstances might call for to avoid interference with con-

tinuous safe passage of the vehicle, and check seals and locks at each stop where time permits.

7. When escorting shipment by aircraft, your security officer escort will not enplane until the cargo area is secured. The escort should preferably be the first person to deplane to observe the opening of the cargo area. Advance arrangements with the airline need your attention.

8. Notify the consignor by the fastest means available if there is an unforeseen delay en route, an alternate route use, or if an emergency happens. When appropriate and if the security of the shipment is involved (especially when a government shipment), the security officer needs to notify the nearest office of the Federal Bureau of Investigation.

9. Armed security officers escorting the shipment need coordination before departure of the shipment with law enforcement agencies in the areas where the shipment will pass through.

QUICK REFERENCE GUIDE
FOR
INTRANSIT CARGO AND SHIPMENT SECURITY

- Analyze your company's position and situation.
- Bring logistics management concepts into your security program for cargo and shipment security.
- Consider the modes of transportation with their advantages and disadvantages, and how each affects your security arrangements.
- Identify your company's problems and find viable solutions.
- Educate and seek company management cooperation.
- Develop audit trail procedures for stolen cargo.
- Research and understand applicable laws affecting cargo and shipping including security officer escorts.
- Decide how to train and use security officers effectively as cargo and shipping escort officers.

15 Executive Protective Security Operations

With increased incidents of terrorism, hostage taking, kidnapping, and violence directed at corporate and industrial executives from disgruntled employees, former employees, and others blaming them for their problems, your security program needs to include protecting company executives from harm. Security of corporate and industrial executives (and often their families) involves normal security measures at your company, along with special techniques related to their homes, public appearances, and travel. The skill of protecting persons from harm involves many aspects that can fill a book in itself; however, the reliable, effective guidelines in this chapter greatly enhance your security program.

PRINCIPLES OF EXECUTIVE SECURITY

Every phase of your executive security program needs careful planning. The possibility of sudden changes of itinerary, however, means that flexibility has to be the keynote in planning.

Physical protection includes a series of protective cordons, each complete in itself. These protective cordons include security officers (in uniform or civilian attire) or physical barriers, or a combination of both. An example of this type of security is the protection established around the executive's home. It may also apply to certain workplace offices, depending on location. A protective cordon includes these steps:

1. Several security officers walking patrols around the grounds to establish a protective cordon (may also serve as an effective deterrent)

2. A series of fixed security officer posts at entrances also create another type cordon

3. Security officers stationed within the residence for the third echelon of protection (security in depth or layered security)

Central direction and unity of effort are your keys and of special importance because of the difficulty often experienced in this type assignment. Your coordination with all elements is necessary and includes a close liaison with local law enforcement agencies.

Your choice of security officers for assignment to this task calls for essential traits, including, but not limited to

1. *Maturity.* Your security officers must have good judgment and common sense. They also need to have the maturity to avoid pranks within the security force; being distracted by a variety of other elements could allow an intruder to penetrate the security cordon.

2. *Experience as a security officer.* This characteristic also includes law enforcement experience.

3. *Acceptable physical appearance and bearing.* Often, the presence of a security officer (either in uniform or civilian attire) serves as an effective deterrent. According to the situation, you need to select security officers who project an image that most people do not want to challenge.

4. *No personal problems.* Domestic or severe financial problems that preoccupy the security officer's mind create an often unobserved distraction. You need to know your officers well and screen them carefully before entrusting the life of an executive and his or her family to them.

In many of your protective activities, bringing technical assistance into the assignment serves your program effectively, for example, mechanics to inspect automobiles, alarm experts, landscaping experts to create natural screens and cordons, building inspectors, aircraft experts, and so forth.

Routes and means of transportation used by the protected executive and his or her family must remain confidential and interchangeable. Often, the itinerary receives wide publication. It may be necessary that he or she address public audiences, accept invitations to local civilian functions, and meet visitors at railway stations and airports. Attentive scrutiny of the normal itinerary will reveal many details you should not release to the public. Do not release the routes to and from appointments. If a series of appointments is scheduled for a particular location, routes need to be varied. Do not permit publicity about the protective assignment. Maintaining secrecy on the movements of your protected executive and family is an effective technique of minimizing the opportunity for attack.

CONTINGENCY PLANNING

Your security planning needs flexibility. Weather and mechanical failures (including lighting) are two ever-present potential hazards. The unexpected arrival of many visitors is another situation often encountered. Last-minute changes in the schedule of events happen routinely. Your security plan must be sufficiently fluid to cover these and many more eventualities, all which present potential life-threatening hazards.

CREATING YOUR OPERATIONS PROGRAM

The following format supplies you with a reliable way of formulating your protective plan. Requirements include

- Assignment description
- Concept of assignment
- Coordination and liaison
- Itinerary areas of interest
- Personnel and equipment requirements
- Cooperation and intelligence
- Communication
- Logistical support
- Public relations
- Emergency information
- Command and control

You need to write your plan with its length and other elements included dependent on the assignment size, length, and depth. The plan, including drafts and notes, must have the highest possible security controls. That control includes persons having knowledge of what information your plan contains. The more the plan develops, the greater problem your security becomes. You may also need to compartmentalize information you provide to others, including the officers assigned to the task. A careless comment about the security operations overheard or passed along innocently creates significant, often critical situations. The problem of leaking information is not always life threatening; however, the consequences can contribute to life-threatening opportunity for the perpetrator. For example, the executive might be a high-profile person who wants to get away from the media spotlight with his or her family. However, a security officer or company staff member having knowledge of a secret trek to a secluded location tells someone (normally trying to impress someone that he or she knows all the company secrets) who passes on the information and the media learn of the location. When your security team arrives with the executive and family, a group of media is waiting. Since their location is then publicized, a perpetrator quietly tracking the executive you are protecting now has an advantage of knowing where the family is vacationing. The secluded location might supply another advantage of penetrating defenses and carrying out his or her scheme.

The key to successful completion of your executive security assignment includes detailed, continuous planning and careful selection, training and use of security officers. It is also important to include one assistant in your planning, preparations, and command control, so that should you be unable to continue, your assistant has sufficient knowledge to take control. Each security officer assigned to the task should also have a reserve counterpart.

COLLECTING INTELLIGENCE

Much of your success when protecting an executive and family depends on collecting reliable intelligence on possible threats and adversaries. This information is available from commercial agencies and law enforcement agencies. Law enforcement agencies normally cooperate with protective security elements because they prefer not to have any such crime committed in their jurisdiction and suffer the wrath of an after-crime charge of failure to cooperate.

Maintaining Detailed Records

During your planning phases and throughout the protective assignment, keep detailed, chronological records of events. You need to include

1. All instructions received

2. All agreements made

3. Other information and decisions about the assignment

Keeping a detailed log throughout the assignment serves as a permanent legal record and is useful in conducting "lessons learned" critiques. You also need to write an after-action report. Combined, these records help you to learn from experience, improve your security, and help during planning and implementation of later assignments.

A loose-leaf, three-ring notebook is convenient for keeping this group of records. The book needs one section for the chronological events log and separate sections for each major phase or geographical area involved.

The Office, Residence, and Other Important Logs

Your security officers performing executive security assignments need to maintain an accurate record of all events affecting the office, residence, or other area where the executive and family are. Ruled, three-ring pages fastened in a hardback binder provide a convenient form for this record. The binder arrangement can also serve the residence watch log, baggage security instructions, lapel button accountability forms, visitor-package-telephone register forms, photographs and other important information used in ready-reference, and other pertinent protective service information.

Baggage accountability and control become simplified and reliable using color-coded baggage tags and with baggage accountability forms. When responsibility for baggage is first assumed, make an accurate count coupled with using a written record filling in a baggage accountability form. Color-coded baggage tags should be affixed to each piece of luggage and changed often during travel without any prearranged system, instead using a random, spur of the moment decision of the color to use. (The same technique applies for lapel pins of security officers and visitors.)

Baggage of the executive and family during travel is an excellent way for a perpetrator to plant a bomb or just steal the baggage creating an inconvenience. Your security for an executive and family includes every aspect of their life, including the baggage while traveling, deliveries addressed to them, mail and packages, people having access to them, their vehicles, the staff at the restaurant where they eat, and so forth.

Effective protection means you need to plug every possibility and every opportunity with a security countermeasure.

PRE-ASSIGNMENT ORIENTATION

Before the executive protection assignment, you need to ensure each member of the protective group knows what they will do You need to emphasize the following:

Security officers are assigned to these duties because of their appearance, alertness, and intelligence, and ability to act quickly and correctly in unforeseen circumstances. You need to ensure they understand the importance of not taking risks with the safety and well-being of protected persons. To perform their duties efficiently, protective security officers must understand the mechanics and terminology peculiar to an executive security assignment of this type. For example, an executive security assignment might need a single bodyguard or a security group and escort groups.

The assignment might include direct or indirect protection or escort duty. Direct protection is open and obvious; indirect is generally a surveillance measure. The security group may operate as interior security and may have one or more officers stationed at fixed posts. Security officers need to know the identity of persons in the party of the executive, including family and staff members.

The attitude of the protected person must be assessed by the security officers and in your planning. Sometimes the presence of security personnel is unpleasant to the executive and his or her family. This is understandable because of the lack of privacy inherent in personal security assignments.

Security officers must be aware of this natural reaction, anticipate it, and adhere to strict policies of nonirritating conduct. In the early planning stages, you need to search for ways to avoid all potential embarrassment to the executive and family. It is normally good policy to avoid direct contact with the executive on details of arrangements. When necessary, coordinate with a close assistant to the executive who is designated for this purpose.

When the protected person ignores measures taken for his or her protection, security officers continue to perform their duties as directed. When appropriate, you need to offer suggestions tactfully.

Restriction on the movement of persons needs strict enforcement. Before allowing any person to approach the executive, his or her property, or family, the person must be checked carefully for identification and the authority for his or her presence verified by a reliable staff or family member. Protective officers should quickly learn to recognize all employees and regular visitors cleared for calling on the executive. Other precautions include the following:

1. Having advance lists when a group of visitors is expected. Arrange with your executive to have a reliable person available to identify and vouch for any unrecognized visitor.

2. Admitting visitors only at specified entrances and maintaining control to ensure that they proceed directly to their approved destinations. Members of the security unit must be especially tactful and diplomatic in performing this function to avoid offending an unrecognized but invited person.

Your security officers need posting at locations so they can observe everyone and everything in the immediate vicinity of the protected person. However, also ensure they understand effective protection includes watching or observing "away" from the executive instead of looking at and watching the executive. The danger comes from others, and not the executive who is unlikely to harm him or herself.

THE PERSONAL BODYGUARDS

Your security officers assigned as personal bodyguards need attentive selection and training. They need to dress similarly to the executive and often appear as a business associate or aide as opposed to a bodyguard. They must exercise constant vigilance over the protected person, remain always a short distance from him or her, and afford constant protection. The bodyguards are the last layer within the in-depth or layers concept of security.

Bodyguards need to be armed, be experts in the use of weapons and first aid measures, know the fundamentals of martial arts, be well briefed about the itinerary of the protected executive, and be well rehearsed in responding to emergencies.

However, bodyguards should not enter conversation between the protected person and other individuals. Information should be given only when solicited, and all dealings with the protected person and family and associates should be on a formal basis. Security personnel should never become involved with providing personal services for executives or members of their parties. Attempts to ingratiate themselves only serve to degrade the security assignment and lead to an undesirable relationship. When the protected person, family, or associates are friendly in their approach to the security group, security personnel should react accordingly. An impersonal, businesslike approach to personal contact should be the rule.

USE OF WEAPONS

There is always the danger of accidental discharge and injury of innocent persons when carrying weapons in a stressful environment. All protective personnel must qualify to fire the weapons they carry on duty. The number and types of weapons carried need to be appropriate to the situation and indicated threat based on credible information:

1. Security officers in close contact with the protected persons should carry handguns, with at least a 9mm or 0.38 special caliber capability. Semiautomatic pistols should contain a fully loaded magazine with a round in the chamber and the safety on.

2. In areas where attacks may fire from a distance, a rifle is valuable. When attacks made in force by armed groups, a machine gun may repel the attempt. The machine gun is also used when attacks come from vehicles and when attackers are behind shields or barricades.

3. Shotguns should be available when the attack comes in a congested area where there is danger of injuring innocent persons when using long-range weapons. They are also effective against persons using suicidal attacks.

4. Use of nightsticks and riot control agents (teargas) can be considered in certain conditions. However, in each category and situation, you need to ensure the officers understand force must match the threat.

CROWD CONTROLS

Your security planning might need provisions for crowd control. The officers you assign for executive security need to understand the principles of crowd control. They should not show prejudice or sympathy, or become involved in any grievances expressed by the crowd. Some of the principles are the following:

1. When force is necessary, protective forces should move with speed and surprise. They also need responsive coordination with law enforcement agencies in the area. When the crowd is well within private property under your security jurisdiction, and at the first sign of disorder, all leaders need to be apprehended by security personnel or law enforcement officers at the scene. The real troublemakers are usually to the rear of the crowd.

2. Protective security officers should not be fooled or deterred by mob leaders who arouse the mob and use females and children in front ranks to shield themselves from aggressive action by protective personnel. The crowd's retreat should never be hindered; it should be moved in the direction where there is space to disperse.

Conduct and demeanor, use of weapons, and crowd control are just a few of the many topics to include in your orientation or training of officers preparing for executive security assignments.

SPECIAL REQUIREMENTS OF EXECUTIVE SECURITY OPERATIONS

Advance Security Arrangements

Normally, accomplishing your advance security arrangements happens with a team of experienced security officers trained in executive security operations. Their duties include coordinating and developing cooperation from appropriate law enforcement and other agencies and previewing all the areas pertinent to the travel or visit in distant places. It is essential that the advance party officer be fully briefed in phases of the planned activities, including

1. Complete list of the persons traveling with the executive

2. Duration of the visit, including arrival and departure times

3. Names of persons to contact at the distant location when applicable, such as a host

4. List of buildings, residences, restaurants, or other known areas to be visited by the executive.

In each area, their activities follow a similar pattern. The advance team contacts local authorities, they collect necessary maps and diagrams, they survey all areas to be visited or occupied by the executive, and they assess potential hazards and amount of protective officers needed. They need to conduct a detailed reconnaissance of the executive's routes of travel to various locations within the area and develop a plan to send to you well before departure for the area. When more than one distant location is involved in the protective assignment, the advance security team moves to the next area and repeats the process.

Area and Building Surveys

All areas to be occupied or visited by the protected executive need to be surveyed. The procedure for building inspections is complete and thorough. Often, the protected executive is a house guest or may stay in a hotel occupied by many other guests. All the inspection elements shown are not feasible in every situation.

The security officer advance team must use common sense and sound judgment in establishing the best security possible under existing circumstances. Sometimes the advance team can simplify security measures by arranging for a separate house or separate floor or wing of a hotel for the executive and his or her party. Often, arrangements might precede the team's arrival; however, they need to survey them and report any doubts or problems to you immediately for possible changes.

Proper building inspection technique includes a thorough examination from roof to basement. Blueprints of the building should be obtained. Rooms and hallways are measured visually and compared with the dimensions shown on the building plan to locate possible hidden passageways or alcoves. Each room needs systematic examination. Walls, ceilings, and floors are mentally divided into 3-foot squares and each square minutely examined for cracks, evidence of recent repairs, and any unnatural appearance.

Suspicious areas need satisfactory explanation by reliable operating or maintenance personnel. Examine furniture carefully, with all doors opened and drawers removed as a check for concealed compartments. Trace all wires leading into or leaving the various rooms, and identify all devices connected with them. Heating radiators, plumbing pipes, and similar equipment need attentive examination for dummy installations. All locks and locking mechanisms are inspected. After the inspection is finished the room or building is secured until used.

TECHNIQUES OF EXECUTIVE PROTECTION

Protection demands teamwork. Your success depends on the cooperation and assistance of others. The failure of one person may nullify the efforts of your entire security effort. All security officers need training for the ideal system and attempt to approach that system as closely as circumstances permit. Protective security officers need intensive training to respond to an emergency, despite excitement and emotion. They must respond instinctively and make correct decisions. Officers must be familiar with the characteristics of all phases of a protective assignment to include the special techniques for protecting the executive when he or she is traveling by motor vehicle, train, air, or small boat, or while walking and at public assemblies.

Travel Security

A protected executive may be in more danger while traveling than while in a static situation. Important factors in planning travel security include the weather forecast, the terrain and the nearness to known hazards, and unfriendly persons. Your goal includes moving the executive as safely and rapidly as possible with the least amount of exposure.

Protection While Riding in Vehicles

The selection of the type vehicle used needs careful thought with the following guidance.

All automotive equipment needs to be in excellent mechanical condition and should be regularly inspected for signs of tampering. Drivers need to be well trained and reliable. Vehicles always remain secured during the security assignment. An escort vehicle should precede the protected vehicle.

The security vehicle should follow the protected vehicle closely, consistent with driving safety. An advance car should precede the group about $\frac{1}{2}$ mile to observe hazards and report on any unusual conditions.

A reserve vehicle should follow the convoy for use in emergencies. The escort, follow-up, and other security vehicles should maintain radio contact. Whenever possible, a member of the security detail is placed in the protected person's vehicle. Under extreme conditions, when greater security is necessary, one or two dummy vehicles, carrying persons similar in appearance to the protected executive may accompany the group.

Place fixed posts at bridges, underpasses, and railroad crossings when thought necessary. An alternate route should be planned and surveyed for emergency requirements. Unless indicated, the vehicle group will conform to local traffic regulations and maintain a rate of speed consistent with road conditions.

Each situation is evaluated to determine security that is practical and necessary. The security vehicle may drop behind and follow at a discreet distance when hazards are minimal. Good judgment by the security officers will be necessary in solving the various situations that arise.

Travel by Train

Generally, the greatest potential security hazards exist at the points where the protected executive boards or leaves the train. Usually, this is a congested area with many persons carrying all sorts of bags, packages, and containers. In the study of assassination techniques, the large number of attempts in this type of location is noteworthy.

When a private car is assigned to the executive and traveling group, it is best to attach it to the rear of the train. The security group should be in control of all entrances of the car. When the train makes stops, security officers need to assume observation positions covering all avenues of approach to the car.

If the protected executive leaves the train constant security should be maintained on the train until the protected person returns and the train departs. Prior coordination with railway officials supplies reliable and exact scheduling of stops en route. Railroad police and local police at scheduled stops can be contacted for standby assistance.

Travel by Air

Normally, corporate or industrial executives travel by air with a special or private corporate plane. The most dangerous periods include the boarding and departures at airports, train stations, and other locations. However, before departure and during nonoperational time, the aircraft needs careful inspection and security maintained to prevent unauthorized persons from approaching the plane.

Enough transportation is normally scheduled for the protected person and his or her traveling party. However, arrangements made by the executive's office might exclude the security teams and you must ensure transportation for accompanying security personnel, and that is best served by having an advance team present to meet the incoming aircraft.

Travel by Small Watercraft

When planning for a cruise, the boats selected should be of a type and size capable of withstanding weather and surf conditions that may be encountered. A thorough inspection of the boat designated for the protected executive needs to include a responsible watercraft expert. The inspection is primarily for unauthorized persons stowing away and for any suspicious objects or packages. An added check includes the on-board inventory for adequate life-saving and emergency facilities and general structural and engine reliability. Security officers need to be alert for other craft approaching the protected executive's watercraft. Your arrangements must include boats that precede and follow the protected boat.

Protection While Walking

One of the best protective measures is varying the selected walking times and routes. The security officers protecting the executive need to be positions that cover all avenues of access. Additional security officers should be available in the area. A security vehicle should cruise the immediate vicinity. Local police agencies can be of special value in adding background security in these instances.

Protection While in Residence

You need to develop at least a three-layered defense with security officers. There must be a pass system for the executive's staff and frequent visitors. Food supplier verification and food selection and handling need tight control. Mail and packages need to be fluoroscoped. Periodic inspections made of premises for safety hazards, lethal devices, and sufficiency of security equipment serve to ensure effective security. Adequate communications should be maintained. All possible emergency situations need your consideration. Persons supplying personal or domestic services for the executive, family, or the party should be screened in advance and should receive a security briefing before the executive's arrival. Accomplishing this task is the responsibility of the advance security team.

YOUR CRITIQUE AND AFTER ACTION REPORT

Your critique is the final stage of the security assignment. It is conducted so that all participants will have a clear idea of what happened properly and happened improperly. To improve operations, intelligent, tactful, and constructive criticism is necessary. The critique can be most effective if held immediately after the assignment is completed.

The critique is so important that it needs to stay a part or phase of the security assignment itself. The effectiveness of the critique phase depends on your flexibility. In conducting your critique, even when dissatisfied, you must not be sarcastic. You must make your criticism or comments in a straightforward, impersonal manner. You should criticize persons in private and praise them in public. Participants should leave the critique with a favorable attitude toward the security assignment and a desire to improve the next one. Examples of personal initiative or ingenuity, types of errors, and ways for correcting them should be covered specifically. You must encourage active participation in the critique process by the protective security officers in a controlled businesslike discussion. They feel then that the critique is a period for learning instead of a time set aside for criticism of their performance.

Steps in Conducting the Executive Security Critique

Your critique cannot be planned as thoroughly as other phases of the assignment, because the points to be covered are influenced directly by the performance of the protective security officers. Planning can include the time and place of the critique and the general outline. During other stages but detailed planning is not practical. However, you can ensure complete coverage of the important elements by following this general procedure

Restate Objective of the Assignment

This will enable participants to start on a common ground. This is necessary because the participants who were concerned with a particular aspect of assignment might have forgotten the overall objective.

Review Procedures and Techniques Used

In this step briefly summarize the methods used to attain the objective.

Evaluate Performance

This is the essential part of your critique. Using notes taken during the assignment, list and discuss the strong points. Then you bring out the weaker points and make suggestions for improvement. You must be cautious not to talk down to the group. All your remarks must be specific and impersonal. Your security officers will not profit from generalities.

Control the Group in Discussion

You need to discuss the points you mentioned and suggest other points for discussion.

Summarize

Your critique ends with a brief but comprehensive summation of the points brought out. You can suggest study and practice to overcome deficiencies. Your critique is businesslike and must not degenerate into a lecture.

Your After Action Report

Your after-action report highlights the executive security assignment, written in narrative style. You need to write it as soon after completion of the assignment as practicable. Composing your report,

1. You can use notes taken by supervisory security officers working on the protective group during operations, your notes, the logs and other information contained in your executive security assignment book.

2. You can use notes from the advance security teams, including their maps, diagrams, and other information generated during their work.

3. You must emphasize the difficulties encountered and the procedures necessary to eliminate them.

4. You must make recommendations for improvement, especially in the areas of planning, coordination, personnel, and equipment.

Illustrations 15–1 through 15–8 are examples of an executive security operation plan guide, a residence watch operations procedure and visitors log, a visitors' identification badge or lapel pin guide and issue log, a baggage security operations procedure, a baggage control log and accountability report, and a trip personnel record form.

Illustration 15–1

EXAMPLE OF AN EXECUTIVE SECURITY ASSIGNMENT PLANNING GUIDE

Executive Security Operations

Name of executive: _____

Name of others: _____

_____

_____

Date assignment begins: _____

Date assignment ends: _____

References:
Itinerary
Biographical Extract
Maps
Other Material

1. Situation
   a. Threat (see Annex A, Intelligence)
   b. Supporting Resources. Describe those resources available to your planning for supporting operations (e.g., law enforcement agencies, para-medical and hospital facilities, and fire departments)

2. Assignment
A concise statement of the executive security task to be accomplished. Include the who, what, when, where, and why elements of the assignment.

3. Execution.
Concept of Operations. Normally, executive security operations are phased as follows:

Phase I	Planning and Coordination
Phase II	Advance Team Activity
Phase III	Movement or Travel
Phase IV	Arrival
Phase V	Residence (permanent or temporary)
Phase VI	Public Appearances
Phase VII	Departure and Return

You need to describe the conduct of executive security officer operations during each phase. Subordinate or standby elements might be required to develop separate operations guides depending on the complexity of the assignment. Details

(continued)

Illustration 15–1 (continued)

pertaining to security badges, baggage control, and vehicle and aircraft (or other types of transportation) security procedures or operating procedures need to be detailed and placed in annexes to this planning guide).

Coordinating Instructions. Direct coordination normally includes the supervisor or supervisors responsible for various elements of the security assignment and other agencies necessary, for example, local police. Details regarding rehearsals and critiques should be included in this paragraph.

4. Administration and Logistics

Security control needs to be clearly stated. Alternate control procedures should be established. List each support agency and explain, in detail, the type and level of support to be provided. Special equipment needs designation. Support control of this equipment needs explanation, as for example, when nonsecurity technicians become a part of the assignment, subordinate to but separate from the security elements.

5. Command and Communications

This section contains information regarding command channels (e.g., who is ultimately responsible and makes the key decisions, who is authorized to make decisions, and how much authority they have)

Communication outlines the types of communications used throughout the assignment, including primary and alternative modes, call signs, frequencies, code words, and other pertinent information.

6. Annex Section
   A. Intelligence
   B. Communications
   C. Other information as needed

Distribution Authorization and Log:

Itemize who is authorized to see this plan. Each copy needs a control number and a note at the top and bottom showing the reader the information is CONFIDENTIAL and NOT TO BE COPIED.

Illustration 15–2

EXAMPLE OF AN EXECUTIVE SECURITY OPERATION
RESIDENCE WATCH OPERATIONS PROCEDURE

The purposes of the operations procedure help clarify exactly what the responsibilities of the security officers assigned to this task are. You can place your instructions here in the detail and extent needed. To accomplish this purpose you or the person you designate will carry out the following duties:

1. Conduct a security inspection of the executive's residence, and at the hour specified in the operations plan, establish the residence watch on a 24–hour basis.

2. Maintain a residence watch consisting of three 8–hour shifts by designated security officers (supported by local law enforcement in certain cases).

3. Ensure that the security officers assigned to the residence watch do not leave their assigned positions until properly relieved, or unless it is necessary to escort the executive, should he or she leave the residence at times when no other member of the traveling security group is present.

4. Interview all persons desiring to visit the executive and obtain verification from a member of the executive's staff. (Be certain to have reliable staff members designated. Keep in mind that an executive's staff are not trained security officers and do not think in terms of security. A staff member might authorize a perpetrator to enter simply because he or she thinks it is business related. Choose and brief the authorizing staff members carefully).

5. Maintain a register of all visitors and packages, list receipts for internal identification lapel buttons, and maintain a log of all incidents occurring.

6. Examine all packages and mail for harmful materials before being released to a member of the executive's staff. All packages and mail will be removed from the residence and appropriate technical persons called to examine it for harmful contents. Whenever the item cannot be safely moved, escort the executive, family, and staff to a place of safety until the threat is neutralized.

7. Make periodic inspection of floors above and below the executive's suite (in a hotel or other accommodations) looking for suspicious items in hallways, unlocked rooms, elevators, washrooms, or utility areas.

8. Immediately notify the security officer supervisor responsible for the assignment about any incident threatening to the executive or for instructions not explained in this operations procedure.

Special Instructions: _____

_____

Illustration 15–3

EXAMPLE OF A VISITOR LOG

Time and Date: _____

Name of Person Admitted: _____

Affiliation: _____

ID Badge No: _____

ID Verified by: _____

Security Officer: _____

Time and Date Departed: _____

Time and Date: _____

Name of Person Admitted: _____

Affiliation: _____

ID Badge No: _____

ID Verified by: _____

Security Officer: _____

Time and Date Departed: _____

Illustration 15–4

EXAMPLE OF ID BADGE OR LAPEL BUTTON LOG

Inventory and accountability: (show numbers and colors designated and in control of appropriate security officer control point):

ISSUE LOG
REFERENCE TO VISITOR LOG

ID No.	Name	Date of Birth	Sex	Initials
_____	_____	_____	_____	_____
_____	_____	_____	_____	_____
_____	_____	_____	_____	_____
_____	_____	_____	_____	_____
_____	_____	_____	_____	_____

Illustration 15–5

EXAMPLE OF BAGGAGE SECURITY OPERATION PROCEDURES

The purpose of this operational procedure is to establish a method for the control and accountability of the baggage of the protected executive, his or her family, and staff during travel. Uncontrolled baggage provides an excellent opportunity for a perpetrator to plant a bomb or other device and maybe steal luggage for the inconvenience factor or to obtain business information. Managing and controlling baggage is an important executive security function while traveling with the executive, his or her family, and staff members. To accomplish this purpose the security person responsible will ensure a written procedure is understood by all security officers working on the assignment and given the baggage security task.

1. Obtain a list of all persons traveling in the executive's party, including security officers.

2. Develop an inventory of baggage (number of pieces) with a description of it (including security officers traveling with the party).

3. Obtain room assignments for each person traveling in the party at each location.

4. Determine the appropriate time for baggage collection and conduct a security examination before loading aboard aircraft. (Coordinate with the executive's designated staff member.)

5. Ensure a system of recovering the baggage from the aircraft, watching to be certain no preapproved bags or items are slipped among it, and placed in the appropriate rooms on arrival at the hotel or other location to control what goes into the rooms. On departures, any acquired items or luggage at the stop need to be identified, logged, and tagged.

6. Develop a color tag system to help quickly identify all bags authorized. For example, use security controlled number tag that is affixed by security officers at the time each piece is collected before departure (use a separate color for the various members of traveling party to help distinguish the luggage when the group includes many people). When the baggage is brought to the hotel and placed in the rooms, the tags are removed and returned to the controlling security officer. The tags need to be a type that is secured well, be large enough for easy identification, and has a large number. Your luggage tags for a travel assignment should be in a variety of colors and unique design, and the controlling officer chooses at random the color of the tags for a specific movement so that no one can predetermine what color tag will be used. Once the bags are assembled, inspected against the inventory, and tagged, they remain in tight control of a security officer to prevent any changes.

(continued)

Illustration 15–5 (continued)

7. Security officers will not handle baggage. Baggage handlers need to be hired locally, screened by the advance security team, and always supervised attentively by escorting security officers.

Illustration 15–6

EXAMPLE OF A BAGGAGE CONTROL INVENTORY

Use a separate sheet for each person. A three-ring notebook supplies an excellent means of maintaining this traveling record. When arranged alphabetically, the information is readily available for reference.

Person: _____

Position: _____

Description of Baggage:

_____

_____

_____

Illustration 15–7

EXAMPLE OF A BAGGAGE ACCOUNTABILITY REPORT

This report serves as a record of baggage handling and responsibility to ensure all luggage and items are collected, loaded, unloaded, and not lost or excess items slipped into the party's baggage. This record, as all logs and documents involved with an executive security assignment, needs to be a part of the after action report and a permanent record. (It is prudent to have at least two security officers on a baggage security task so the count and other aspects are double-checked and witnessed.)

Location: _____ Date: _____

Security Officer (s) responsible:

_____

_____

On-Load and Off-Load

Residence/Hotel (   )   Aircraft/Other (   )

First Count (quantity): _____

Second Count (quantity): _____

Baggage Handlers: _____

_____

_____

Remarks:

_____

_____

_____

Illustration 15–8

EXAMPLE OF A TRIP PERSONNEL RECORD

This record serves as a permanent record useful not only in documenting immediate activity but also as a reference resource for later assignments going to the same area. A separate form needs completion for each location.

Assignment: _____

Date: _____

Location: _____

Residence Locations and Type:

_____

_____

Persons in Traveling Party:

_____

_____

_____

_____

Transportation and Baggage Information:

_____

_____

_____

_____

(continued)

Illustration 15–8 (continued)

Security Officers Participating and Role:

_____

_____

_____

_____

Local Support Names/Agencies (e.g., law enforcement and others):

_____

_____

_____

_____

Transportation Information (e.g., aircraft and pilots, vehicle types and drivers' names, rail and names of assisting persons):

_____

_____

_____

_____

Medical, Fire, Bomb Squad, Others:

_____

_____

_____

_____

(continued)

Illustration 15–8 (continued)

Location Advance Team:

_____

_____

_____

_____

Executive Staff Member Contacts and Role:

_____

_____

_____

_____

Remarks:

_____

_____

_____

_____

P A R T 5

Managing Security Officer Career Development

Training is the key to competence and professionalism. Corporations with 100 or more employees report they currently spend about $40 billion each year for training employees, recognizing the long-term, cost-effective benefits. However, training management for security officers bears certain responsibilities not common to other company positions. It also needs to be "career oriented," opposed to meaningless sessions serving only to satisfy a requirement or to create an illusion for dealing with an image problem.

The demand, challenges and experiences of the security mission itself calls for a professional attitude. Gone are the days when a person could be placed on duty as a "guard" or "watchman" without any clue of the essential skills, knowledge, and judgment necessary for modern security officers. However, security doesn't always have the benefit recognition of other corporate positions and budget limits often prevent meaningful training attempted in a traditional sense. That problem, coupled with limited management skill about how to develop and conduct effective security officer training, often leads to the easy way out, including no training or very little. A lack of training for security officers often leads to increasing dilemmas of lawsuits stemming from security officer actions or omissions. Last, but surely not least, it involves the massive losses experienced by companies, often stimulated by a lack of security officer training, but effectively prevented through training and continued training.

Part Five brings you several chapters packed with training information, skills, and techniques that enable you to achieve the needed training even when your security budget places time and other resource restrictions on you. The valuable information includes a chapter on important dimensions of security officer authority based on state law samples and court findings. You should not attempt to conduct training without first researching and developing these aspects. Next, you'll find the best approach to conducting security officer training, and what your training curriculum needs to include. Other key elements bring you the information and techniques needed for effective in-service training, firearm training and qualification, and unarmed defense measures easy to learn and work effectively when necessary. Added bonuses include forms and a variety of training points and tips that help you create a dynamic security officer training program from A to Z.

16 Dimensions of Security Officer Authority

Before you can train your security officers effectively, you need to have a clear understanding of the dimensions of authority. There is no clear representation of the security officer dimensions of authority in any *one body of law*; instead the important aspects are found indirectly in the law including (1) constitutional, (2) court case law, (3) statutory law, and (4) administrative rule making. Law does not serve you as a detailed book of reference concerning the exact parameters of legal authority. Rather, law establishes precedents to be used as guidelines for preventing injuries (legal terms for violating the legal right of another or inflict an actionable wrong) and damages that may result in lawsuits or lead to criminal actions against the officer and maybe the employing company. Laws often supply you with a source of authority instead of supplying you with a clear definition of authority. It is essential before initiating or revising any training program for security officers, for you to identify the sources of your security authority and limitations. It's also essential that, when you understand all the legal aspects, you ensure each officer knows and understands each fully and then has the skill needed to use them to follow procedures effectively.

This chapter will supply you with the following essential elements:

- Outlines of the bodies of law associated with the dimensions of authority for security officers.

- Examination of the major categories of law shaping security performance, coupled with the pertinent laws and court case precedence.

- Reviews of possible legal sources of privileges and immunities for security officers.

- Discussions and analyses of problem areas related to legal restraint of security officers.

- Important training points and tips.

Generally, security officers have the same powers as private citizens to arrest, to defend themselves, to investigate, and to carry firearms. Normally, security officers generally do not have special police powers, although about 50% of the 5 million or so security officers in the United States reportedly now have limited police powers. Most laws framing legal authority of security officers stem from those outlining private citizens' rights and limitations.

SOURCES OF LEGAL AUTHORITY FOR SECURITY OFFICERS

The legal system attempts to strike a balance between the rights of persons and companies to protect lives and property from outside interference. It also tries to defend the rights of private citizens to be free from the power or intrusions of others. That balance, dealing with competing and conflicting interests, becomes apparent in the security profession. In one aspect, a company uses proprietary or contractual security officers to protect their employees' lives and company property and assets from criminal elements. Another aspect that affects the security role relates to the legal protection ensuring that all citizens are entitled to be free from assault, unlawful detention, or arrest; injury to reputation; intrusion into personal privacy and solitude; and illegal invasions of their personal property. Security officers often must walk a tightrope between permissible legal protective activities and unlawful interferences with the rights of private citizens. The precise limit of security officer authority rarely, if ever, appears clearly described in any one source of legal guidance. That stems from the perception that security officers normally are legally only private citizens. To find the answers, and you must have those answers, you must look at a number of sources to define, even in a rough sense, the dividing line between proper and improper security behavior. Your sources include the following:

Constitutional Law

The U.S. Constitution places many limits on the criminal justice system and other government agencies, but says little about the rights of private citizens in relationship with other citizens. Most constitutional rights of people pertain to government or state action and not to activities of other private persons or corporations. In six specific instances, however, constitutional restrictions could apply to your security officers:

1. *When security officers act as agents for public law enforcement agencies.* For example, when a law enforcement officer asks a security officer to watch for a particular person or circumstance, apprehend a person, or

supply information about a person's activities, the security officer becomes an "agent" of public law enforcement. As a law enforcement "agent," he or she must observe the same constitutional restrictions placed on public officials.

2. *When the security officer acts in concert with public law enforcement officials.* For example, when a security officer accompanies a law enforcement officer to apprehend a suspect even when on corporate property, the security officer acts in concert with a public law enforcement officer and must adhere to public police rules.

3. *When a security officer gathers evidence for criminal justice agencies for use in a prosecution.* For example, when the police ask a security officer to help them with crime scene searches and collect evidence that identifies a company employee as the suspect, the security officer then begins to act for the law enforcement agency.

4. *When the security officer acts with deputized police powers.* For example, when a security officer holds a special officer or auxiliary commission with a law enforcement agency that compels him or her to uphold the state laws, that security officer makes an arrest of a person for a crime, although on private property where he or she is working as a security officer, their law enforcement responsibilities and obligations take precedence, and they cannot claim their actions as a private citizen.

5. *When a security officer acts with limited police powers granted by a licensing or regulatory body.* For example, when a security officer receives a temporary deputization from a government agency empowered to do so for some specific situation, that might include escorting company property manufactured for a government agency during the delivery process.

6. *When a security officer is hired by a public authority (normally contractual).* For example, when a security officer is working for a public authority, they are acting with authority of state law and subject to constitutional restrictions on the exercise of power (*Williams* v. *United States*, 341 U.S. 97, 1951).

Training Points

- Ensure that each officer understands his or her specific circumstance and *exactly* the scope of his or her authority for his or her security position.

- Ensure that each officer understands why his or her authority and actions have limits and where that guidance comes from. Don't infer the controls come from the company; however, point out the company policies stem from the constitutional restraints.

Criminal Law

Criminal codes, state and federal, are sources of restraint for the security officer. In criminal law, the term "social harm" describes an offense answerable to society, not a specific person. However, criminal offenses call for "intent" to commit a crime, and the prosecution must prove intent and guilt beyond a reasonable doubt. The criminal laws generally establish broad limits on the behavior of security officers instead of a day-to-day regulatory mechanism.

Training Points

- Ensure that each officer understands the criminal code of your state as it pertains to his or her security position.
- Ensure that each officer understands his or her need to temper enforcing security and protection of company assets aligned with the proper criminal code and rules of criminal law. For example, theft of company property such as a typewriter requires "intent" to steal as opposed to just taking it home with permission to work on a company project. Although the policy might state "no employee may take company property home," there are exceptions to every rule, and an overzealous security officer might create many problems including liability for himself or herself and the company.

Tort Law

Tort law is a body of law that governs the civil relationships between persons. There is no one body of tort law, it varies from state to state. This is law that spawns lawsuits. Tort law differs from criminal law because private parties are suing and the suing parties are seeking relief for themselves and not punishment of the offending parties. The remedies given by a court deciding for the plaintiff includes equitable (the enjoining of certain conduct, an action called for by the defendant under supervision of the court) or legal action (the recovery of money damages for a legal injury received).

Tort law does not supply authority for security officers; however, it does vaguely define some limits on their conduct. It allows a person to bring a lawsuit for damages and injuries caused by what the plaintiff perceives as improper conduct of a security officer. (The company and officer(s) might jointly be named and sued within tort law when the officer was acting in his or her official security capacity.) This legal action (tort) usually views security officers as having status equivalent to a private citizen. Security officers (and their employing company) can incur liability in a tort case on three grounds:

1. Intent to cause harm
2. Negligence
3. Liability without intent or negligence

Many tort cases involve aspects of both negligence and intent to do harm. Intention may involve overzealous self-defense or protection of property while negligence normally involves a failure to establish probable cause before making an arrest or detention. Liability without fault evolving from situations not involving carelessness or intent to cause harm is not generally applicable to security officers; however, action might be brought against the employing company because of a security officer's actions while acting for the company. An example might be a perception of "sexual discrimination" that doesn't necessarily create liability for the officer but for the company he or she represents.

Training Points

- Ensure that officers understand the problems that stem from "torts" generally created by their actions or handling of a situation.
- Ensure that officers understand that torts and lawsuits based on a perception often come from their words and attitudes as much as their actions. Sexual discrimination or quality of language that is offensive to people can create many problems.

Contract Law

Contractual arrangements might have importance to the authority of your security officers, as when, for example, your company hires security forces from a security company as a supplement or instead of hiring added proprietary officers. You may limit the private security officer's authority and define more stringent standards of behavior than defined in law. The contract between the security agent and the hiring company normally needs to define and govern the liabilities of all parties using the contractual security service. The contract usually establishes who is to be responsible and carry insurance for liability risks. However, although the contract states that the contractual security company is responsible for its own security officer actions, your company still retains in a legal sense a degree of responsibility. The contract elements dealing with responsibility and liability generally allow actions by your company against the contracted company but do little to defend during a lawsuit based on a perceived tort.

Training Points

- When security officers work under a contract, ensure that they have full knowledge of their responsibilities and limitations agreed upon in the contract.

Regulatory Laws

Restraints on the behavior and performance of your security officers also stem from a variety of state and local statutes, rules, ordinances, and regulations governing security operations. Often, these restraints apply only to private security agencies offering security officers for hire instead of corporate or industrial proprietary security forces.

About 38 states have established private security agency licensing (normally exclude proprietary) on a statewide basis. In 5 states, regulation is for revenue purposes only, and 11 states do not have any state statutes regulating private security. Of the 38 states licensing, 11 do so through an established regulatory board while the remaining states generally name a state agency, for example, the state police or department of commerce.

Normally, arrest or police powers are not conferred on security officers by state statute; however, some states, through enabling legislation or county and local ordinances, grant special police powers to licensed private security officers under specific conditions. Further, 45 states, through state statute or common law, permit arrests by private citizens that include most security officers.

You need to research your situation carefully, because a variety of laws and local controls may apply to your geographical area. For example, in California, there are 8 counties and 63 cities that have separate ordinances regulating some aspect of private security. You might, for example, be legal in one county or city and your officers working at another facility in another county or city might have different laws to follow. Ensure you make certain what they are in each circumstance and include them in your training, regular briefing, and on-site "situational plans and directives." The best advice begins with a visit to the local prosecutors, followed with guidance added by your company's legal counsel.

Training Points

- Ensure that officers not only understand state laws but local laws, ordinances, and regulations governing their position and conduct.

- When your company facilities extend to areas in two or more separate counties or municipalities, ensure that each officer knows the differences. For example, a local ordinance regulating the conduct and authority of security officers in that city might not be applicable to a jurisdiction located in a twin city just across the river where your company has warehouses. When security officers have revolving assignments, they need to understand their legal positions at each location.

MAJOR LEGAL ISSUES CONFRONTING SECURITY OFFICERS

Training plays an important role in the following issues. Your training removes the misunderstandings, myths, and actions by security officers that often create liability for both the officers and employing company. The following guidance offers additional research sources with a caution that
you should always work closely with your local prosecutor and company legal counsel when creating the training and situational plans for security officers in most areas, especially those following.

Elements of Arrest

An arrest happens when a person is lawfully deprived of personal freedom. The arrest, under real or assumed authority, is the custody of another for holding or detaining him or her to answer a criminal charge or civil demand. References include court case precedence (*State* v. *Ferraro*, 81 N.J. Super. 213, 195 A. 2d 227; *People* v. *Wipfler*, 37 Ill. App. 3d 400, 346 N.E. 2d 41, 44). Merely touching a person may be classified as an arrest and the officer (and company) may be liable for battery, false arrest, or false imprisonment if the officer is not privileged by law to do so. The elements of arrest generally defined a court decision in *People* v. *Howlett*, 1 Ill. App. 3d 906, in which the court said: "Every arrest involves authority to arrest, assertion of that authority with intent to make an arrest and restrain the person arrested." Unless granted special police powers or having been deputized, your security officer normally makes an arrest under the rules of a "citizen's arrest." Although you must check your state laws regarding that action, generally, using the California Penal Code, paragraph 837 as a reference, a citizen (security officer without specific arrest powers) may under certain circumstances make an arrest, generally for a felony or misdemeanor or amounting to breach of the peace. That code cites that a private person may arrest another (1) for a public offense committed or attempted in his or her presence; (2) when the person arrested has committed a felony, although not in his or her presence; and (3) when a felony was committed, and he or she has reasonable cause for believing the person arrested to have committed it.

Arrest with a Warrant

The Fourth Amendment to the Constitution protects persons against "unreasonable searches and seizures." This amendment also limits the issuance of warrants to probable cause supported by "oath or affirmation" that describes the person or thing to be seized (arrested) or place searched (*Draper* v. *United States*, 358 U.S. 307, 1959). Only a sworn law enforcement officer can arrest with a warrant; a private person (security officer), unless given special authority, does not have this power. The only arrest a security officer can make (absent special powers) lawfully is one that does not call for the issuance of a warrant.

Arrest Without a Warrant: Under Common Law Rule

Under common law, a felony arrest by a private citizen (security officer) was permitted "to protect the safety of the public" and arrest for a misdemeanor "creating a breach of the peace: was permitted by a private citizen" when immediate apprehension was necessary to preserve or restore public order (*Wong Sun* v. *U.S.*, 371 U. S. 471, 83 S. Ct. 407, 9 L.Ed. 2d 441).

Without any deputized or special policing powers supplied through state statute or county and local ordinance, security officers are essentially acting as private citizens in effecting arrests. They have no powers or immunities by virtue of their being in a protection function other than the common law or statutory powers of arrest granted an ordinary citizen or "citizen's arrest." Now 14 states rely on common law for citizen's arrest privileges. In a citizen's arrest, the arrest is valid under the limitations only if the security officer has intention to and does turn the arrestee to the "proper authorities" when practicable. The arrest power may not serve any purpose other than to transfer the person to proper authorities for a felony or misdemeanor committed; it should never serve to obtain a confession.

When a security officer (or any citizen) induces a police officer to make an arrest without a warrant, the burden of proof that the person arrested was guilty of the crime rests with the security officer (private citizen). References to review include (*Green* v. *No. 35 Check Exchange, Inc.* 222 N.E. 2d 133, 111 App. 1966).

On occasion, courts said that a private citizen (including security officers with no special powers) is not liable who mistakenly informed the police that the suspect committed a crime (*Armstead* v. *Escobedo*, 448 F. 2d 509, 1974) or if he did not act in malice in identifying the plaintiff (*Tillman* v. *Holsum Bakeries, Inc.*, 244 So. 2d 681 La. App., 1971).

Arrest with a Warrant: Under Statutes

The circumstances, or elements, of arrest and the specific offenses, vary greatly in each of the states. For example, in some states the felony must be committed in the presence of the arresting person; however other states require only an element of reasonable cause. Now 31 states provide felony arrest privileges for private citizens, and 23 states permit arrest by private citizens for misdemeanors. The common law tradition that designates only breach of the peace as an offense for citizen's misdemeanor arrest continues in some states. You must research the variety of laws about your specific situation and then coordinate with local prosecutors and company counsel before integrating this important guidance into your training program.

Arrest Without a Warrant: With Special Police Powers

In many states, security officers have the power of arrest through state statute, state enabling legislation, or county and local government ordinances that confer police powers on them. This practice often includes giving ancillary police titles such as "special deputy sheriff," "special police officer," and "auxiliary police officer." These powers often include limits to specific geographical area or place of employment and assignment. Supplying a power of arrest in these instances is to allow the security officer to operate under the "color of the law" in apprehending a suspected law violator. In practice, the security officer is often merely afforded the greater civil and criminal protection of a police officer while detaining a suspect until a law enforcement agency can assume formal custody of the suspect.

THE PROBLEM OF FALSE IMPRISONMENT

A false arrest leads to the problem of false imprisonment. Such arrest consists in unlawful restraint of a person's personal liberty or freedom (*Johnson* v. *Jackson*, 43 Ill. App.2d 251, 193 N.E.2d 485, 489). An arrest without proper legal authority is a false arrest, and because an arrest restrains the liberty of a person, it is also false imprisonment. The gist of the tort is protection of the personal interest in freedom from restraint of movement. Neither ill will nor malice is an element of the tort, but if these elements are shown, punitive damages may be awarded in addition to compensatory or nominal damages.

It is unnecessary to restrain, confine, or touch a person physically to establish a false imprisonment. In *Riley* v. *Stone*, (174 N.C. 588, 94 S. E. 434), the court held that a false imprisonment may be committed by "words alone, or by acts alone, or by both," and that "any exercise of force or express or implied threat of force, by which the other person is deprived of his liberty, compelled to stay or go where he does not wish to be is an imprisonment." To be unlawful or a false imprisonment, the detention or restraint of the person must be involuntary. When giving the consent does not involve force, the a false imprisonment has not happened. (*Martinez* v. *Sears, Roebuck and Company*, 467 P. 2d 37 N.M., 1970). What is consent, however, is debatable. A false imprisonment may also happen through deception as in *Winans* v. *Congress Hotel* (277 Ill. App. 276, 1922), in which a security officer said he had a warrant for arrest of a person when no warrant existed.

Reasonable cause is usually a requirement for a lawful detention. The legal arrest requirement of reasonable cause creates a false imprisonment offense stemming from a false arrest (*Shelton* v. *Barry*, 66 M.E. 2d 697 Ill. App., 1946). Often, false arrest and false imprisonment are interchangeable, the difference being in the plaintiff's suit. Reasonable cause for a detention on "mere belief of a third person that somebody did or did not do something," cannot be a defense, as held in *J. C. Penney Company* v. *Cox* (246 Miss. 1, 148 So. 2d 679, 1963). However, in *Meadows* v. *F. W. Woolworth Company* (254 F. Supp. 907, 909 N.D. Fla., 1966), the court said a store manager had probable cause to detain shoplifting suspects who "generally fit the description" of teenage girls believed to be shoplifting, after he was forewarned by the police of their activities in the area. If there is reasonable cause to detain but the detention is handled in an "unreasonable manner," the detention privilege will be lost (*Wilde* v. *Schwegmann Bros.*, 160 So. 2d 839 La. App., 1964). There, a supermarket store detective held Wilde 30 minutes against her will until she signed a confession. But in a similar time element (27 minutes) for search of the plaintiff's purse in *Cooke* v. *J. J. Newberry and Co.* (96 N.J. Super. 232 A. 2d 425, 1967), the court said the detention was reasonable. An earlier decision held that a detention by a store detective was permitted if it was reasonable collectively in time and manner (*Collyer* v. *S. H. Kress and Co.*, 5 Cal. 2d 175, 54 P. 2d 20, 1936).

Training Points

- This action can create many problems for the security officer and company. Ensure each officer fully understands the effect of his or her actions by simply detaining a person.
- Ensure that each officer knows the proper procedures to follow and the reasonableness of their suspicious about a person before detaining them for any length of time.

SEARCH AND SEIZURE PROBLEMS

The federal statutes and the U.S. Constitution protect the rights of the person with respect to searches. The powers to "search and seize" is highly restricted, and its exercise is generally dependent on the execution of a lawful arrest by a sworn peace officer, the issuance of a valid search warrant, or the consent of a person.

Security officers often conduct searches for suspected stolen property, to recover merchandise, to collect evidence for internal investigation or prosecutions, and to gather information for clients. The Constitution, on its face, does not limit the powers of private security officers, like those of public law enforcement, to conduct searches of persons or property. This applies despite whether the search happened under a lawful arrest (*Burdeau* v. *McDowell*, 256 U.S. 465, 1921). While common law authority for a private search is sparse and inconclusive, there appear to be four instances when a search by a security officer would be permissible:

1. Actual consent by a person

2. Implied consent as a condition of employment or as part of an employment contract (for example, a union contract)

3. Incidental to a valid arrest

4. Incidental to a valid detention

These circumstances parallel the condition under which public law enforcement may conduct warrantless searches. A citizen's arrest, when valid, appears to be similar to an arrest by a law enforcement officer, and a search incidental to arrest would be allowable. In a challenge to search incidental to arrest of a shoplifter by a store security officer in *People* v. *Santiago* (278 N.Y.S. 2d 260, 1967), for example, the court stated that the "rationale that justifies searches incident to lawful arrest as outlined in *United States* v. *Rabinowitz*, 70 S. Ct. 430, apply with equal force whether a law enforcement officer or a private citizen make the arrest."

Conditions of employment and union contracts often express or imply consent to search employees and their belongings, but search of patrons, visitors, or customers in nonarrest situations is a clouded legal issue. This would include situations such as visitor-access control points, inspections of briefcases in office buildings, package inspections of entering nonemployees, and visual searches of automobiles parked in or leaving parking lots. Without consent there is no clear authority to detain and search in these situations.

Training Points:

- Ensure that each officer understands he or she cannot act in these circumstances unless it falls within the legal authority. Being on private company property doesn't in itself supply authority for search and seizure.

- Have solid, researched legal counsel approved policies that conform to the specific state and local laws and ordinances, and ensure that each officer fully understands all aspects of them.

Evidence Obtained from Searches

When a search conducted by a law enforcement officer is not within a lawful arrest or valid warrant, then evidence seized is generally inadmissible at the defendant's trial. This exclusionary rule of evidence stems from the Forth Amendment and applies to the states through the Fourteenth Amendment (*Mapp* v. *Ohio*, 376 U.S. 643, 1961). In *Burdeau* v. *McDowell*, noted earlier, the court found this exclusionary rule of evidence not applicable to private parties. Security officers could, however, be subject to tort liability for actions taken during the search such as assault, battery, theft, trespass, and so on. Several court decisions have relied on *Burdeau* v. *McDowell* to rule on the admissibility in a prosecution of evidence obtained from a search by a private person (*United States* v. *Berger*, 355 F. Supp. 919, 1973; *People* v. *Bryant*, 243 N.E. 2d 354 Ill. App., 1968;

Barnes v. *United States*, 373 F. 2d 517 C.A. 5th, 1967). Constitutional limitation on searches by law enforcement offers will, however, apply to the conduct of security officers when they act as agents for the police or in concert with the police or obtain the evidence with the intent of furnishing it to the police for use during a pending prosecution. In any of these contexts, the exclusionary rule would apply to evidence seized by the security officer. Cases supporting that fact include *United States* v. *Small* (297 F. Supp. 582 B. Mass., 1969) and *Stapleton* v. *Superior Court of Los Angeles County* (73 Cal. Rptr. 575, 1969). In *California* v. *Fierro* (46 Cal. Rptr. 132, 1965), the court held that evidence obtained illegally in a joint operation between a motel manager and sheriff's office was not admissible in court.

Training Points

- Ensure that each officer is skilled in collecting and managing evidence properly.
- The task of collecting and managing evidence needs to be supported by easy-to-use forms and procedures (found in the appendix), and each officer must receive training in the process.

SECURITY INVESTIGATIONS AND INTERROGATIONS

Security officers often conduct investigations of internal and external theft, employee misconduct, embezzlement and fraud, and other problems in their function of asset protection and loss reduction. Generally, there are no restrictions against soliciting voluntary answers to questions from employees, especially when conditions of employment and union contracts mandate cooperation in such matters. Similarly, when you conduct interviews of employees on the company premises or in the normal working environment, the activity would not constitute "custodial interrogation." In the case of an arrest or detention by security officers, there is no clear prohibition on asking questions, if the arrest or detention is lawful or reasonable in time and manner.

Public law enforcement officers are restricted in custodial interrogation by the *Miranda* rule that calls for police to inform suspects of the right to remain silent (*Miranda* v. *Arizona*, 86 S. Ct. 1602, 1966). Some court decisions show the *Miranda* warning not applicable to security officers (*People* v. *Frank*, 275 N.Y.S. 2d, 570 Sup. Ct., 1966; *United States* v. *Castreel*, 476 F. 2d. 152, 1973). It was explicitly stated in *United States* v. *Antonelli* (434 F. 2d 335, 1970) that the "Fifth Amendment privilege against self-incrimination does not call for the giving of constitutional warnings by private citizens or working security officers who take a suspect into custody."

However, if the security officer has a pertinent official or existing connection with any public law enforcement agency, then the court probably has inclination to find the security officer was acting for or at the direction of the police, in which case the *Miranda* rule would apply with a requirement for warnings and waiver obtained before interrogation can begin. Last, clearly an incriminating statement shown to be "involuntarily" given to a private citizen, security office or private police, or actual or implied law enforcement officer will be totally tainted and inadmissible.

When a security officer invites the cooperation of public law enforcement, it is questionable whether the *Miranda* rule, coupled with other exclusionary rules of evidence and constitutional restrictions, should apply. Although constrained by civil tort remedies, generally security officers may have greater powers of interrogation than the public police. A key issue for consideration is whether the courts will continue to refuse application of *Miranda* rule to security officers and whether confessions obtained from such interrogations will later be admissible in a criminal prosecution.

When security officers decide to file formal complaints for criminal charges, there is generally no liability for "malicious prosecution" if the charges are not sustained. While the security officer had probable cause to believe the person committed a criminal offense and submitted the fact of his or her investigation to the proper authorities in good faith and without malice, he or she has no responsibility for malicious prosecution. A plaintiff would need to be acquitted or have had charges dropped, demonstrate injury or damage, and assume the burden of proof for malice by the security officer to obtain a civil tort judgment.

When your security officer has special police powers, either related to the position or as a private pursuit, he or she comes under the law enforcement officer rules. Use the *Miranda* rule when arresting a suspect and a noncustodial warning other times. Both appear later in this chapter. Use of the *Miranda* or noncustodial rights warning by security officer routinely surely does no harm and shows a concern for people's rights and professionalism.

Another important point about using the *Miranda* rule stems from *People v. Jones* (47 N.Y. 2d 528, 1979) where the Court of Appeals called for a need of *Miranda* rule warnings given to a suspect questioned by a security officer. If a person confesses to a security officer and the prosecutor wants to offer that confession through the testimony of the security officer, the court and jury will still look at the total circumstances and determine whether the confession was voluntary. (*University of Chicago Law Review* 555, 573–82).

Training Points

- Confessions and admissions often come whether solicited or not. Security officers must know the proper procedures when a person voluntarily confesses.
- Security officers must know how to approach an investigation, for example, a reported burglary at a tool shed within an industrial complex. Before notifying law enforcement agencies, the security officer needs to establish

a burglary and theft happened. During the investigation, a guilt-ridden employee comes to the officer and confesses the crime was staged to cover pilferage or even unexplained losses. The officer at that point needs to know exactly what procedure to follow. Depending on the circumstances, referring the situation to the police might not happen; however, dismissing an employee needs as much care and documentation as going to court.

USE OF FORCE BY SECURITY OFFICERS

Generally, persons who reasonably believe that others intend to do them harm have the privilege of using force to repel attack, but such force must be reasonable under all the circumstances. (*State* v. *Anderson*, 230 N.C. 54, 51 S. E. 2d 895). The degree of force used to repel attack may be commensurate with the degree of force used by the attacker and sufficient to repel the attack. The person might face a charge of assault and/or battery if the degree of force is excessive or beyond common expectations of what is reasonable. Under the common law, security officers may also use force to repel an attack of the safety and lives of other persons.

Protecting Company Property

The common law recognizes that individuals have the right to use force to protect their own property or to recapture it while in "hot pursuit." Security officers hired to protect the property of a company are benefited by the privilege of "protection of one's own property." Deadly force is never sanctioned for the defense of property because the value of property could never surmount that of life.

The Question of Arrest

When a security officer is without authority to arrest, the use of force, despite its degree, is not permitted. However, a lawful arrest assumes a certain level of privileged force. Both the law enforcement officer and the security offer may use reasonable force to effect a lawful arrest. The reasonableness of that force will depend on what is necessary under all the circumstances, viewing the severity of the offense, resistance, and other related factors. Excessive force may be grounds for making the arrest illegal and subject the security officer to liability charges.

Crime Prevention Efforts

The common law recognizes a privilege to use force for those who intervene to prevent crime. This privilege is intertwined with such other privileges as self-defense, defense of others, and defense of property. Generally, these privileges are available to all persons if the intervention is not accompanied by force that is excessive or unreasonable decided by all the facts. Without legislation, there is no privilege in common law to use force, and such use of force amounts to battery in both criminal and civil laws when it is excessive or beyond common expectations of what is reasonable.

The crime will determine the force permitted. At one time a private citizen, in common law, was authorized to use deadly force to stop a fleeing felon or to prevent the commission of a felony. This rule developed when any felony was punishable by death. With the changes of current state criminal codes, the privilege has changed about use of deadly force. It applies only to prevent or end action of a deadly felony (one likely to cause death or serious bodily harm, such as murder, robbery, or arson). Prevention of other crimes using reasonable force not amounting to deadly force has a requirement of law.

Self-defense and Deadly Force Involving Security Officers

While self-defense is a justification for use of deadly force (*People* v. *Joyner*, 278 N.E. 2d Ill., 1972), mere threat is not enough justification to use deadly force (*People* v. *Odum*, 279 N.E. 2d 12, Ill. App., 1972). It is axiomatic that deadly force is never permissible in defense against nondeadly force (*Etter* v. *State*, 185 Tenn. 218, 205 S.E. 2d 1, 1947). The right to use deadly force in defense of oneself is a less uniform doctrine and needs viewing in general terms. Deadly force is permitted to repel an attack believed to include the risk of death or serious bodily harm. In some states, the defender must retreat by any reasonable means before the use of deadly force, for example, retreating to the wall, while other states do not require a retreat rule. Whether the law or court requires a retreat usually depends on the circumstances of the particular case.

Under the common law, the use of deadly force was never permitted for the sole purpose of stopping on fleeing from arrest on a misdemeanor charge. Courts have said that shooting at the escaping car of one charged with a misdemeanor is such criminal negligence to support a charge of manslaughter if death should result (*People* v. *Klein*, 205 Ill., 141, 137 N.E. 145, 1922). However, the common law permits a private person to kill a fleeing felon who could not otherwise be taken (*Bircham* v. *Commonwealth*, 239 S.E. Ill., Ky., 1951). For a private citizen, such force is not privileged unless the arrestee was guilty; a reasonable belief that the arrestee was guilty, who was innocent, will not justify the killing. When deadly force has justification, the killing of an innocent victim is not a crime (*People* v. *Adams*, 291 N.E. 2d 54 Ill. App., 1972). However, if the physical force is not justified, then the killing of an innocent victim is a crime

(*People* v. *Thomas*, 290 N.E. 2d 418, Ill. App., 1972). As noted, deadly force is never justified for solely protecting property.

Training Tips

- Ensure that each officer has total knowledge and understanding of the points noted here regarding arrest, authority, use of force, and other aspects. These points have vital importance from a safety, professional, and liability point of view.

THE QUESTION OF SECURITY OFFICERS AND FIREARMS

An issue closely related to legal restraints on the use of force are the carrying and use of firearms by security officers. Firearms create the means of potentially deadly force when used and may also be an excessive use of force. About 50% or more of persons employed as security officers carry firearms on duty. The key, however, to the fears created by many about firearms and security officers stems from the general lack of adequate training that creates competence and knowledge about the proper use of firearms. Normally, the horror stories that make the news represent a tiny percentage of officers carrying a duty firearm. Chapter 21, on firearms training, shows you how to create the competence you need when your security officers carry firearms.

Training Reminder

- No security officer, or any person, should carry a firearm unless fully qualified to do so and be competent in its use.
- No security officer should carry a firearm unless he or she is competent, when its use is lawful, and when he or she is mentally ready to use it within the lawful limits. A person carrying a firearm who is not competent, afraid of it personally, and doubts that he or she could use it despite the situation should not be placed in that position.

PROBLEMS OF DEFAMATION

A problem to guard against largely through training and supervision stems from defamation liabilities created by security officers, normally not recognizing their actions. The essential element in defamation is not whether the person's feelings were injured but that "damage" was caused to that person's reputation in the eyes of other persons. Sometimes in slander, only the injurious words need be proven. Actual harm need not be proven but assumed. In other cases, actual damages and malice must be specifically shown as noted in *Whitby* v. *Associates*

Discount Corporation (59 Ill. App. 2d 337), where five types of slander were reviewed for the decision:

1. Imputing the commission of a criminal offense
2. Imputing infection with a communicable disease that would tend to exclude one from society
3. Imputing inability performing or want of integrity in the discharge of duties of office or employment
4. Prejudicing a particular party in his or her profession or trade
5. Defamatory words that, though not actionable in themselves, occasion the party special damages.

Training Tips

Security officers, when apprehending a suspect or detaining a person, must be extremely cautious in the use of language not to accuse the suspect in front of others of stealing, being a thief, or generally of committing a criminal offense. This may be actionable not only as slander but also as intentional infliction of mental distress that does not require that oral statements be defamatory. Security officers must be cautious, in dealing with the public in either a protective or an investigative capacity that their conduct not be outrageous or so coercive that it is likely to cause mental strain on others, and they should refrain from making accusatory statements in public perceived defamatory.

The right of businesses to conduct investigation of employee wrongdoing has been consistently upheld in court decisions, but exercise care to prevent disclosing to other employees statements considered defamatory made by an employee in an investigation. In *Cook* v. *Safeway Stores, Inc.* (511 P. 2d 375 Or. 1973), a store manager told three employees that a former coworker had been discharged for stealing from the company. The Supreme Court of Oregon held that these words were actionable and that a general recovery of damages be made without proof of harm, since they imputed commission of a crime by the plaintiff and that he was unfit to perform the duties of his employment. In *Picard* v. *Brennan* (307 A. 2d 833 Me., 1973), the Supreme Court of Maine considered the issue of slander for a statement that an employee was discharged or fired, without a stated reason for the discharge. Although the statement itself was false, the court held that a general statement that a person was discharged or fired is not slanderous, but probably considered slanderous when a statement of discharge of an employee for reasons shown to be false.

THE KEY TO READING COURT CITATIONS

Throughout this chapter and in other parts of the book you'll see legal citations such as *Miranda* v. *Arizona* (384 U. S. 436, 1966). That is the short citation for that case. The long citation reads: *Miranda* v. *Arizona*, 384 U.S. 436, 86 S.Ct. 1602, 16 L.Ed.2d 694 (1966).

Although a legal citation may appear forbidding, it merely serves as an identification method for finding the cited case in the books of law.

The *Miranda* decision, *Miranda* v. *Arizona*, 384 U.S. 436, 86 S.Ct. 1602, 16 L.Ed.2d 694 (1966) shows that you find

- *Miranda* v. *Arizona* in Volume 384 of the *United States Reports* on page 436 or
- Volume 86 of the *Supreme Court Reporter* on page 1602 or
- Volume 16 of the *Lawyer's Edition*, 2nd edition, on page 694
- The decision handed down in the year 1966

Another way of understanding the breakdown of the citations is *Miranda* (plaintiff) v. (versus) *Arizona* (defendant), 384 (Volume 384) U.S. (*United States Reports*) 436 (page 436), 86 (Volume 86) S.Ct. (*Supreme Court Reporter*) 1602 (page 1602), 16 (Volume 16) L.Ed. 2d (*Lawyer's Edition*, 2d edition) 694 (page 694), 1966 (year of the case).

BEING CONCERNED ABOUT PEOPLE'S RIGHTS

There is much concern about how to prevent having to advise a suspect of his or her rights. Many information sheets and checklists have appeared and continue to appear since the landmark *Miranda* rule handed down by the U.S. Supreme Court in 1966. The lists tell us when we must and when we don't have to tell a suspect what and how to exercise his or her rights. The result leads to confusion and prosecutions lost because that point is a favorite line of attack for defense attorneys. The best rule is to do exactly what the Fifth Amendment to the Constitution says to do and what its framers intended when they wrote it—be concerned about people's rights—it's the signal of genuine professionalism. The *Miranda* rule only interpreted what already existed in the Fifth Amendment and requires "custodial" advisement. However, instead of concern about schematics, why not create a routine procedure? When a person is suspect, whether in custody or not, why shouldn't you let him or her know where he or she stands and inform the person of his or her rights? There is a difference between the rights when in custody and not in custody in some aspects, and the following guides provide you with the procedures that always mark security officers as professional and avoid challenges in court and lost cases when it's important. Earlier in the chapter, a note about the courts requiring *Miranda* warnings in the *People* v. *Jones* case and the opinion noted in a law review indicate that the requirement might one day change for security officers.

NONCUSTODIAL RIGHTS

Noncustodial rights need to be a key tool of security officers. Any time a security officer questions a suspect, not arrested, the following rights should be read and explained to the person. It is always best to have the person and the security officer sign a form containing the rights, along with the time, date, and place the reading happened. Illustration 16–1 is one format you can use.

Illustration 16–1

STATEMENT OF NONCUSTODIAL RIGHTS

I am a Security Officer for the XYZ Corporation, Any City, Any State. I am investigating a possible criminal offense against the Company. The offense is (state the offense, e.g., theft of widgets). I would like to ask you some questions about this investigation and because of circumstances need to consider you as a suspect.

I must inform you however that under the Fifth Amendment of the U.S. Constitution you cannot be compelled to answer any of my questions or submit any information that you feel might incriminate you in any way.

Also, anything you say and any documents you submit about the matter I've explained or any related matter that involves an offense can be used against you in a criminal or administrative proceeding.

You may, if you desire, obtain the assistance of an attorney before responding to any of my questions. You do not have to answer my question, and you are free to leave or discontinue this interview whenever you want.

Do you understand these rights as I have read them to you?
Record answer: _____

Do you wish to contact your attorney now?
Record answer: _____

Do you wish to answer my questions voluntarily now?
Record answer: _____

Do you read, write, and understand the English language?
Record answer: _____

_____
Security Officer

Date: _____ Time: _____ Location: _____

I have read the above statement and understand my rights as explained to me. Knowing these rights, I voluntarily and willingly waive my right to call my attorney and agree to answer questions. I also affirm no coercion, threats, or promises were made to me by the security officer.

_____
Signature of Person Being Questioned

Date: _____ Time: _____

File this form with your case report. You should retain a copy for your files.

THE *MIRANDA* RULE—CUSTODIAL WARNING

The general legal rule excludes most security officers from advising suspects of their rights because the security officer's arrest is normally a "citizen's arrest" made for the purpose of detaining a person until releasing him or her as soon as possible to a public law enforcement officer. However, you can never go wrong by advising the person of his or her rights, although the law enforcement officer assuming custody will also probably do that. A good rule to follow is that regardless of what the conventional routines seem to dictate, no matter what the strict letter of the law, you are the person on the spot and you are the person that might create liability—against you! Always protect your interests, and in doing so, you protect the suspect's interests.

When you have special police or deputized powers, you must certainly inform a person of his or her rights. You should also use a form for this statement of rights. Never leave yourself in a position of having a suspect later say you did not inform him of the rights; document the event and you can be certain of your position and the suspect will know his or her position. Illustration 16–2 shows the *Miranda* rule rights.

Illustration 16–2

STATEMENT OF RIGHTS FOR ARRESTED PERSON
(FOR SECURITY OFFICERS AND CITIZEN'S ARREST)

I am a Security Officer for the XYZ Corporation, Any City, Any State and I have placed you under arrest as a suspect of _____ (explain the reason for the arrest and note that in this space) _____.

You will be released to the proper law enforcement agency when an officer arrives to take you into custody and he or she will explain to you the process after that time. I will not be questioning you; however, the law enforcement officers will, and I want you to understand your rights.

You have the right to remain silent. You are not required to say anything or answer any questions about the offense for which you have been arrested. Anything you do say to me or the law enforcement officers can be used against you in court.

You have the right to talk to a lawyer for advice before answering any questions and have an attorney with you during any questioning you agree to participate.

If you cannot afford a lawyer, and want one, a lawyer will be appointed for you free of charge.

If you decide to answer questions without advice from a lawyer or without a lawyer present, you have the right to stop answering at any time. You also have the right to stop answering questions at any time until you have the opportunity to consult with a lawyer before saying any more and before making any further decisions.

Do you understand your rights as I have read them to you? Record answer: ___

Do you read, write and understand the English language? Record answer: ____

_____
Security Officer

Date: _____ Time: _____ Location: _____

I have read the above statement and understand my rights and why I have been arrested.

_____
Signature of Suspect

Date: _____ Time: _____

Released to (name of officer and department): _____

(continued)

Illustration 16–2 (continued)

At: _____ (time) _____ Date: _____

Comments:
(List any pertinent information or any spontaneous statements the suspect made without your asking him or her any questions.)
File this form with your case report. (You should retain a copy for your personal files.)

How to Prepare and Conduct
17 Performance-Oriented Training

Training in a traditional sense supports the idea that "hearing is learning." It is instructor centered and it doesn't work! We've often heard that the best teacher is experience, and that's true when the quality of experience has the right ingredients. Performance-oriented training enables the student to learn by doing, except under systematic, controlled conditions. Often, experience comes at the expense of others, and often at the expense of the novice who gets into serious trouble. The security profession cannot allow inexperienced people to perform duties that call for competence. To develop and maintain a career-oriented security force, you need to develop basic and continued training that counts, and that happens when you have student-centered, performance-oriented training. Throughout this chapter you'll discover how it works, how easy it is, the benefits and advantages, and how you can make it fit nearly any budget, despite how austere.

ASK YOURSELF THREE IMPORTANT QUESTIONS

Training is hard work. You cannot afford substitutes or shortcuts during your training. However, developing efficient, effective training of all types requires solid direction, and you must answer some questions before going further. Ask yourself,

1. *Where am I going?* What must the security officers do as a result of their training? Answering this question gives you a clear picture of your desired results of training.
2. *Where am I now?* What can my security officers do now, compared to what

I want them to be able to do because of training? Answering this question gives you a clear picture of current levels of training versus desired level of training.

3. *How can I best get from where I am to where I should be?* What training techniques, training methods, and organization styles offer me the most effective and efficient use of available resources? Answering this question gives you a clear picture of how to conduct your training.

PLANNING FOR LEARNING AND MOTIVATION

Your training should increase a security officer's knowledge and skill. When your training has that goal, certain conditions need consideration and must be present. There are six key points to consider:

1. The security officer required to attend training must realize he or she needs training.
2. The officer must understand what you expect him or her to learn.
3. The officers receiving training must have an opportunity to practice what they learn.
4. The officers must get reinforcement they are learning.
5. They must progress through training in a logical sequence.
6. Your officers must be willing to learn and improve.

If the first five conditions are present, you create an environment conducive to learning and motivate officers. The characteristics and advantages of performance-oriented training help to establish those conditions.

CHARACTERISTICS OF PERFORMANCE-ORIENTED TRAINING

Performance-oriented training is characterized by training objectives that state precisely what the officer must be able to do at the completion of your training. A properly structured training objective contains the following three elements:

1. Task to be accomplished.
2. Conditions for achieving the task.
3. Training standards of acceptable performance.

When you develop your training with the precise expression of task, conditions and standards, the student officers understand that if they can already perform the task to acceptable standards, fine; if not, they must know what to learn to achieve the standard. The first two conditions of learning include satisfying them with training objectives. Further, you readily understand your training purpose by the clear nature of training objectives.

Job- and Duty-Related Training Objectives

Since the goal of your training is preparing security officers for job and duty performance, your training objectives must relate to those requirements. For example, first aid training for security officers would not be the same as those objectives established for security officers certified as emergency medical technicians (EMT). Training standards for officers you want qualified as EMTs will call for special instructors and meet the state certification requirements. The first aid instruction; however, probably will be conducted by a certified Red Cross instructor and involves certain basic steps.

Officers Need to Have Training in an Active Job Environment

Your performance-oriented training needs to hold lectures and conferences to a minimum. Some subjects you'll present in your training curriculum need that type of presentation because actual "performance" of the knowledge is not possible. Knowing which type of training is applicable to the subject presented comes from knowing if the training objective is knowledge, such as laws regulating the officer's conduct, company policies, and other information related subjects. However, when the officer needs to learn a skill, he or she needs to have performance-oriented training. The great bulk of your training time must include controlled practice of a task. That practice ensures the security officers being trained become capable of performing the tasks needed by their jobs. Because you're devoting the bulk of training time to skill practice, you're satisfying the third condition of learning. Further, because your training objectives relate to specific job skill of the officer, he or she will be better able to understand that they need training.

Evaluation of Your Training

Evaluation of your performance-oriented training is a continuous process. Because of your emphasis on "learning by doing," the trainer receives continuous response on the progress of those officers being trained and on the efficiency of the training. Using this training technique, an added benefit includes reducing the need to wait for the end of a training session for test results. The very end of a training session is a poor time to find that little or no learning has taken place. This happens often with traditional types of training such as lectures, for which according to a variety of studies show retention totals about 5 to 10% of the material heard. That figure often decreases as time passes, as hearing or retaining doesn't create skills, only knowledge.

Just as important, because of the active role involved with performance-oriented training, student officers receive a steady flow of indicators on how well they are progressing. They, too, do not need wait until completing their training to assess how well they can perform a task or skill. Because each objective has a training standard, the officer can receive immediate response and reinforcement that he or she has achieved the training objective satisfying the fourth objective for learning and motivation. When the officer reaches the last training objective by a progression from simple to difficult tasks, that completes the fifth condition.

ADVANTAGES OF PERFORMANCE-ORIENTED TRAINING

Three key factors supply the advantages of performance-oriented training, and you need to consider each when developing your security training at all levels.

Clear Training Objectives

When you have precise training objectives, you or your trainers and the student officers share an understandable, common focus for their efforts. That reduces to a minimum the varied, occasionally conflicting, interpretations that arise when terms such as "proficiency, familiarity, and working knowledge" are used to describe the desired results of training.

Training Resources Used Efficiently

Because you write your training objectives in precise, measurable terms, your trainers and those officers they train understand exactly what the training achieves. Your planning for training resources (human, physical, and time) necessary to complete and accurately estimate each training objective improves through the precise, measurable terms. This factor becomes increasingly important as you prepare training, request or get training aids and devices, write training plans, and conduct rehearsals when needed.

Training Is Officer Oriented Instead of Trainer Oriented

In performance-oriented training, security officers perform job-related tasks under the conditions specified until they prove proficiency established by the training standards. Officers who quickly master a particular training objective can shift to help slower learners (a form of peer instruction) or continue their own skill development in other areas. The training focus is on officer performance instead of a trainer's ability to present instruction.

DIFFERENCES BETWEEN PERFORMANCE-ORIENTED AND CONVENTIONAL TRAINING

- Conventional training relies on the lecture as its chief method of instruction. Performance training uses short demonstrations and "learning by doing" as its main technique of instruction.
- Conventional training selects content to what the instructor can present or cover in a certain amount of time. Performance training develops content into a set of high-priority skills important for officers to learn in the time allotted for training.
- Conventional training uses "grades" to rate what the officer has learned. Performance training sets standards all officers must meet. When the officers do not meet the standards, they practice until they can.

QUICK REFERENCE GUIDE FOR DEVELOPING PERFORMANCE-ORIENTED TRAINING

- The purpose of your training is preparation for performance.
- Your training must relate to each officer's job.
- Your training needs precise training objectives.
- Your training must permit efficient use of resources.
- Your training focuses on the officer, not the instructor.
- The key to a definitive training objective includes
  - The task necessary to perform.
  - The conditions of the performance.
  - The standards for acceptable performance.
- Your training objective serves as the basis for
  - Preparing training.
  - Conducting training.
  - Evaluating training.

YOUR THREE-STEP PLANNING PROCESS

Step One: Describe Your Desired Results of Training

You need to decide exactly what you want the security officers to achieve during their training and what they must be able to do at the completion of training.

Start with the Requirements

When you have developed a curriculum for your basic, in-service, or other training, the requirements guide what you do. In some states a minimum standards law for security officers sets requirements to satisfy their desires; however, you can exceed those. Some companies have requirements that might not be directly security related but require each employee, despite position, to learn. Whatever your requirements might be, you need to bring them into focus to continue with your training effort. You also need to include

- Who will receive the training
- When will the training occur
- Where will the training happen
- Why the training is needed—what requirements did it satisfy

Step Two: Prepare to Conduct Training

You need to develop intermediate training objectives in a logical, progressive sequence coupled with the administrative requirements, such as training plans, aids, and facilities.

Your Objective Is the Key

It is only a slight exaggeration to state that your performance-oriented training approach begins and ends with the training objective. For a given skill, a properly structured and complete training objective is both the training and the test. Your objective can also contribute to the evaluation of training needed and the training conducted for that skill. This performance approach creates an equation:

$$\text{Training objective} = \text{Training} = \text{Test} = \text{Evaluation}$$

Keep this equation in mind as you continue to read Chapter 17: its meaning will become clearer in the following paragraphs.

Developing Your Training Objective

Your training objective needs three elements:

1. Task necessary to perform. What skill do you want the officers being trained to acquire?

2. Conditions of performance. Under what conditions do you want these officers to demonstrate the skill acquired?

3. A training standard of acceptable performance. How well do you expect these officers to perform?

Establish Your Intermediate Training Objectives

The need for intermediate objectives will depend on the complexity of the total objective. If your training objective is simple (for example, learning to fill out a form properly), then how you train the officer is easy to determine. However, if your training objective is complex, then tasks the officers must do and complete to standards, and how you will train them to do it, becomes more difficult.

The need to develop intermediate objectives becomes obvious as you examine your total objective and ask yourself the following question: "What must the student officers do to perform the required objective successfully?" By answering this question, you can "talk" yourself through how to perform the objective and include identifying the tasks necessary to complete it. The number and complexity of these tasks give you a sound basis for determining the requirement of intermediate objectives. Remember, you are not concerned, for the moment, with how to teach the subject matter inherent in this objective; you are only determining all the separate tasks a security officer must do to perform the total objective. For example, when you train newly hired security officers, a part of their training might be emergency medical techniques or what is commonly called first aid. It's not feasible to believe that officers can learn all the techniques they need to know, practice them, and become proficient in one training session. Your intermediate training objectives divide the completion objective into parts designed to be practical for the time available at each training session; however, to stay effective, each intermediate objective continues to use the same planning format. That includes the task, conditions, and standards discussed earlier. For example, you might be training 20 new security officers, and you need to have intermediate objectives of CPR during one or two training sessions, how to splint broken bones temporarily when medical aid is not readily available, how to bandage wounds, and how to use other techniques normally associated with emergency medical aid. Each phase calls for one training session, and each session becomes an intermediate objective leading to the completed training objective of being proficient and competent when giving first aid.

Another advantage of intermediate training objectives includes taking the necessary time to ensure each officer is genuinely proficient. For example, you might be limited on training aids, such as the CPR dummy regularly used to practice this skill. The importance of learning to perform CPR overrides rushing everyone through and betting someone's life that he or she can perform the skill properly. Instead, you need to use the intermediate objective to ensure that the officers reach the standard and it may need delaying other types of training. The only way you can evaluate their proficiency is with performance-oriented training and having the precise measurement advantage of an intermediate objective. When all officers meet the CPR standards you have developed, then move to the next training objective, which might include splinting broken bones. You may have five or ten intermediate training objectives that enable you to reach the completed training objective.

Develop Your List of Tasks

When your analysis of the complete objectives shows a necessity for intermediate objectives, you must first identify the specific tasks needed to do that complete objective. In developing your task list, you need to identify only those tasks essential to the officer's achieving the complete objective. Expertise in judging how detailed you should make the task list will improve with experience. The task list also relies on how well you or the trainer knows the subject; that is, it should neither break down tasks excessively nor retain tasks too complex.

Establish the Performance Conditions

The conditions element of a training objective is necessary to tell clearly how student officers must perform a task while on the job. Conditions specify the personnel, equipment, and procedures used, and the environment where officers must work while doing a specific task. To understand this better, consider the following task: Each officer will splint a broken leg. There are many different types of splints that an officer could use (e.g., plastic, inflatable, or traction splints). However, access to any of these splints is a deciding factor. The conditions in your objective should be as close as possible to those the officers receiving training are likely to find when and if needed to perform the task on the job. For example, suppose that a severe storm hits the area or there is an industrial accident of large proportion and local support medical teams can't handle all the casualties. The officers need the training as a stopgap measure; however, train them only to use what resources will be readily available should a need arise.

Step Three: Conduct Your Training to Standards

You or your trainers should continuously monitor and evaluate the conduct of training to ensure the officers' performance meets the training standard you have developed.

Establish a Comprehensive Training Standard

The last element of the training objective that you must develop is the training standard. This ensures officers receiving training will be able to perform the objectives. Training standards normally need expression with measurement terms (e.g., time, distance, accuracy) or with specific procedures following.

When you are developing training standards for intermediate objectives, you should first examine the training standards established by your requirements. This will ensure that training standards you develop for your intermediate objectives will not relax or, conversely, become more stringent than the needed training standard.

DETERMINE AND ORGANIZE TRAINING REQUIRED

With training objectives and appropriate intermediate objectives established, your job is to translate them into orderly, progressive training. This is accomplished by (1) determining how much training is required and (2) organizing the training required. Doing this will enable the officers receiving training to progress from easier to more difficult tasks in a manner that uses the available resources efficiently.

Determine How Much Training You Need

The intermediate training objectives you established specify what the student officers must be able to do to achieve your required objective (e.g., the required objective includes being proficient at emergency medical aid or first aid). Now, you should determine how well the officers can perform the intermediate objectives before beginning training. That determination allows you to (1) select for training only those objectives that the officers cannot perform without further training, and (2) make a determination of how much training will ensure the officers can meet the standards of your intermediate training objectives (e.g., the officers may need only brief "refresher" or they may need extensive practice to become proficient). To determine how well the officers can perform each intermediate training objective (i.e., their current proficiency), you can obtain and evaluate past performance results or you can conduct diagnostic testing.

When you have a large force of security officers, a good source of information might be their personnel records regarding experiences, or you can develop and have supervisors circulate a form for each officer to complete. It should ask for experience in the categories you'll include in your training curriculum. Also, determine experiences of newly hired officers for that information. For example, 5 of 20 new hires might be certified EMTs, and 12 have Red Cross first aid completion cards. That makes your training in that category less complicated and the EMTs might serve well as instructors to present and supervise the others as they practice first aid techniques.

When the information obtained appears unreliable (i.e., outdated, lacking or inappropriate for consideration), you may use a second approach—diagnostic testing. A diagnostic test determines how well officers can perform a specified objective (task, conditions, and training standard) before the start of your training. This action helps a trainer to determine how much training, if any, is needed to ensure the officers can perform an intermediate objective and meet its training standard.

Intermediate training objectives also work when used as a diagnostic test by randomly choosing a few of the officers you will train and have them perform each intermediate training objective. The results will give you a good sign whether the officers can meet the established training standard or how close to meeting it in each objective. Random choice means that you don't call for each officer to perform each objective; a few officers are chosen similar to drawing names out of a hat. This ensures a valid cross section of officers scheduled for training. The few evaluated prevents choosing only the most proficient or least proficient. When most of the officers randomly selected successfully perform an intermediate training objective, the officers need no further training (or very little) for the objective. Conversely, when most of the officers do not meet the training standard established for a particular objective, you would have determined a gap between current proficiency and desired proficiency. This gap represents the training needed.

Organizing Your Required Training

Performance-oriented training lends itself to a training session (i.e., a class or block of instruction) having three primary phases. You need to understand them and keep each in mind as you organize your training.

Phase I:

The trainer states a purpose of the training to the student officers and explains or demonstrates how to perform the objectives. Essentially, the trainer is transmitting information to the officers. Because this part of the training session is what the trainer does (not what the student officers must do), it should be as brief as possible. It should provide only essential information and conserve time better devoted to ensuring the officers can perform the objectives and meet the establishes standards.

Phase II:

The student officers practice the objectives to acquire proficiency called for by your training standard. During this phase the officer is receiving skills through performance. Once acquiring these skills, officers may need to continue practicing them to develop higher levels of proficiency. You must provide enough time and other resources (training aids, devices, equipment, assistant trainers, etc.) to ensure the officers do an acceptable level of proficiency before moving into phase III.

Phase III:

The officers are tested by performing the objective. The results show whether the officers can or cannot meet the established training standard. Your objective equals the test.

Organizing Your Training in Three Important Steps:

Step One: Determining the Order of Objectives

When you have determined training requirements, you're ready to arrange the intermediate training objectives into the order of presentation and conduct (i.e., a sequence that will lead to an orderly, progressive training session).

Two overriding considerations emerge as you determine how to organize your training. The first is expressed in the question: "Are any of the intermediate objectives a prerequisite to beginning training in the others?" If the answer is yes, teach those objective first.

Occasionally, your arrangements of intermediate objectives will have no effect on the conduct of training. For example, when the subject is first aid, normally it won't matter which part of the total objective comes first since each part has separate applications (i.e., managing broken limbs, bandaging cuts, CPR, and other aspects have separate aid functions; however, collectively qualify the officer to handle all types of situations).

The second consideration depends on resource limitations: "Do your resources dictate how you must organize the intermediate training objectives?" For example, when several officers have certifications as EMTs and others in Red Cross first aid, that increases your training resources. However, when 20 officers must have training and none has any past training, the resources change dramatically. There is also a problem of equipment and space when all 20 need all the training. In another example earlier, the problem of having many students for CPR training and only one dummy training aid calls for shifting of objectives. You can solve the problem by conducting two, three, or more intermediate objectives simultaneously in adjacent but separate areas. Divide the 20 into four groups, with one group participating in CPR, another splinting broken limbs, another bandaging serious injuries, and another dealing with persons in shock. As each group meets the training standards for that part, they rotate and begin the new intermediate objective. When all have finished each part to standards, they have reached the needed total training objective of first aid proficiency.

Step Two: Estimating the Resources and Choosing the Training Techniques

You can estimate and accurately allocate the resources in phase I because you're controlling most of the factors that influence the decision. Specifically, your intermediate objectives enable you to reduce a complex task to a logical series of smaller, simpler tasks. You are using the aids and devices and facilities. By rehearsing, you can determine the time you need to explain the objectives. You can even allow time for student officers' questions. Also, with diagnostic testing, you have determined the current level of skill proficiency of the officers.

Determining your training resources (including time) in phase II can prove the most difficult of the three phases. That difficulty stems from the officers performing (practicing). Because you have little control over these factors, and the time the officers need to learn and practice (phase II), your determination must wait until after you have found the time requirements for phase III.

The resources needed for phase III generally stay fixed because after enough practice, the officers should be able to perform the objective to the established training standards. Because your objective states what the officer will use in performing the task and usually time in which he or she must do it, you can determine the resources accurately.

Using this information, you now have an accurate method for estimating time for phase I and III. To estimate better time for phase II, do the following:

- Start with the total amount of time you allocate for training.
- Subtract the estimated time needed for your explanation (phase I).
- Subtract the estimated time needed for testing (phase III).
- Subtract the administrative time needed to conduct the training.

Time remaining will be the time available for phase II (officers' practice). If this amount of time is, in your judgment, too short, then you must consider the following steps:

1. Reduce the time expended in phase I. One way to save time is to use homework assignment techniques. These assignments should provide officers with reasons for training (i.e., training objectives and reasons for the training), explanation, if necessary (i.e., procedures they will follow during phases II and III), and the knowledge they will use during phase II and III (i.e., characteristics of first aid for example).

2. Acquire more training aids, devices, or equipment, as that will reduce the time for practice.

3. Rethink your requirements.

Step Three: Completing Administrative Requirements

The performance-oriented training approach indicates the most useful training plan should contain the following information:

- Your final training objective
- Your intermediate training objectives, if any
- When, where, to whom, and by whom the training is given
- Time-phased sequence of the training process
- Any safety restrictions and measures
- Other administrative information pertinent

There are still two things you must do before you conduct training—check the administrative support requirements and conduct your rehearsal. A good rule of thumb for training is, "Don't take anything for granted—check everything." Administrative requirements vary with each training session. The following checklist may help to ensure that you don't overlook anything.

- Check training facilities.
- Obtain or make training aids.
- Notify any assistant trainers.
- Inform officers about training attire.
- Prepare and reproduce handouts, if appropriate.
- Coordinate for special items and instructors.
- Ensure job schedules have allowed time for training.

EVALUATING YOUR TRAINING PROGRAM

Your training evaluation looks for the effectiveness and efficiency of security training. Training effectiveness emerges through how well your security officers undergoing training can meet or exceed established performance standards you set in your training objective(s). Training efficiency depends on how well you or your trainer used what was available (i.e., the training resources—time, personnel, facilities, equipment, funds) to train security officers.

The following checklist supplies the items necessary for you to make a self-evaluation of how well you prepared and conducted training. It will help make training more efficient and effective.

SELF-EVALUATION CHECKLIST

1. Preparation of Training

Were specific training objectives (intermediate and required) developed and stated in terms of task, conditions, and measurable training standards?

Did the training plan contain the following minimum elements of information?

- The required training objective?
- All intermediate training objectives (if any) listed in sequence?
- Administrative instructions:
  - When training will be conducted.
  - Training location.
  - Who will be trained.
  - Principal and assistant trainers.
  - Training aids/devices and equipment needed.
  - Any key references.
  - Training activity sequence and estimated time.
  - Any safety restrictions.
  - Added information.
- Did you rehearse:
  - Explanations, presentations?
  - Practice periods controlled by your assistant trainers?
  - Performance tests?
  - Films or audiovisual training aids integrated into training?
- Before training, did you check the following:
  - Arrangement of the classroom or training area?
  - Arrival of special equipment?
  - Working order of equipment?

2. Conduct of Training

a. Phase I (Explanation and Demonstration)

- Did you
  - Tell officers the training objectives including performance standards?
  - Give a reason for learning the skill?
  - Demonstrate how to perform the objective from officer's viewpoint?
  - Demonstrate each step of the objective in the order performed?
  - Give information necessary for performance of each step?
  - Where proper, call for officers to perform each step immediately after your demonstration and explanation?
  - Emphasize critical (key) points?
  - Avoid giving unnecessary information?
  - Pace demonstrations to correspond with the officers' learning ability?

(continued)

b. Phase II (Practice)

    (1) *Walk through*

- Did you
  - Correct officers if they made errors?
  - Tell officers what to do when they needed that help?
- When coaching, always require officers to perform all the steps or parts of the steps you demonstrated?

    (2) *Individual Practice*

- Did you
  - Tell officers when they were ready for skill practice?
  - Prompt officers when necessary by asking questions?
  - Ask officers questions?
- If task result varies with conditions, give officers practice situations that differed from each other and from demonstration and walk-through situations?

c. Phase III (Test)

- Did you
  - Explain or read testing instructions clearly and slowly to the officers being tested?
  - Observe complete performance of officers being tested?
  - Avoid correcting errors before test was finished?
  - Arrange testing conditions so officers could not watch and copy each other?

d. General

- Did you
  - Speak so officers could hear well?
  - Use understandable words?
  - Encourage officer questions?
  - Always answer relevant questions?
  - Always defer irrelevant questions?
  - Be patient with officers?
  - Reinforce correct performance?
  - Avoid giving officers unnecessary help?
  - Create an environment for learning (e.g., minimizing distractions)?

INSPECTING TRAINING

Evaluating training includes more than walking into the training area and watching. A good evaluator is not overly impressed with the "eye wash" of training. Instead, you need to have concern with the conduct of training. Your evaluation should concentrate on whether complete performance-oriented training objectives have been developed and whether, as a result of the training, the officers can perform the objective(s) and meet or exceed the established training standard(s). All other items are secondary, but by evaluating them, future training may be made more efficient. The following training inspection checklist is supplied as a guide for developing one for your department. Remember, in performance-oriented training, the goal is for all the officers to successfully perform all the training objectives.

PERFORMANCE-ORIENTED TRAINING INSPECTION CHECKLIST

1. Did the trainer have specific training objectives to accomplish?
   Comments:

2. Did the student officers perform successfully?
   Comments:

3. Were the resources adequate to complete the training?
   Time?
   Equipment?
   Training area or classroom?
   Training aids and devices?
   Trainers?
   Comments:

4. Did the training progress in a logical sequence to satisfy the required objective(s)?
   Comments:

5. Did the student officers appear to be motivated?
   Comments:

6. Did the trainer:
   a. Inform the officers of the training objective(s) to accomplish and give reasons?
   b. Arrange training area so all could see and hear?
   c. Use understandable words?
   d. Demonstrate how to perform the objective(s)?
   e. Give necessary information?
   f. Avoid giving unnecessary information?
   g. Require "walk-through" performance of the objective?
   h. Encourage questions?
   i. Exhibit adequate knowledge of the subject matter?
   j. Show interest in helping the officers learn?
   k. Make acceptable use of training aids?
   l. Use assistant trainers to best advantage?

(continued)

    m. Require practice to ensure achievement of the training standards?

    n. Test officers' ability to perform the required training objective?
       Comments:

7. Would you consider this training adequate?
   Specific recommendations:

18 Training Security Supervisors

Security supervisors normally come from within a security force, promoted from a senior security officer position, while security managers normally come from outside recruiting. The problem of promoting security officers from within a security force, to a security supervisor, is the tendency for the new supervisor to remain torn between being a "boss" and "one of the officers." Another problem develops when an outstanding security officer becomes a supervisor and disappoints management because of poor performance. Both problems stem from a lack of supervisory training and a clear understanding of what a security supervisor needs to do. In reality, a security supervisor becomes a "trainer."

The security supervisor, a job often misunderstood, has responsibility to manage a shift of security officers, ensuring they do their job and handle all problems they cannot. That translates into training, on the job, every day. The supervisor has the responsibility to supply "continuing" training to each officer on the shift and help him or her to develop and become a competent, exemplary officer. This chapter shows you how to train and develop supervisors by supplying them training for the job, and when doing so, convert them into security trainers. When you approach the supervisor problem this way, you also create the advantage of having department trainers available to develop new officers and conduct formal in-service training. You also have the benefit of their attentive "continuing" training of officers on the job.

PEOPLE-CENTERED SECURITY SUPERVISORS

Many studies have shown that when supervisors have concern for their subordinates as human beings, the subordinates become more competent and productive than the average security officer. A part of your supervisors' training program must include a people-oriented instead of job-centered approach. The best way to show interest and concern for subordinates stems from helping them grow professionally, and that stems from continued training while the officer is on the job. You must also supply the supervisor with training in leadership skills, and the complexities of interpersonal relations with the officers he or she is responsible to supervise.

CREATING YOUR SUPERVISOR TRAINING COURSE

To make your security supervisor training course logical and progressive, you should break it into two major parts. The first part should include a course to teach supervisors how to conduct training, including on-the-job (continuing), in-service, and basic security types. The second part should focus on how supervisors develop into effective leaders or leadership trainers. Although leadership is in itself a form of training, often supervisors need to lead their subordinates through performance and personal problem counseling and appraisals.

Your first part needs also to focus on the techniques of performance-oriented training discussed in Chapter Seventeen. Gaining the skill to conduct effective training enables you to develop competent trainers for all types of training requirements, basic through continued, and has a cost-effective advantage for your department. The following training plans (lesson plans) supply you with the best technique of training trainers. Part one of your supervisors' training also needs to have two parts, with the first teaching them how to prepare for training others and the second, how to conduct the training effectively. As your supervisors complete their basic training course, they have the basic skills necessary to develop more complex presentations. Illustrations 18–1 and 18–2 supply training plan examples for supervisor training. Illustration 18–3 is a student training plan example for use during supervisor training during part two—conduct.

Illustration 18–1

TRAINING PLAN ONE—TRAINING SECURITY SUPERVISORS TO PREPARE TRAINING

A. Training Objective

Task: Each supervisor (trainer) will prepare a training session for the basic security course, another for in-service training.

Conditions: Given complete security management training guidance that includes

- A security manager's training objective specifying the task to perform, performance conditions, and the training standard the student officers must meet or exceed. (Note: The security manager's objective should be complex enough to need the development of at least one intermediate training objective.)
- Who will receive the training.
- When the training happens.
- Where the training happens.
- Reasons for training.
- Coordinating instructions for resources obtained, if applicable.

Training Standard: Supervisor (trainer) must complete a training plan (lesson plan) that includes all elements of the training you direct. All intermediate objectives must support the security manager's objective and written in performance terms (i.e., task, conditions, and training standard). The activity sequence and time estimates must provide for conducting all three phases of performance training (i.e., phase I—state objective(s), explain, and demonstrate, if necessary, how to perform objective(s); phase II—practice; and hase III— test).

B. Intermediate Training Objectives

Intermediate Training Objective 1

Task: Each supervisor trainer will develop (write) one or more intermediate training objectives.

Conditions: Given a complete security manager's objective (i.e., train all officers sufficiently to qualify for administering first aid and CPR competently) requiring the development of at least one intermediate training objective.

Training Standard: Each intermediate training objective developed must contain the following elements:

- A task statement performed as a part of the security manager's objective.
- A statement that describes the performance conditions for each task. The

(continued)

Illustration 18–1 (continued)

conditions must be consistent with the conditions of the security manager's objective.

- A measurable training standard that clearly describes how well the student officers to be trained must perform the objective. The training standard must be consistent (neither too relaxed nor stringent) with the training standard of the security manager's objective.

Intermediate Training Objective 2

Task: Each trainer will determine the training required.

Conditions: (1) A complete security manager's training objective and its list of intermediate training objectives (each specifies a task, conditions, and measurable training standard), and (2) information about the past performance results for each intermediate training objective.

Training Standard: Consistent with the information supplied, the trainer chooses all intermediate training objectives for further training as needed.

Intermediate Training Objective 3

Task: Each trainer will estimate the time the other resources needed to conduct training.

Conditions: (1) Complete security manager's training guidance using (2) the intermediate training objective(s) for further training as needed, along with (3) information about the current proficiency of the student officers to be trained within the intermediate training objective(s) and (4) information about the available training resources (e.g., time, equipment, facilities, assistant trainers, training aids, and devices).

Training Standard: Sufficient to estimate the time and other resources needed to

- State purposes of training and explain and demonstrate, if needed, how to do each intermediate training objective and the security manager's training objective.
- Permit the student officers undergoing training to practice each objective to achieve the proficiency needed to meet established training standards.

C. Administrative instructions

1. When training will happen: _____

2. Training location _____

3. Who will be trained: _____

4. Principal and assistant trainers: _____

(continued)

Illustration 18–1 (continued)

5. Training aids and equipment used—one handout per student officer specifying complete security manager's training guidance for separate tasks: _

6. References: _____

D. Sequence of activity and estimated time

1. State the training objective and each intermediate training objective. Explain that each student trainer will learn how to perform the objectives largely though his or her own efforts. Specifically, each student, working at his or her own pace, will prepare a training session by developing a training plan that contains all the elements, including
   a. Read and study the security department and company policies and requirements of training.
   b. Complete practical exercise on writing training objectives.
   c. Based on the security manager's training guidance, research appropriate training procedures and develop a complete training plan.

2. Each student supervisor has complete guidance and told to prepare a complete training session.

3. Meet with each student supervisor (trainer trainee) and evaluate the quality and completeness of their training plans and session plans. Depending on the results of your evaluation, the student meets the training standard or, if not, supplies added work to complete to correct deficiencies.

E. Safety Restrictions: _____

F. Additional comments and information as needed

G. Time requirement for training: 24 training hours

Illustration 18–2

TRAINING PLAN TWO—TRAINING TRAINERS TO CONDUCT TRAINING

A. Training Objective

Task: Each supervisor (trainer) will conduct a separate training session.

Conditions:

- A complete training plan containing all elements of a training plan
- Enough time to study the lesson plan and rehearse the training
- Any equipment and material necessary to conduct the training

(continued)

Illustration 18–2 (continued)

Training Standard: Student supervisor (trainer) must train security officers in training or other student supervisors to perform the security manager's training objective successfully (i.e., meet or exceed training standard specified).

B. **Intermediate Training Objectives**

Intermediate Training Objective 1

Task: Each supervisor trainer will conduct phase I (explanation and demonstration) of a training session.

Conditions:

- A complete training plan for a specific security task
- Sufficient time to study and rehearse the training
- Any equipment and materials necessary to conduct the training

Training Standard: During phase I, trainer supervisor accomplished the following:

- Told the students the training objective(s) including the standards of performance they must meet.
- Demonstrated, if applicable, how to perform the objective(s) from the student's point of view.
- Demonstrated, if applicable, in a location that allow all students to see clearly.
- Demonstrated, if applicable, each step of the objective in the order performed.
- Gave all information necessary for the performance of each step.
- When applicable to the training, required students to do each step immediately after showing and explaining how to do it.
- Avoided giving needless information.
- Paced the demonstration, if applicable, by the students' learning ability.

Intermediate Training Objective 2

Task: Each supervisor trainer will conduct phase II (practice) of a task in a training session.

Conditions:

- A complete training plan for a security task
- Enough time to study and rehearse the training
- Ample equipment and materials to permit all the students in training to practice.

Training Standard: During phase II, the supervisor trainer accomplished the following:

(continued)

Illustration 18-2 (continued)

- Did a walk-through of each objective (observed students practicing).
- Corrected students if they made errors.
- Told students what to do when they needed the help.
- Showed students what to do when they needed that help.
- Told students what to do when they needed that help.
- Told students when they were ready for skill practice.
- Used faster learners to help slower learners.
- Supervised practice to ensure each student received enough practice to perform successfully the training objective(s).

Intermediate Training Objective 3

Task: Each supervisor trainer will conduct phase III (test) for a training session.

Conditions:

- A complete training plan for a security task
- Ample time to study and rehearse the training
- Any equipment and materials necessary for the test.

Training Standard: During phase III, the supervisor trainer accomplished the following:

- Explained testing instructions clearly and slowly to student officers being tested.
- Observed complete performance of students being tested.
- Avoided correcting errors of students being tested until test ended.
- Arranged testing conditions so students could not observe each other.
- At completion of test explained error(s), if any, and if any student officer does not meet specified standards, assigning him or her to an assistant or peer trainer for remedial training (time permitting).

Intermediate Training Objective 4

Task: Each supervisor trainer will evaluate a training session.

Conditions: Given an opportunity to observe an entire training session conducted by a student trainer.

Training Standard: Well enough to determine if the training session was effective (i.e., whether each student in training can meet or exceed the training standards specified in the training objective) and if they cannot, why not. (Note: To obtain answers to the latter, use the training standards of intermediate training objectives 1, 2, and 3.)

(continued)

Illustration 18–2 (continued)

C. Administrative Instructions

1. When training will happen: _____

2. Training location: _____

3. Who attends training: _____

4. Principal and assistant trainers. (Note: This training best serves small groups of about ten or fewer students per trainer. This permits organization of the training session so one student conducts training while five students act as student in training and four students evaluate the training conducted. Positions rotate until each student has conducted one training session.) _____

    _____

5. Training aids and equipment used (list according to subject): _____

6. References: _____

D. Sequence of Activity and Estimated Time

1. State the training objective. Explain that each student will conduct a short (20- to 30-minute) training session and he or she must meet the training standard specified. State each intermediate objective. As possible you need to videotape the training exercises and sessions for review with the student supervisors. When used, ask students to evaluate each of the taped sessions. Discuss conduct of training regarding that done correctly and the errors observed.

2. Provide each student with a complete training plan and all equipment and materials necessary to conduct the training called for by the plan. Permit each student to rehearse (practice) his or her training session. Supervise practice; answer questions.

3. Test each student by requiring each person to conduct the training called for in the training plan. Use other students to act as student officers in training (about five when possible) and as training evaluators (about four). Rotate the positions until each student conducts a training session. (Note: Have student evaluators use the training standards of the objectives to make the evaluations. Have students review each session and then summarize.)

    Total time: 24 training hours

E. Safety restrictions: _____
F. Additional comments and information as needed.

Illustration 18–3

EXAMPLE OF TRAINING PLAN FOR TRAINING SUPERVISORS AS TRAINERS FIRST AID TECHNIQUE FOR DISASTER INJURIES

A. Training Objective

Task: Each student will apply a bandage for severe disaster-related injury.

Conditions: Use supplied bandages and simulated injured person or dummy.

Training Standard:

- Application of dressing and bandages within 2 minutes.
- Application of dressing without touching (contaminating) the sterile parts of the dressing.
- Dressing must cover the injury.
- Student must apply pressure to the injury either with the attached bandages or with the hand over the dressing, until determined by the trainer that bleeding has stopped.
- The bandages secure the dressing on the injured limb and tied securely over the dressing.

B. Intermediate Training Objectives: None

C. Administrative Instructions

1. When training will occur: _____

2. Training location: _____

3. Who will be trained: _____

4. Principal and assistant trainers: _____

5. Training aids and equipment—one dressing and set of bandages per student: _

6. References: _____

D. Sequence of Activity and Estimated Time

1. State training objective and reason for learning the task: 5 minutes.
2. Show application of the dressing and bandages: 3 minutes.
3. Conduct walk-through by having the students switch positions and apply the dressing step by step. Have each student go through a walk-through as the student applies the dressing: 10 minutes.
4. Conduct practice session until students feel they are ready for testing: 10 minutes.

Illustration 18–3 (continued)

5. Test students separately: 10 minutes.

6. Retrain and retest students who don't meet standards: 10 minutes.
Total time needed: 38–45 minutes

E.   Safety Restrictions: None

F.   Additional Comments and Information: None

TRAINING SUPERVISORS FOR LEADERSHIP

After developing security supervisors into formal trainers for the classroom and training facilities, you need to move them to the second part of their training responsibilities: leadership counseling. Primarily, the security supervisor supplies continued training to security officers through performance counseling or performance appraisals. Using those approaches a supervisor can develop perceptions of training an officer might need and help the officer to understand how he or she needs to improve their job performance.

Training Supervisors to Counsel Subordinates

Counseling skills need to be a part of your supervisor training program. Since acquiring counseling skills evolves self-study, experimental training, and diligent practice, each supervisor is largely responsible for the development of his or her own skill. However, you need to provide the framework in your training program that allows the supervisor to understand clearlythe skill so their development follows the right course.

Supervisory counseling is one of the key elements of leadership. Counseling aims at changing things for the better in the relationship, behavior, and functioning of persons. It is a process for helping a person to find answers to his or her problems. It is helping a person to help himself or herself.

Counseling is the art of communicating advice, instruction, or judgment with the intent of influencing a person's attitude or behavior either formally or informally. It may range from a "pat on the back" for doing a good job to having a person come into an office for a private but pointed discussion of serious job deficiencies. It may in any location, but no matter how or where counseling occurs, it is an essential and good part of supervisory leadership.

The Effective Supervisory Counselor

Your training program for supervisors and the counseling skills begin with ensuring that the supervisors admit to themselves that they have particular likes, dislikes, biases, and prejudices and that they must not let these interfere with the relationship between themselves and the security officers they supervise. Recognizing the possibility of intrusion into the life of a subordinate, the supervisor must maintain a reputation for being able to keep a confidence. Also, instead of trying to solve every problem him or herself, they should encourage the counselee to solve his or her own problems. Avoid the approach, "I had a problem similar to yours." The counselee has interest in solving his or her own problems, not those of the supervisors. A supervisor as a counselor does three things:

1. He or she provides encouragement and support for change in the subordinate.

2. He or she provides information as knowledge and sources of knowledge that will help the counselee improve.

3. He or she plays a reinforcing or an evaluation role through strengthening the counselee's expression of feelings or presentation of ideas that will tend to help him or her improve performance or solve his or her own problems, avoiding ideas that do not help the subordinate and need no reinforcement. To prevent reinforcement of the ideas not related to the problem, guide the discussion away from them.

Supervisors must be observant, able to communicate, and flexible in their use of a variety of counseling techniques. They must see the subordinates they are counseling as well as listen to them. Observation of the person's actions during counseling will tell the supervisor whether the person understands what's said and whether the person accepts what he or she says. This information will help the supervisor to know what needs elaboration, what needs follow-up, and what point to emphasize.

Communication is a two-way flow of information. Supervisors must learn to communicate clearly, concisely, and without "beating around the bush." They must express themselves in understandable terms. They must also be good listeners. If the supervisor is conscious only of what he or she feels and what he or she will say next, the subordinate isn't getting the attention and assistance he or she needs.

Creative Training Sessions

Training supervisors for this important role calls for creativity on your part. You should always stay committed to performance-oriented approaches and supply a variety of challenges for the student supervisor to practice and achieve. You can best use other supervisor students or, when you don't have many to work with, use established supervisors who can also profit by learning or improving their skill. Do not use security officers as the person the student supervisor practices the skill on and with. It's important in this type training to maintain distance from subordinates and keep the training among supervisors and managers. Having described the performance-oriented approaches and how to supply training to supervisors through that process, the following information supplies the material to convert into training plans and develop training sessions. This type of training can be desirable for in-service training, but only when the training session has only supervisors and managers in attendance.

Training Supervisors the Counseling Techniques

Successful supervisory counseling calls for the sensitive and flexible use of a variety of interviewing techniques. It is not enough to use proper English or read a number of points for improvement from a list. The supervisor's objective must remain to influence the course of the interview in ways to motivate the subordinate to participate in a way most likely to cause understanding by both parties. There are three key approaches the supervisor must learn.

The Directive Approach

The best way for the supervisor to decide whether to be directive involves determining where there's necessary information to solve the person's problems. In the directive counseling approach, the supervisor may give advice and make certain decisions such as the type of information that would be meaningful to the subordinate. In directive counseling, the supervisor can take the needed action to the actual decision. The decision is always more satisfactory when counselee reaches it themselves. Supervisors may seek out the person who needs counseling in the directive approach. However, they should avoid giving advice and direction in a way that hinders the subordinate in his or her self-expression and the development of their own self-reliance. Directive counseling serves for things such as unsatisfactory performance and financial problems that begin affecting job performance. This approach works best in performance counseling.

Nondirective Approach

Supervisors need to learn how to help their subordinates solve problems, especially involving personal problems, through guidance instead of advice. This can serve by helping a person examine the problem logically and to develop a feasible solution. The nondirective counselor takes the approach that the person with a problem must take full responsibility for solving the problem and the counselor aids the counselee in its solution only by helping him or her to remove self-constructed obstacles. With the nondirective approach, the person with the problem begins the counseling relationship. The counselor (supervisor) listens to the problem, helps the counselee to gain insight, and provides information as the counselee requests it. Throughout the relationship, the counselor gives the counselee the feeling that he or she has found a fellow human being who has interest in trying to understand him or her and concerned with helping him or her find a solution to a troublesome situation. The nondirective counselor must be a good listener. Nondirective counseling serves in situations when a person has dissatisfaction with the job, requests career guidance, or is having financial difficulties.

Electic Approach

The last approach, the electic approach, combines the directive and nondirective approaches to help a person to make the proper adjustments or to solve his or her own problems as efficiently as possible. The supervisor (counselor) may be more directive initially, until the subordinate (counselee) "opens up." The supervisor then could resort to being nondirective and hear the counselee out by being a good listener, commenting and responding where necessary. As in the other approaches, the counselor must encourage a counselee to make the final decision about his or her problem and take the necessary action.

Key Signals of Subordinates with Problems

Not all people will ask for help. The supervisor must know his or her subordinates well enough to recognize their need for assistance. Some indications of silent cries for help that supervisors should learn to recognize and answer include the following:

- A good performer begins to perform his or her job below par consistently.
- An attentive person suddenly displays a lack of attentiveness or concentration.
- A moderate drinker begins to drink excessively.
- A person becomes involved in deliberate acts of misconduct or refuses to follow instructions.
- A person lingers after a meeting to talk, posing such questions as, "What if a person has a problem?"

Counseling serves many reasons such as

- Fact finding
- Informing
- Altering opinions, feelings, and behavior

The counseling interview is really nothing more than a communicating process where a supervisor interviews a person to find out something from that person, to tell that person something, or to effect some change in that person. It is possible for an interview to have more than one purpose, but ordinarily, one purpose will predominate.

Establishing Performance Standards

A major part of your supervisor training in this category must point out clearly that although they receive much guidance from your standards for the department operations, your supervisors also need to develop their own standards. However, their standards, as must yours, must remain reasonable and credible. When establishing performance standards for security officers, and throughout the department, the following criteria should serve as your guide.

Standards must stay realistic and within the capability of the subordinate officers. Factors that need consideration when determining realistic standards include

- *Personnel.* Are the security officers capable of doing the job? Have they experienced proper training? Are there enough security officers to satisfy the operational requirement?

- *Time involved.* Can the security officer, and the security shift, realistically and adequately accomplish the security operations task in the time allocated?

- *Equipment available.* Are equipment and materials needed for the security task available or easily acquired?

- *Facilities.* Are facilities for security officers and equipment adequate for the security task?

Standards must be realistic and within the security department's mission. Because of varying situations it is impractical to establish the same standards of performance for each security task.

Standards must be clearly stated, concise, and complete. As you establish standards, the words or phrases you use should not include unfamiliar abbreviations or excessively technical terms. Subordinates must clearly understand standards to avoid failure based on misunderstanding of the requirement. The subordinate receiving the assignment must know requirements exactly, the range of his or her authority and responsibility, and the resources available to him or her.

TEACHING SUPERVISORS APPROACHES THAT MOTIVATE SUBORDINATES

Ensure supervisors know that in reviewing performance, it's more useful to present solutions and points for improvement than to dwell on deficiencies. This approach can develop a climate that motivates their subordinate officers to improve their performance and a form of influence used by the supervisor. Influence may take many forms. During an appraisal interview, the supervisor may need to use one or many forms depending on the course taken by the interview and by the reactions of the subordinate. The options to teach supervisors in your training courses include the following:

Mapping Alternatives

Suggest several optional actions the subordinate officer might take. The officer needs to make the decision about alternatives.

Recommending

The supervisor can recommend a certain course of action. Although whether the subordinate decides to accept the supervisor's recommended action remains the officer's discretion.

Persuading

A supervisor can try to persuade the subordinate officer that a given course of action is in his or her best interests. The supervisor tries to sell them on taking this certain course of action but still expects the officer to make his or her own decision. Successful persuasion depends on the supervisor's credibility. For example, does he or she have the expertise to critique the subordinate's performance and is there an atmosphere of mutual trust between the supervisor and subordinate security officer?

Urging

This is the strongest form of persuasion without resorting to authority. The supervisor exerts every effort to convince the subordinate officer that he or she should take a given course of action. However, there is still no suggestion of a command.

Advising

This technique is somewhat stronger than recommending. The supervisor advises the subordinate that it is in his or her best interests to take a given course of action.

Commanding

The supervisor orders or demands the subordinate officer takes a specific course of action. There must be no possibility of the subordinate's misunderstanding that it involves a command. This is an "either or" situation.

Preparation for Counseling

When preparing for a counseling interview, the supervisor should consider advance notice, allotment of time, plan of action for conduct of the interview, physical setting, and the general atmosphere. Whenever possible, the subordinate counselee needs notification before the time of the interview. That permits him or her to think about their performance or problems and prepare to discuss it. Enough time allotment needs consideration for the interview so neither the counselor nor the counselee will feel rushed. While a large amount of work to be accomplished may place restrictions on time available, the supervisor should try to allow sufficient time. No interview can be a success if the participants feel rushed.

Learning to Make Plans

A general plan of action for the conduct of the interview needs development by the supervisor. However, since flexibility is important in counseling, a detailed plan doesn't serve well. For a general interviewing plan, the supervisor must have his or her objective clearly in mind. Supervisors should review all background information so that they can develop a general plan for conducting the interview. This will primarily involve the sequence of that he or she wishes to discuss and the point he or she wants to make about each item.

Selecting the Right Place

The place where the interview happens is also important. An uncomfortable or disturbing location causes distractions and reduces motivation of the counselee to take part in the interview. Privacy is also essential, both to prevent distractions and to maintain a confidential atmosphere.

The supervisor should try to create an informal atmosphere. That means the counselee needs to know if he or she can sit, smoke, and freely discuss the items with the supervisor. High levels of formality are not conducive to good motivation and openness during the interview.

Conducting the Interview

Having properly prepared for the interview, the next step for the supervisor includes interviewing the person. The opening few minutes are probably the most critical phase of the interview because it is in this time that the atmosphere becomes created for the entire interview. Accordingly, an objective of the supervisor during the opening phase should include establishing a relationship with subordinate in which both feel as ease. From the start, the supervisor needs to relieve any tension. This happens by showing acceptance of the counselee, letting him or her feel that his or her view is important and that he or she can avoid discussing it. An explanation of the interview objectives may happen here and the counselee drawn into the discussion quickly.

In the discussion, the supervisor would guide the interview, to invite the subordinated back from detours, escapes, fruitless conversation, and other factors using brief questions.

In almost every situation, the counselee needs a way to "save face." This means that the supervisor should not push the counselee into a position where he or she cannot retreat without embarrassment. This point is important because an assault on the personal integrity of the subordinate drastically reduces his or her motivation. Under no circumstances should the counselor allow himself or herself trapped into an argument with the person being counseled.

Sometimes the discussion may slow down however; momentum revives by keeping counseling purposes in mind and by asking questions. The questions asked need adaptation to the counseling session; so no one set of questions will do for every interview. Certain types of questions serve to advantage in almost all interviews or counseling sessions. The "W" questions, who, what, where, when, and why are extremely valuable because they fit so may situations. They are especially useful in getting detailed answers and in saving time. Although "yes-no" questions may commit the counselee or to get a better understanding, they should be used sparingly. The "yes-no" question must precede another question to get more detailed and useful information.

As the interview purpose concludes, close the conversation and dismiss the counselee in graceful manner and in a friendly atmosphere. The interview should be closed when all points have been covered, when the counselee has had enough time to understand, and when the conversation is at a natural stopping point. If any action was taken by the counselor, such as submitting a report, making a record of the session, and so on, the counselee should be so informed. If time is critical and the counselee appears to want to continue a general discussion of their situation, suggest the interview continues later at a convenient time. Although the counseling interview is over that doesn't mean the job is over. Certain follow-up actions must happen. The supervisor must continue to evaluate performance and must check to ensure the personal problems no longer exist. If problems still exist, further counseling is necessary.

Preparation for Counseling

When preparing for a counseling interview, the supervisor should consider advance notice, allotment of time, plan of action for conduct of the interview, physical setting, and the general atmosphere. Whenever possible, the subordinate counselee needs notification before the time of the interview. That permits him or her to think about his or her performance, or problems and prepare to discuss it. Enough time allotment needs consideration for the interview so neither the counselor nor the counselee will feel rushed. While a large amount of work to be accomplished may place restrictions on time available, the supervisor should try to allow sufficient time. No interview can be a success if the participants feel rushed.

Learning to Make Plans

A general plan of action for the conduct of the interview needs development by the supervisor. However, since flexibility is important in counseling, a detailed plan doesn't serve well. For a general interviewing plan, the supervisor must have his or her objective clearly in mind. The supervisors should review all background information so that they can develop a general plan for conducting the interview. This will primarily involve the sequence in which they wish to conduct the session and the points they want to make about each item.

ABCs OF COUNSELING—A CHECKLIST

Your training program for supervisors needs to use the following guidelines that can also serve as an effective checklist for continuing review. Counseling supervisors should use it as their framework reference to develop counseling skills.

- Be friendly, natural, personable, and relaxed when counseling subordinates.
- Put aside unfinished business and concentrate on the counseling task.
- Do something to put your counseling session at ease. If the subordinate had difficulty during the beginning conversation, introduce a topic of mutual interest or discuss some of his or her achievements.
- Exhibit a keen interest in the subordinates and their statements. Provide for simple "acceptance." Let them tell their own story in their own way. This may be all the help they need.
- Find out what the subordinates consider to be important. Discuss their attitudes and why they take the position they do.
- Give them enough opportunity to tell the story. Let them talk freely without interruption if he or she seems so inclined.
- Help them to see their own problem. Try to help them see these problems in proper perspective. Help them to become more objective about their own statements.
- Ask about the steps they have already taken to solve their difficulties. Determine, if possible, how much interest they have in wanting to find better solutions.
- Judge their actions objectively, if they have to be judged. Relate their attitudes to their standards and welfare.
- Remain friendly, sympathetic, and helpful, but don't assume the responsibility for finding solutions to the subordinate's problems.
- Lead subordinates to develop a deficit plan of action for themselves. When

appropriate, suggest some possible next steps. Help them choose those plans that may prove most helpful, but leave the final decision to him or her. It is their life and they should have freedom to make their own choices.

- Mention by title and location books and other materials that might help.
- Name people or agencies that help people with problems.
- Observe any signs of disappointment or discontent. These may be a clue to the real problems or may disclose the counseling session moved to embarrassing topics to the counselee.
- Pursue the main problems until satisfied the counseling session has ended on a positive note.

TRAINING SESSION TECHNIQUES FOR COUNSELING

The best technique for training supervisors for counseling involves the performance-oriented approach. Using this technique, each supervisor plays the role of the counselor and counselee in view of the other supervisor students. This method helps all supervisor students because of the practice involved and learning experience from watching others practice. This technique also enables immediate feedback and rotating through several practice sessions enables them to improve by using that critique information to correct shortcomings. Whenever possible, use videotaping equipment and use that as an added feedback training tool. The idea is improvement, not criticism, and student supervisors need to understand that at the onset. The final period of time for training should be devoted to a practical test. It should include

- Giving a valid measure of the supervisor's skill to counsel.
- Evaluating the supervisor as they role play at least two separate counseling situations.
- Receiving student supervisor responses. Their responses enable you to respond content (what is said) and process (what is happening).

MOVING SUPERVISORS INTO CONTINUED TRAINING APPLICATIONS

Ongoing or continued training should not be confused with in-service training. There are certain differences between the two types of training. Ongoing training, unlike in-service training has no formal program or specific number of hours devoted to its conduct. Instead, it relies on supervisors to supply training to officers at roll call and supply training guidance to officers on the job. Other techniques include training bulletins that offer tips and procedures, information about changes in company policy and laws, coupled with anything that has an immediate need for implementation. The supervisors have a responsibility to ensure that their subordinates understand and integrate the new information into their job routine. Supervisors, then, have a strong leadership role and realistically their job includes being continuous trainers.

QUICK REFERENCE REVIEW AND GUIDE
FOR
TRAINING SECURITY SUPERVISORS

- View Security Supervisors as Trainers
- Train Supervisors as People Centered Instead of Job Centered
- Create an Effective Supervisor Training Course
- Develop Comprehensive Performance-Oriented Training Plans
- Train Supervisors for Leadership Counseling
- Train Supervisors for Performance and Personal Counseling
- Move Supervisors into Continuous Ongoing Training Responsibilities

19 Important Basic Security Training

The extent and types of training needed for your security force will vary according to the importance, vulnerability, size, and other factors affecting your protective responsibilities. The objective of the training program for security officers ensures that each can perform routine duties competently and meet emergencies quickly and efficiently. Efficient and continuing training is the most effective means of obtaining and maintaining maximum proficiency of security force officers. Despite how carefully you choose security personnel for your department, seldom do they initially have all the qualifications and experience necessary to do the job well. Further, new and revised job requirements often mean that security officers must have training from different jobs and skills. The bridge between skill and job requirement happens with performance-oriented training. When developing your security officer training program, remember that all people do not have the same training needs. It is a waste of valuable time and resources to train a security officer in subject matter that he or she has already mastered, and it is a source of dissatisfaction to the person when subjected to instruction he or she knows has no importance to his or her job. Experience, training, acquired skills, and security assignment and responsibility need evaluation for each person as an aid in planning an effective training program. Illustration 19–1 shows the relationship of basic, in-service, and continued job training (within the supervisor's purview) and it's value.

Illustration 19–1

THE BENEFITS AND ADVANTAGES OF TRAINING

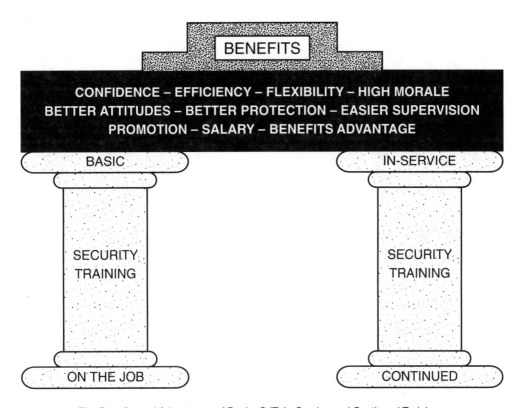

The Benefits and Advantages of Basic, OJT, In-Service and Continued Training

DEVELOPING BASIC SECURITY TRAINING CURRICULUM

Because of the diversity in corporate and industrial security, no one routine or standard training course can satisfy all specific needs. However, there are basic skills each security officer must know, and those categories plus the performance-oriented training time suggested for each follows. Add subjects to fit your situation or drop subjects accordingly. For example, when your security responsibilities include protecting a toxic chemical plant, you need to add that to your curriculum. When none of your security officers carries firearms, you can drop that from the training. The following guide supplies a general process for developing and evaluating the training curriculum suited for your department and company.

● *Before Determining Curriculum*

1. Review job descriptions prepared for the positions where the student officers will work.

2. Conduct a job analysis providing you a systematic and precise identification of the skill requirements through review of job descriptions.

3. Determine the frequency and importance of the functions; enabling accurate assignment of training time needed to prepare the student security officer for the job.

● *During Curriculum Preparation*

When developing your training curriculum, remember the interrelation of all levels of training. A necessary and progressive program begins with basic security training, but the full potential cannot develop unless supervisors continue the training on the job and you ensure a meaningful in-service program reinforcing the basic training. You should also

1. Ensure you identify each job function in both the curricula and training plan.

2. After each element of the curriculum, develop a response mechanism to ensure the student officers have sufficient skill for the next phase of instruction. For example, when preparing the officer to perform the job function of "controlling personnel access to a given location," the officer should learn the following information:
   a. Legal and company policy authority to restrict access
   b. Techniques for gaining cooperation from others without the use of force
   c. Use of minimal force to stop persons from gaining access
   d. Procedures to follow if someone illegally gained access.

During Curriculum Evaluation

1. Ensure training standards focus the student officers enabling them to apply the information effectively on the job. For example, avoid abstract hypothetical situations that don't focus directly on what task the officer needs to perform once placed on the job.

2. Allow student officers an opportunity to review their performance testing and strengthen any training deficiencies through explanations or retraining, if needed.

3. Evaluate student officers after training and when on the job and ensure supervisors continue their training through on the job training (OJT).

4. As necessary, assess your training program to ensure training stays job related. This has importance because job functions change periodically and your training needs to adapt to the changes.

• Suggested Curriculum and Time Requirements

The following suggested curriculum for basic security officer training should apply to all security officers in your department. Although generally perceived as a course for new officers hired, when your present officers have not received the training, you should at the earliest opportunity supply them the opportunity of the basis course. The "training hours" noted here show a 50-minute block of instruction, the standard for training and education curriculums.

Illustration 19–2

SUGGESTED CURRICULUM FOR BASIC SECURITY OFFICER TRAINING

● **Crime Prevention Measures**   **5 Training Hours**

    The primary presence of security includes prevention, and the secondary element involves dealing effectively with situations not prevented. You should ensure that crime and other types of prevention training follow basic training through in-service sessions and continued training by supervisors. Much of this session deals with employee or visitor pilferage and prevention through security officers knowing the factors of most crimes, including motive or desire, opportunity, and means.

● **Authority and Jurisdiction—Persons and Places**   **5 Training Hours**

    You can avoid many problems and confusion within the security force by including this element of training in your basic course. Although the five hours allotted might be few for such a broad subject, supervisors need to continue reinforcing the training when officers begin working.

● **Civil and Criminal Law Review**   **4 Training Hours**

    Although security officers don't enforce the law in a technical sense as public police do, they need a basic knowledge of crimes that might affect your company, including the elements of proof. For example, often people use the term "robbery" when they describe a "burglary." Each officer needs to learn the differences in various crimes and what elements must be present to make an event a crime.

● **Restraints and Use of Force**   **2 Training Hours**

    An important part of your authority and jurisdiction training includes the extent and limits of restraints and use of force. For example, a security officer must understand the laws, and company rules about both when on duty.

● **Legal Rights and Warnings**   **3 Training Hours**

    A problem many security officers often express involves confusion about regarding their need to observe a person's legal rights and the *Miranda* rule warning. Although security officers normally have exclusion from this concern, some courts have held that a security officer making an arrest might do so within the gray area of public authority. Also, some security officers within a department may have special police powers conferred on them by local authorities. This is a subject best taught by a local prosecutor or at least an attorney.

(continued)

Illustration 19–2 (continued)

● Search and Seizure of Property   3 Training Hours

Security officers need this training since search and seizure of property, especially at exit points could be a problem when officers don't understand the authorizations of search and the seizure of property even when believed to be company property.

● Elements of Proof   4 Training Hours

A continuation of the authority and action sessions noted earlier includes ensuring all elements necessary enable probable cause to act. For example, before acting on an event that appears a crime, run a mental checklist ensuring all elements of proof become clear.

● Court Testimony   4 Training Hours

Security officers might appear in court regularly or rarely, depending on the type of protective role your department supplies. Each security officer needs to have a sound knowledge of the court procedure and how to testify should he or she be called to do so. A minimum of training needs to include:

1. The security officer needs to review the case reports before the testimony.
2. He or she needs to wear a proper uniform as prescribed by department and company policy and bear in mind the importance of personal appearance upon entering the courtroom and during testimony.
3. The officer needs to report to the court, always maintaining a professional bearing throughout the testimony.
4. The officer must avoid mannerisms when testifying and look at and talk directly to the members of the court.
5. He or she needs to learn to answer questions asked directly and simply, with facts only, and give deliberate, considered answers. He or she must explain and clarify an answer if necessary, but not volunteer information not asked for.

● Arrest of Persons   4 Training Hours

Although authority discussions in earlier sessions include the right to arrest or the lack of it, this session needs to discuss how to arrest a person. For example, what must the security officers do and say when arresting a person. Much of this session might also include company and department policy on the subject. Your training needs to include a minimum of the following procedures:

1. Approaching with caution, and making an estimate of the situation, security officers might, depending on the situation and location, need to make a

(continued)

Illustration 19–2 (continued)

mental observation of the area, noting details and conditions and courses of action he or she needs to take when the person arrested tries to escape or becomes belligerent:

   a. Observing the attitude of the suspect and determine whether he or she is belligerent, boisterous, aggressive, surly meek, mile, or cooperative.

   b. Calling for help whenever he or she expects trouble from the person. Often, a display of no-nonsense force prevents aggressive action from the suspect.

2. Security officers in training need to learn how to make a plan of action when deciding what to do or how to handle a situation. With practice, a security officer can learn to develop the plan mentally immediately.

3. Whenever possible the officer should make arrests at a location that offers maximum advantages to his or her and minimum to the suspect.

4. Approaching the suspect, the security officer's actions should include

   a. Assuming that the suspect might be dangerous. Be firm, decisive, and courteous, but restrained.

   b. Identifying themselves when in civilian clothes and often in uniform to ensure the person knows they have a right to be there.

   c. After following all procedures noted, arresting the suspect.

5. Develop a policy on use of handcuffs by your security officers.

● Drug Abuse and Company Policy   2 Training Hours

A present problem in corporations and industries employing hundreds and thousands of employees is drug abuse in the workplace. Many companies call for involvement of security managers and the security force officers with the company policy on this subject. Your officers need to have a clear understanding about the company policy and be able to respond effectively when called upon to do so.

● Interviews and Interrogations   4 Training Hours

Often, security officers have needed to interview and maybe interrogate a person or employee suspected of a crime within company property. Each officer needs a sound knowledge of the proper and improper techniques of both categories and the differences between the two. The training session needs a minimum of the following elements.

1. What is an interview?

2. What is an interrogation and when to apply the techniques?

3. Admissions and confessions.

4. The correct process of taking a written statement.

(continued)

Illustration 19–2 (continued)

● Ethics of the Security Profession   2 Training Hours

Generally, each department and company has certain ethical standards set for security officers. The standards create a guide that helps maintain a professional attitude and performance. Further, some codes of ethics have evolved from security associations, societies, and other guiding forces behind increasing the professionalism of security officers. However, you establish a guideline of ethics for your security force, the subject needs to be a part of your basic training.

● Report Writing and Administrative Tasks   8 Training Hours

A security officer normally has a requirement to complete report forms and other administrative tasks inherent with his or her job. Often confusing and intimidating to new security officers, the procedure and standards you want come to the officer in this session. Earlier in the book, the case reports and other reports create the foundation for your training during this session.

● Traffic Collision Investigation (Company Property)   4 Training Hours

Large industrial plants often have hundreds, maybe thousands, of motor vehicles entering and departing the company daily. Any time concentrations of vehicles happen, collisions also happen regularly. Most have minor damage; however, most law enforcement agencies don't like to or cannot investigate unless the collision has serious injuries or fatalities. Generally, investigating the collision on company property you protect includes a responsibility of investigating and completing a report on such collisions. Your training needs to include procedures for the following elements as a minimum:

1. Arrive at the scene and take charge. During hours of darkness, use flashing warning devices to protect the scene and prevent further collisions from unsuspecting drivers approaching the area. Use a security vehicle to block and protect the injured at the scene. Other warning devices include flags or flares.

2. Establish traffic control, calling for added officers when necessary.

3. Provide first aid as needed and summon medical help if necessary to the scene for injured persons.

4. Note positions of vehicles—photograph scene when possible. Collect and protect personal property of the injured when necessary.

5. Request support elements as needed, for example, fire trucks, wreckers, and others.

6. Record observations of the accident scene including weather conditions, road and traffic conditions, measuring skid marks, final resting position of

(continued)

Illustration 19–2 (continued)

involved vehicles, point of impact, contents of involved vehicles, and other pertinent information.

7. Collect evidence when needed, tagging, marking, and packaging it for safe-keeping.

8. Identify and interview witnesses, obtain written statements when needed.

9. Prepare a sketch of the scene including all measurements and triangulation information.

10. Clear the scene and prepare a full report of the collision and officer actions.

● **Traffic Control & Parking (Company Property)**   **2 Training Hours**

This session serves two distinct purposes. First, officers learn how to control traffic, and second, officers need to have a sound concept of how the company and you want cars parked. Some large security forces even use traffic radar and issue speeding tickets. The tickets, however, do not go to court; instead they go to supervisors, and when an employee has habitual poor driving standards, the necessary information goes to the higher echelons of the company. When your company has a large number of employee and company vehicles, your new security officer needs to have a knowledge and skill of identifying parking permits and matching them with the proper parking areas.

Also, when your company has heavy truck traffic, making deliveries and pickups, officers need to control and direct their movements, check manifests, and often make inspections of cargo. Officer may also need to conduct basic safety inspections on vehicles when employees or vendors apply for parking permits. Use of a variety of control applications depending on the size and needs of the problem.

● **Emergency Medical Aid (First Aid) and CPR**   **16 Training Hours**

Each security officer needs this course as a minimum; however, more hours would normally be a prudent idea. Much of the time needed to be proficient in first aid and CPR depends on equipment available and who teaches the course. Whenever possible have an EMT, doctor, or both teach CPR and elements of first aid whenever possible. A minimum training objective needs to include

1. The four lifesaving measures
   a. Check the injured person's air passages.
   b. Stop bleeding.
   c. Treat for shock.
   d. Protect the injury.
2. Treatment of injuries caused by cold
3. Treatment of injuries caused by heat
4. How to immobilize a fracture
5. Treatment for burns

(continued)

Illustration 19–2 (continued)

---

6. Medical kit applications and improvising

7. CPR techniques

● Security Relationship with Law Enforcement Agencies   2 Training Hours

The type of protection your department and officers provide governs the amount and levels of contact security officers have with law enforcement officers. However, at some point contact probably happens and officers need to know how to maintain a professional working relationship with law enforcement officers and agencies. Often a lack of training or distancing attitude creates friction between security departments and law enforcement agencies. Law enforcement officers often look down on a security officer's abilities, and question their judgments, believing them to be untrained. However, when the liaison between your department has teeth, and your officers receive this part of training, including basic, in-service, and continuing, law enforcement officers and agencies begin having high regard for your officers. Also, whenever it is possible, you should coordinate with the local law enforcement agencies and invite law enforcement officers to act as instructors for key elements of your training, both basic and in-service. The bond and mutual respect will develop favorably in those conditions.

● Observation and Description Techniques   2 Training Hours

An important part of a security officer's duties includes observing and supplying accurate descriptions when needed. Normally, the most common event of that activity happens with people. Appendix C contains a valuable guide and checklist for instruction and later application for security officers working in most areas.

● Investigative Procedures   4 Training Hours

Security officers often have a responsibility of early investigations, maybe in-depth probes into internal company matters. When your security department has that responsibility, each officer, even those considered novices, need a basic course on procedures to enable them to develop correctly and effectively later. This session leads to added sessions noted next.

● Crime Scene Protection   2 Training Hours

When security officers find a probable crime, such as burglary, attempted arson, or other event, they need to have the basic knowledge of how to secure and protect the crime scene until arrival of a supervisor and maybe the police. Minimum elements you should include are the following:

1. Understanding the importance and establishing authority on arrival at the scene.

2. Clearing people who may be curious.

(continued)

Illustration 19–2 (continued)

3. Protecting life for any injured people at the scene through first aid measures and calling for medical aid.

4. Protecting and securing items of potential evidence value.

5. Sealing areas pending arrival of supervisor and police when applicable.

6. Identifying any person related to the incident and any witnesses.

7. Taking notes and later writing a complete report. Take photographs when possible.

8. Briefing the supervisor or police on their arrival.

• Preservation of Evidence   2 Training Hours

Whenever a security officer comes upon a probable crime or becomes responsible for investigating an internal company matter, he or she must know how to preserve and handle items believed evidence in the case. Companies often have the prerogative of reporting most crimes or events to the police and prefer to handle the problem internally. However, company action often relies on various types of evidence, and when a security officer handles it poorly, neither the company nor the police can act appropriately. Include the following minimum elements:

1. Identify potential physical evidence, no matter how large or microscopic following these procedures:
   a. Identify movable evidence, such as tools, weapons, clothing, glass and documents. (Movable evidence can be picked up at the crime scene or other location and transported elsewhere.)
   b. Identify fixed or immovable evidence, such as walls, telephone poles, and other items not easily removed from a crime scene because of its size, shape, or makeup.
2. Identify fragile potential evidence such as footprints, fingerprints, body fluids and other items that might deteriorate rapidly or easily be destroyed in weather or confusion.

• Security Patrol Operations   4 Training Hours

This session shows security officers the proper way to conduct a patrol according to your department and company policy. For example, in some industrial or corporate environments, fire or chemical spills might be important, and company management wants security officers to be watchful for violations of safety policies or to report any situation he or she believes could evolve to a dangerous event. Other aspects might include how to detect intruders by observing changes in areas being patrolled, such as open windows, lights broken, and other like situations.

• Security Operational Communication Systems   2 Training Hours

When your security department uses radios for communications, new officers

(continued)

Illustration 19–2 (continued)

need training in proper use and procedure. The training needs to include radio operation and maintenance and an awareness generally of the department's communication policy.

● **Company Personnel Movement Control Measures**   **2 Training Hours**

This session generally acquaints the new officer with your department and company policies and procedures. Posting an untrained security officer invites problems and on-the-job training with an experienced officer without a formal training period might teach the officer something wrong or the novice misunderstands the casual nature of the veteran and decides that represent your policy.

● **Identification Systems and Procedures**   **2 Training Hours**

This course acquaints the new officer with your company and department identification systems and procedures and the principles behind it. Always present the new officer with the proper procedure and techniques.

● **Access Control Systems**   **2 Training Hours**

This session has the same purpose.

Intrusion Alarm Systems   **2 Training Hours**

This session has the same purpose.

● **Bomb Threat Procedures**   **2 Training Hours**

Bomb threats happen periodically at large companies and industrial areas. Although normally a hoax, security officers need to know and prepare to implement immediate procedures to protect the employees and prevent any person from entering the suspect area until cleared by qualified bomb disposal persons, normally from the local police or fire departments. Appendix A contains a guide for security officers confronted with company bomb threats.

● **Managing Difficult People**   **2 Training Hours**

Whenever security officers must deal with hundreds or thousands of people each day, some might become difficult, especially when directed to do something they perceive as unnecessary. You need to develop procedures within your company policies and ensure each officer knows what to do when confronted with this type situation.

● **Managing Mentally Disturbed People**   **2 Training Hours**

Mentally disturbed people might appear at entrances to the company. Security officers working on gates need to know proper procedures to handle the situation until summoned help can arrive, often from the local law enforcement agency. Instruction

(continued)

Illustration 19–2 (continued)

for this session needs competent medical or law enforcement expert participation whenever possible.

- **Basic Unarmed Defensive Measures**   **8 Training Hours**

    Each officer needs to learn reasonable and easy-to-apply unarmed defense measures when necessary. Although not often attacked, an intruder caught in the act might resist arrest or a person trying to exit a gate and stopped by a security officer for suspected theft might attack the officer in panic or anger. Appendix B supplies applicable techniques normally adequate in most security applications.

- **Fire Prevention and Control Systems**   **2 Training Hours**

    Fire prevention in the company area has significant importance, and often an alert security officer can alert the proper people or agency, or handle the dangerous situation immediately. Alert security officers often avert a fire by watching for probable hazards and enforcing company policy on smoking areas, storage of flammable materials, and other fire prevention measures.

- **Emergency Situation Notification**   **2 Training Hours**

    This training often involves a notification procedure, for example, "When situation X happens, this is whom you notify or contact for assistance. Clear procedures need to be the department rule; however, each new officer must not have any misunderstanding or confusion about what to do in each contingency. Don't allow your operations to be bogged down in bureaucratic procedures that confuse officers trying to determine protocol instead of making the important calls in the order of priority.

- **Disaster Relief Operations**   **2 Training Hours**

    This training part establishes awareness and action procedures for security officers confronted with a disaster that strikes company areas and employees while at work. Officers also need to have clear procedures for threatening major disaster, imminent serious conditions, and other situations. These situations may include hurricanes, tornadoes, storms, floods, high water, wind-driven water, and earthquakes. For example, security officers working in an earthquake-prone area need to have clear training and instructions on action to take should that happen. Officers in the South or Midwest especially need training on tornadoes and what to do before and after one strikes at the company area.

- **Basic Fire Rescue Measures for Employees**   **2 Training Hours**

    This session concerns the emergency situation procedure specific to fires and ensures that the security officers have the responsibility of protecting life instead of property. You should try to have professional fire fighters and rescue people supply

(continued)

Illustration 19–2 (continued)

your officers with this training. You should merge the training into the framework of emergency situations and fire fighting segments.

- **Basic Fire-Fighting Procedures**   **4 Training Hours**

This course should be taught by qualified fire fighters from a local fire department. Normally, the security officer's exposure to fire fighting is limited to the proper use and application of fire extinguishers, along with the rescue procedures noted earlier. It might also include shutting off electricity or other fuel sources pending arrival of fire fighters.

- **Firearms Training**   **24 Training Hours**

This course needs to include a minimum of

1. Company policy on use of weapons
2. Legal limitations
3. Firearms safety
4. Care and cleaning
5. Range firing
6. Qualification for record

Chapter twenty-one discusses firearms training and procedures suited for armed corporate and industrial security officers.

THE IMPORTANCE OF TRAINING RECORDS

Records supply a yardstick of performance. Records showing curriculum and security officers successfully completing basic in-service, and special training are a priority. Training records serve well in nearly any reasonable format and need to be complete. On request, you should supply each security officer with a copy of his or her training record. Proof of courses a security officer attends at his or her own expense, including college courses, needs to be entered in the department training record. A good training record is an excellent planning tool and a supporting document for budget requests. Training records also aid in establishing career development, programs, supervisor appraisals, and promotion lists. llustration 19–3 is an example of a useful security officer training record.

Illustration 19—3

EXAMPLE OF A TRAINING RECORD

Name: *John Doe*	SSAN: *000-00-0000*

Date of Birth: *00-00-0000*	Date of Hire: *00-00-0000*

Assignment Record: *Gate 3 – Rotating Shift 00/00 thru 00/00*

Gate 1 – Shift 2 – 00/00 thru 00/00

Control Center – Shift 1 – 00/00

Subject	No. Hours	Training Date	Skill Level
First Aid	*12*	*00/00*	*Level 3*
Fire Rescue	*8*	*00/00*	*Level 5*
Use of Force	*4*	*00/00*	*Level 3*

XYZ Company –
Security Form 12

20 In-service Training for Security Departments

Corporate and industrial in-service security training differs from basic or continued on-the-job (OJT) training mostly because of the difficulty in scheduling. For example, when your company decides to have training for the marketing department, all members of the department attend for a day or two. The operations of marketing can shut down during the training time without any problem, and the cost of inactivity is offset by the increased abilities after the sessions. Your security department, however, cannot shut down for training and leave the company unprotected; instead, you have to find other ways of scheduling training. Your job of designing, developing, and conducting in-service training for security officers has great importance, but it is often difficult to manage. This chapter will help you to find the proper mix of training and offers creative ways of getting the important job done properly. You'll also discover how important instructors are to in-service training and how to choose the right mix of instructors to receive the maximum benefit from the effort.

CREATIVE WAYS TO FIND IN-SERVICE TRAINING FACILITIES

When we think of training, we think of classrooms, probably because that tradition runs from the days of kindergarten forward. Although some elements of in-service training need a classroom environment, you should try to locate facilities that relate to the security jobs and keep your training focused. A classroom is often like attending a movie. When you depart the movie and return to reality, your memories of the movie soon fade. In schools and colleges, the classroom serves as a base of instruction over several months; however, in-service training normally lasts about two hours, just as the movie referred to.

Whenever possible, have your in-service training sessions in a nearby working environment, such as a warehouse. The surroundings will have a familiar feel because that's where the officers work, and it removes the problem of leaving training in a controlled, sanitized place and reentering the real world. When using performance-oriented training techniques, the familiar work environment setting also trains the officers in the same place they will later apply the training during their daily work. To obtain the most from your in-service training, keep the training environment realistic.

WHY BOTHER WITH IN-SERVICE TRAINING?

A person who states he or she has 20 years of experience in corporate and industrial security might be saying he or she actually has 1 year of experience 20 times, often making the same errors repeatedly. Seldom will a person learn from their own experience alone; however, with meaningful controlled training, and collective experience supplied systematically, the person can have professional growth through his or her own personal experiences. The key element of training involves an objective and goals, rarely achieved by just showing up for duty and getting through the shift.

Security skills not practiced by officers soon fade. For example, baseball teams have spring practice before each new season to retrain players who have not used their skills during the winter. Just as a baseball team's manager plans and conducts practice, as a security manager, you must develop your department's in-service training program by keeping close watch on your officers' proficiency levels and then supplying in-service training in areas of poor performance. You also must renew training in skills already known and "fine-tune" many to ensure security officers remain competent and prepared for any contingency.

HOW TO DESIGN YOUR IN-SERVICE TRAINING PROGRAM

Your first step in designing an in-service training program stems from considering the training gains and proficiency level needed for your department and company. Remember, the process of training, when conducted properly, causes people to change. They change through receiving accurate information and professional techniques altering their attitude and creating competence to perform specific tasks. Your basic security training supplies the foundation for officer performance, and continued training by supervisors supplies important career guidance; your in-service training supplies officers "readiness" capability. This component of your training program ensures each officer has the opportunity to grow professionally and doing so creates benefit and advantage to your department and company.

● *What Techniques Work Best*

Normally, you should use performance-oriented training for your in-service program. However, also recognize that some training, such as supplying information about new company or department policies, new or changed laws involving your department operations, and similar information-oriented subjects necessarily must have lecture presentations. Depending on the requirement, you might have a combination of lecture and performance oriented, or in firearms include an exercise such as qualification firing. Remember, however, the old adage supporting differences among lectures, videos, and performance-oriented approaches: "Tell me, I will forget. Show me, I may remember. Involve me, and I will remember."

● *About the Curriculum*

Your in-service training curriculum design needs to focus on whatever your protective responsibility calls for and your company's expectations. For example, whenever company pilferage figures climb, security officers controlling storage areas, gates, and other structures probably need added training about controlling pilferage through prevention and detection, coupled with what action to take when detecting pilferage. Other subjects to consider for in-service training include first aid, fire prevention and rescue, and authority and jurisdiction. Whenever company policy changes affect security operations, you should ensure a full understanding by your officers through in-service training. The key to your in-service training curriculum stems from need, instead of a standardized curriculum much as you use in basic security training. Also, choose subjects that have the potential of creating problems, such as use of force, arrest, and detection.

● *Using a P-I-E and O-M-R Design Approach*

Because your in-service training is "sandwiched" into daily operations denying the luxury of other training, such as basic courses where officers attend "school" and not concerned then with working, you need to use a slightly different approach to designing how you'll achieve your training goals.

Often, especially in large corporations with diversified security operations, or private security companies supplying services to several client corporations, a problem of keeping abreast of directives, changing methods, and floods of administrative requirements and training leads to dropping in-service training from the agenda. However, there is a solution by adopting a sound training management application to prevent becoming overwhelmed. The technique that can solve your dilemma includes the P-I-E system (plan-implement-evaluate) that helps you unravel the confusion and develop your in-service training design.

During your design planning phase, ask yourself what objectives, methods, and resources (O-M-R) you'll need in your in-service training program. This element creates the O-M-R approach that supports the P-I-E. The more you plan, the less trouble you will have implementing your in-service training program, because a well-developed plan shows you how. Your plan should also include what objectives (outcomes) you expect to achieve and what methods you will use according to the situation (i.e., performance oriented, lecture, or both coupled with other aspects). Also include resources you will require (e.g., space, audiovisual aids, time). The O-M-R strategy is your personal aid for designing in-service training. The implementing phase occurs when you are conducting the training. Remember to keep checking to see if your in-service training is going according to your plan. Keep your outcomes, methods, and resources in mind as you move to the actual training.

Evaluating the effectiveness of your in-service training program requires that you have a clear idea of what Outcomes (standards) you are expecting. Evaluate training Objectives first, and then the program's Methods and Resources. You achieve the objective when the student officers can do a certain thing according to the standards you formulate.

Evaluation becomes easier for you through developed training and learning objectives for your training. Assure, however, that your objectives get at what you want for outcomes. That is, be sure your written objectives match the objectives you are looking for in your program. Otherwise, you may end up measuring how perfect your "apples" are when you really wanted "oranges." There is a time dimension to evaluation; you can evaluate your training program as you go or immediately after the training completion when using performance-oriented techniques.

Illustration 20–1 shows an example diagram of the P-I-E and O-M-R design approach to consider when creating your in-service security training.

Illustration 20–1

P-I-E AND O-M-R MODEL EXAMPLE
FOR
IN-SERVICE TRAINING PROGRAM DESIGN

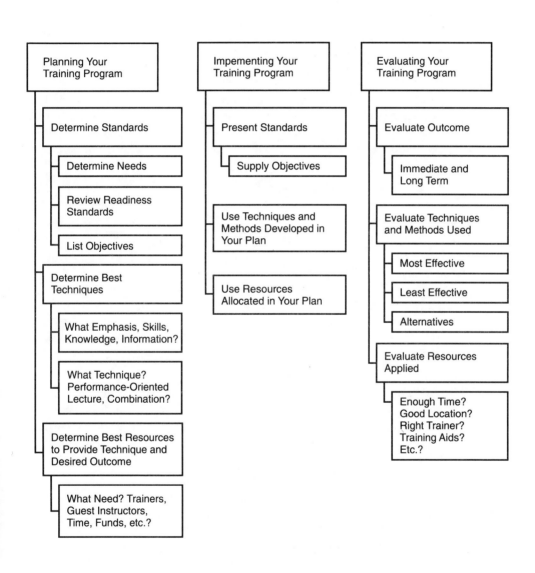

SCHEDULING IN-SERVICE TRAINING

Your next step after designing your in-service training program involves developing a schedule that supplies meaningful, regular training within your department budget. Several aspects need your consideration when working out a schedule. A few key questions to answer follow:

1. When will the training location (s) be available for department use? Depending on your situation, you probably share training facilities with the rest of the company. You will need to coordinate with whoever controls the facility uses and find acceptable dates.

2. When will your training materials be available? This could include equipment also shared by the company, or it might be a firing range, or special equipment you need to order or borrow from local agencies, such as a CPR dummy, and other items that your company probably would not have in its inventory.

3. What is the training capacity of the facility you will use? When you have a large security force this factor has importance. For example, when the company training facility has a capacity for 20 people and you have 40 people, your scheduling needs to accommodate each group.

4. When will your officers be available for in-service training? Certain times and days have better advantage than others. For example, weekends normally have less need for maximum security officer presence than weekdays. Other considerations might be specific days when shipping and receiving take place while other days of the week have less traffic and activity. Can you afford overtime and will officers object to training on weekends or days off even when paid extra for it? These are important questions that must factor in your scheduling.

5. What about rescheduling makeup classes for officers who miss important scheduled training? Rarely will you have 100% attendance, considering illness, added and unexpected last minute security requirements and other reasons for less than planned for attendance. Normally, the best course of action for scheduling training includes two or three identical sessions for the same group to allow those who can attend at one session.

6. How much time will each session need? In-service security training has importance, but because you must sandwich it into a busy operational routine, the best method includes trying to limit each session from two to four hours. Normally, in a two-hour session when planned prepared properly and when "intermediate objectives" used, the training is productive and over time reaches the total training objective. It's better to take two

months or more to reach the objective than to not have training because you don't feel there's enough time.

7. What subjects have priority over others, and how does that affect the other questions? When designing your training, you determine how you're going to achieve your in-service training objectives; however, now you need to take your list of subjects and decide how to fit them into the schedule. Always create a priority list with the essential subjects first and lesser subjects last. Then decide how many training hours each call for, and factor that into your scheduling effort.

8. Do you have the trainers and guest instructors figured into your scheduling? Often the complicated task of working out in-service training schedules gradually moves into a final draft, but make certain those persons acting as trainers, or guest instructors from the local police or fire department, EMTs, and others you might call on will be available when you schedule the session.

How to Consider the Time Factor

The old tradition of one-hour or 50-minute training sessions creates many problems for managers who somehow feel they must adhere to this schedule. For example, a presentation that takes 20 minutes efficiently and effectively stretches to one hour to "fill the time." Also, when subjects that need two hours are squeezed into an hour, important information doesn't reach the student officers. In either case, limited available training opportunity is misused. You need to do your best to be flexible in scheduling to allow training events that require significantly more or less time than an hour. When the training objective is achievable in 20 minutes, then schedule 20 minutes.

Don't Keep Your Training Schedule a Secret

The best rule of thumb for planning in-service training schedules is annually. You should always have a detailed schedule with all arrangements in place quarterly and post it for officers to see. You'll find that when people become well informed, they have better reception to whatever task needs their attention. Instructors and trainers also appreciate knowing what they must do well before time to do it. There will be changes when some unexpected event happens, and that's an easy task of posting the changes whenever they become known. It's a good idea to build in options, such as alternate trainers, alternate facilities, and other aspects that allow the scheduled training to continue even when certain elements need changing to achieve it.

CHOOSING AND MANAGING IN-SERVICE TRAINING INSTRUCTORS

In-service security officer training differs from other forms of training because of the time restrictions and operational responsibilities. It also differs because officers attending the training have experience, some a few months, others 20 years. The instructor of in-service training must have a different personal approach than in basic or continued training, since basic training normally involves "aspiring" new security officers while continued training involves a "shift" rather than a collected group from each shift as normally found with in-service training. An instructor that fares well in basic or continued categories of training might not do well within the in-service category. The following guidelines can help you to choose the best instructors for the session, including guest instructors from local agencies. Depending on your situation and skill levels of officers, you might choose a security officer as opposed to a supervisor to instruct a specific course. For example, when your in-service session involves a first aid or CPR review, one of your officers might be an EMT or certified in other ways as an instructor in the subject. He or she would be best qualified to instruct in that subject as opposed to a supervisor who might teach elements of first aid to student officers in the basic course. The key point with choosing instructors for in-service training can include finding a variety of highly qualified persons who have established expertise in a specific subject as opposed to an all-around instructor or trainer who might normally instruct in a variety of subjects. However, an expert qualification does not guarantee the person can successfully convey the information and knowledge to others. An EMT who saved 50 lives using CPR might not be able to teach another person how to perform the task properly. Conveying information and knowledge needs certain attributes, and the following guidelines can help you select the right person by understanding the general principles of instruction beyond expertise in a specific subject.

General Qualifications to Look For

There are certain qualifications that an in-service training instructor must possess if he or she is to do an effective job of teaching.

1. *Knowledge of the Subject.* Obviously, instructors must know the subject if they will teach it to others. They should know more about the subject than they will have time to teach and should have enough background material and ready to answer any question on the subject.

2. *Knowledge of Techniques of Instruction.* A knowledge of how to instruct is a definite prerequisite to good instruction. The person needs to be equally proficient in performance oriented, lecture, or a mix of each.

3. *Personality of the Instructor.* A good personality is essential to good in-

struction. Personality is the sum of all those things about a person that cause responses from other people, either favorably or unfavorably.

4. *Training Leadership.* Instructors who are good leaders can develop proper habits, attitudes, appreciation, and character traits in their students and teach the information needed. The skill of leadership might be in any person for specific situations. For example, your supervisors must have a form of leadership to achieve their responsibilities; however, a good security officer might display leadership teaching CPR but in a broader sense on the job lack comparable leadership qualities.

5. *Professional Attitude.* The instructor having the proper professional attitude continuously adds to his or her store of knowledge and skills in their subject and makes every effort to improve their teaching ability. He or she also has a sympathetic understanding of his or her students' problems and is fair in dealing with each person.

PRINCIPLES OF IN-SERVICE TRAINING INSTRUCTION

The desired outcome of all instruction is student learning. When student officers cannot perform a skill better at the end of a training session than before it, no learning has resulted from the instruction. Instructors must realize that if the student failed to learn, the instructor failed to teach. Instructors must accept responsibility for their students' learning and look first to themselves and their presentation for the cause of any failure.

• *The Three-Step Instructional Process*

The instruction process is the basic method for teaching intermediate objectives or the entire training objective. It is a three-stage process: presentation by the instructor, application or practice by the student officers, and evaluation by the instructor. Within this framework, the instructor applies specific instructional methods and techniques for achieving the most effective teaching-learning situation.

Presentation

In this stage of the instructional process, students gain the basic concept of what they will learn. They may gain the concept by completing a task, by listening to the instructor's explanation, or by watching a demonstration by the instructor. For most subjects, effective presentation has a combination of these activities.

Application

In this stage of the instructional process, students receive an opportunity to apply or practice the new concepts gained in the presentation stage. Although all three steps of the instruction process are necessary for effective learning, application is the most critical. All learning calls for conscious and successful response by the student. In planning and conducting instruction, the instructor should remember that it is not so much what the instructor does or says that teaches; instead it is what he or she causes the student to do.

Evaluation

In this phase of the instructional process, the instructor checks student response, keeps students informed of their success or progress, and prevents them from practicing incorrect responses. Evaluation includes formal testing of students ending the session or phase of instruction; however, the important type of evaluation is informal and is concurrent with the presentation and application stages of the instructional process. Accomplishing the evaluation stems from questions to the group following the explanation or demonstration of a teaching point and by close observation of students during practical work to detect errors and make on-the-spot corrections.

Eight Principles of Instruction

The eight principles of instruction are generalizations that describe conditions and requirements for effective teaching and efficient learning. They should guide the instructor using instructional process and in selecting and using specific methods and techniques of instruction. They all involve motivation. Your security officers attending in-service training must want to learn and improve before they can respond to the instruction. A major requirement for effective in-service teaching involves an instructor who can motivate the officers to have strong interest in the training and understand how it can help them professionally. The instructor must

1. Show a Need

You cannot assume security officers recognize the importance of learning or improving through in-service training. The instruction must begin with a clear reason and benefit for the officer attending the training session.

2. Develop an Intent to Learn

Before instruction, the security officers must realize that they are responsible for learning. It is not enough that they are physically present for training; they must be mentally willing to learn. Instructors must check their progress often and insist that each person apply himself or herself. Traditionally, security officers learn more when they feel responsible for learning.

3. Maintain Interest

Security officer interest is essential when in-service training achieves success. The use of strong personal force and enthusiasm, examples, and illustrations will help officers maintain a keen interest in the training. The more interesting the material is to the officers, the more readily they learn the skill. The instructor, however, must keep in mind that his or her responsibility is to teach not to entertain.

4. Encourage Early Success

Early success is a motivating force that sets the stage for further learning. A person's success tends to drive him or her to further effort and added successes. To the normal person, achievement brings a certain pleasure and satisfaction and is a stimulus to greater activity. During the stages of a training program, your instructor should have officers work at only worthwhile activities they can complete successfully.

5. Give Recognition and Credit

Recognition and credit provide strong incentives for learning. Officers desire, and have a right to expect, credit for work well done. Instructors must mention the good points of officers' performance and not dwell entirely on their mistakes. Start with favorable comments; then lead into suggestions for improvement.

6. Avoid Feelings and Emotional Responses That Interfere with Efficient Learning

Feelings affect learning. Security officers who become angry, resentful, embarrassed, frightened, or otherwise upset during training think about the source of their disturbance instead of the subject of the training session.

7. Use Competition

Friendly competition stimulates learning. However, avoid the problems that can stem from competition as those stated in principle 6. The competition needs attentive crafting for in-service training exercises on a win-win basis, so that, although one person or group does better, the other also has notable achievements. Competition normally works best when the comparison is nearly or actually tied.

8. Use Rewards

Rewards are powerful incentives. They can be as simple as a letter recognizing achievement or a certificate of training or as significant as a promotion. When an officer clearly has outstanding skill or potential, the instructor needs to recognize that and ensure you have the opportunity to authorize a reward appropriate to the situation.

QUICK REFERENCE GUIDE TO EFFECTIVE IN-SERVICE TRAINING

- **Objective:** Learning is most efficient when the security officer knows exactly what he or she is to learn and what you expect from him or her.
- **Response:** A security officer learns only what he or she responds to. His or her response may take many forms, such as listening, observing, reading, recalling, taking notes, reciting, writing, practicing, or solving problems.
- **Reinforcement:** Efficient learning calls for the security officer to know whether his or her responses are correct.
- **Realism:** This principle calls for constant considers to ensure the learning activities in training approximate situations in actual practice.
- **Background:** Learning stems from collective experience; new experiences correlate with past experiences. Your training is collective and workable experience presented systematically in a controlled training environment.

THE VALUE OF HANDOUT PACKETS

Because your in-service training for security officers is necessarily short sessions, maximum use of the opportunity grows with training handouts. For example, fires and arson have a prominent place in the security officer's responsibility of prevention and detection. One of your in-service training subjects annually should include instruction on fire prevention and arson detection, best presented by members of a local fire department. However, the training for this subject, limited to a couple of hours, hardly will enable a security officer to absorb all aspects and remember them later. Excellent guidance supplementing training happens using a handout that reviews the training and supplies additional information and procedures. Security officers prove valuable witnesses for fire investigators, either official or from insurance companies because normally the officer discovers and reports the fire and may be the only witness to its progress until arrival of fire fighters. Even after their arrival, they have so much to do, that little time is available for observing key elements that can later determine the cause, especially when not apparent and arson is suspected. The observations of the officer can also help identify the perpetrator in arson cases and in doing so serves your department and company well. In additional to training, the officer provided a handout as the one shown in Illustration 20–2 enables him or her to supply the information noted earlier competently. Develop a similar handout packet for each of your in-service training sessions regardless of the subject.

Illustration 20–2

EXAMPLE OF AN IN-SERVICE TRAINING HANDOUT PACKET

ARSON AND EXPLOSIVES

You can be a valuable witness aiding fire investigators, the security department, and company. That begins through an understanding of what information you can provide and what information helps the experts through knowing how they investigate a fire. Use the following information as your background study and review, coupled with creating a guide for your observations and notes. Whenever you discover a fire, call for help and immediately take notes on your observations. Whenever possible, call for a supervisor with a camera and color film to photograph the fire in progress. After the fire, write your case report, attach you notes or copies of them, and leave the matter to the security manager.

● The Fire Investigation Approaches

A fire investigation hinges on proving fire cause and origin. These facts cannot be established until all possible fire-causing factors except one have been conclusively disproven. Fire investigation is a cautious process of elimination, and this process must squarely consider the various possibilities of natural or accidental causes, including the possibility of arson. Arson remains among the most difficult investigations encountered.

Fires originating from electrical sources comprise a major category of accidental fires, and fires caused by improper or defective electrical wiring are a chief component of this category. Shorted electrical wiring also receives the blame often as a defense for arson.

Fires can begin in myriad ways. For example, flames often applied directly and intentionally to physical objects with an open-flame device like a cigarette lighter, a lit cigarette, or all manner of incendiary devices and often accelerated by a flammable liquid like gasoline, kerosene, or charcoal lighter fluid. Gunpowder trails strategically placed within a structure and ignited among combustibles are an effective means of arson. Also, chemicals combined will create fire, often with the aid of a time-delay device such as a chemical-filled prophylactic suspended over another carefully situated chemical. Burning will happen when one chemical eats its way through the condom and falls into the chemical below. And a simple lit match applied to paper can make great havoc in a room packed with combustibles.

Long-term neglect of frayed electrical wiring and overloading of available circuitry with too many simultaneously operating appliances can cause a short circuit, arcing, and the spitting of flames into an open atmosphere. Natural gas lines, heating appliances, and electrical wiring components can be defectively manufactured or improperly installed, eventually leading to an explosion or fire.

Lightning can strike timber or other combustibles, causing the eruption of flames. Under certain environmental conditions, oily rags improperly stored in a confining but

(continued)

Illustration 20–2 (continued)

unsealed space can spontaneously combust. Even the sun reflected through a prism can sometimes generate enough heat to make dry vegetation burst into flames.

Occasionally, the cause of a fire is readily apparent, as when you may find two separate corners of wood paneling consumed by fire near the baseboard, in a V pattern, with charred crumpled paper lodged against the wall in both locations, loose matches, and a box of matches on the floor nearby. The obvious cause of this fire is arson. However, as finding a body with five bullet holes in vital areas you know the crime of murder happened, the big question is: Who is responsible? Usually, a fire's cause will not be immediately obvious. Nor is it prudent practice for you to assume the obvious and neglect to eliminate painstakingly every conceivable cause of the fire. Many arson fires are never detected, and of those detected, few are successfully investigated with the perpetrator prosecuted.

A fire investigation needs two separate approaches: (1) a quest for positive physical evidence showing a fire's most probable cause or (2) establishing the cause of a fire through negative proof. You should always watch for positive physical evidence, but such proof often is ellusive, especially when a skilled, professional arsonist is the perpetrator.

Negative proof tends to support the truth of fire causation through a compilation of evidentiary artifacts that were not present at the fire scene. In forming a theory based on negative proof, you must carefully sort through and consider all data collected. Using the approach of negative proof, arson can sometimes be proven to be the only plausible way a fire began. Certainly, if no electric current or natural gas was flowing at the time of a fire, for example, if neither electric nor gas utilities service connected at the time of a fire in a building, that fact supplies absolute negative proof that the fire could not have resulted from accidental reasons related to natural gas or electricity.

Electricity and electrical wiring are often closely identified with the eruption of fire. Three of the most infamous and costly fires in America have been attributed to electrical sources. For example, a fire at the MGM Grand Hotel, Las Vegas, Nevada, during 1980 that killed 85 persons was directly traced to an improperly connected flexible metal conduit.

There's always have good reason to suspect electricity and electrical wiring as having played a part in any structural or vehicular fire where electrical current was or could have been running through a circuit. Yet it seems that electricity and faulty wiring too often serves as the whipping posts of fire causation. They are convenient scapegoats to pin fire cause, normally concealing disinterest or incompetence of investigators. It is also a handy scapegoat for desperate criminal defendants seeking to ward off blame where arson is alleged. Also, it's a favorite misdirecting element for a professional arsonist or a person who researched fires at the public library and recognizes the ease in which most investigators' will accept electrical causes for fires.

(continued)

Illustration 20–2 (continued)

• For Security Officer Observers

Examining the burning building is important while the fire is in progress, noting if windows, doors, or other openings are closed, open, or locked. Observe walls to note any suspicious condition, such as a breakthrough that might have happened from an explosion or a burned-out section where the fire might have originated. You should walk completely around the building at a distance, observing the smoke patterns on the tops of the windows and doorways. The pattern will show the direction the fire is burning because of drafts and ventilation.

You should note the location and extent of the fire, and whether it's concentrated in a specific part of the building. Also, when more than one burning happens within the location you should observe their relationship to each other when possible and record the observation in your notes. Two or more separate fires at one location may show arson. However, there might have been only one original fire, with other fires created by other circumstances. For example, when observing the burning residue,

- You should carefully note the color and location of flames, which may indicate the intensity of the fire and the type of materials burning.

- Steam and smoke, particularly at the start of a burning, may aid you in determining what substances are burning and the type of substance that started or accelerated the fire. Attentive observation of the smoke can be of considerable importance because its appearance and its odor, including its chemical composition, may yield information that may be of definite value.

- Smoke is largely of carbon, mineral ash, and partly consumed organic materials, with a variety of invisible gases that give to the smoke most of its odor. Oil, gasoline, creosote, tar, paint, and like organic materials having a petroleum base usually burn with a black carbonaceous smoke. Black material in smoke is indicative that some such material is being burned and is of great importance in arson because of the common use of like materials in starting fires.

- Wood smoke is usually gray or white, although sometimes, when appearing black, may show where the air supply is poor or the wood is green, making a lower burning temperature. It is unlikely that a dry wood fire will show much black in the smoke.

- White clouds appearing before the fire fighting equipment extinguish a fire indicates combustion of moisture laden substances.

- Reddish-brown or yellow smoke indicates burning of nitric acid, nitrates, nitrated plastics, celluloid, or products having a nitrocellulose base. The presence of reddish-brown or yellow smoke in premises where materials of

(continued)

Illustration 20–2 (continued)

this type are seldom present shows uses of a substance to aid the spread of the burning (accelerants).

- Grayish smoke emerges from loosely placed substances, such as straw and hay that give off flying soot and ash.

- Smoke odor is an added means of identifying the substances being consumed by fire. Ammonia, used by an incendiary keeps fire fighters away from the burning and offsets the odor of gasoline, is readily recognizable. Gunpowder, gasoline, rubber, alcohol, manufactured gas, linseed oil, turpentine, paints, thinners, and lacquers have distinguishable odors. Feathers, wood, and hair give off a typical sulfurous odor because of their high sulfur content. Vegetable materials may produce acrid or aromatic odors, which may give you some indication about the fuel used.

- Note the manner of burning, whether slow or rapid, to learn whether accelerants used or whether highly combustible materials are burning.

- Circulate through the crowd. Watch faces and actions of onlookers and take note of any spectator who seems to be getting personal satisfaction from the fire. Pyromaniacs enjoy flames and excitement. The best place to look for them is at the scene of his or her own fire.

- Note weather during the burning. Take color photographs and make sketches during the burning when possible.

• Burning Factor Reminder

Combustion or burning is the rapid oxidation of substances accompanied by generation of heat and light. Burning happens only when three essential ingredients are present:

1. Fuel
2. Oxygen
3. Temperature high enough to maintain combustion.

Withdrawal of the fuel, elimination or exclusion of oxygen, or lowering of temperature will extinguish the burning.

Although fuels may be gaseous, liquid, or solid, combustion usually happens when they are in a finely divided vaporous state. With many materials, oxidizing happens slowly at room temperature. However, for oxidations to reach the point of combustion, the materials must be heated. When heated, an oxidizing agent gives off oxygen, which in turn has an intense attraction for any fuel. When reaching the ignition temperature, a violent reaction happens.

Most ordinary combustibles are compounds of carbon and hydrogen with the frequent addition of mineral matter and oxygen. When they burn completely and freely in air, the carbon reacts with the oxygen to form carbon dioxide, the

(continued)

Illustration 20-2 (continued)

hydrogen combines with the oxygen to form water vapor, and the mineral matter stays behind as ash.

Several factors contribute to the spreading of a fire. Drafts and air supply directly affect behavior of fire. A fire started in a completely closed space will soon become extinguished because of use of the available oxygen and generation of noncombustible gases that smother the fire. Conversely, the combustion rate greatly increases when the slightest chimney action exists where the hot gases and flame from the fire contact combustible material. Disastrous fires have resulted in large buildings where the elevator shafts or stairways served as chimneys to direct the up rushing flames and gases.

• Other Factors that may Influence the Spread of Fire

- Dryness of surrounding vegetation or of the structure itself
- Presence of rain or amount of humidity
- Temperature of the surrounding air
- Building construction, including wooden partitions, unprotected doors and windows, elevator shafts and stairways, overhanging eaves, and wooden shingles.

• Explosive Fires

An explosion is the rapid and violent combustion of a material (solid, liquid, or gas) with resultant pressure and heat. While an explosion is distinguishable from a fire, a fire may result as the final manifestation of an explosion. Sometimes, an explosion and fire may need to be investigated simultaneously.

(continued)

Illustration 20–2 (continued)

SECURITY OFFICER'S GUIDELINES
FOR
DISCOVERY OF THE FIRE OR EXPLOSION

- Date and time of the fire/explosion and exact location where it happened?
- Who discovered the fire/explosion?
- Who gave the alarm and how was it given?
- What was the exact time of notification?
- How long before fire fighters arrived?
- Any delay in the notification of the fire department? Why?
- How was the fire/explosion discovered?
- Color of smoke observed?
- Were windows and doors open?
- Were windows and doors locked?
- Did fire fighters have to force entry to structure?
- Were windows, doors, or other parts blew out?
- Any vapors inside the structure?
- Size of fire and intensity?
- Spread of fire?
- Speed of fire spread?
- Amount of smoke—interior?
- Direction fire traveled while spreading?
- Point of origin of fire when obvious?
- Unusual smells or characteristics of fire?
- Any attempts to hinder the progress of fire fighters? If so, who? If so, reasons?
- Attempts of occupants to extinguish the fire?
- Reactions and attitudes of occupants?

Information from Observation of the Scene Exterior—While Burning

- Color of smoke?
- Smoke venting from (roof, windows, doors, eaves, etc.)?
- All smoke same color—each location?
- Photographs from all sides and angles of structure fire in progress?
- Weather at the time of the burning?

(continued)

Illustration 20–2 (continued)

- Are suspect footprints at the scene? Where?
- Are suspect tire tracks at the scene? Where?
- Footprints and tire tracks photographed and protected?
- Any other suspect items found outside the structure (e.g., gas cans, matches, clothing, tools)?
- Were they photographed and reported?
- Observation of onlookers and take photographs
- Note any interior explosions during structure burning
- Get names and addresses of victims and witnesses
- Get names and official address of fire-fighting personnel.
- Note any other observations or material information.
- Which area of the structure suffered the greatest amount of damage?
- Was it an unusual location for a fire starting or explosion to happen?
- Tampering with warning devices?
- Tampering with fire-fighting equipment or fire control systems?

(continued)

Illustration 20–2 (continued)

QUICK REFERENCE CHECKLIST
FOR
SECURITY OFFICERS AND MANAGERS FIRES,
FIRE PREVENTION, AND ARSON

Conditions Necessary for a Fire to Occur:

1. Adequate fuel (combustibles)
2. Source of oxygen (air)
3. Sufficient ventilation to replenish oxygen supply
4. Application of heat at a temperature high enough to permit ignition

Types of Fire:

1. Flame is the visible result of oxidation of a gas. The gas may be in its natural state, for example, methane (swamp gas), natural gas, or hydrogen. Or gas may be formed by evaporation, for example petroleum products and alcohol, distilled, or pyrolyzed from a solid such as paper and wood.
2. A glowing fire is the absence of flames such as a coal or charcoal fire.

A source of heat is necessary to start a fire. Heat may be transmitted by

A. Conduction

Conductivity Chart   **K Factor**

☐	Copper	.92 {Excellent Conductor of Heat}
☐	Aluminum	.50
☐	Iron/steel	.16
☐	Glass	.0025
☐	Wood	.0005
☐	Paper	.0003 (poor conductor of heat)

B. Convection

☐   Air surrounding the flame is heated and rises.

C. Radiation

☐   Flash points and self-ignition temperatures of some common fuels. (Flash points are the minimum temperatures at which a substance will burn if a source of ignition is available.)

Self-ignition temperature is the point at which a substance burns spontaneously.

(continued)

Illustration 20–2 (continued)

Fuel	Flash Point (°F)	Self-Ignition (°F)	
Acetone	0	1,000	☐
Cellosolve	100	460	☐
Denatured alcohol	60	760	☐
Ethyl alcohol	55	750	☐
No. 1 fuel oil	110–165	490	☐
Gasoline	−50	495	☐
Petroleum ether	−50	475	☐
Mineral spirits	85	475	☐
Toluene	40	1,026	☐
Turpentine	95	488	☐
Methyl alcohol	54	878	☐

Ignition temperatures of wood and wood products

Hard Oak		448–500	☐
White pine		500	☐
Redwood		467	☐
Red cedar		468	☐
Fir		489	☐
Paper		425–475	☐

Note: Prolonged exposure to heat lowers the ignition temperature. For example, white pine exposed to 362 °F for 12 minutes will ignite even though ignition temperature is 500 °F.

(continued)

Illustration 20–2 (continued)

CHARACTERISTICS OF SLOW- & FAST-BURNING FIRES

Slow	**Fast**
• Uniform, widespread damage overhead	• Extensive damage in a smaller area directly overhead
• Wide spreading across surface	• Narrow spreading across surface
• Large cracks in windows glass; heavily stained with smoke	• Small irregular cracks in glass with minimal smoke staining
• Uniform charring of wood and flat alligatoring	• Irregular charring and heavy, shiny alligatoring
• Cement and bricks seldom affected	• Pieces of cement and brick fall off due to intense heat

Note: The source of an interior fire may have been external

- Fire from an adjacent building
- Accelerants piled against the building.

Ignition Sources

- Matches, lighters.
- Sparks from machinery, electric motors, welding equipment and so on.
- Radiant heat; improperly insulated furnace, wood stove, fireplace or sunlight focused by a lens or lenslike object (broken glass, bottles, etc.).
- Friction: improper lubrication of machinery
- Overheated wiring due to improper fusing, wire diameter, wire composition (aluminum wire is known to cause fires).
- Chemical combustion: certain chemicals generate heat which, when confined, may burst into flames.

Melting Points of Substances

Substance	Melting Point (°F)
Aluminum	1150
Glass	1200
Brass (yellow)	1710
Bronze	1910*
Copper	1980
Cast Iron	2150

(continued)

Illustration 20–2 (continued)

Stainless steel	2550
Wrought iron	2750
Steel	2760

*Melting of metals with melting points above 1900 °F may indicate the pressure of accelerants.

Copper Wire Size Versus Amperage Safely Carried

No. 14	15 amps
No. 12	20 amps
No. 10	30 amps

Temperatures of Light Bulbs

25 watt	110 °F
60 watt	260 °F
100 watt	261 °F
200 watt	307 °F
300 watt	389 °F

SMOKE COLOR CHART

Combustible	Color of Smoke
Vegetable compounds	White
Phosphorus	White
Sulphur	Yellow to brownish yellow
Gunpowder	Yellow to brownish yellow
Chlorine gas	Yellow/green
Wood	Gray to brown
Paper	Gray to brown
Cloth	Gray to brown
Cooking oil	Brown
Naphtha	Brown to black
Lacquer thinner	Brown to black
Turpentine	Black to brown
Petroleum products	Black
Tar, coal, plastics	Black
Rubber	Black

(continued)

Illustration 20–2 (continued)

FLAME COLOR VERSUS TEMPERATURE

Flame Color	Temperature	
Faint red	900 °F	480 °C
Red	975 °F	525 °C
Blood red	1050 °F	565 °C
Cherry red	1365 °F	740 °C
Bright red	1550 °F	845 °C
Orange	1725 °F	940 °C
Lemon	1825 °F	995 °C
Light yellow	1975 °F	1080 °C
White	2200 °F	1205 °C
Blue white	2550 °F	1400 °C

21 Qualifying Armed Security Officers

About 50% of corporate and industrial security officers carry firearms and that figure increases each year. Because the responsibilities and liabilities of armed security officers, this chapter supplies the basic firearms training and qualification procedures. Some states now have minimum standards for armed security officers; however, these standards normally apply to private security company officers opposed to proprietary officers. Check with your state and follow the minimum standards firearm guidance; when that is not a factor, use the following procedure. You may also want to use both.

Your armed security officers need a sound basic firearm training course and qualification with reviews and qualification each six months. Your training needs to include the use of deadly force each time you conduct firearms training and qualification. You need to point out specific court decisions regarding the misuse of firearms. That brings home the responsibility that armed security officers have and serves better than just stating laws and company policies. The latter has importance. However, actual civil or criminal prosecutions show the reality of error involving a firearm and the importance of training.

KEY COURT DECISIONS ABOUT LIABILITY FOR MISUSE OF FIREARMS

A key court decision you can apply to caution armed security officers and dispel many myths about the justification for using a firearm and deadly force is *Tennessee* v. *Garner* (105 S.Ct. 1694, 85 L.Ed. 2d 1, 1985), which provided that after notice of the intention to arrest a criminal suspect, and the suspect flees or forcibly resists, "The officer (police, however equally applies to a security officer protecting company property) may use all the necessary means to effect the arrest." The common law recognized a privilege to use deadly force when attempting to arrest a fleeing felon, but not to apprehend a fleeing misdemeanant. However, in this landmark case, the U.S. Supreme Court held justification of such force applies only "where the officer has probable cause to believe that the suspect poses a threat of serious physical harm, either to the officer or others." Any misuse of force in this situation, according to the Court, makes the unreasonable seizure of a person a violation of the Fourth Amendment.

This case involved a nighttime burglary. Two law enforcement officers answered a complaint of a prowler, and while investigating a 15-year-old boy ran from a residence and started to climb a 6-foot chain-link fence behind the property. With the aid of a flashlight, the officer could see the suspect's face and hands, saw no weapon, and were "reasonably sure" the suspect wasn't armed. However, to prevent the escape, the officer fired, killing Garner, the suspect. After the shooting, evidence found on the body included ten dollars in cash and a purse taken during the burglary. The Supreme Court held that the officer did not have probable cause to believe that serious physical harm was imminent.

This case, although involving law enforcement officers, has similarities to situations that an armed security officer might confront when detecting a burglar of a company building, and observing a suspect climbing a perimeter fence to escape.

The U.S. Supreme Court stated that the shooting of a nondangerous fleeing suspect is not such an important component of effective law enforcement that it outweighs the suspect's interest in his or her own life. The Court also held the Tennessee law was unconstitutional and generally that the Fourth Amendment prohibits the use of deadly force to prevent the escape of an apparently unarmed felony suspect unless it is necessary to prevent the escape and the officer has probable cause to believe that the suspect poses a significant threat of death or serious physical injury to the officer or others.

Other cases include *Giant Food, Inc.* v. *Scherry* (444 A.2d 483 Md., 1982). This decision contained an extensive discussion of liability where a security officer of Giant Food, Inc., knew that an escaping car contained robbers, fired two shots from a distance of 15–40 feet, and a bullet passed through a window across the street causing a female there to become emotionally distraught. Any legal privilege to shoot was only related to rights against the criminal. The company was liable for negligence to others. "The context is important in determining the reasonableness of the action taken, but the basic standard seems to be the same." The security officer could have obtained the license plate of the fleeing car. Although the robber had earlier brandished a weapon, he had not fired and had returned it to his belt before entering the car. The security officer should have known that he was untrained and unskilled (this factor would distinguish the case from a trained officer) and that he was "literally shooting into the dark at a rapidly moving target."

Generally, your policy underlying your department firearms training for armed security officers needs to include a strong caution against using a firearm in any situation beyond defending oneself or another against obvious deadly force. Each situation needs a judgment call by the armed security officer, however, no reasonable justification allows deadly force to protect property, only to protect persons.

Your Three Primary Areas of Concern

Studies of security officer mishaps and misuse of firearms while on duty show three primary areas that need to shape your training program for armed officers:

1. Self-injury because of mishandling of the firearm
2. Injury to others, often innocent bystanders, because of lack of skill when firing the weapon.
3. Criminal and-or civil suits against both employers and employees resulting from the actions noted in (1) and (2).

No amount of training can promise elimination of weapons abuses or that firearms accidents will cease to happen. However, a firearm training program, as framed here, can reduce the chance of these types of problems. The necessity of training is apparent; the risks are too great without it.

SUGGESTED TRAINING FOR ARMED SECURITY OFFICERS

Effective firearm training for armed security officers needs two separate sessions. The first, must be classroom, although a mix of lecture and performance oriented. The second, calls for meaningful, realistic practice and qualification exercise on a firing range.

The Classroom

The following topics supply a "basic" or "initial" training program for armed security officers. Also noted are requirements for the postbasic course that armed officers need every six months.

Topic I: Legal and Policy Restraints

Basic or initial training course   3 hours
In-service training course (each 6 mo.)   2 hours

This phase of your firearms training needs to focus on state law, local ordinances, and when appropriate any special regulations governing actions of armed security officers. Supplement that information with company and security department policies and procedures. The topic has a built-in level of boredom calling for creative instruction that ensures each officer remains attentive. You can achieve that through an enthusiastic instructor who presents the topic in segments accompanied by real and hypothetical, but realistic, examples that officer might confront in your protective environment. The instructor needs to encourage the student officers to present their views on action to take according to the hypothetical scenario the instructor frames. The phase needs a comprehensive handout much like the example shown for fires in Chapter Twenty. The handout needs to include key court decisions on cases that relate to a situation a security officer might face, such as *Tennessee* v. *Garner.*

You may shorten the in-service six-month requalification phase; however, the basics need review coupled with any new court decision, laws, or policies that must be presented and discussed in the classroom setting. Prepare a new handout for each officer to review and study.

In any course, each topic presented also needs each officer to sign a statement of company policy, laws, and other information discussed in each session certifying that the officer received the training and confirming who presented it, the duration of training, and the signature verifying he or she understands the topic. When officers need to sign this type document, they have a tendency to grasp the gravity of the situation and show more interest. It also protects the company from lawsuits resulting from firearms misuse should that problem arise out of officer negligence or poor judgment.

Topic II: Firearms Safety and Care and Cleaning the Handgun or Shotgun

Basic or initial training course   2 hours
In-service training course (each 6 mo.)   1 hour

This topic supplies an opportunity for instructors to integrate lecture and performance-oriented training by having each officer "field strip" his or her firearm and inspect each part, spend considerable time cleaning it and reporting any deficiencies. During the initial course, a detailed safety presentation ensures that the officer has no question about the responsibilities he or she has when carrying a firearm on duty. Often, during the basic course, the officer might not have former exposure to firearms or at least the type you authorize them to carry. You're also developing a habit of caring for the weapon, but an added benefit includes getting them over the fear and comfortable handling the firearm through disassembly, cleaning, and reassembly. It is also an excellent time to discuss and inspect ammunition. In the basic session and later in-service training each six months, holsters and leather equipment, coupled with handcuffs and other items, should be cleaned as appropriate and inspected for serviceability by the instructor.

The in-service training sessions each six months should review safety, maybe with any new information and always include care, cleaning, and inspection. A statement of training with the officer's signature should also be completed for this topic. The instructor should verify the serial number of each firearm and record these numbers for later use by the firing range instructor. Also, prepare a comprehensive handout for each officer for this topic each session.

Topic III: Written Examination (1 Hour)

Generally, a 20-question written test based on the material presented in topics I and II should be administered each officer, in both the basic and in-service firearm training. The officer needs to answer 70% of the questions correctly for a passing score, necessary to continue the firearms course. Even officers who have carried a weapon for years and qualified repeatedly need to take the test (different each time) to ensure that they don't fall into an attitude of laxity.

THE FIRING RANGE

Armed security officers subject to the danger of deadly force directed at them differ from law enforcement officers who face peril daily. Security officers have a "defensive" role, normally surrounded by other forms of layered security that an intruder must penetrate to reach the officer. Rarely does a security officer confront a sudden, violent attack and deadly force. Instead, the armed security officer generally creates an effective deterrent to violence, whereas an unarmed officer can do little against an armed intruder. The firing range segment of training needs to focus on competence, accuracy, and systematic applications opposed to "combat or survival" methods necessary for law enforcement officers.

Topic I: Principles of Marksmanship

Basic (initial) training   2 hours
In-service training   1 hour

This part of firearm training needs to focus on the following elements:

Shooting Stance for Handgun or Shotgun

The key element of shooting stance (see Illustration 21–2) stems from what's comfortable for the person, yet provides solid balance. Normally, the stance adjustment stems from one with the feet spread apart with the same general concept of a person taking an important photograph with a camera. When doing that task, the person wants to be well-balanced and steady to focus on the target being photographed and carefully tripping the shutter. The same basic concept applies to firing a handgun. Officers should also learn to fire effectively from behind a barricade cover (also shown later) to simulate a building and from sitting and prone positions. The idea stems from being effective despite the position and helps to strengthen the concept of "readiness" for any contingency. The stances for shooting a shotgun need to apply the same principles, ensuring that the officer can effectively handle the increased recoil without losing his or her balance.

Grips and Gripping the Handgun

The grips on a handgun often create many problems for shooters. Obviously, properly designed grips that fit the person's hand perfectly have much importance in the accuracy of shooting. Often, the grips don't fit small hands or vice versa; however, the varieties of commercially available grips for each type firearm supply the solution to that problem. You should always match the grips on handgun to the size and the type of grip the officer feels comfortable with and can use to control the gun effectively and safetly. Gripping the handgun develops from attentive, slow shooting experience beginning in dry fire exercises. The relationships of grips to a handgun relate to driving a car: with the seat poorly adjusted, the pedals too far or too close, and other problems, the driver can neither feel comfortable nor operate the vehicle effectively and safely. Start with the grips to fit the person's hand; then ensure that the officer develops an effective and safe habit of gripping the handgun during drawing and firing. (Also see sighting, discussed next.)

Sighting

The common stance copied today stems from Sgt. Jack Weaver of the Los Angeles County Sheriff's Department developed over 20 years ago and dubbed "Weaver method." Although the Weaver grip and method have merit, its design intention involved shooting competition, that is, target shooting, and somehow became the standard for law enforcement and most firing range instructors. The problem that comes from forcing shooters to use a certain grip that uses a premise of ensuring correct and accurate shooting is that in a real situation the shooter's mind focuses on doing all the "right things" and not on saving his or her life by accurate shooting. Two-handed shooting no doubt steadies the shooter and enables a good sight picture. However, the officer needs to use a two-handed grip that ensures comfort and promotes effective, accurate, and safe shooting. Illustrations 21–3 through 21–9 show the necessity of developing a natural and accurate sight picture. With practice, using both dry fire and live fire but absent the pressure of which techniques the instructor thinks best or having to fire a certain number of rounds in a few seconds, and enduring all the normal rituals found in "ego" training styles, officers can develop the skill of effective sight pictures.

Trigger Control

The essential element of trigger control stems from smooth operation of it. Jerking the trigger, often the case with novice shooters, destroys a good stance, a good grip, and great sight picture. Learning to control the trigger has great importance to ensure the other efforts work as they should. Although instructors often insist that only the tip of your index finger should rest on the trigger, in theory a correct basic technique, some shooters that have deadly accuracy put their finger much further on the trigger. The rule of thumb remains—if it works for you and enables the desired result, that's what you need to do. Theories, rituals, procedures, and other things that create the framework for teaching a person to handle a gun and shoot well create the starting point. From those basic, the officer must, to be effective, begin to develop and adjust them to his or her specific needs. I've observed instructors "chewing out" a student officer for not using the right positions and techniques, although the officer consistently had 100% deadly hits. Don't allow yourself to become the "ego instructor"; instead lead and guide the student to being the best he or she can be.

Breathing Control

Practicing breathing creates a habit that pays off in a real shooting situation, and that's where breathing becomes a problem. Breathing hard is like jerking the trigger; it spoils everything else that might otherwise be perfect. In reality, hard or erratic breathing moves the gun around and nearly guarantees a miss. You will want to let out part of your breath and then hold it while you squeeze off the rounds needed. When shooting slowly, breathe normally, and let out some and hold it as you make each shot. That will eventually be an unconscious habit that merges with all techniques you learn or teach and modify to make each officer effctive, and safe.

Loading and Unloading Techniques for Handgun or Shotgun

Armed security officers often have little or no experience with handguns or shotguns. You need to keep each segment simple because simplicity plus slow, deliberate procedures create good habits both for shooting competence and safety. The true way to speed and accuracy stems from slow, deliberate and simple practice.

This topic, covering the six elements just listed, has best results when carried out with "dry fire" techniques that involve practicing with unloaded weapons in the same way as though loaded. Much of the problem new and often veteran shooters have involves getting the firearm from the holster to firing position smoothly and quickly. Trying to be fast creates a snatch and grab tendency that wastes time and makes any attempted firing inaccurate. Snatch and grab fast-draw artists often shoot themselves in the foot or leg. The best solution to delivering the handgun to shooting position involves moving the arm and hand in a natural and circular motion as noted in Illustration 21–1. When you teach your officers to draw their handguns slowly and come into firing position in a direct line naturally, their actions become a habit related to the same subconscious effect as when learning to drive or operating a car. You wouldn't think of teaching new drivers or testing veteran drivers by having them drive along a street and slam on the brakes periodically to practice stopping the car fast. Instead, you teach them to stop the car slowly and deliberately. However, when an emergency suddenly appears, the driver learning properly will slam on the brakes without thinking about it. The same effect comes from learning and continuing to practice drawing a handgun slowly and carefully. Remember, the officers aren't competing for a trophy; they are learning to protect themselves and others against any persons threatening them with deadly force. Also, your policy should forbid cross draw and shoulder holsters. They have a time and place, but for experts only, and no regular place in the security officer positions. Sidearms, worn to promote accuracy and safety, will always be on the right or left side depending on whether the officer is right or left handed, and drawn and swept directly up and on line with their target. Their shooting stance needs to be comfortable and supply maximum balance. Illustration 21–1 shows a comfortable stance that promotes accuracy and safety.

Illustration 21–1

EXAMPLE OF CIRCULAR AND NATURAL DRAWING TECHNIQUES FOR HANDGUNS

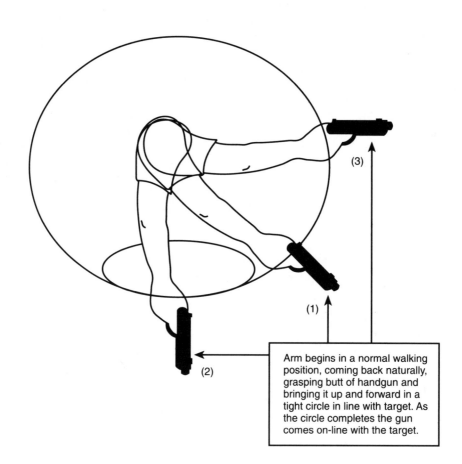

(3)

(1)

(2)

Arm begins in a normal walking position, coming back naturally, grasping butt of handgun and bringing it up and forward in a tight circle in line with target. As the circle completes the gun comes on-line with the target.

Illustration 21–2

EXAMPLES OF VARIOUS SHOOTING STANCES

One Hand Sideways Stance   Two Hand Weaver Stance

Examples of Various Shooting Position Stances

Another important purpose in your dry fire practice involves student officers developing a comfortable and accurate sight picture. This element normally causes most novice shooters great problems and often extends to those who have been shooting for many years but not properly. The fastest way to determine improper sight pictures will be live firing and consistent target misses. The other factors noted—gripping the handgun, trigger control, breathing, and stance—can easily affect the sight picture. You need a qualified, trained, and experienced firearms instructor to supply hands-on training in all the elements; however, Illustrations 21–3 through 21–9 supply examples you should include in handouts of this training topic.

Illustration 21–3

EXAMPLE OF SIGHT ALIGNMENT AND SIGHT PICTURE

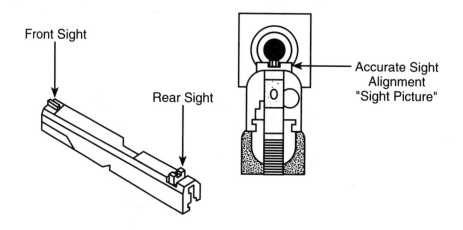

Illustration 21–4

EXAMPLE OF PERFECT SIGHT ALIGNMENT

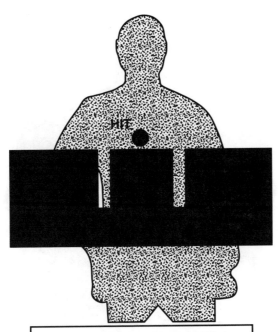

Perfect alignment. Top of front sight blade level with type of rear sight. Equal amount of light on both sides of front sight blade in notch of rear sight. Perfect Hit.

Illustration 21–5

EXAMPLE OF DEFECTIVE SIGHT ALIGNMENT

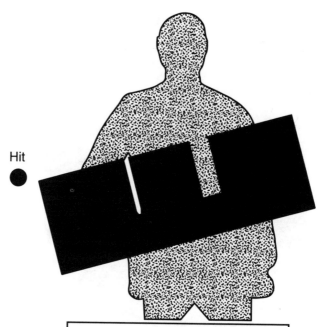

Hit

Top of front sight level with top of rear sight blade. Too much light on right side of front sight in rear sight notch. Handgun canted to left, bullet strikes left of target.

Illustration 21−6

EXAMPLE OF DEFECTIVE SIGHT ALIGNMENT

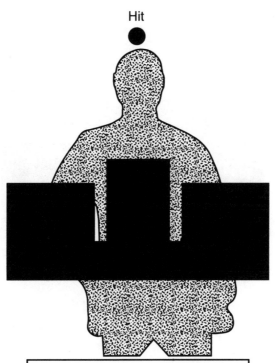

Top of front sight higher than top of rear sight, equal amount of light on both sides of front sight blade in rear notch. Bullet strikes high.

Illustration 21–7

EXAMPLE OF DEFECTIVE SIGHT ALIGNMENT

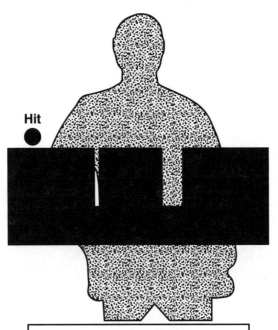

Hit

Top of front sight level with top of rear sight with too much light on the rear side of the front sight blade in the rear sight notch. Bullet strikes to left.

Illustration 21–8

EXAMPLE OF DEFECTIVE SIGHT ALIGNMENT

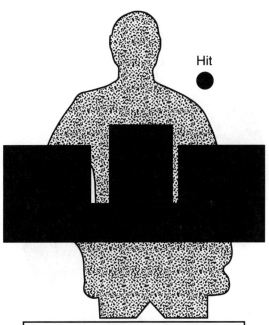

Top of front sight blade higher than rear sight. Too much light on left side of front side blade in rear sight notch. Bullet strikes high and right.

Illustration 21–9

EXAMPLE OF DEFECTIVE SIGHT ALIGNMENT

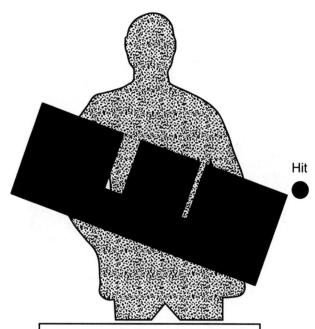

Top of front sight blade level with top of rear sight, too much light on left side of front sight blade in rear sight notch. Handgun canted to right, bullet strikes to right.

Topic II: Live Fire Course One

Practice (8 hours)

Practice courses supply armed security officers with an opportunity to apply all the skills learned and practiced in dry fire except with live ammunition. The concept of practice rounds stems from performance-oriented techniques that allow the student to develop without the stress of testing. The practice course should always be identical to the qualification course discussed later. Student officers should proceed at their own pace during practice fire, and instructors should ensure each receives their attention to correct errors. The following table shows a suggested procedure, however as noted earlier, check with state and local certification officials for the required procedures when they apply to your situation. When those need application, substitute them for those shown here.

DISTANCE	POSITION	NO. ROUNDS
10 feet	Standing, one hand	10 rounds
21 feet	Standing, two hands	10 rounds
35 feet	Standing, two hands	10 rounds
35 feet	Kneeling, two hands	10 rounds
45 feet	Standing, one hand (barricade cover)	10 rounds
45 feet	Standing, one Hand (barricade cover, opposite hand)	10 rounds
55 feet	Prone, two hands	10 rounds
55 feet	Sitting, two hands	10 rounds
75 feet	Standing, one hand (barricade cover)	10 rounds
75 feet	Standing, one hand (barricade cover, opposite hand)	10 rounds

The 100-round course supplies all the positions and training for assuming the positions that a security officer may require should a defensive situation with deadly force develop on the job. The barricades simulate shooting from the side or corner of a building, for example, within an industrial complex, amid warehouses, or waterfront setting. Sitting and prone positions simulate using cover and creating a low profile while gaining the advantage of steadiness for distance shooting. By learning to fire in different positions, the armed security officer increases the "readiness" capability for any contingency. Examples of barricade positions are shown in Illustration 21–10.

Illustration 21–10

EXAMPLES OF BARRICADE COVER
THE BARRICADES CAN BE PERMANENT OR PORTABLE

Topic III—Firearm Qualification Course

Practice 8 hours

Although your local requirements might dictate a timed firing course for qualification, avoid that when you can. Timing or requiring officers to fire a certain position and number of rounds in a few seconds causes significant harm that can cause the death of an officer in a real situation. Dozens of law enforcement officers training in timed conditions (and still have those requirements) were killed by unskilled assilants and found without ammunition having used it all in the same manner taught on the firing range and then becoming vulnerable to the assailant. Timing causes officers to develop a subconscious habit of firing all their ammunition as fast as possible. Most officers carry a full handgun and two reloads, normally the same or similar to ammunition expended during timed sessions requiring it fired within a few seconds. Firing fast also serves no purpose, since few if any rounds under real conditions will hit their target, especially when the intruder is also firing at the officer. Timing inspires panic shooting instead of careful, accurate shooting. On the firing range for qualification, timing causes the officer to be thinking about rituals and about hurrying instead of concentrating on developing accuracy. It's not a volume of rounds fired that matter in a shootout; it's how many rounds fired that hit the assailant that matter. Normally, one or two well-placed rounds will serve to neutralize the assailant.

Qualification scoring often creates more problems than it solves. Having different levels of qualification, for example, "marksman," "expert," "master," and others depending on the location, creates "losers." Remember that motivation has room for some competition, but a "win-win" situation; scoring should be either passing or failing, with failing calling for continuing to try until reaching passing. An exception might be a person who has fear of guns or just cannot develop the skill necessary. Passing a firing session should require a minimum of 60% of the rounds fired during the exercise to hit within an acceptable area of the silhouette target. When instruction is correct and firing happens in a no-stress environment, most scores will be significantly higher.

The armed officers must practice and qualify with each firearm they carry on duty. A log, mentioned earlier, with the make, model, serial number of the weapon used to qualify should remain on file as proof of qualification. Also, attach the time, date, range location, type of course fired, and instructor's names to the log.

When officers carry or might use shotguns (or other types of firearms) on duty, they must receive training and practice, and they must be qualified by serial number also. A shotgun course normally should be fired at a maximum of 35 feet, with other firing positions at 25 feet and 15 feet. Normally, 10 rounds at each position will be sufficient to qualify the officer. Illustration 21–11 shows suggested shotgun firing positions.

Illustration 21–11

EXAMPLE OF PRACTICE AND QUALIFICATION FIRING RANGE

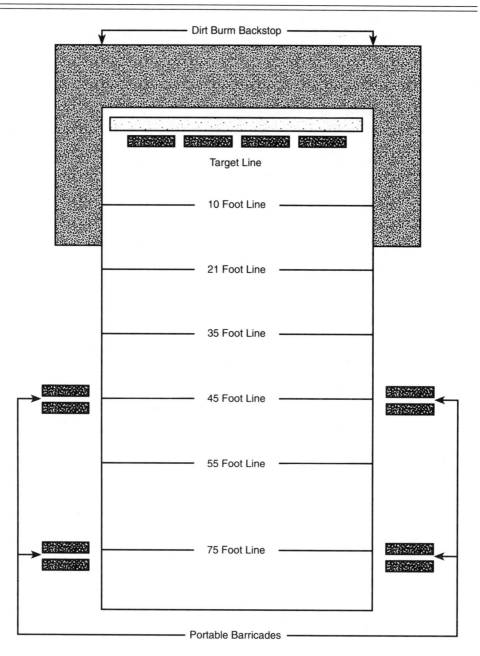

TARGETS AND AMMUNITION

Your firearms training course effectiveness also involves selecting the proper targets for the officers to use on a firing range and what type ammunition they use. Both have significance as explained in the paragraphs that follows.

What Target to Use

The target you use might depend on state requirements for scoring hits, however when you have a choice, use a target that has realistic features. Several companies produce photographic targets showing an actual person holding and pointing a gun at the officer. This type of target serves two important purposes. First, the officer develops a sense of when deadly force can be authorized, that is, a gun being pointed at them by a person, and second, it eliminates the "target shooting" concept of the old bull's-eye or competition shooting, actually a sport. Some companies produce similar targets using a cartoonlike person pointing a gun; these are better than a standard silhouette target, but still are a second choice. Last, you can choose a silhouette target, for example, the FBI style that has no scoring rings are best. The farther you can move from the bull's-eye concept, the better, and the more realism you can create, the less liability problem you might face later. The extra cost of using photographic targets far outweighs an officer shooting without reason or probable cause and where a person loses his or her life or is injured needlessly, coupled with your company becoming judged responsible and paying huge sums of money resulting from a court judgment. The officer might also lose economically and could face criminal charges that ultimately stem from your lack of adequate training techniques.

How to Choose the Best Ammunition

The ammunition an officer uses for live fire practice and qualification must always be the same ammunition he or she carries on duty. The first consideration comes from liability possibilities. For example, you go to great lengths to ensure proper training, everything is the best, and you spare no expense or time to ensure that each officer has a high degree of competence and judgment, but you use reloaded wad cutters on the firing range. In a lawsuit situation, a good lawyer will show that your training ammunition differs from that used by the officer on duty and during the shooting that led to the suit. What you've done is neutralize the qualification. As noted earlier, the serial number of the firearm and other details involving the firearm a security officer uses for training and carries on duty have importance for records of training and qualification coupled with proof of competence. Even when ammunition is interchangeable, the differences in actual firing are great, so always use the same ammunition carried and used on duty when you're training and qualifying armed security officers.

QUICK REFERENCE REVIEW AND GUIDE
FOR
CHAPTER TWENTY-ONE

- Begin your firearms training with key criminal and civil liability court cases and the laws pertinent to use and misuse of firearms.
- Stimulate interest and discussion among student officers through presenting real and realistic hypothetical situations similar to what they might face and collectively find solutions and actions acceptable.
- Give a realistic written examination on classroom subjects to further stimulate officer interest and attentiveness.
- Move to a firing range for teaching proper shooting techniques. Supply the basic framework and allow officers to develop adaptations that enable them to become accurate, responsible, and safe with firearms.
- Conduct dry fire exercises under actual range conditions.
- Conduct live fire practice exercises.
- Conduct firearms qualifications with realistic targets
- Use the same ammunition carried by officers on duty in the training sessions, and keep an accurate log of all events, including the serial numbers of the handguns used in training and qualification.

Appendix A
Physical Security Plan Guide

It is essential, in the best interest of security, that you develop and use a detailed physical security plan. Your plan should include at the least special and general security officer instructions, access and assets control, protective barriers and lighting systems, and so forth.

Appendix A supplies a sample physical security plan guide.

PHYSICAL SECURITY PLAN

1. **Purpose.** State the purpose of your plan.

2. **Area Security.** Define the areas, buildings, and other structures considered critical and establish priorities for their protection.

3. **Control Measures.** Define and establish restrictions on access and movement into critical areas. These restrictions can be categorized as personnel, vehicles, and material assets.
   a. Personnel (employee, visitor, vendor) access.
      (1) Controls pertinent to each area or structure.
         (a) Authority for access.
         (b) Access criteria for
            i.   Company employees.
            ii. Visitors.
            iii. Vendors.
            iv. Maintenance persons.
            v.   Contractor persons.
            vi. Others.

(2) Identification and control.
    (a) Describe the system to be used in each area. If a badge system is used, a complete description covering all aspects should be used in disseminating requirements for identification and control of persons working or conducting business within the company areas.
    (b) Application of the system to include
        i.   Company personnel.
        ii. Visitors to restricted areas.
        iii. Visitors to administrative areas.
        iv. Vendors.
        v.   Contractor persons.
        vi. Maintenance persons.
        vii. Others.
b. Material control.
    (1) Incoming.
        (a) Requirements for admission of material and supplies.
        (b) Search and inspection of material for possible sabotage hazards.
        (c) Special controls on deliver of supplies or other shipments into restricted areas.
    (2) Outgoing.
        (a) Documentation required.
        (b) Controls.
        (c) Sensitive shipments (when applicable).
c. Vehicle control.
    (1) Policy on company vehicles.
    (2) Policy on employee vehicles.
    (3) Policy on vendor and visitor vehicles.
    (4) Controls for entrance into restricted and administrative areas.
        (a) Employee vehicles.
        (b) Company vehicles.
        (c) Emergency vehicles.
        (d) Vendor, visitor, contractor, and other vehicles.
d. Vehicle Registration Policy and Procedure.
4. Aids to Security. Indicate the manner in which the following listed aids to security will be implemented within the company areas.
a. Protective barriers.
    (1) Definition.
    (2) Clear zones.
        (a) Criteria.
        (b) Maintenance.
    (3) Signs.
        (a) Types.
        (b) Posting.

(4) Gates.
    (a) Hours of aeration.
    (b) Security requirements.
    (c) Lock security.
b. Protective lighting system.
  (1) Use and control.
  (2) Inspection.
  (3) Action to be taken in the event of power failure.
  (4) Action to be taken in the event of a failure of alternate source of power.
  (5) Emergency lighting systems.
    (a) Stationary.
    (b) Portable.
c. Intrusion detection systems.
  (1) Security classification.
  (2) Inspection.
  (3) Use and monitoring.
  (4) Action to be taken in event of "alarm" conditions.
  (5) Maintenance.
  (6) Alarm logs or registers.
  (7) Sensitivity settings.
  (8) Fail-safe and tamperproof provisions.
  (9) Monitor panel location.
d. Communications.
  (1) Locations.
  (2) Use.
  (3) Tests.
  (4) Authentication.

5. **Security Forces.** Include general instructions that would apply to all security force officers (fixed and mobile). Detailed instructions such as policy and procedures need attachment as annexes.
a. Composition and organization.
b. Length of duty shifts.
c. Essential posts and routes.
d. Weapons and equipment.
e. Training.
f. Use of sentry dog teams.
g. Reserve security forces.
  (1) Composition.
  (2) Purpose or mission.
  (3) Weapons and equipment.
  (4) Location.
  (5) Utilization concept.

6. **Contingency Plans.** Indicate required actions in response to various emergency situations. Detailed plans such as bomb threats, disasters, fire, and so forth need attachment as annexes.

   a. Individual actions.

   b. Alert or reserve force actions.

   c. Security force actions.

7. **Use of Air Surveillance.**

8. **Coordinating Instructions.** Indicate matters that require coordination with outside agencies (e.g., fire departments, law enforcement, and others).

   a. Integration with certain plans and needs of agencies.

   b. Liaison and coordination.

     (1) Local authorities.

     (2) Local support elements.

Annexes

A—Intelligence Collection

B—Company Security Status Map

C—Contingency Plans

D—Special Instructions to Security Officers

E—Other

Appendix B
Physical Security
Inspection Checklists

The checklists contained in this appendix are intended for use only as guides for physical security inspections by your department. Their most important function is to act as reminders for your inspections including what to look for in each of the situations they include.

PHYSICAL SECURITY INSPECTION CHECKLIST

General Purpose

1. Is the perimeter of your company or facility defined by a fence or other type of physical barrier?
2. If a fence is used as the perimeter barrier, does it meet the minimum specifications for security fencing?
3. Is the fence of chain-link design?
4. Is the fence constructed of no. 11 gauge or heavier wire?
5. Is the fence mesh opening no larger than 2 inches square?
6. Is the fence selvage twisted and barbed at top and bottom?
7. Is bottom of fence within 2 inches of solid ground?
8. Is the fence top guard strung with barbed wire and angled outward and upward at a 45-degree angle?
9. Are physical barriers at perimeter lines damaged or deteriorated?
10. If masonry wall is used, does it meet minimum specifications for security fencing?

11. Is the wall at least 7 feet high with a top guard similar to that required on a chain-link fence or at least 8 feet high with broken glass set on edge and cemented to the top surface?

12. If building walls, floors, and roofs form part of your perimeter barrier, do they provide security equivalent at least to that provided by chain-link fence?

13. Are all openings properly secured?

14. If a building forms a part of your perimeter barrier, does it present a hazard at the point of juncture with the perimeter fence?

15. If so, is the fence height increased 100% at the point of juncture?

16. Are openings such as culverts, tunnels, manholes for sewers and utility access, and sidewalk elevators that permit access to the activity properly secured?

17. Do the doors exceed the number required for safe and efficient operation?

18. Are doors constructed of sturdy material?

19. Are all entrances equipped with secure locking devices?

20. Are they always locked when not in active use?

21. Are hinge pins to all entrance doors spot welded or peened?

22. Are all ventilators or other possible means of entrance to the buildings covered with steel bars or adequate wire mesh?

23. Are all windows securely fastened from the inside?

24. Are all windows not accessible from the ground adequately secured?

25. Are all openings less than 18 feet above uncontrolled ground, roofs, ledges, and so on, protected by steel bars or grill?

26. Are openings less than 14 feet directly or diagonally opposite uncontrolled windows in other walls, fire escapes, roofs, protected by steel bars or grills?

27. Has a key control security officer been designated?

28. Are locks and keys to all buildings and entrances supervised and controlled by a key control officer?

29. Does the key control officer have overall authority and responsibility for issuance and replacement of locks and keys?

30. Are keys issued only to authorized employees?

31. Are keys issued to other than company employees?

32. Is the removal of keys from the premises prohibited?

33. Are keys not in use secured in a locked, fireproof cabinet?

34. Are records maintained indicating buildings and entrances for which keys are issued?

35. Are records maintained indicating number and identifications of keys issued?

36. Are records maintained indicating location and number of master keys?

37. Are records maintained indicating location and number of duplicate keys?

38. Are records maintained indicating issue and turn-in of keys?

39. Are records maintained indicating location of locks and keys held in reserve?

40. Is a current key control policy in effect?

41. Are locks changed immediately upon loss or theft of keys?

42. Are inventories conducted at least annually by the key control officer to ensure compliance with directives?

43. If master keys are used, are they devoid of marking identifying them as such?

44. Are losses or thefts of keys promptly investigated by your department?

45. Must all requests for reproduction or duplication of keys be approved by the key control officer?

46. Are locks on inactive gates and storage facilities under seal?

47. Are locks checked periodically by security officers?

48. Are locks rotated within the company areas at least semiannually?

49. Where applicable, is manufacturer's serial number on combination locks obliterated?

50. Are measures in effect to prevent the unauthorized removal of locks on open cabinets, gates, or buildings?

51. Is there a safe located within the building?

52. Is safe adequately secured to prevent removal?

53. Is the safe in a position where it can be observed from the outside by a security officer?

54. Is an alarm system used by the company or facility?

55. Is it a local alarm system?

56. Is it a central station system?

57. Is it a proprietary system?

58. Is it connected to your security department?

59. Is it connected directly to a location outside the activity proper?

60. Is there any inherent weakness in the system itself?

61. Is the system backed up by properly trained security officers?

62. Is the system tested before activating it for nonoperational periods?

63. Is the alarm system inspected regularly?

64. Is the system tamper resistant?

65. Is the system weatherproof?

66. Is an alternate or independent source of power available for use on the system in the event of power failure?

67. Is the emergency power source designed to cut in and operate automatically?

68. Is the alarm system properly maintained by trained security or technical specialists?

69. Are frequent tests conducted to determine the adequacy and promptness of response to alarm signals?

70. Are records kept of all alarm signals received including time, date, location, action taken, and cause for alarm?

71. Is protective lighting provided during hours of darkness?

72. Does it provide adequate illumination for all sides of the company area?

73. Are there provisions for emergency or standby lighting?

74. Are repairs to lights and replacement of inoperative lamps effected immediately?

75. Is there an auxiliary power source?

PHYSICAL SECURITY INSPECTION CHECKLIST

Warehouse Activities

1. Is there a specific procedure in effect that assures strict accountability of all company assets?

2. Are the records of this activity subjected to periodic audits?

3. Are sufficient and comprehensive physical inventories conducted?

4. Are inventories conducted by disinterested company employees?

5. Is fixed and real property accounted for?

6. Are stock record or bin cards maintained?

7. Are stock levels on these cards verifiable through records of incoming stock?

8. Are issues recorded on these cards indexed to specific requisitions?

9. Are inventories recorded on these cards?

10. Is there excessive use loss or damaged asset reports?

11. Is there a specific and secure procedure for the receipt of incoming property?

12. Are there any weaknesses in the present system for the physical unloading and storage of merchandise or materials?

13. Are delivery persons required to produce a bill of lading or other listing of the delivery?

14. Is an accurate tally conducted before acceptance?

15. Are delivery records checked against requisitions or purchase orders?

16. Is acceptance of deliveries limited to specific employees?

17. Are incoming shipments carefully checked for signs of pilferage, damage, and so on?

18. Are shipping and receiving platforms free of trash and are shipments neatly stacked for proper observation and counting?

19. Are unauthorized persons kept from store rooms and storage areas?

20. Is a current employee access list maintained?

21. Are supplies adequately protected against pilferage?

22. Are adequate protective measures afforded open storage?

23. Is material in open storage properly stacked, placed within, away from, and parallel to perimeter barriers, to provide unobstructed view by security officers?

24. Are adequate locker and "break area" facilities provided for employees?

25. Is there a secure place to keep broken cases of damaged merchandise to prevent pilferage?

26. Are employees permitted to carry packages in and out of their work areas?

27. Are provisions made for parking employee owned vehicles to ensure that they are not parked in an area offering an opportunity to remove items from the building to the vehicle undetected?

28. Are trash collectors permitted in the building?

29. If so, are trash containers inspected to assure no assets are secreted in the containers?

30. Is there a specific procedure in effect for the issue and shipping of company property?

31. Are there any weaknesses in the present system for the physical issue or shipment of company property?

32. Are receivers required to receipt for the company assets?

33. Are signature cards used for all authorized receivers?

34. When issues are made by shipment, is there a means to verify their arrival at the requesting facility or customer?

35. Are shipments or deliveries receipted to the carrier or the person making the delivery?

36. Are adequate controls maintained over company property in storage?

37. Is the responsibility for company property fixed?

PHYSICAL SECURITY INSPECTION CHECKLIST FOR CORPORATE

Retail Chain Stores or Similar Activities

1. Does the manager of each store, at the end of each business day, inspect the premises to ensure that all windows, doors, safes, and so on are closed and that no person is hidden in restrooms or elsewhere? Is an intrusion detection device or system installed?

2. Are service entrances locked from the inside when not in use for business operations?

3. Is a strong light used to illuminate the offices and safes during nonbusiness hours? Is it visible to law enforcement or security patrols checking the building?

4. Does the store or any part of it lend itself to pilferage or shoplifting?

5. Are trusted employees available to observe customers discreetly as a deterrent to shoplifting?

6. Are all employees familiar with procedures in handling shoplifters?

7. Is there a tally-in or tally-out system, as appropriate, for checking supplies and merchandise shipped against shipping documents?

8. Are there any shortages in high-value items such as cameras, watches, jewelry, and so on?

9. What action is taken when high value, identifiable items are missing?

10. Do sales slips (when applicable) contain serial numbers of items?

11. Are critical or sensitive items such as watches, cameras, and so on, stored in separate secured storage in stockroom or other area?

12. Are any items of comparatively high value and sensitivity displayed in a way they could be readily stolen with little chance of discovery?

13. Are issues of sensitive items to salesclerks for display and sales documented in any way?

14. Are service doors under the security of responsible employees when open?

15. Are unauthorized persons permitted to enter the storerooms or kitchen serving area of a store food activity?

16. When it is necessary for employees of vendors, or maintenance persons, or other persons not company employees to enter the stock rooms, are they always accompanied by a company employee?

17. Are garbage and trash inspected before removal to assure that they are not being used as a means of removing merchandise or material with authorization?

18. Are employees required to check all personal packages or parcels with the manager?

19. Are employees required to check with the manager before leaving the premises of the store?

20. Are female employees permitted to take their purses into the aisles of the store?

21. Are employees required to enter and depart the store though one door under the supervision of management persons?

22. Are employees permitted to ring up their own purchases?

23. Are all sales recorded on cash register systems?

24. If not, how are sales controlled?

25. Are excessive quantities of money removed from cash registers during daily operations?

26. Are the funds immediately turned in to an office cashier or manager?

27. Are amounts rung up on cash registers observable by customers?

28. Are surprise counts of cash conducted?

29. Are all cash register drawers equipped with operative locks and keys?

30. Are cash register drawers kept locked when unattended?

31. Are change funds from each cash register bagged and turned in to the officer or manager at the close of each business day?

32. Are customers desiring to cash checks, money orders, or traveler's checks required to produce identification prior to cashing them?

33. Are postdated checks accepted?

34. Are credit cards examined and verified for all purchases?

35. Is adequate control maintained over items taken into fitting rooms?

36. Are frequent inventories conducted?

37. Are inventory shortages reconciled or investigated promptly?

38. Are employees assigned lockers or provided other facilities to secure their personal property?

39. Are cash funds restricted to the minimum consistent with needs?

40. Are petty cash funds maintained? Are controls and accountability adequate?

41. Is commingling of funds between sales clerks permitted?

42. Are interdepartmental exchanges or sales properly controlled and recorded?

PHYSICAL SECURITY INSPECTION CHECKLIST FOR CORPORATE FOOD RETAIL STORES

Supermarkets and Convenience Stores

1. Is door construction adequate from a security viewpoint?

2. Are all floor openings, other than doors, in excess of 96 square inches barred, grilled, or covered with chain-link material?

3. If openings are not secured, is it required?

4. Is there a crawl way beneath the building?

5. Does the crawl space provide a means of gaining unauthorized access to the building?

6. Are heating ducts arranged so that they provide an avenue for unauthorized access to the building?

7. Is the service entrance to the store secured so that it can be opened only from the inside?

8. Is the service door kept locked at all times except during loading or unloading operation?

9. Are door hinge pins either of the lock-pin variety or welded to prevent their removal?

10. Are padlock hasps, if any, installed in ways to prevent their removal?

11. Does the arrangement of the store lend itself to maximum observation of attempted pilferage or shoplifting?

12. Is there a tally-in or tally-out system for checking merchandise received or shipped against shipping documents?

13. Is the system effective?

14. Do inventory records indicate shortages in excess of allowable percentages?

15. Are shortages confined primarily to certain items?

16. If shortages are confined primarily to certain items, has corrective action been taken?

17. Is destruction of meat supplies considered unfit for human consumption witnessed or verified by managers?

18. Are fat trimmings that are not sold to customers weighed and reported on a daily record?

19. Are there adequate cross-checks regarding the amount of meat received, amount on hand, amount sold, amount of waste, and other factors that verify no thefts occurred?

20. Are cash register tapes and cash receipts reconciled and verified at the end of each business day?

21. Are checks cashed for amounts greater than the sums due with the difference returned in cash?

22. Are controls adequate to accept checks from customers?

23. Are deposits of monies made at the close of each day's business,, or as soon as practicable?

24. Is there any record maintained of overages in cash receipts?

25. Is there any record maintained of shortages in cash receipts?

26. Doe the records show enough detail to track potential theft problems, need for added training, or incompetence?

27. Are locks and keys to all buildings and entrances under the control of the manager?

28. Are keys issued only to employees authorized access by the manager?

29. Do persons other than the manager or authorized assistants possess keys to the main entrance or other doors?

30. Are all keys to entrances or exits turning in and placed in a key locker or other secured container at the close of each business day?

31. Are locks changed immediately upon loss or theft of keys?

32. Is a record kept of the location of keys to all locks in use?

33. If master keys exist, is access to such keys restricted to the manager and designated assistants?

34. Are master keys kept in a secure place when not in use?

35. If combination locks are used, has the manufacturer's serial number been obliterated?

36. Are measures in effect to prevent the unauthorized removal of opened padlocks from doors, buildings, or storage rooms?

37. Are safe combinations restricted to the minimum number of persons necessary?

38. Is an intrusion detection system installed? Is one needed?

GENERAL SECURITY INSPECTION CHECKLIST

For All Company Operations

1. Are physical security inspections conducted regularly?

2. Are employees bonded?

3. Are audits conducted regularly?

4. Are inventories conducted regularly?

5. Are shortages reported and investigated properly when known?

6. Is preemployment screening conducted? Is it handled properly?

7. Is temporary fire fighting equipment available in the facility?

8. Are first aid supplies and equipment available in the facility?

9. Are employees briefed daily on any changes?

10. Are employees trained properly and do they receive periodic continued training and updates?

Appendix C
Managing Corporate and Industrial Bomb and Terrorism Threats

===

Bomb threat planning is an important facet of any corporate or industrial security program. Whether for a single building, a facility, or a complex, your security force needs training and preparation for a prompt and effective response to this common threat.

Bomb threats or "bomb scares" have become increasingly frequent in recent years, paralleling increases in civil disturbances, periodic labor and student unrest, and similar manifestations of dissidence or dissatisfaction. The threats often include businesses, corporations, and industries. Often, the perpetrators attempt to blame the incident on others or have their own specific motives.

There are many more motives for bomb scares than for actual bomb detonation. Excitement may make a dull day interesting for some people. A chance for publicity or money from a news media for reporting information may cause a person to make his or her own news.

About 5 to 10% of bomb threats received involve a real bomb; however, it is not a matter to shrug off since that threat might be one within the real bomb percentage. In other instances an anonymous call received could set a trap drawing the police and victims to create injuries when a bomb does explode. Or the person calls to prevent innocent victims from being injured. A bomb scare also ties up security, police, and fire officers providing a perpetrator with an opportunity to commit crimes elsewhere with less risk of discovery.

While there is no foolproof method of preventing such threats, or preventing their being carried out, the physical security measures and procedures previously discussed will assist you in lessening their chances of success. In times of disturbance or unrest, or on any other indication of dissidence or dissatisfaction, control measures need intensification.

Especially important are personnel identification and control and package and material control. All building occupants and security and maintenance personnel should be alert to persons who look or act suspicious. All personnel should be alert to observe and report suspicious objects, items, or parcels that do not appear to belong in the area where such items or parcels are observed. Security and maintenance personnel need instructions to ensure periodic checks of all rest rooms, stairwells, areas under stairwells, and other areas of the building. This activity ensures that unauthorized personnel are not in hiding in these areas or otherwise appear to be reconnoitering or conducting surveillance of the area.

It is also extremely important that doors be security locked when not in use, to restrict the access of unauthorized personnel. Doors to utility closets, boiler rooms, fan rooms, telephone wire closets and switchboards, and elevator machinery rooms are especially vulnerable. Keys must be readily available, however, if searches need to happen quickly.

Terrorism associated with bombs and bomb threats is often misunderstood. Most corporate and industrial threats come from quasi-terrorism, a description applied to activities incidental to the commission of crimes of violence that are similar in form and method to true terrorism, but that lack its essential ingredient. Quasi-terrorism is the use of terroristic techniques or tactics in situations that are not terroristic crimes per se; it is different from common crimes that involve terror for this reason.

The taking of hostages is a prime example of a common terroristic technique that has been adopted by quasi-terrorists. In the true terrorist situation, the victims who are seized and threatened serve as bargaining chips to coerce authorities to comply with the terrorist's demands. This situation, when exploited, serves their "cause" for publicity purposes and in other ways. It has become increasingly common in recent years for ordinary criminals, who have no original terroristic purpose, to take hostages during commission of a conventional crime of violence, such as bank robbery.

Bomb threats in corporate and industrial situations normally stem from the quasi-terrorist, maybe a former employee or activist having some perceived unresolved grievance toward the company or its employees instead of the government authority. Although in some environments you may have the threat of true terrorists, normally your problems stem from the quasi-terrorist.

• DEALING WITH THE BOMB THREAT

A bomb is a device capable of producing damage to material and injury or death to people when detonated or ignited. Bombs are classified as explosive or incendiary. An explosive bomb causes damage by fragmentation, heat, and blast wave. The heat produced often causes a secondary incendiary effect. An incendiary bomb generates fire-producing heat without substantial explosion when ignited.

A bomb threat is a message delivered by any means and the message may or may not

- Specify location of the bomb.
- Include the time for detonation or ignition.
- Contain an ultimatum related to the detonation or concealment of the bomb.

A bomb incident involves any occurrence concerning the detonation or ignition of a bomb, the discovery of a bomb, or execution of a bomb threat.

● HANDLING BOMB THREATS

Bomb threats may be received either by telephone or in writing. In either case, the immediate question arises about whether the threat is genuine. Your dilemma includes whether a bomb has actually been placed or whether the threat is false, maybe only for the purpose of causing a disturbance or creating a diversion. In some instances notification of the placement of a bomb is made so that damage is caused to property or equipment but not to persons.

Telephone Threats

Bomb threats generally are received over the telephone. Security and corporate employees likely to receive such a call need briefing on what to say to the caller and use the following procedures:

1. Attempt to keep the caller on the line as long as possible.
2. Make notes including the exact words of the caller. Attempt to ascertain the location of the bomb, type of device, what it looks like, and expected time of detonation.
3. Attempt to determine the sex, the approximate age, and the attitude of the caller, specifically any reasons or motives for his or her actions in placing the bomb.
4. Note any background noise that might provide a clue to the caller's location.
5. Note any accent or peculiarity of speech that may help to identify the caller.
6. If time permits, ask the caller "Who is calling, please?" or "What is your name?" In some instances, the caller may react unthinkingly and reply.

A checklist to collect information from bomb threat callers follows. You can use it when all persons in your company who are likely to receive bomb threat calls have it readily available.

A Call-in Bomb Threat Checklist

Instructions: Be calm. Be courteous. Listen. Do not interrupt the caller. Notify supervisor or the security department by prearranged signal while the caller is on the line whenever possible.

Caller's Identity

Sex: Male ☐
      Female ☐

Adult: Adult ☐   Juvenile ☐

Approximate Age: _____

Origin of Call

☐ Local   ☐ Booth   ☐ Internal   ☐ Long distance

Voice Characteristics		Speech	
☐ Loud	☐ Soft	☐ Fast	☐ Slow
☐ High pitch	☐ Deep	☐ Distinct	☐ Distorted
☐ Raspy	☐ Pleasant	☐ Stutter	☐ Nasal
☐ Intoxicated	☐ Other	☐ Slurred	☐ Lisp
		☐ Other _____	

Language		Accent
☐ Excellent	☐ Good	☐ Local
☐ Fair	☐ Poor	☐ Not local
☐ Foul	☐ Other	☐ Foreign

Manner		Background Noises
☐ Calm	☐ Angry	☐ Factory machines
☐ Rational	☐ Irrational	☐ Bedlam
☐ Coherent	☐ Incoherent	☐ Music
☐ Deliberate	☐ Emotional	☐ Office machines

☐ Righteous ☐ Laughing   ☐ Mixed
                                             ☐ Street traffic
                                             ☐ Trains   ☐ Animals
                                             ☐ Quiet   ☐ Voices
                                             ☐ Aircraft   ☐ Party

Bomb Facts

Pretend difficulty with your hearing. Keep caller talking. If caller seems agreeable to further conversation, ask such questions as, When will it go off? Hour? Time remaining? What kind of bomb? Where are you now? How do you know so much about the bomb? What is your name and address? (Often, the person will respond or provide significant information that provides clues to the identity.) If the building is occupied, inform caller that detonation could cause injury or death. Did caller appear familiar with plant or building by his or her description of the bomb location?

       Write out the message in its entirety and any other comments on a sheet of paper and attach to this checklist.

Action to Take Immediately After Call

Notify your supervisor and the security department immediately. Talk to no one other than as instructed by your supervisor and representatives of the security department.

       The recipient of such a call should be interviewed, following the call, by a competent interviewer. Add to the report any information that the person will later recall, when interviewed items of information that they momentarily overlooked, perhaps due to the stress of the incident. Your interview must remain patient and quiet, and designed only to supplement or expand on the reported information.

Written Threats

Written threats must not be handled more than necessary since crime laboratory technicians might develop latent fingerprints of the sender or other clues to the writer by examination of the handwriting. Excess handling reduces, or may prevent, successful examination. The entire message, including the envelope, if any, must be preserved until released to the appropriate criminal justice agency.

● *Setting Priorities to Effectively Deal with Bomb Threats*

Whenever a bomb threat is received, your first priority (concurrent with notifying the appropriate authorities and bomb disposal experts) is evacuation of employees, visitors, vendors, and others who may be in the area. You need a carefully thought-out plan of evacuation since people rushing out can create a serious breach in otherwise tight security systems. The problem often experienced is having everyone rush out into parking lots and streets and then returning to work when the all-clear signal comes down. However, in the rush and excitement, often the normal entry security is waived and people stream back in, maybe the real bomber among them. Whenever you evacuate, and open the cleared area for employee return, you must handle the incoming persons in the same way as when they arrive for work at the beginning of the day or shift! It is the only way to maintain your security systems with confidence the area remains secure!

Appendix D
Security Officer's Quick Reference Checklist for Any Type Corporate or Industrial Crime

- *WHO questions*
  - Who discovered the crime?
  - Who reported the crime?
  - Who saw or heard anything of importance?
  - Who had a motive for committing the crime?
  - Who committed the crime?
  - Who helped the perpetrator?
  - With whom did the suspect associate?
  - With whom are the witnesses associated?

- *WHAT questions*
  - What happened?
  - What crime was committed?
  - What are the elements of the crime?
  - What were the actions of the suspect?
  - What do the witnesses know about the case?
  - What evidence was obtained?
  - What was done with the evidence?
  - What tools were employed in the crime?
  - What weapons were utilized in the crime?

- What knowledge, skill, or strength was necessary to commit the crime?
- What means of transportation was used in the commission of the crime?
- What was the motive?
- What was the modus operandi?

- *WHERE questions*
  - Where was the crime discovered?
  - Where was the crime committed?
  - Where were the suspects seen?
  - Where were the witnesses during the crime?
  - Where was the victim found?
  - Where were the tools and weapons obtained?
  - Where did the suspect live?
  - Where did the victim live?
  - Where did the suspect spend his or her leisure time?
  - Where is the suspect now?
  - Where is the suspect likely to go?
  - Where was the suspect arrested?

- *WHEN questions*
  - When was the crime committed?
  - When was the crime discovered?
  - When was notification received?
  - When did the police arrive at the scene?
  - When was the victim last seen?
  - When was the suspect arrested?

- *HOW questions*
  - How was the crime committed?
  - How did the suspect get to the scene?
  - How did the suspect get away?
  - How did the suspect get the information necessary to enable him or her to commit the crime?
  - How was the crime discovered?
  - How did the suspect obtain the tools and weapons?
  - How were the tools and weapons used during the crime?
  - How much damage was done?

- How much property was stolen?
- How much skill, knowledge, and strength were necessary to commit the crime?
- *WHY questions*
  - Why was the crime committed?
  - Why were the particular tools utilized?
  - Why was the particular method employed?
  - Why are the witnesses reluctant to talk?
  - Why was the crime reported?

Appendix E
Criminal Description
Guide and Checklist

Illustration E-1

QUICK REFERENCE GUIDE—CRIMINAL DESCRIPTION SHEET

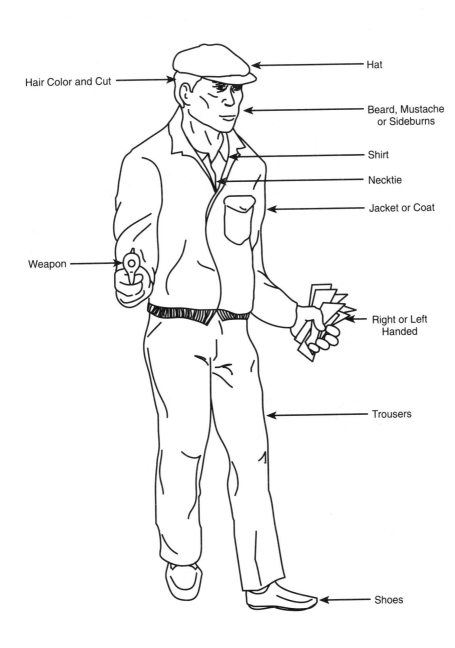

Hair Color and Cut

Weapon

Hat

Beard, Mustache
or Sideburns

Shirt

Necktie

Jacket or Coat

Right or Left
Handed

Trousers

Shoes

FAST GENERAL DESCRIPTION OF SUSPECT

☐ Male   ☐ Female
☐ Caucasian   ☐ Black
☐ Asian   ☐ Other _____
☐ Height _____   ☐ Weight _____
☐ Nationality_____   ☐ Complexion_____
☐ Build_____   ☐ Posture _____
☐ Eye color _____   ☐ Eyeglasses _____
☐ Eyes alert _____   ☐ Eyes normal _____
☐ Eyes droopy _____ ☐ Tattoos _____
☐ Marks, scars _____ ☐ Age estimate _____
☐ Hat _____   ☐ Hair color _____
☐ Mustache _____   ☐ Beard _____
☐ Sideburns _____   ☐ Haircut style _____
☐ Shirt _____   ☐ Necktie _____
☐ Jacket _____   ☐ Coat _____
☐ Suit _____   ☐ Blazer _____
☐ Trousers _____   ☐ Shoes _____
☐ Weapon _____   ☐ Other _____

SUPPLEMENTAL INFORMATION ABOUT SUSPECT AFTER PRELIMINARY INVESTIGATION FEATURES AND OTHER CHARACTERISTICS

SEX

☐ Male   ☐ Female

RACE

☐ Black   ☐ Caucasian
☐ Asian   ☐ Native American

HEAD SHAPE AND SIZE

☐ Round   ☐ Flat on top
☐ Long   ☐ Broad
☐ Narrow   ☐ Flat behind
☐ Square   ☐ Bulging behind
☐ Small   ☐ Egg shaped

HAIR AND HAIRCUT

☐ Long   ☐ Short
☐ Full   ☐ Thinning
☐ Bald   ☐ Curly
☐ Kinky   ☐ Crew cut
☐ Straight   ☐ Wig/toupee
☐ Red   ☐ Hazel

- ☐ Black
- ☐ Brown
- ☐ White
- ☐ Mussed

- ☐ Blond
- ☐ Gray
- ☐ Neatly combed
- ☐ Other _____

COMPLEXION

- ☐ Normal
- ☐ Blotched
- ☐ Pale
- ☐ Acne
- ☐ Medium

- ☐ Scarred
- ☐ Pock marked
- ☐ Florid
- ☐ Fair
- ☐ Dark

EYE SPECIFICS

- ☐ Blue
- ☐ Black
- ☐ Green
- ☐ Large
- ☐ Medium
- ☐ Round
- ☐ Cocked
- ☐ Sunken
- ☐ Albino
- ☐ Glassy
- ☐ Piercing
- ☐ Close set

- ☐ Brown
- ☐ Hazel
- ☐ Crossed
- ☐ Squint
- ☐ Small
- ☐ Slanted
- ☐ Bloodshot
- ☐ Multicolored
- ☐ Protruding
- ☐ Blinking
- ☐ Dull
- ☐ Bags under

EYEGLASSES

- ☐ Plastic
- ☐ Plain lens
- ☐ Thick
- ☐ Bifocal

- ☐ Wire frame
- ☐ Dark lens
- ☐ Normal
- ☐ Monocle

EYEBROWS

- ☐ Heavy
- ☐ Dark
- ☐ Bushy
- ☐ Average

- ☐ Thick
- ☐ Light
- ☐ Thin
- ☐ Other _____

NOSE

- ☐ Large
- ☐ Wide
- ☐ Narrow
- ☐ Turned up
- ☐ Short
- ☐ Pug

- ☐ Small
- ☐ Medium
- ☐ Hooked
- ☐ Long
- ☐ Flat
- ☐ Pointed

MOUTH SIZE AND FEATURES

☐ Small
☐ Large
☐ Normal
☐ Dry lips
☐ Lipstick

☐ Medium
☐ Thin lips
☐ Thick lips
☐ Moist lips
☐ Color _____

BEARD AND MUSTACHE

☐ Mustache/color _____
☐ Beard/color _____
☐ Long
☐ Trimmed
☐ Full

☐ Short
☐ Unkept
☐ Other _____

TEETH

☐ Normal
☐ Large
☐ Cracked
☐ Irregular
☐ Braces
☐ Stained
☐ Gaps

☐ Missing _____
☐ Small
☐ Protruding
☐ Wide spaced
☐ Close spaced
☐ Fillings
☐ Other _____

EARS

☐ Small
☐ Large

☐ Medium
☐ Other _____

CHIN

☐ Jutting
☐ Pointed
☐ Square
☐ Dimpled

☐ Receding
☐ Normal
☐ Double
☐ Short

NECK

☐ Short
☐ Thick
☐ Other _____

☐ Long
☐ Slender

SHOULDERS

☐ Small
☐ Broad

☐ Medium
☐ Stooped

HANDS AND FINGERS

☐ Small
☐ Large
☐ Stubby
☐ Rings _____
☐ Missing _____

☐ Average
☐ Short fingers
☐ Long fingers

TRUNK OF BODY

Chest

- ☐ Large
- ☐ Narrow
- ☐ Average
- ☐ Sunken

Back

- ☐ Straight
- ☐ Humped
- ☐ Curved
- ☐ Bowed

Waist

- ☐ Small
- ☐ Large
- ☐ Average
- ☐ Protruding stomach

Hips

- ☐ Broad
- ☐ Thin
- ☐ Average
- ☐ Other _____

Legs

- ☐ Long
- ☐ Average
- ☐ Straight
- ☐ Short
- ☐ Bowed
- ☐ Muscular

Feet

- ☐ Small
- ☐ Large
- ☐ Average
- ☐ Other _____

MARKS/SCARS/TATTOOS

- ☐ Tattoos _____
- ☐ Scars _____
- ☐ Marks _____

SPEECH

- ☐ Normal
- ☐ Coarse
- ☐ Whisper
- ☐ Soft
- ☐ Deep
- ☐ High
- ☐ Vulgar
- ☐ Cultured
- ☐ Articulate
- ☐ Explain _____
- ☐ Rough
- ☐ Lisps
- ☐ Strained
- ☐ Harsh
- ☐ Average
- ☐ Raspy
- ☐ Accent
- ☐ Drawl
- ☐ Dumb sounding

DRESS/APPEARANCE

- ☐ Hat or cap, kind and color

_____

- ☐ New ☐ Old ☐ Faded
- ☐ Blouse, kind and color

_____

- ☐ New ☐ Old ☐ Faded

☐ Dress or skirt (female), kind and color

_____

☐ New ☐ Old ☐ Faded
☐ Purse/other (female), kind and color

_____

☐ New ☐ Old ☐ Faded
☐ Trousers, kind and color

_____

☐ New ☐ Old ☐ Pressed
☐ Shoes, kind and color

_____

☐ New ☐ Old ☐ Shined
☐ Shirt ☐ Sweater ☐ T-shirt

Color _____
☐ New ☐ Old ☐ Worn
☐ Necktie ☐ Bandana ☐ Ascot

Color _____
☐ New ☐ Old ☐ Worn
☐ Suit ☐ Blazer ☐ Jacket

Color _____
☐ New ☐ Old ☐ Worn

PROSTHETIC DEVICES

☐ Crutches ☐ Hearing aid
☐ Cane ☐ Braces
☐ Other _____

OVERALL APPEARANCE

☐ Neat ☐ Unkept ☐ Rumpled
☐ Dirty ☐ Clean ☐ Cologne
☐ Groomed ☐ Mannered ☐ Crude

OVERALL BUILD

☐ Large ☐ Average
☐ Small ☐ Tall
☐ Short ☐ Straight
☐ Stooped ☐ Agile
☐ Clumsy ☐ Muscular

MANNERISM AND HABITS

☐ Calm   ☐ Nervous
☐ Twitches   ☐ Facial tics
☐ Smokes   ☐ Chews tobacco

SUBCONSCIOUS MANNERISM

☐ Pulling an ear
☐ Scratching or pulling nose
☐ Jingling keys or change
☐ Hitching up pants
☐ Running hand through hair
☐ Other _____

Appendix F
Suggested Corporate and Industrial Security College-Level Education and Training Programs

There is a need for education and training in the security profession. Developing professional responsibility coupled with greater needs and lessening law enforcement involvement within the corporate and industrial environment calls for specialized, college-level education and training. The continued effort includes noncredit and credit seminars and courses, and the following guide supplies a list of possible courses for professional security officers and managers.

SUGGESTED COURSES AND SEMINARS FOR OPERATIONAL PERSONNEL (SECURITY OFFICERS AND INVESTIGATORS)

- Arson Investigation Courses and Seminars
- Background Investigation Seminars
- Bomb Threats Courses and Seminars
- Civil Disturbance Seminars
- Cooperation with Law Enforcement Agencies Seminars
- Employee Security Seminars and Courses
- Fire and Safety Seminars and Courses
- Firearms Training Courses
- First Aid and Paramedical Courses
- Internal Theft Investigation Courses

- Interviewing Seminars
- Law and the Security Role Courses
- Note Taking and Report Writing Courses
- Security Patrol Seminars
- Physical Security Courses and Seminars
- Preliminary Investigation and Crime Scene Preservation Courses and Seminars
- Public Relations for Security Services Courses and Seminars
- Security Techniques and Procedure Courses
- Shoplifting Prevention Seminars
- Surveillance Technique Seminars

COURSES AND SEMINARS FOR MANAGEMENT PERSONNEL

- Crime Prevention Through Environmental Design
- Disaster and Emergency Planning
- Bomb Threat Management
- Law Management for Security Operations
- Executive Protection
- Security Management
- Security Administration

ASSOCIATE DEGREE PROGRAMS

A useful starting point for security professionals desiring advancement through increased education is the acquisition of an associate degree (awarded after two years of study) when they do not have a college degree. This degree is awarded by community colleges that cost less and offer greater flexibility than four-year colleges and universities. The degree also creates a foundation and credential for further development when a four-year bachelor degree or higher is later pursued. Each college, either a two or four year, has a variety of courses and many necessary to achieve a degree although not directly related to your security profession. But you can attend more than one college or university to take the professional courses needed to further your career. The following suggested curriculum serves as a guide that meets the professional goals with an associate degree. (This is an example that, depending on the college or university, might vary in some areas.)

SUGGESTED CURRICULUM FOR CORPORATE AND INDUSTRIAL CAREER DEVELOPMENT WITH AN ASSOCIATE DEGREE

FIRST YEAR

FIRST SEMESTER	Credits	SECOND SEMESTER	Credits
English I	3	English II	3
General Psychology	3	Introduction to Sociology	3
Criminal and Civil Law I	3	Criminal and Civil Law II	3
Introduction to Security	3	Security Administration	3
Elective	3	Elective	3
Electives			
Accounting I	3	Accounting II	3
Economics I	3	Economics II	3
Science I	3	Science II	3
Administration of Justice	3	Civil Rights/Liberties	3
Principles of Interviewing	3	Report Writing	3
Industrial Relations	3		

SECOND YEAR

FIRST SEMESTER	Credits	SECOND SEMESTER	Credits
Fundamentals of Speech	3	Criminal Investigation	3
Social Problems	3	Criminology	3
Human Relations	3	Labor and Management	3
Principles of Loss Prevention	3	Current Security Problems	3
Elective	3	Elective	3
Electives			
Document and Personnel	3	Commercial/Retail Security	3
Business Mathematics	3	Field Practicum	3
Emergency Preparedness	3	Industrial Fire Protection	3
Environmental Security	3	Security Education	3
Physical Security	3	Security Education	3
Safety and Fire Prevention	3	Special Security Problems	3

COLLEGES AND UNIVERSITIES OFFERING EDUCATIONAL PROGRAMS IN SECURITY, POLICE SCIENCE, AND CRIMINAL JUSTICE SUBJECTS RELATED TO NEEDS OF THE CORPORATE AND INDUSTRIAL SECURITY PROFESSIONAL

A reasonable effort has been made to ensure the accuracy of this information; however, colleges and universities add and delete specialized curriculum according to demand. Moreover, when a college or university listed here or in your area does not offer the specific courses, you may, through a corporate-sponsored arrangement, encourage them to provide the courses needed along with required courses leading to associate or bachelor degrees.

Alabama

Auburn University, Auburn
Auburn University at Montgomery, Montgomery
Enterprise State Junior College, Enterprise
Faulkner State College, Bay Minette
Gadsden State Junior College, Gadsden
George C. Wallace Community College, Dothan
Jacksonville State University, Jacksonville
Jefferson State Junior College, Birmingham
John C. Calhoun Community College, Decatur
Lurleen B. Wallace State Junior College, Andalusia
Northeast State Junior College, Rainsville
Samford University, Birmingham
Southern Union State Junior College, Wadley
Troy State University, Montgomery
University of Alabama Birmingham, Birmingham
University of Alabama Huntsville, Huntsville
University of Alabama, University
University of South Alabama, Mobile

Alaska

University of Alaska, Fairbanks

Arizona

Arizona State University, Tempe
Arizona Western College, Yuma
Central Arizona College, Coolidge
mesa Community College, Mesa
Northern Arizona University, Flagstaff
Phoenix University, Phoenix
Pima Community College, Tucson
University of Arizona, Tucson
Yavapai-College, Prescott

Arkansas

University of Arkansas at Little Rock, Little Rock

California

Allen Hancock College, Santa Maria

Bakersfield College, Bakersfield

Butte Community College, Durham

Cabrillo College, Aptos

California Baptist College, Riverside

California Lutheran College, Thousand Oaks

California State College, Dominquez Hills

California State College, San Bernardino

California State College, Stanislaus, Turlock

California State University, Fresno

California State University, Fullerton

California State University, Los Angeles

California State University, Sacramento

Cerritos College, Norwalk

Chabot College, Hayward

Chaffey College, Alta Loma

Chapman College, Orange

Citrus College, Azusa

College of the Desert, Palm Desert

College of Marin, Kentfield

College of the Redwoods, Eureka

College of San Mateo, San Mateo

College of the Sequoias, Vislia

College of the Siskiyous, Weed

Contra Costa College, San Pablo

Cuesta College, San Luis Obispo

Diablo Valley College, Pleasant Hill

East Los Angeles College, Los Angeles

Fresno City College, Fresno

Fullerton College, Fullerton

Golden Gate University, San Francisco

Golden West College, Huntington Beach

Frossmont College, El Cajon

Hartnell College, Salinas

Lassen College, Susanville
Loma Linda University, Riverside
Long Beach City College, Long Beach
Mira Costa College, Oceanside
Miramar College, San Diego
Modesto Junior College, Modesto
Monterey Peninsula College, Monterey
Moorpark College, Moorpark
Mt. San Antonio College, Walnut
Mt. San Jacinto College, San Jacinto
Napa College, Napa
Ohlone College, Fremont
Palo Verde Community College, Blythe
Palomar Community college, San Marcos
Pasadena City College, Pasadena
Rio Hondo College, Whittier
San Joaquin Delta College, Stockton
San Jose State University, San Jose
Santa Ana College, Santa Ana
Santa Barbara City College, Santa Barbara
Santa Rosa Junior College, Santa Rosa
Shasta College, Redding
Sierra College, Rocklin
Southwestern College, Chula Vista
University of California, Berkeley
University of California-Irvine, Irvine
University of California-Santa Barbara, Santa Barbara
University of Southern California, Los Angeles
West Hills College, Coalinga
West Valley College, Saratoga

Colorado

Arapahoe Community College, Littleton
El Paso Community College, Colorado Springs
Metropolitan State College, Denver

Trinidad State Junior College, Trinidad

Connecticut

Eastern Connecticut State College, Willemantic
Housatonic Community College, Bridgeport
Manchester Community College, Manchester
Mattatuck Community College, Waterbury
Northwestern Connecticut Community College, Winsted
Norwalk Community College, Norwalk
Tunxis Community College, Farmington
University of Connecticut, Storrs
University of New Haven, West Haven

Delaware

Brandywine College, Wilmington
Delaware Technical and Commercial College, Georgetown
Delaware Technical and Commercial College, Newark
University of Delaware, Newark
Wilmington College, New Castle

District of Columbia

American University, Washington, D.C.
Trinity College, Washington, D.C.
Washington Technical Institute, Washington, D.C.

Florida

Biscayne College, Miami
Brevard Community College, Cocoa
Broward Community College, Fort Lauderdale
Central Florida Community College, Ocala
Dhipola Junior College, Marianna
Daytona Beach Community College, Daytona Beach
Edison Community College, Fort Myers
Florida Atlantic University, Boca Raton
Florida Junior College at Jacksonville, Jacksonville
Florida State University, Tallahassee

Florida Technological University, Orlando
Gulf Coast Community College, Panama City
Lake City Community College, Lake City
Manatee Junior College, Bradenton
Miami Dade Community College, Miami
Palm Beach Junior College, Lake Worth
Pensacola Junior College, Pensacola
Polk Community College, Winter Haven
Rollins College, Winter Park
St. Petersburg Junior College, St. Petersburg
Santa Fe Community College, Gainesville
Seminole Junior College, Sanford
South Florida Junior College, Avon Park
Tallahassee Community College, Tallahassee
University of Florida, Gainesville
University of South Florida, Tampa

Georgia

Albany Junior College, Albany
Andrew College, Cuthbert
Armstrong State College, Savannah
Augusta College, Augusta
Clayton Junior College, Morrow
Columbus College, Columbus
DeKalb Community College, Clarkston
Floyd Junior College, Rome
Georgia Southern College, Statesboro
Georgia State University, Atlanta
Gordon Junior College, Bannesville
Macon Junior College, Macon
Middle Georgia College, Cochran
Savannah State College, Savannah
Valdosta State College, Valdosta
West Georgia College, Carrollton

Hawaii

Chaminade College, Honolulu
Honolulu Community College, Honolulu
Kauai Community College, Kauai
University of Hawaii at Hilo, Hilo

Idaho

Boise State University, Boise
Lewis-Clark State College, Lewiston
North Idaho College, Coeur d'Alene

Illinois

Aurora College, Aurora
Belleville Area College, Belleville
Black Hawk College, Moline
College of Lake County, Grayslake
Community College of Decatur, Decatur
Illinois Central College, East Peoria
Illinois State University, Normal
Illinois Valley Community College, Oglesby
Joliet Junior College, Joliet
Kankakee Community College, Kankakee
Kishwaukee College, Malta
Lewis and Clark Community College, Godfrey
Lincoln College, Lincoln
Loop College, Chicago
McHenry County College, Crystal Lake
Moraine Valley Community College, Palos Hills
Northwestern University, Evanston
Parkland College, Champaign
Prairie State College, Chicago Heights
Sangamon State University, Springfield
Southern Illinois University, Carbondale
Southwest College, Chicago
Thorton Community College, South Holland

Triton College, River Grove
University of Chicago Law School, Chicago
University of Illinois at Chicago Center, Chicago
Waubonsee Community College, Sugar Grove
Western Illinois University, Macomb
William Rainey Harper College, Palatine

Indiana

Anderson College, Anderson
Ball State University, Muncie
Calumet College, East Chicago
Indiana Central College, Indianapolis
Indiana State University, Terre Haute
Indiana University, Bloomington
Indiana University East, Richmond
Indiana University at Kokomo, Kokomo
Indiana University-Purdue University at Indianapolis, Indianapolis
Indiana University at South Bend, South Bend
Vincennes University, Vincennes

Iowa

Des Moines Area Community College, Ankeny
Hawkeye Institute of Technology, Waterloo
Indian Hills Community College, Ottumwa
Iowa Central Community College, Fort Dodge
Iowa Lakes Community College, Esterville,
Iowa Wesleyan College, Mt. Pleasant
Iowa Western Community College, Council Bluffs
Kirkwood Community College, Cedar Rapids
Mount Mercy College, Cedar Rapids
Muscatine Community College, Muscatine
Saint Ambrose College, Davenport
Simpson College, Indianola
State University of Iowa, Iowa City
Western Iowa Tech, Sioux City

Kansas

Allanen County Community Junior College, Iola
Barton County Community College, Great Bend
Buthen County Community College, El Dorado
Colby Community College, Colby
Cowley County Community College, Arkansas
Hutchinson Community Junior College, Hutchinson
Hohnson County Community College, Overland Park
Wichita State University, Wichita

Kentucky

Eastern Kentucky University, Richmond
Murray State University, Murray
Paducah Community College, Paducah
Thomas More College, Mitchell
University of Kentucky, Hopkinsville Community College, Hopkinsville
University of Louisville, Louisville
Western Kentucky University, Bowling Green

Louisiana

City College-Loyola University, New Orleans
Louisiana State University, Baton Rouge
Manesse State University, Lake Charles
Northeast Louisiana University, Monroe
Saint Mary's Dominican College, New Orleans
Southeastern Louisiana University, Hammond
University of Southwestern Louisiana, Lafayette

Maine

Bangor Community College of the University of Maine, Bangor
Southern Maine Vocational Technical Institute, South Portland
University of Maine-Augusta, Augusta
University of Maine, Portland-Gorham, Portland

Maryland

Anne Arundel Community College, Arnold
Catonsville Community College, Catonsville
Cecil Community College, North East
Charles County Community College, La Plata
Chesapeake College, Wye Mills
Community College of Baltimore, Baltimore
Coppin State College, Baltimore
Hagerstown Junior College, Hagerstown
Montgomery College, Rockville
Prince George's Community College, Largo
Towson State College, Baltimore
University of Baltimore, Baltimore
University of Maryland, College Park

Massachusetts

American International College, Springfield
Berkshire Community College, Pittsfield
Boston University-Metropolitan College, Boston
Bristol Community College, Fall River
Bunker Hill Community College, Charlestown
Cape Cod Community College, West Barnstable
Clark University, Worcester
Dean Junior College, Franklin
Greenfield Community College, Greenfield
Holyoke Community College, Holyoke
Massachusetts Bay Community College, Watertown
Massasoit Community College, Brockton
Middlesex Community College, Bedford
Mount Wachusett Community College, Gardner
North Shore Community College, Beverly
Northeastern University, Boston
Northern Essex Community College, Haverhill
Springfield College, Springfield
Westfield State College, Westfield

Michigan

Alpena Community College, Alpena
Bay de Noc Community College, Escanaba
Charles S. Mott Community College, Flint
Eastern Michigan University, Ypsilanti
Ferris State College, Big Rapids
Grand Valley State College, Allendale
Henry Ford Community College, Dearborn
Jackson Community College, Jackson
Kalamazoo Valley Community College, Kalamazoo
Kellogg Community College, Battle Creek
Kirtland Community College, Roscommon
Lake Michigan College, Benton Harbor
Lake Superior State College, Sault Ste Marie
Lansing Community College, Lansing
Macomb County Community College, Mt. Clemens
Michigan State University, East Lansing
Northern Michigan University, Marquette
Northwestern Michigan College, Traverse City
Saginaw Valley College, University Center
St. Clair County Community College, Port Huron
Wayne County Community College, Detroit
Wayne State University, Detroit

Minnesota

Inver Hills Community College, Inver Grove Heights
Lakewood Community College, St. Paul
Mankato State College, Mankato
Metropolitan Community College, Minneapolis
Moorhead State College, Moorhead
Northland Community College, Thief River Falls
Rochester Community College, Rochester
St. Cloud State College, St. Cloud
University of Minnesota at Duluth, Duluth

University of Minnesota, Minneapolis

Mississippi

Hinds Junior College, Raymond
Jones County Junior College, Ellisville
Mississippi Gulf Coast Junior College, Gulfport
Northeast Mississippi Junior College, Booneville
Northwest Mississippi Junior College, Senatobia
University of Mississippi, University
University of Southern Mississippi, Hattiesburg

Missouri

Central Missouri State University, Warrnesburg
Culver-Stockton College, Canton
Drury College, Springfield
Florissant Valley Community College, St. Louis
Forest Park Community College, St. Louis
Hannibal-La Grange Junior College, Hannibal
Lincoln University, Jefferson City
Mayville College, St. Louis
Meramec Community College, St. Louis
Metropolitan College, St. Louis
Missouri Southern State College, Joplin
Missouri Western State College, St. Joseph
Penn Valley Community College, Kansas City
Rockhurst College, Kansas City
Southeast Missouri State University, Cape Giradeau
State University, Kirksville
University of Missouri at Kansas City, Kansas City

Montana

Carroll College, Helena
College of Great Falls, Great Falls
Dawson College, Glendive
University of Montana, Missoula

Nebraska

Chadron State College, Chadron
University of Nebraska, Lincoln
University of Nebraska-Omaha, Omaha

Nevada

University of Nevada, Las Vegas
University of Nevada-Reno, Reno

New Hampshire

River College, Nashua

New Jersey

Atlantic Community College, Mays Landing
Bergen Community College, Paramus
Brookdale Community College, Lincroft
Burlington County Community College, Pemberton
County College of Morris, Dover
Glassboro State College, Glassboro
Gloucester City College, Sewell
Jersey City State College, Jersey City
Mercer County Community College, Trenton
Monmouth College, West Long Branch
Ocean County College, Toms River
Rutgers, New Brunswick
Rutgers University School of Criminal Justice, Newark
Somerset County College, Somerville
Stockton State College, Pomona
Trenton State College, Trenton
Union College, Cranford

New Mexico

New Mexico Highlands University, Las Vegas
New Mexico State University, Las Cruces
University of Albuquerque, Albuquerque

New York

Adirondack Community College, Glen Falls

Auburn Community College, Auburn

Broome Community College, Binghamton

City University of New York (John Jay College of Criminal Justice),
    New York City

Community College of Fingerlakes, Canadaigua

Dutchess Community College, Poughkeepsie

Erie Community College, Buffalo

Genesse Community College, Batavia

Hudson Valley Community College, Troy

Jamestown Community College, Jamestown

Mohawk Valley Community College, Utica

Monroe Community College, Rochester

Nassau Community College, Garden City

New York Institute of Technology, Old Westbury

Niagara University, Niagara

North Country Community College, Saranac Lake

Onondaga Community College, Syracuse

Pace University in Westchester, Pleasantville

Rochester Institute of Technology, Rochester

Rockland Community College, Suffern

St. John's University, St. Vincent's College, Jamaica

Schenectady County Community College, Schenectady

State University of New York-Albany, Albany

State University of New York-Brockport, Brockport

State University of New York-Buffalo, Buffalo

State University of New York-Canton, Canton

State University of New York-Farmindale, Farmingdale

State University of New York-Oswego, Oswego

Suffolk County Community College, Selden

Ulster County Community College, Stone Ridge

Westchester Community College, Valhalla

North Carolina

Campbell College, Buies Creek
Central Piedmont Community College, Charlotte
Cleveland County Technical Institute, Shelby
East Carolina University, Greenvile
Forsyth Technical Institute, Winston Salem
Guilford College, Greensboro
Pfeiffer College, Misenheimer
Pitt Technical Institute, Greenville
University of North Carolina at Charlotte, Charlotte
Wake Technical Institute, Raleigh
Wilson City Technical Institute, Wilson

North Dakota

Minot State College, Minot

Ohio

Bowling Green State University, Bowling Green
Columbus Technical Institute, Columbus
Cuyahoga Community College, Cleveland
Hocking Technical College, Nelsonville
Jarrerson County Technical Institute, Steubenville
Kent State University, Kent
Lakeland Community College, Mentor
Miami University, Oxford
Ohio University-Chillicothe, Chillicothe
Owens Technical College, Perrysburg
University of Akron, Akron
University of Cincinnati, Cincinnati
University of Dayton, Dayton
University of Toledo, Toledo
Youngstown State University, Youngstown

Oklahoma

Claremore Junior College, Claremore
Connors State College, Warner
Northeastern State College, Tahlequah
Oklahoma City University, Oklahoma City
Oklahoma State University, Oklahoma City
Tulsa Junior College, Tulsa
University of Oklahoma, Norman
University of Tulsa, Tulsa

Oregon

Chemeketa Community College, Salem
Eastern Oregon State College, La Grande
Lane Community College, Eugene
Portland Community College, Portland
Portland State University, Portland
Southern Oregon College, Ashland
Southwestern Oregon Community College, Coos Bay

Pennsylvania

Bucks County Community College, Newtown
Community College of Allegheny County, Monroeville
Community College of Beaver County, Monaca
Community College of Philadelphia, Philadelphia
Indiana University of Pennsylvania, Indiana
King's College, Wilkes-Barre
La Salle College, Philadelphia
Lehigh County Community College, Schnecksville
Mansfield State College, Mansfield
Mercyhurst College, Erie
Montgomery County Community College, Blue Bell
Penn State University, University Park
Reading Area Community College, Reading
Saint Joseph's College, Philadelphia
Temple University, Philadelphia

University of Pennsylvania, Philadelphia
Villanova University, Villanova
York College of Pennsylvania, York

Rhode Island

Bryant College, Smithfield

South Carolina

Central Wesleyan College, Central
Greenville Technical Education Center, Greenville
Orangeburg-Calhoun Technical Education Center, Orangeburg
Spartanburg Methodist College, Spartanburg
Tri-County Technical College, Pendleton
University of South Carolina, Columbia

South Dakota

Augustana College, Sioux Falls
Sioux Falls College, Sioux Falls
University of South Dakota, Vermillion

Tennessee

Cleveland State Community College, Cleveland
East Tennessee State University, Johnson City
Memphis State University, Memphis
Middle Tennessee-State University, Murfreesboro
University of Tennessee at Martin, Martin
Walters State Community College, Morristown

Texas

Amarillo College, Amarillo
Austin Community College, Austin
Baylor University, Waco
Bishop College, Dallas
Central Texas College, Kileen
East Texas State University, Commerce
El Paso Community College, El Paso

Galveston Community College, Galveston
Henderson County Junior College, Athens
Houston Community College, Houston
Lamar University, Beaumont
Midland College, Midland
San Antonio College, San Antonio
South Texas Junior College, Houston
Southern Methodist University, Dallas
Southwest Texas State University, San Marcos
Tarrant County Junior College, Hurst
Temple Junior College, Temple
Texarkana Community College, Texarkana
Texas Christian University, Fort Worth
Tyler Junior College, Tyler
Tyler State College, Tyler
The University of Texas at Arlington, Arlington
University of Texas, El Paso
University of Texas, Odessa
West Texas State University, Canyon
Western Texas College, Snyder
Wharton County Junior College, Wharton

Utah

Brigham Young University, Provo
Southern Utah State College, Cedar City
Weber State College, Ogden

Vermont

Castleton State College, Castleton
Champlain College, Burlington
Norwich University, Northfield

Virginia

Blue Ridge Community College, Weyers Cave
Central Virginia Community College, Lynchburg
Dabney S. Lancaster Community College, Clifton Forge

Danville Community College, Danville
George Mason University, Fairfax
J. Sargeant Reynolds Community College, Richmond
Northern Virginia Community College, Annandale Campus, Annandale
Old Dominion University, Norfolk
Piedmont Virginia Community College, Charlottesville
Southside Virginia Community College, Keysville
Virginia Commonwealth University, Richmond

Washington

Central Washington State College, Ellensburg
Clark College, Vancouver
Everett Community College, Everett
Green River Community College, Augurn
Highline Community College, Midway
North Seattle Community College, Seattle
Olympic Community College, Bremerton
Seattle University, Seattle
Shoreline Community College, Seattle
Tacoma Community College, Tacoma
University of Puget Sound, Seattle
Washington State University, Pullman

West Virginia

Parkersburg Community College, Parkersburg
West Virginia State College, Institute

Wisconsin

Blackhawk Technical Institute, Beloit
Carthage College, Kenosha
College of Racine, Racine
Madison Area Technical College, Madison
Milwaukee Area Technical College, Milwaukee
North Central Technical Institute, Wausau
University of Wisconsin, Madison

University of Wisconsin, Milwaukee
University of Wisconsin, Plateville
University of Wisconsin, Superior

Wyoming

Casper College, Casper
Laramie County Community College, Cheyenne
Western Wyoming Community College, Rock Springs

Guam

University of Guam, Agana

Canada

Algonquin College of Applied Arts and Technology, Ottawa, Ontario
Douglas College, New Westminster, B.C.
Humber College, Rexdale, Ontario
Lethbridge Community College, Lethbridge, Alberta
Mount Royal College, Calgary, Alberta

Index